The World's Greatest
Horse Stories

The World's Greatest Horse Stories

Edited by J. N. P. Watson

PADDINGTON PRESS LTD

NEW YORK & LONDON

By the same author

The Book of Foxhunting
Victorian and Edwardian Sports from Old Photographs
Captain-General and Rebel Chief: the Life of James, Duke of Monmouth

Library of Congress Cataloging in Publication Data
Main entry under title:
The world's greatest horse stories.
1. Horse – Literary collections. 2. Horsemanship – Literary collections. I. Watson, J.N.P.
PN6071.H73W67   808.8'036   79-10676

ISBN 0 448 23171 9 (U.S. and Canada only)
ISBN 0 7092 0874 X

Filmset in England by Tradespools Ltd., Frome, Somerset.
Printed and bound in the United States.

Designed by Patricia Pillay

In the United States
PADDINGTON PRESS
Distributed by
GROSSET & DUNLAP

In the United Kingdom
PADDINGTON PRESS

In Canada
Distributed by
RANDOM HOUSE OF CANADA LTD

In Southern Africa
Distributed by
ERNEST STANTON (PUBLISHERS) (PTY.) LTD.

In Australia and New Zealand
Distributed by
A.H. & A.W. REED

To Lavinia

CONTENTS

7

ACKNOWLEDGMENTS

I AM EXTREMELY GRATEFUL for the generous cooperation of many writers and artists, and to their publishers and representatives, for allowing me to quote from their books and reproduce their drawings.

In particular I should like to thank J.A. Allen Ltd for the description of cavalry in the First World War and of the character of Sir Gordon Richards from the late Major Jack Fairfax-Blakeborough's autobiography, *J F-B*; Bodley Head Ltd and the executors of the late Capt. J.H. Marshall for his description of a trooper in riding school, taken from *Horseman*; and the same publishers and the author for the story *The Night before the Fair* from *Tally Ho* by Moyra Charlton. To them and the artists' executors for the drawing by the late Lionel Edwards (*He has a wicked oi on him*) which accompanies that story, and for the Lionel Edwards sketches reproduced from R.C. Lyle's *Royal Newmarket*.

Jonathan Cape Ltd and the executors of the late Ernest Hemingway for the description of picadors in *Death in the Afternoon*; Cassell Ltd and the author for the piece from *Jump for Joy*, by Pat Smythe; and Jonathan Clowes for the verses of *The Groom's Story* by the late Sir Arthur Conan Doyle. To Collins Ltd and the author for Alastair Boyd's dissertation on riding in Andalucia, from *The Road to Ronda*; to Pers Crowell for his account of quarter horses in *Cavalcade of American Horses*. And to Constable Ltd for the verses by Will Ogilvie.

To David and Charles Ltd and J.M. Brereton for permission to use the description of the Mongols from *The Horse in War*; J.M. Dent Ltd for the late W. Heath Robinson's drawing (*Mine Arms Are Mine Ornaments*) from their edition of Cervantes' *Don Quixote*; and Andre Deutsch Ltd and the artist, Brian Robb, for his illustrations to *The Adventures of the Celebrated Baron Munchausen*. Doubleday and Co. and the author for my two pieces on Arabians from *Drinkers of the Wind*, by Carl Raswan. To Ronald Duncan for allowing me to quote his tribute to the horse, written for the *Horse of the Year Show* program. To Faber and Faber and the executors of the late Siegfried Sassoon for the quotation from *Memoirs of a Foxhunting Man*; and to the same publishers and the executors of the late Major John Board for the extracts and illustrations from *Polo*.

To Hamlyn Ltd, the authors and, where applicable, the artists, for a variety of extracts and drawings – in particular from *The Mind of the Horse*, by R.H. Smythe; *My Early Life*, by the late Winston S. Churchill; *Advice to Players* from Marco's *Introduction to Polo*; the description of training the showjumper from Colonel Talbot-Ponsonby's *Harmony in Horsemanship*; and the incident from Percy Westerman's *The Young Cavalier*. To Harrap Ltd and the author for the reminiscences quoted from *My Horses, My Teachers*, by Colonel Alois Podhajsky. To Hart-Davis Ltd and the executors of the late Dorothy Duchess of Wellington for her poem, *Horses*.

To William Heinemann Ltd and the executors of the late G.D. Armour for his sketches from John Masefield's *Reynard the Fox*; and Heinemann again and the executors of the late Enid Bagnold for my selection from *National Velvet*, together with one of Laurien Jones's sketches from that novel. To the Editor of *Horse and Hound* for permitting the description of Fred Winter's "*Win without Reins*" by "Audax" to be reproduced.

To John Johnson Ltd and the executors of the late author for the passage I have taken from *Tschiffely's Ride*, and the horses' prayer in *Round and About Spain*, also by A.F. Tschiffely. And to Michael Joseph Ltd and the authors for the quotations from *The Sport of Queens*, by Dick Francis, *Up Up and Away*, by Lucinda Prior-Palmer and *Great Moments in Sport*, by Dorian Williams.

To Methuen and Co. and the author's executors for the description of a point-to-point meeting, taken from the late H.V. Morton's *In Search of England*. To John Murray Ltd and the authors for the description of preparing for a ride in Spain in *Two Middle-Aged Ladies in Andalusia*, by Penelope Chetwode, and for the description of Gerard and the fox-hunt from the late Sir Arthur Conan Doyle's *The Adventures of Brigadier Gerard*. Phaidon Press Ltd and the author for the account of George Stubb's work from *Stubbs*, by Basil Taylor. Pitman Ltd and the author's executors for my selection from the late Sir Alfred Munnings's *An Artist's Life* and the sketch we have reproduced from that autobiography; and also to Pitman Ltd and Hutchinson Ltd, and John Hislop for the piece on race-riding tactics from his *Steeplechasing*.

To Seeley Service and Cooper Ltd for the piece on conduct in the hunting-field from the late Major-General Geoffrey Brooke's *The Way of a Man with a Horse* (Lonsdale Library). To Warne Ltd and Stella Walker for her account of the evolution of the horse in Summerhay's *Encyclopaedia for Horsemen*. To A.P. Watt Ltd, the National Trust, the Macmillan Co., of London and Basingstoke, and the late author's estate for Rudyard Kipling's polo story, *The Maltese Cat*, and to A.P. Watt Ltd, the National Trust and Eyre Methuen Ltd for the same author's verses, *The Undertaker's Horse*.

Finally to Audrey Guy, Sarah Huntington, Blanche Massey and Virginia Pinkham who helped type the passages from the books. And to my wife, Lavinia, who typed my preface, introductory commentaries, many of the passages and all my correspondence connected with this book.

J.N.P.W.

PREFACE

THE VERY WORDS "horse" and "rider" evoke romance and adventure. The literature surrounding them is enormous. I believe this collection embraces a larger number of extracts and a wider variety of authors than any comparable anthology in the English language. But, far from being exhaustive, it does not pretend to represent much more than a tip of the iceberg of equine and equestrian writing.

Anthologies take their character from personal taste and inclination, and in this case from the directions of my own equestrian experience. I was fortunate, some years ago, to serve in the Household Cavalry and to go through its equitation course; and, by virtue of the encouragement and generosity of that famous Corps, and a number of fortuitous army secondments, I went on, from my predilection for foxhunting, to indulge in polo, race-riding, showjumping, hunter trials, and the pentathlon. In addition to these activities, which often took me abroad, I also made a number of riding expeditions through the *sierras* of Andalusia. Naturally my selection has been influenced by these particular involvements, coupled with my preoccupation with history.

From the beginning of recorded history to the present century no creature has been closer to us than the horse. No other living agent has endowed us with greater power or has been more influential in helping us to extend and defend, and generally shape, the frontiers of our world. For, prior to the age of the combustion engine and wireless, equine power implied superior mobility and communications, as well as sheer physical strength.

The early peoples of Asia and Europe were enabled both to spread their power and protect their territories by harnessing horses into cavalry formations. Genghis Khan built his empire through the might of the warhorse. If Mahomet had not encouraged horse-breeding at the time of his rise there could have been no diffusion of Islam. If Harold had fielded a significant force of cavalry, the Normans could not have won England. The leaders of those tiny bands of Spaniards setting forth to conquer continents, Cortès in Mexico, and Pizarro in Peru, vowed that "next to God we owed our victories to our horses." And it was, above all, with the horse that "the West was won."

The ancients treasured their horses, sometimes even worshiped them: the Emperor Lucius Verus's horse, Celer, was stalled in the imperial palace, covered with a cloth of royal purple, and fed on almonds and raisins; while Caligula went so far as to appoint his Incitatus priest and consul of Rome, giving him an ivory manger and a golden bucket from which to drink wine.

Classical myth is steeped in references to the horse as a symbol of power: using its giant image in wood, the ancient Greeks took Troy; Castor and Pollux rode the "mighty Cyllaros"; the winged Pegasus flew Perseus to Andromeda's rescue and carried Bellerophon to the home of the gods, atop Mount Olympus; and Xanthos, the horse of Achilles, was reputed to be "human to all intents."

All through history horses have been associated with celebrated names; Bucephalus with Alexander the Great, Kantaka with the Buddha, Orelia with Roderick, Veillantiff with Roland, Babieca with El Cid, Black Saladin with Warwick, Roan Barbary with Richard II, White Surrey with Richard III, Savoy with Charles VIII of France, Carman with the Chevalier Bayard, Marengo with Napoleon, Copenhagen with Wellington, and Ronald with Cardigan. So, too, in the field of fiction is Rozinante linked with Don Quixote, Black Bess with Dick Turpin, and Orlando with Brigliadoro; while countless names stand out on their own: Black Beauty, Silver Blaze, Mare Swallow, Flicka, Pinto. . . .

This collection includes not only the "greatest stories" of its title, but also a host of vignettes of horse lore: poems, snatches of equestrian philosophy and personal experience, excerpts from novels and plays and many other pieces which, though "small" in literary terms, contain much charm and wisdom. But the book, to some extent, has been curtailed by the necessity to keep it to a reasonable length; and, after some painful decision-making, in order to strike the right balance, reluctantly I found myself cutting out pieces by such good authors as Armitage, Fillis, Gould, Grand, March Phillipps, de Maupassant, Thompson Seton and Wynmalen.

My included choices are grouped in twelve sections, each heralded by a brief introduction. The first, "Handsome Is . . .", deals with the evolution and nature of the horse, and continues with discussions by over twenty writers, from Shakespeare to Sassoon, on the characters of a diversity of horses and riders.

The second section, "Youth," is all about young people and their aspirations and adventures with ponies and horses. The third, "Equitation," includes five comments on the art of riding; and the fourth, "Cavalry," which is devoted to the warhorse and the warrior, portrays the glamor and trials, the glory and the tribulations of the horsed cavalry.

The Western Hemisphere has the next part to itself – "The West," with four vignettes of adventure from the United States and two from South America. Part six, "Spain," features the country, about whose horses more has been written, I think, than any other's.

Then come four sporting sections. "The Race Track" and "The Hunting-Field," each owning extensive literatures of their own, are the longest; with "Polo" next. Showjumping and eventing – "Leaping" – being very late on the stage, lack depth of literary material. But, so widely popular are they that I felt they merited a section to themselves, and I hope the choice of authors – Jack Talbot-Ponsonby, Dorian Williams, Pat Smythe and Lucinda Prior-Palmer – will provide ample enticement.

When you read of the vivid and exciting nineteenth-century coaching scenes, from both fact and fiction, in the penultimate section, "Old Coaching Days," it will not surprise you that so many good writers were attracted to that milieu. The descriptions which I have chosen come from the pens of Dickens, Washington Irving, Nimrod and Leigh Hunt.

The twelfth and last batch, "Adventure and Adversity," is composed of a variety of fictional dramas casting the horse in a dozen different roles – villainous and heroic, perilous and carefree, tragic and joyful – ending, appropriately, if gruesomely, with Kipling's tribute to the undertaker's horse.

I only hope you will derive as much fun and pleasure from reading this collection of equestrian writings as I have had in compiling it.

J.N.P.W.

HANDSOME IS...

~~~~~~

"Handsome is that handsome does," said my master. "You are only taking him on trial, and I am sure you will do fairly by him, young man; and if he is not as safe as any horse you ever drove, send him back."

ANNA SEWELL,
Black Beauty

HORSES COME IN A very wide variety of breeds, and between them these continue to fulfil many functions. And since the horse which wins the Grand National is unlikely to put up a good performance in the dressage ring, and the one that shows perfectly in the arena may be quite useless at drawing a cart, it follows that there can be no such creature as the perfect horse. Since the horse is diverse in character and employment, yet subject to a certain standard requirement in looks, I begin this section with an account of the evolution of the horse by Stella Walker. I follow it with the passage on conformation from the classic *Horsemanship*, by Waldemur Seunig, a graduate of Saumur, who went on to become famous in the Riding Instructors' Institute and as an instructor at the Spanish Riding School, at Vienna.

We know a good deal now about the faculties of horses. R.H. Smythe, a former examiner in surgery to the RCVS recorded his knowledge in *The Mind of the Horse*, from which I have quoted part of his essay on eyesight. A few years ago, H.N. Blake revealed the findings of forty years' research into horse communication, in his fascinating *Talking with Horses*, a central message of which follows Smythe's piece.

From there we turn down the ages for commentaries on equine quality from Virgil, Marco Polo, Shakespeare and Gervase Markham; and for sidelights on man's pride in his horse by listening to some of Shakespeare's lines for the Duke of Orleans in *Henry V*. In *Venus and Adonis* Shakespeare imagines a horses's capacity for love, and so, too, in *A Tree Grows in Brooklyn*, does Betty Smith. Then we have a beautiful panegyric on a horse in foal, by Vernon Watkins.

Of all the breeds the Arabian has probably been most widely upheld as

18

the most "handsome." Four centuries after Shakespeare's zenith, Wilfrid Blunt, the poet and publicist, and his wife Lady Anne, daughter of the Earl of Lovelace and grand-daughter of Byron, were traveling the northern deserts of Arabia in search of the best blood on which to found their Arabian stud at Crabbet, near Three Bridges, and Newbuildings near Horsham, in Sussex. I have taken a passage from Lady Anne's *Bedouins of the Euphrates*, in which she eulogizes about a horse typical of the quest, which was paraded for them during their first journey in 1878.

Thirty-three years later, when a young German, Carl Raswan, drawn by a romantic ideal, went to live among the bedouin of Egypt and Arabia, he learned to love their horses, and, above all, to find devotion in a horse called Ghazal. In my two excerpts from his book, *Drinkers of the Wind*, he explains how the Arabs recorded their horses' pedigrees, why the Arabian was by then in decline, and the charming way in which he meets Ghazal. To give an indication of the Westerner's continuing admiration for the breed I have put in Major John Board's assessment from his *Horse and Pencil*, together with his drawing of an Arab warrior mounted on his charger.

> *Blood arab, pedigree, no name*
> *All horses are the same . . .*

So wrote Dorothy, Duchess of Wellington, and the following poem from which those lines come, showed that she believed the best of all the breeds have an equal claim to beauty. And so, obviously, does Ronald Duncan who wrote the stirring epilogue for the Horse of the Year Show, which

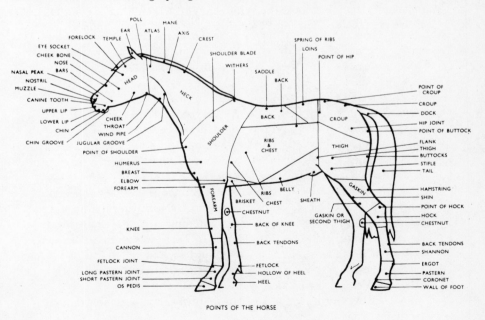

POINTS OF THE HORSE

comes next. But " . . . handsome is that handsome does"? How about that invention of Rabelais, Gargantua's hideous mare, who " . . . as soon as ever they were entered into the . . . forest, and that the wasps had given the assault, she drew out her tail, and there with skirmishing did so sweep them, that she overthrew all the wood along and athwart . . . in such sort that never since hath there been either wood or wasp." Or Modestine, the unprepossessing donkey which Robert Louis Stevenson chose in favor of a horse to carry him through the Cevennes a hundred years ago? Both of them are here.

Handsome is . . . We may also apply the maxim to a host of humans, who, in fact or fiction, have been involved with horses – flatteringly in five of the seven examples given: Chaucer's Monk who had "full many a dainty horse in stable"; Prince Harry "witching the world with noble horsemanship," from *Henry IV, Part I*; Gulliver explaining the usage of horses in the human world to the Houyhnhnms; Stubbs hoisting the carcases of dead horses into life-like positions in order to anatomize them; Raspe's ingenious Baron Munchausen, and Peter Donovan, the horse-breaker, whom Edith Somerville remembers from her childhood in the autobiography she wrote jointly with her partner and cousin, Martin Ross. Peter was handsome and did handsomely – "like a little elderly Dresden china shepherd . . . he was thrown and killed while showing-off a young horse at a fair, and it was said, in apology for his overthrow, that he had drink taken. He must have been over seventy, and, after all, it was a good way of escape from old age and its limitations, and of getting back – as we may believe – to the days of his 'bloom.' " The last two alas do less handsomely than they look: the White Knight, whom Alice encounters in *Through the Looking Glass*, and Siegfried Sassoon's "fussy colonel."

"I am Thor!"
"Thilly boy! Why not ride thide-saddle?"

THE EVOLUTION OF THE HORSE

Stella A. Walker

1975

MOST SCIENTISTS BELIEVE that the first animal capable of producing our modern horse was found originally in both the Eastern and the Western hemispheres, but the distribution of fossils seems to show that it became extinct in the Old World and that the first equine ancestor proper (*Eohippus*) lived approximately fifty-five million years ago in North America.

It has been deduced that it was a creature the size of a fox with short hair, thick neck and stumpy tail. Its fore-feet were divided into four toes and the "splint" of a fifth toe, and the hind feet had three toes with either one or two additional "splints".

As swamp was gradually replaced by forest and grassland this prehistoric animal, over a period of many millions of years, appears to have adapted its conformation to the new physical conditions. The legs became longer, the head was raised higher and the toes started to contract on the harder ground. This growth made concealment from its enemies difficult, so speed was developed as a means of escape. Increased movement brought further leg and muscular expansion until a three-toed horse with a good turn of speed, and the size of an Exmoor pony, gradually evolved. It is interesting to note, though, that at six weeks the modern equine embryo of today still has the three-toed foot conformation. The necessity for increased speed may have caused the broadening of the central toe until the lateral toes became mere "pettitoes" and the final major evolutionary change to a foot of one toe resulted in the *Equus* of the Pleistocene Age. It is this animal which is readily recognizable as the forerunner of the modern horse: and this is the broad theory of the evolution of the horse held by most scientists today. It is borne out by fossils found in many parts of the United States, especially in the asphalt pits of California. As recently as 1953 eight practically perfect skulls of *Eohippus* have been found in a fossil bed in Colorado.

There were many types of this primitive horse in North and South America, its growth varying with geographical conditions from mere pigmy size to the *Equus giganteus* of 20 h.h. (204 cm) which inhabited Texas. Eventually some cause, possibly disease perhaps spread by a primitive tsetse fly or a form of rabies, and the coming of the Glacial Age rendered the horse extinct in the Western hemisphere, and it was not seen there again until the invasion by Cortès in the sixteenth century.

Before the complete disappearance of the horse in the Americas, however, herds must have crossed to the eastern hemisphere by the still

21

existent land bridges between the continents. Here it had escaped extinction by the Glacial Age, as only the more northerly regions of Europe and Asia were affected; but the ultimate subsidence of the land connecting the eastern and western worlds eventually made the horse an inhabitant solely of the Old World.

There were two distinct types of horses. The first was a northern dun species which is still represented today by the wild pony of Western Mongolia known as the Przevalski horse, after the nineteenth-century Russian explorer. It is the only truly wild horse still in existence and is about 12 h.h. (122 cm) high with an ungainly head, short erect mane and no forelock. It is yellowish-dun in colour with a light muzzle and narrow, ass-like feet. Certain characteristics of this northern type of horse are seen today in the ponies of Norway and Iceland.

It seems possible, though scientifically unproved as yet, there may have been a subdivision of this Northern species into a European forest type, heavily built, large boned and hairy legged, which became the primitive ancestor of our Shires and Clydesdales.

The second type was the Southern Horse, living in the Caspian and Mediterranean areas. It was a thinner skinned animal, less heavy, quicker in movement and intelligence and darker in colour. It can be claimed as the prehistoric forerunner of the Arab, Barb and Turk.

These herds of wild horses were very common and were hunted and killed extensively by Palaeolithic man for food. The bones of tens of thousands have been found outside one prehistoric cave settlement near Lyons.

Domestication of the horse did not occur until many hundreds of years later, possibly about 2500 BC amongst tribes of the Near East, being tamed probably first for its milk and flesh, then for haulage and much later for riding. Marauding forays into Babylonia and Syria spread this domestication westwards until we have evidence in 1900 BC of the horse being driven and ridden by the Egyptians.

Among the isolated and nomadic tribes of Arabia the Southern Horse seems to have possessed even then the qualities unequalled by those in other regions. Some authorities trace the real genesis of the Arabian horse to Libya and Morocco, and others to India. The fact remains that, wherever its origin, it is the Arab type of horse that has always been used down the ages to improve the northern stock. We hear of this Arab strain being imported by the horse-loving Greeks; the Arab blood was used also by the Romans to improve the native ponies in their conquests in Northern Europe, Asia and Africa.

War has always been an incentive to the development of a better type of horse. Saracen invasions brought the Barb to France; Moorish occupation introduced it into Spain. The ever-increasing use of armour in mediaeval warfare made weight and size the supreme aim in horse-breeding, and the Percherons of today are the descendants of those weight-carriers of the

Middle Ages. Eventually the arrival of firearms rendered obsolete the huge load of armour on man and beast and the end of the sixteenth century brought a demand for a lighter horse of speed and dexterity. In England racing and hunting became enormously popular under the Stuarts and as a result Barbs, Arabs and Turks were imported in great numbers. Between 1689 and 1730 there arrived the three famous stallions, the Byerley Turk, the Darley Arabian and the Godolphin Arabian, and from these three horses all modern English Thoroughbred stock can trace its descent. This alliance of the sturdiness and vigour of the Northern Horse to the beauty, speed and stamina of the Southern Horse has resulted in the superb English Thoroughbred, an animal unsurpassed by any other horse in the world, and epitomizing the miracle of evolution.

CONFORMATION (1)

Waldemar Seunig

1956

THE FIRST IMPRESSION we get as the horse is shown to us should leave us in no doubt that the flat, long, muscular hindquarters are connected with sloping shoulders and a long, well-carried neck through a back that is not too short, and through long, pronounced withers. Its steps should be rangy and elastic.

Enough time must be allowed for observation, from *all sides*, that is, in front and behind, during, before, and after movement, in the stable and in the pasture if at all possible, and in the demonstration ring only if absolutely necessary. This will enable the average judge to make a closer study of the individual parts of the body and their relationship to one another.

A lean, finely chiselled *head*, with strong masseteric muscles, well developed in height and breadth, is an index of great value. Leanness is evidence of mobility and nerve, and divergence of the angles of the lower jaw and adequate space between them testify to good development of the molars, so necessary to digestion.

Concavity of the bridge of the nose, with wide nostrils, is evidence of greater energy of breathing produced by compression and warming up. A slight arch of the line of the forehead between the eyes often indicates a strongly developed wilfulness, which may develop into intractability.

One of the principal attributes of a perfect head is the large *eye*, which should reflect guileless confidence. It should be set low, that is, down towards the nostrils, and should not be sunken. Such an eye will be able to orient itself in the immediate neighbourhood without moving the head, since the large cornea enables much light to enter the eye, and its low position enables the horse to see the ground immediately in front of it without having to lower its head.

The expression of the eye and the set of the ears provide hints of character. An unsteady eye or one that looks "far away" indicates psychological disturbances; a "tranquil ear" indicates inner equilibrium, and short, deeply arched ears are evidence of sensitivity and ability to learn.

But not all breeds can have the heads of Arabs, and we find noble horses of balance and achievement with heavy heads among the Irish and Lipizzan breeds, for example.

The *neck* should be long and free, wide in gullet, that is, thinning down as it approaches the head, with a slightly curved topline and a straight bottom line, the two lines enclosing a broad base that is "set on" the shoulders. Short, heavy necks that are set on low down do not aid equilibrium and hence should be rejected for any usage. But if the set of the neck is good, such a neck can be shaped by stretching it to meet the bit, and its steadiness will make the rider's work much easier. If the neck is thin and set on low, the only thing one can hope for in training is making it steady; one should not try to do violence to nature by demanding that it be held higher as a result of collection.

As a balancing rod that promotes motion, the neck plays an extremely important role in the total mechanism of motion. That is why natural carriage of the neck that is altogether too high becomes an obstacle to rapid travel over rough terrain.

Low, short *withers* will never provide a good base for the saddle. The rider's weight thrown too far forward will prevent the horse from achieving balance, the transition to the extended gaits will turn into rushing, and these gaits will never develop smoothly and in correct tempo from freely carrying hindquarters. When we add the danger of pressure owing to the saddle's sliding forward, we can say that blurry "mutton withers" will be a source of perpetual dissatisfaction, no matter how the horse is employed.

If the *shoulder* is long and slopes forward from the withers, we have further guarantee of the formation of a good position for the saddle. A horse with a long neck and withers gives the rider "a lot in front of him," which not only increases his safety but makes it easier for him to have calm nerves in difficult terrain and to maintain the necessary easy control of the reins.

An *arm* of suitable length, connected at approximately a right angle to a shoulder blade covered by well-contoured muscles, guarantees a long-striding step, provided the impulsion and thrust reaching it from the hindquarters are adequate. Without the latter, however, the most splendid pair of shoulders are practically worthless.

Large posterior projections of the ulna in the *elbow joint* are particularly desirable in horses that are destined to do much galloping. If these bony processes (which are important levers) are not "slicked down" and are separated from the side of the chest by at least a finger's width, it may be generally assumed that such an "elbow-free" horse will be able to get out of critical situations skilfully and always remain on its four legs, which will not interfere with one another. Then trotting is done behind the vertical as well as in front of it.

The *forearm* should be long compared to the front cannon and like the latter, should be broad. Though it cannot be too heavily muscled, the tendons must be well marked on the cannon, and the impression of leanness must not be impaired by any blurredness.

The *front knee* and *fetlock* will do their job best if they are large enough to provide favourable points of attachments for ligaments and tendons. But both of these joints will not possess much staying power if they are "puffy".

The connection between the cannon and the hoof should be made by a rather long and elastic but strong *pastern*. Too steep a pastern can make an otherwise outstanding horse practically useless. Aside from the fact that the grounding reaction, thudding, is communicated from the hoof to the joints with practically no interruption, thus making premature wear very likely, the inelastic tread also causes premature fatigue of the rider. We might add that horses with upright pasterns take short steps because of the almost vertical, pricking step in their gait, which has little swing to it because it has no phase of suspension; these horses seem to find every little stone in the terrain to stumble over, making one mistake after another.

In conclusion, let me say that if you have to choose between a very soft pastern and one whose angle exceeds 45 degrees, even if only slightly, do not hesitate to choose the "defective" soft one in which the axis of the toe is bent somewhat to the rear; you will not regret it. Owing to its active elasticity, the system of ligaments and tendons that supports and surrounds the treading pastern is much stronger than the bones and joints, which are inevitably damaged if the pastern is too steep. The softer pastern not only ensures a natural mitigation of the impact (landing after a jump) but also promotes the so-called compensating sliding, which allows even hoofs that wear calked horseshoes to slide a bit forward when they land on hard ground. This protects the coffin joint and assists the mechanism of the hoof.

Though catchwords are of little value in judging a horse, where all criticism can be only relative, that is, related to efficiency and kinetics – the way in which a horse makes use of its means of locomotion – I should like to make an exception in this case and repeat the old truism "Without a pastern, no horse."

We may suppose that the "necessary evil" of shoeing has not caused any damage in the hoofs of horses that have grown up in the open air. Such horses should be left unshod as long as possible – at most, they should be shod with crescent-shaped shoes on their forefeet. This will greatly promote the circulation of the blood and the breathing of the hoof – gymnastics of the frog. The unshod hoof adheres to smooth ground better, though it cannot be denied that the Mordax antislip calks are very useful on glazed frost or that calked hind horseshoes are necessary for jumping on slippery tournament turf. What one should look for in foals out at pasture is good development of the bars. They act as shock absorbers and protect the joints just as correctly angled pasterns do.

The fore and hind hoofs differ in that the former are somewhat larger and rounder (supporting surface) and the latter are somewhat ovoid (to facilitate thrust). That is why the slope of the hind pasterns (about 60 degrees) should be somewhat steeper than that of the front pasterns.

Backs that are too stiff and straight are passable today only for draft animals; but if we intend to ride, we must remember that only a certain length of the back makes possible an unconstrained interaction of the ring of muscles from the croup through the back, the neck, and the belly, and allows the entire mechanism of the horse to swing freely. The length of the back must, of course, be the combined result of long withers, long, straight breastbone (girth furrow!), and a loin of moderate length. Then the loin will be satisfactory, with well-developed lower ribs lying close to the haunches. Such a horse will probably be able to do well on short rations and thus be cheaper to maintain.

A short, "square" horse, in which the distance from the shoulder to the pelvis does not exceed the height at the withers, will always find it hard to keep its balance because of the shortness of its area of support. A long neck – which is a rarity in such horses – may facilitate equilibrium, compensating by its free balancing action.

Much as a pronounced "low point" of the back, in the region of the fifteenth spinal vertebra and at the end of the smoothly sloping withers, is desirable from the standpoint of the rider, extremes should be avoided; unmistakable sway-backs, and "hog backs" are causes for rejection. Such backs make extension difficult, imperilling correct dressage as well as the development of speed.

Narrow-chested, long-legged horses will grow tired rapidly, not for want of muscle power, but because the length and curvature of the ribs are too small to provide the heart and the lungs, that is, the breathing apparatus, the necessary room for action. In school training such horses tend to be "cross-legged" in the lateral movements, and since the outer hind foot steps out too far to the side, in the *travers* (also called "*haunches in*"), for example, crossing the line that passes through the centre of gravity, they lose their impulsion and with it their poise and carriage. Moreover legs that are excessively long tend to drag, especially in the collected gaits.

If the *breadth and depth of the chest* are so highly developed that the chest is out of proportion to the rest of the body, we must suppose that such a horse will display a lack of manoeuvrability during dressage, and insufficient speed.

The *hindquarters* should be long. This is especially true of the distances between the hips and the point of the buttocks, the hip joint and the stifle joint, and the stifle joint and the hock. The latter joint should be as close as possible to the ground, thus providing the desired shortness of the hind cannon. If the angle between the ilium and the thigh bone at the hip joint is just less than a right angle, the stifle joint will lie far in front as a visible sign of this bone structure, and the gluteus maximus muscle will act at a right angle upon the great trochanter of the thigh. Stretching and bending then occur under the best circumstances, without any loss of power, and thus promote the gait. If the stifle and hock project to the rear, there is a lack of harmony between the thrust and the ranging action; this results in the ugly "remaining behind" of the hindquarters and interferes with the harmony of motion, a defect that, like being built too high, is hard to compensate even by perfection of forequarters and back.

Broad and strong musculature of the *lower thigh* depends chiefly on the location and size of the most important of the six bones of the *hock*. The longer this bone is and the greater the angle between its axis and that of the tibia, the more room for the development of strong muscles, for then the Achilles tendon is far from the gaskin. And the gaskins are good and wide. This development of the biggest bone in the hock also determines the length and width of the hock itself, to which we must add its depth – the distance between the inner and outer surfaces, the transverse diameter. All three of these dimensions are equally necessary to give this third strongest joint in the horse's body the ability to distribute the pressure of the load of horse and rider (which is often extraordinarily high when striking the ground) and to throw it forward and carry it by means of favourable lever action. The bones and ligaments of this joint must be well defined under a thin skin and must blend imperceptibly into the broad front surface of the hind cannon. These parts of the hind leg, like all the others, must be judged in accordance with the same principles as those used for the forelegs.

If the position of the thigh is correct, steep hocks need not cause too much worry, especially if the hind fetlock is somewhat soft and contributes to absorbing the shock. The forward reach of the hind leg suffers somewhat at the walk, but horses with this conformation can be very useful at the trot and the gallop. The slight extensibility of the angle (which is naturally too wide open in this case) is balanced out by the thrust – the impulsion – which is particularly effective in this case in the suspension phases of these two gaits. But if we try to get from such a horse real flexion and extension, which are required for a correctly ridden middle trot, or an elastic, spirited, springy step in flexion, in complete collection, we will meet the difficulty and realize that nature sets bounds to even the greatest art. However, a hock that is somewhat too sharply angled will certainly not harm a dressage horse if the stifle is at the right location and the thigh is long and sloping. Too open a stifle angle, to be sure, interferes with an otherwise excellent freedom of movement of the hock. It renders long strides in the direction of the centre of gravity impossible, and the hind-quarters drag.

EYESIGHT

R. H. Smythe

1965

HOW FAR DOES a horse see?

It is likely that with head held reasonably high with forehead and face perpendicular to the ground, in open country the horse will see, when nothing else crosses the field of vision, all the landscape for several hundred yards around by the alternate use of frontal and lateral vision. By careful adjustment of the head the horse might recognise another horse or group of horses a quarter of a mile distant. It must not be imagined, however, that a horse can see a tiny speck on a hillside half-a-mile away, which we might recognise as a man or a woman and translate it into an enlarged mental image. This is most unlikely as it would require a deal of imagination, and a memory for detail which few animals below the Primates possess.

The horse does not see a landscape as we do. In the first place, being colour blind, the horse fails to see green fields, blue skies and water, and the spring and autumn tints of trees. The eyes of the horse are quite incapable of breaking up the visual image into trees, grass, bridges, gateways, arches, patches of cover and areas of space. It sees the land ahead as a mosaic in shades of grey, including dark areas and a modicum of shadow.

It cannot sort out a grey rabbit from among a patch of green cabbages, unless the rabbit moves – in fact in a landscape free of movement the horse might be unable to sort out anything other than masses forming the greater part of the picture. These would be represented by woods and trees, areas of grassland, or large patches of water, but as all would differ . only in tone and not in colour, there is no proof that the horse would have any knowledge as to their exact nature when viewed from afar.

We possess the advantage of knowing that large expanses of green represent grassland. We can distinguish cornland from land growing roots, all by colour shades, but no horse can do this as we can. It must depend for its visual information upon brightness rather than upon colour. It recognises movement by the change of brightness in parts of the mosaic as various parts of the moving object reflect or refract light, as well as upon the changing relationship of the moving body to other fixed bodies.

Nor does the young horse receive verbal or visual teaching from a fond parent who points out objects, gives them a name and explains what they are. The horse knows only what it can teach itself by experience, using mainly the principles of trial and error. Horses learn little by the sense of touch, except perhaps that jumps are hard. They seldom go up to an object and touch it with lips or tongue, neither have they any fingers.

Their knowledge is confined to objects in constant reach such as pails and mangers, rugs and grooming equipment – not a great background upon which to found knowledge.

In the wild state the horse might satisfy its own curiosity. If it viewed a flat grey surface and wondered whether it represented grazing land; or if it saw a patch of brighter grey and hoped it was water, it could find out by approaching it and making a close-up investigation.

With a rider on its back it goes only where the rider wishes.

LANGUAGE

H.N. Blake

1975

WHEN WE STARTED RESEARCH into animal communication, we decided to try to compile a short dictionary of horse messages, and for this we started by following the path that had been trodden by most people in the same field. Since we use sounds ourselves to communicate, it seemed obvious to start by studying horse sounds, so we decided to try to deduce some pattern from the sounds horses make. In these early stages we had a certain degree of success. We found that the whicker of welcome and the neigh of alarm were sounds that were common to very nearly all horses. But the more research we carried out, the more we discovered that we could not rely on set patterns as a guide to interpreting the sounds used by horses as a species. It became clear that different horses use the same sequence of sounds to convey different meanings, each horse having its own language, only similar to that of its associates and not identical. So we had to go back and start again.

We did this first by looking at how human beings communicate, and we discovered that as much is conveyed by the tone of voice and the manner of delivering a phrase as by the actual words themselves. For example, an

Englishman, an Irishman, a Scotsman and a Welshman all speak English. They can understand each other, but their means of conveying any meaning is different. They will use different words, different phrases in different forms. In other words, people of different cultural background, even though they speak the same basic language, will use different words and phrases to convey a single meaning. And even within one culture, people of different nature and temperament will use divergent word-forms to convey a single meaning. Certain sounds on the other hand are standard to all people of the same race and are used at certain times: the word "hello" for instance is common to all English-speaking people. It is in the same sense that the whicker of welcome is common to all horses. And just as the cry of "help" is used by all people who speak English, most horses have a neigh or scream of alarm.

We also looked at the importance of the tone of voice to meaning. We found that the tone of voice used by human beings to convey a standard message can vary both its meaning and its force. For example, a man or a woman using the phrase "come here" can vary its whole sense by the tone of voice. If the words are murmured by a woman in a soft and seductive voice, it can be an invitation to make love. If the tone of voice is sharp or harsh it is a command to be obeyed instantly, and if screamed "come here" can be a cry for help. In the same way the horse can vary its message by a raising and hardening of the voice, so that similar sounds can mean anything from "come here, darling" to, in its highest and hardest impera- tive, "if you do not come here immediately I will have your guts for garters." And exactly the same message can be used as a cry for help.

The second thing we found we had to take into account was that habits of communication vary according to sex; and whereas among human beings there are only two sexes, male and female, among domesticated horses there are three sexes, male, female and neuter. This is important, since the note and tone of each sex is different: the range of notes used by a stallion and a mare are completely different, and the gelding will come somewhere between the two. This is not so important when you are in contact with a single horse, but it is extremely important to remember if you are handling a large number of horses, or are trying to understand what a strange horse is saying, since the same sequence of notes used by a mare, a gelding and a stallion can mean different things.

Before you can even start to interpret a message made by sound, therefore, you have to know the sex of the animal. We also discovered that it is important to take into account the age of the horse, because obviously the range of tones and notes used by a foal is completely different from the notes and range he will use as a stallion four or five years later.

On the other hand the stallion, mare, gelding, foal and yearling will all have the same number of tones and notes, and they will be made in eleven different ways. Nine of the eleven different tones of voice are made by exhaling, that is to say they are made by breathing out. First there is a snort, which is made by using the nostrils alone as a sound box, and at times the imperative is expressed by crackling the nostrils at the same time. The stronger note with the crackling of the nostrils is used to draw attention as a signal of alarm, as a sign the horse is excited or to denote strong emotions. The whicker is also made by using the nostrils as a sound box, but this is a much more caressing note and can vary from a very gentle blowing through the nostrils to quite a strong sound, used usually as a greeting or to show affection of some sort. Then there is the whinney, which is a much higher-pitched enquiring sound, and the neigh, which is stronger again than the whinney. In these two the voice box is used. In addition we know the squeal of the mare, and the bell of the stallion, each of which can have a distinctive sexual tone to them, or may sound aggressive or be used as a warning. These both come from the upper nasal regions of the voice box and are used in sex play, in anger or to display temper. The stallion has a whistle which he uses to call the mare; and all horses have a scream of fear, pain or anger which comes as a gust of terror from the lungs. These are all exhaling sounds. The breathing-in-sounds consist of a snuffle, which corresponds to the snort. Each of these notes has a definite meaning for another horse.

The stallion has the greatest vocal range, and some of his notes are frightening, while others will be very beautiful to hear. But he has a somewhat limited range of messages to deliver with his voice, simply because in his natural state he is concerned only with three things: sex, danger and food. So his messages are confined to these three subjects. In fact you might say he has only got three subjects of conversation, fear, food and female, which makes him very like man, except that man has one further topic of conversation, and that is how best to avoid work. So in addition to "let's eat", "let's make love", "let's bugger off", mankind also adds "let's strike"!

A mare on the other hand, while she has her sexual sounds and her sounds for food and danger, also has a range of sounds for the care and protection of her foal, and probably her yearling as well. She has to call her young to her for food, she has to call them in case of threatened danger and she has to teach them discipline, so her range of messages will be far greater than that of the stallion. A gelding, which of course does not exist in the wild, has a vocal range which may vary from that of a stallion, if it has been cut very late, to that of a mare if it is over-protective to the person who looks after it. A foal equally will have its own messages and vocal range concerning food and fear; it will have no sexual messages but it will have a range of sounds asking for protection and reassurance, and these will change as he gets older. He will retain some of his foal phrases as a yearling and even as a two-year-old. Then, when he starts feeling a man in his two-year-old summer, and certainly as a three-year-old, unless he has already been cut, his messages and voice will change to that of a stallion; or a filly will develop the language of a mare.

31

ROME

Virgil

c. 30 BC

DISCRIMINATING CARE is requisite for a breed of horses. But still, on those which you intend to bring up for the hope of the race, bestow your principal diligence immediately from their tender years. The colt of generous breed from the very first walks high throughout the fields, and nimbly moves his pliant legs; he is the first that dares to lead the way, and tempt the threatening floods, and trust himself to an unknown bridge; nor starts affrighted at vain alarms. Lofty is his neck, his head little and slender, his belly short, his back plump, and his proud chest swells luxuriant with brawny muscles: (the bright bay and bluish grey are in most request; the worst colours are the white and sorrel). Then, if he by chance hears the distant sound of arms, he knows not how to stand still; he pricks up his ears, trembles in every joint, and snorting, rolls the collected fire under his nostrils. Thick is his mane, and, waving, rests on his right shoulder. A double spine runs along his loins, his hoof scoops up the ground, and deep resounds with its solid horn. Such was Cyllarus, broken by the reins of Amyclaean Pollux, and such (which the Grecian poets have described) the harnessed brace of Mars, and the chariot-horses of great Achilles. Such Saturn too himself, swift at the coming of his wife, spread out a full mane on his [assumed] horse's neck, and flying filled lofty Pelion with shrill neighing.

Him too – when with sickness oppressed, or now enfeebled with years, he fails – shut up in his lodge, and spare his not inglorious age. An old horse is cold to love, and in vain drags on the ungrateful task, and if ever he comes to an engagement, he is impotently furious, as at times a great fire without strength among stubble. Therefore chiefly mark their spirit and age; then their other qualities, their parentage, and what is the sorrow of each when vanquished, what the pride when victorious.

See you not? when in the rapid race the chariots have seized the plain, and pouring forth rush along; when the hopes of the youth are elevated, and palpitating fear heaves their throbbing hearts: they ply with the twisted lash, and bending forward give full reins: the axle flies glowing with the impetuosity. And now low, now high, they seem to be borne aloft through the open air, and to mount up into the skies. No stop, no stay: but a thick cloud of yellow sand is tossed up; the foremost are wet with the foam and breath of those that follow. So powerful is the love of praise, so anxious the desire of victory.

First Erichthonius dared to yoke the chariot and four steeds, and upon the rapid wheels victorious to stand. The Pelethronian Lapithae first mounted on horseback applied the reins, and turned him in the ring; taught the horsemen under arms to spurn the plain, and with proud ambling pace to prance along. Either toil is equal; with equal care the masters in either case seek after a [steed that is] youthful, of warm mettle, and eager in the race: [they do not make choice of an old horse] though often he may have driven before him the flying foes, may boast of Epirus, or of warlike Mycenae for his country, and derive his pedigree even from Neptune's breed.

These things observed, they are very careful about the time [of generation], and bestow all their care to plump him up with firm fat whom they have chosen leader, and assigned stallion to the herd: they cut downy herbs, and supply him with plenty of water and corn, that he may be adequate to the soothing toil, and lest the puny sons should declare the meagreness of their sires. But they purposely attenuate the brood mares with leanness: and, when now the known pleasure solicits the first enjoyment, they both deny herbs, and debar them from the springs; often too they shake them in the race, and tire them in the sun, when beneath the beaten grain the barn floor deeply groans, and in the rising zephyr the empty chaff is tossed about. This they do, that excessive pampering may not blunt the powers of the genial soil, and choke up the sluggish passages; but that it may with eagerness drink in the joys of love, and lay them up more deeply within.

Again the cares of the sires begin to fail, and that of the dams to succeed; when now, their months elapsed, they rove about pregnant: let no one suffer them to drag the yokes of heavy waggons, or to leap across the way, scamper over the meads with sprightly career, and swim the rapid floods. They ought then to feed in spacious lawns, and beside full rivers, where moss, and grassy banks of prime verdure, and caves may shelter them, and over them a shady rock project.

THE BREED OF BUCEPHALUS

Marco Polo

Late 13th Century

THE PROVINCE OF Balasham is a cold country. The horses bred here are of superior quality and have great speed. Their hoofs are so hard that they do not require shoeing. The natives are in the practice of galloping them on declivities where other cattle could not or would not venture to run. They asserted that not long since there were still found in this province horses of the breed of Alexander's celebrated Bucephalus, which were all foaled with a particular mark in the forehead. The whole of the breed was in the possession of one of the king's uncles, who, upon his refusal to yield them to his nephew, was put to death; whereupon his widow, exasperated at the murder, caused them all to be destroyed; and thus the race was lost to the world.

CONFORMATION (2)

William Shakespeare

1593

Look, when a painter would surpass the life,
In limning out a well-proportion'd steed,
His art with nature's workmanship at strife,
As if the dead the living should exceed;
   So did this horse excel a common one,
   In shape, in courage, colour, pace and bone.

Round-hoof'd, short-jointed, fetlocks shag and
   long,
Broad breast, full eye, small head, and nostril
   wide,
High crest, short ears, straight legs, and passing
   strong,
Thin mane, thick tail, broad buttock, tender
   hide:
   Look what a horse should have he did not lack,
   Save a proud rider on so proud a back.

RICHARD II DETHRONED AND DEHORSED

William Shakespeare

1597

   Enter a Groom of the stable.
GROOM Hail, royal Prince!
K. RICH. Thanks, noble peer!
   The cheapest of us is ten groats too dear.

What art thou? and how comest thou hither,
Where no man never comes but that sad dog
That brings me food to make misfortune live?
GROOM I was a poor groom of thy stable, King
When thou wert king; who, travelling towards York,
With much ado at length have gotten leave
To look upon my sometimes royal master's face.
O, how it ern'd my heart, when I beheld,
In London streets, that coronation-day,
When Bolingbroke rode on roan Barbary –
That horse that thou so often hast bestrid,
That horse what I so carefully have dress'd!
K. RICH. Rode he on Barbary? Tell me, gentle friend,
How went he under him?
GROOM So proudly as if he disdain'd the ground.
K. RICH. So proud that Bolingbroke was on his back!
That jade hath eat bread from my royal hand;
This hand hath made him proud with clapping him.
Would he not stumble? would he not fall down,
Since pride must have a fall, and break the neck
Of that proud man that did usurp his back?
Forgiveness, horse! Why do I rail on thee,
Since thou, created to be aw'd by man,
Wast born to bear? I was not made a horse;
And yet I bear a burden like an ass,
Spurr'd, gall'd, and tir'd, by jauncing Bolingbroke.

THE ENGLISH HORSE

Gervase Markham

1616

I DO DAILY FIND in mine experience, that the virtue, goodness, boldness, swiftness, and endurance of our true-bred English horses is equal with any race of horses whatsoever. Some former writers, whether out of want of experience, or to flatter novelties, have concluded that the English horse is a great strong jade, deep-ribbed, side-bellied, with strong legs and good hoofs, yet fitter for the cart than either saddle or any working employment. How false this is all English horsemen know. The true English horse, him I mean that is bred under a good clime, on firm ground, in a pure temperature, is of tall stature and large proportions; his head, though not so fine as either the Barbary's or the Turk's, yet is lean, long, and well-fashioned; his crest is high, only subject to thickness if he be stoned, but if he be gelded then it is firm and strong; his chine is straight and broad; and all his limbs large, lean, flat, and excellently jointed. For their endurance I have seen them suffer and execute as much and more than ever I noted of any foreign creation. I have heard it reported that at the massacre of Paris (St. Bartholomew) Montgomerie, taking an English mare in the night, first swam over the river Seine, and after ran her so many leagues as I fear to nominate, lest misconstruction might tax me of too lavish a report. Again, for swiftness, what nation has brought forth that horse which hath exceeded the English – when the best Barbarys that ever were in their prime, I saw them overrun by a black hobby at Salisbury; yet that hobby was more overrun by a horse called Valentine, which Valentine neither in hunting or running was ever equalled, yet was a plain-bred English horse both by sire and dam? Again, for infinite labour and long endurance, which is to be desired in our hunting matches, I have not seen any horse to compare with the English. He is of tolerable shape, strong, valiant and durable.

BETTER A HORSE THAN A MISTRESS

William Shakespeare

1600

CONSTABLE OF FRANCE. Tut! I have the best armour of the world. Would it were day!

DUKE OF ORLEANS. You have an excellent armour; but let my horse have his due.

CON. It is the best horse of Europe.

ORL. Will it never be morning?

THE DAUPHIN. My Lord of Orleans and my Lord High
Constable, you talk of horse and armour?

ORL. You are as well provided of both as any
prince in the world.

DAU. What a long night is this! I will
not change my horse with any that treads
but on four pasterns. Ça, ha! he bounds
from the earth as if his entrails were hairs;
le cheval volant, the Pegasus, chez les
narines de feu! When I bestride him I
soar, I am a hawk. He trots the air; the
earth sings when he touches it; the basest
horn of his hoof is more musical than the
pipe of Hermes.

ORL. He's of the colour of the nutmeg.

DAU. And of the heat of the ginger. It is
a beast for Perseus; he is pure air and
fire; and the dull elements of earth and
water never appear in him, but only in
patient stillness while his rider mounts
him; he is indeed a horse, and all other
jades you may call beasts.

CON. Indeed, my lord, it is a most
absolute and excellent horse.

DAU. It is the prince of palfreys; his
neigh is like the bidding of a monarch, and
his countenance enforces homage.

ORL. No more, cousin.

DAU. Nay, the man hath no wit that
cannot, from the rising of the lark to the
lodging of the lamb, vary deserved praise
on my palfrey. It is a theme as fluent as
the sea: turn the sands into eloquent
tongues, and my horse is argument for them
all; 'tis a subject for a sovereign to reason
on, and for a sovereign's sovereign to ride
on; and for the world – familiar to us and
unknown – to lay apart their particular
functions and wonder at him. I once writ
a sonnet in his praise and began thus:
"Wonder of nature" –

ORL. I have heard a sonnet begin so to
one's mistress.

DAU. Then did they imitate that which I

compos'd to my courser; for my horse is
my mistress.

ORL. Your mistress bears well.

DAU. Me well; which is the prescript
praise and perfection of a good and
particular mistress.

CON. Nay, for methought yesterday your
mistress shrewdly shook your back.

DAU. So perhaps did yours.

CON. Mine was not bridled.

DAU. O, then belike she was old and
gentle; and you rode like a kern of Ireland,
your French hose off and in your strait
strossers.

CON. You have good judgment in horsemanship.

DAU. Be warn'd by me, then: they that ride so,
and ride not warily, fall into foul bogs.
I had rather have my horse to my mistress.

LOVE

William Shakespeare

1593

*Sometimes he scuds far off, and there he
    stares;
Anon he starts at stirring of a feather;
To bid the wind a base he now prepares,
And whe'r he run or fly they know not
    whether;
  For through his mane and tail the high
    wind sings,
  Fanning the hairs, who wave like
    feath'red wings.*

*He looks upon his love and neighs unto her;
She answers him as if she knew his mind;
Being proud, as females are, to see him woo
    her,
She puts on outward strangeness, seems
    unkind,*

Spurns at his love, and scorns the heat
   he feels,
Beating his kind embracements with her
   heels.

Then, like a melancholy malcontent,
He vails his tail, that, like a falling plume,
Cool shadow to his melting buttock lent;
He stamps, and bites the poor flies in his
   fume.
   His love, perceiving how he was enrag'd,
   Grew kinder, and his fury was assuag'd . . .

THE MARE

Vernon Watkins

1935

The mare lies down in the grass where the nest of the skylark is
   hidden.
Her eyes drink the delicate horizon moving behind the song.
Deep sink the skies, a well of voices. Her sleep is the vessel of
   Summer.
That climbing music requires the hidden music at rest.

Her body is utterly given to the light, surrendered in perfect abandon
To the heaven above her shadow, still as her first-born day.
Softly the wind runs over her. Circling the meadow, her hooves
Rest in a race of daisies, halted where butterflies stand.

Do not pass her too close. It is easy to break the circle
and lose that indolent fullness rounded under the ray
Falling on light-eared grasses your footstep must not yet wake.
It is easy to darken the sun of her unborn foal at play.

THE BLUNTS IN SYRIA

Lady Anne Blunt

1878

ALL DAY LONG people have been bringing horses and mares for us to look at, for we have given out that we wish to exchange Tamarisk for something better, and a very interesting sight it has been. The Welled Ali themselves are not remarkable for their horses, but we saw one very pretty grey horse, Seglawi Jedran of Ibn Nedéri's breed, which had no defect but that of size. It was only fourteen hands. A Gomussa, however, came in later with a magnificent three-year-old, a Samhan el Gomeáa, a bay with black points. This is the most powerful animal we have yet seen. He stands fifteen hands, and has tremendous forearms and quarters, though still coltish. His action was less good, though it is difficult to judge from the extremely bad riding of the man who brought him. Horses, in the desert, are always ill-broken compared to the mares, for they are seldom used for riding purposes. But our chief delight was to follow, when Beteyen ibn Mershid, sheykh of the Gomussa, rode up to Mohammed Dukhi's tent to pay a visit. He had just purchased from one of his people the "bridle-half" of a three-year-old mare, an Abeyeh Sherrák, and was riding her home when he heard that we were at Mohammed Dukhi's tent. The mare is so much more remarkable than the man, that I must describe her first. She is a dark bay, standing fifteen hands or over. Her head, the first point an Arab looks to, is a good one, though I have seen finer, but it is perfectly set on, and the *mitbakh*, or join of the head and neck, would give distinction to any profile. Her neck is light and well arched, the wither high, the shoulder well sloped, and the quarters so fine and powerful that it is impossible she should be otherwise than a very fast mare. Her length of limb above the hock is remarkable, as is that of the pastern. She carries her tail high, as all well-bred Arabians do, and there is a neatness and finish about every movement, which remind one of a fawn or a gazelle. We are all agreed that she is incomparably superior to anything we have seen here or elsewhere, and would be worth a king's ransom, if kings were still worth ransoming.

THE TRULY NOBLE BORN

Carl R. Raswan

1938

I HAD NOT COME to live in a dream world. I must face realities, not only those of Aristotle, but of Nick, the manager, and his friends in Egypt, who expected me to purchase as many good mares as possible.

In past centuries only a few mares had come out of desert Arabia. The Bedouins refused to sell them, saying, "They are our soil. We cannot sell the earth."

I realized that I would have a hard task not only to purchase mares but to find them, for mortality among horses in the desert was great. The gradual desiccation of inner Arabia and the consequent years of prolonged drought had their tragic effect upon horse-breeding. Hunger and thirst took a high toll.

A large number of animals had also died in raids and in murderous wars, when the Turks invaded Arabia in the eighteenth century and occupied the Hejaz and the province of Hassa. Many tribes then lost their horses, and the settled princes of the oases, ignorant of pure breeding, crossed pure desert mares with Turkish cavalry stallions.

No wonder that I found only thirteen hundred mares among the Ruala and not more than three or four hundred mares in foal. Hardly enough fillies survived to replace the natural loss of mares each year. Colts were sold as yearlings to the Agheyl (camel traders) and others who shipped them to Iraq and India, to Syria and Egypt; some even went as far as Europe and America. Only the purest and most promising colts were kept in the tribes – among the Ruala not more than a dozen!

Slowly the horses of the Arabian desert were dying out, although the Bedouins had made supreme sacrifices for them. In times of drought, even the women and children would go hungry to let the mare and her filly have sufficient milk. I have seen the foals of camels killed in order that the milk-camel's sustenance could be given to a mare and her filly. And I have often seen a colt (the good colt of a good mare and a good sire) killed to let his mother have the little remaining food. Only one out of every hundred Arabian horses to reach Europe during the past ages may have been a mare, or perhaps only one in two or three hundred.

Later I found similar conditions among eighteen other tribes with whom I migrated during twenty-six years. But in all my twelve journeys to the Bedouins, I exported only ninety-one horses from the desert to Egypt and Europe.

Even in 1912 it was almost impossible to find in Arabia a horse at once pure-in-the-strain and outstanding as to physical perfection and Arab characteristics.

Pedigree, conformation and type:

These were the three things I must consider.

But with the first – the pedigrees – I had difficulty. Written pedigrees were not ordinarily kept in Arabia. However, if a purchaser demanded one, the chief of the tribe or owner of the horse dictated to his secretary (usually a slave, for all manual work is despised by the aristocratic Bedouin!) the history of the descent of the horse. At least two witnesses set their seal to it, thus verifying the truth of the statements.

This precautionary measure was unnecessary because so many mares changed hands in raids. The Bedouin who had lost his horse in this manner must, according to all laws of chivalry, inform the new owner about her descent before witnesses.

The history of desert horses, though, is not complicated. The Bedouin, with his fabulous memory, recalls all that his father and grandfather and other old people of the tribe have told him. The information will be strictly true, for to lie about the history of a horse is considered a great crime. The owner is marked; his horse automatically becomes "kedish" (ordinary), and no one will breed to this "unwitnessed" horse.

And there are *different* types of Arabian horses, with well-defined qualities. A careless mixture of strains results in an unbalanced, less typical and therefore less desirable steed. Thus, to the fanatic Bedouin breeder even the proof of desert descent is not sufficient. He will adjudge outstanding only the horse whose ancestors have been bred – since time immemorial – *pure-in-the-strain*. This horse, the fountain-head of a certain type, he calls the genuine Asil, the truly noble-born (from ASL, the root).

GHAZAL

Carl R. Raswan

1938

SHEYKH AMMER LED me to his tent, where a slave tended the coffee hearth.

From one of the beaked cans that stood in the glowing embers, the old chief poured coffee into a tiny cup.

"Welcome to the threshold of our sanctuary," he said with exquisite formality.

In the wilderness every home is a retreat where the stranger's stay may lengthen into years, where his past will be his own.

Abraham entertained angels unaware. Since that day the Bedouin says: "We look upon the visiting stranger as an envoy of our lord."

I settled down with my new friend beside his fireplace. It was comfortable in the nomad booth. The coarsely woven black goat hair allowed the air to circulate freely. Another advantage of the goat hair curtains, I learned, was that in a rainstorm the fleece absorbed moisture and contracted the covering until it became waterproof.

At my left a camel saddle was placed for me to lean upon. I found a great advantage in that position close to the ground. The horizon was brought almost to a level with my eyes, and the interior of the tent could also be seen from an unusual angle. Such differences in the mode of life were not only novel but carried me suddenly closer to the natural perspective of Arabian existence. Spiritually, perhaps, they were symbolic of the humble and close-to-the-earth attitude of the desert man.

The pounding of the heavy wooden pestle in the brass coffee mortar was a strange new sound. The slave's own deep, soft humming accented the rhythm of the coffee ritual. I liked the strong aroma of crushed coffee beans and the scented smoke of tamarisk wood.

My view through the tent opening revealed Ghazal and a chestnut mare with her foal standing in the shade of the tamarisk bushes. The long-legged youngster pushed his nose very hard into his mother's side. A girl of about twelve years old hurried from the women's part of the tent to aid the baby foal. The child unloosened a rope from the back of the mare to which a bag had been attached for the protection of the udder. With gentle hands the girl guided the head of the suckling foal to the source of its sustenance.

The Sheykh told me that the mare and her foal were of the Saqlawi strain, the same to which Ghazal belonged. But he was not the sire of the baby colt.

Ghazal was only six years old and a typical representative of the showy Saqlawi type: beautiful and full of grace. Even the stallions of this strain have a feminine beauty, though they are endowed with great strength and endurance.

A slave had taken care of my horse Filfil, shackling both forefeet and one hind foot of my stallion with woollen hobbles. One hind pastern was fettered by a rope not only to the forefeet but also to another rope stretched out between two stakes behind the horse.

This was the Bedouin fashion, a most practical way to picket a stallion in the open yet allow him freedom of movement. Without interference to his head he could step a few feet in each direction.

Sheykh Ammer explained that Bedouins never tie the head of a horse to a solid object except by the long rope of the headstall which is secured to a tent rope *above* the animal. There is play in that method, too, in case the horse – suddenly frightened – turns his head to ascertain the danger.

After unbuckling the girth of my English saddle, the slave had rubbed Filfil with wisps of barley straw. Then he threw a rug of coarsely woven wool in front of the horse and placed upon the mat a pile of desert herbs.

With surprise I observed that Ghazal was not hobbled but walked freely about. I asked the sheykh if the stallion would not disturb the mare and her foal. And would he not run off into the desert?

Ghazal, the Bedouin assured me, knew what was expected of him as a member of the family. However, another owner and a new environment might make a different horse of him.

The old man continued by telling me that he had met with no difficulty in teaching Ghazal the meaning of thirty-seven words.

"Ghazal's understanding mind," he added, "has also learned many signs of my hands and legs."

Urged on by my interest, the sheykh offered to show me still another example of Ghazal's intelligence.

As we walked away from the tent, Ghazal's head was at once attentively directed to his master.

The sheykh asked me to stay behind while he approached my own horse. Suddenly the old man stumbled – purposely, of course – and threw himself full length upon the ground.

Ghazal snorted in fright. He wheeled about and raced at full speed toward the prostrate form of his master; there he pawed the ground and neighed loudly as if calling to him. But when the sheykh did not answer, Ghazal began to turn the man's body over cautiously with one of his hoofs.

Ghazal nipped at Sheykh Ammer with anxious little caresses. Then the stallion tossed his head and neighed tremulously.

"Ghazal!" whispered the sheykh.

At once the horse sought the ground, his muzzle close to the man's face.

"Naum – sleep!" the sheykh said.

With a little moan Ghazal went down on his forelegs, bent his hocks and settled upon the sand, rolling over on his side and stretching his limbs.

The sheykh crawled across Ghazal's withers, seated himself upon his back.

"Goom – arise!" he called out.

With no apparent strain Ghazal lifted his body to a kneeling position, then rose from his haunches to stand firmly on his feet.

Rewarding Ghazal with a friendly slap on the croup, the sheykh commanded: "Zatt – throw!"

Instantly Ghazal threw himself forward. He pawed the air, his whole body aquiver. Though his hands were buried in Ghazal's mane, Sheykh Ammer lost his hold and slipped from the back of the horse and landed safely on his feet.

Almost absent-mindedly I touched the shoulder of Sheykh Ammer as I congratulated him.

"Beware!" cried the sheykh, and I was thrown down by Ghazal who had rushed boldly between his master and me. Courteously the sheykh reached out a helping hand. While I brushed the dust from my back, the old man scolded Ghazal and sent him away with a single gesture, saying "Enough of these tricks."

The sheykh turned to me. "I did not expect Ghazal to treat you so roughly, my guest. He ought to have known that you are friend, not foe. But woe to him who dares to lift his hand against me when Ghazal is near.

"Ta'al – come here!" the sheykh called to Ghazal who had walked off to the threshold of the women's quarters. Immediately the stallion returned to us and stood obediently before his master.

The old man pointed out a deep scar on Ghazal's neck.

"It happened last year," he told me, "when I rode him from Medain Saleh to Amman and fell in with the Beni Sakhr. I alighted at one of their tents. My host took Ghazal from me to shackle his feet. But I knew the treachery of these people. They dwell in the Harra, the volcanic mountains, and their souls are as black as the rocks among which they live."

Sheykh Ammer had sensed his host's plans to steal Ghazal and do harm to himself. When he saw the slave pick up a rifle, the sheykh called as loudly as he could, "Dakhil!" Ghazal tore himself loose, knocked down

44

their host (who was leading him away) and made a dash to his master's side. The slave fired his rifle just as Ghazal rushed between them. The bullet struck Ghazal's neck and threw him to the ground.

Sheykh Ammer's voice trembled as he recalled that scene. " 'Ayb – shame on thee!' " I cried to the men. To their honour be it they rued their attempt to steal the horse and murder their guest.

"Such are the Beni Sakhr and their allies! But God is compassionate. Ghazal grew well again."

THE GOOD ARABIAN

Major John Board

1950

FROM THE PURELY aesthetic viewpoint there is no created being comparable with the good Arabian. To try to draw him is like trying to draw the angels or beautiful women. And he has other even greater qualities. Though a small animal, the recognized normal height being about 14.3 hands, the Arab, despite his slender bone and general air of delicacy, has the most phenomenal stamina and will carry an enormous weight for great distances, day after day without distress. The ivory-like quality of his bone, the wonderful consistency of his feet, make him exceptionally sound: his short back and the barrel-like spring of his ribs (of which he has one less than any other breed, as he has one fewer lumbar vertebra) gives him his amazing capacity to carry weight up to 18 stone. The concave skull and circular eye-socket are unique in this most ancient breed. He has inherited through countless generations, indeed millenniums, the most wonderful temperament. In his native Nejd the Arab foal is brought up in the tent and with the family of his breeder, and that constant association on intimate terms with mankind seems to have given him a singular

intelligence and "kindness". It is a fact that the Arab can learn his job far quicker than any other horse can be taught. The one defect of the Arab, from the English point of view, is the comparatively straight shoulder and shortness of rein, though this is a fault more apparent than real. Also, compared with the thoroughbred, he lacks pace, very naturally, for the Arab horse is properly a warhorse, accustomed to travelling long distances, with heavy weight up, for days on end, while the thoroughbred is a specialized product, designed to gallop at exceptional speed over short distances. It is also alleged – and it must be admitted that there is abundant evidence of the fact – that the Arab is apt to "chuck it" at polo and will not "go in" properly to ride off. This, however, is not to deny the otherwise high courage of the Arab: rather is it comparable with the dislike of many far from cowardly people for playing Rugby Football. On the other hand, the suggestion that he cannot jump is untrue, for he can and, for his size, compares well with any.

ALL THE BREEDS

Dorothy Wellesley, Duchess of Wellington

c. 1930

Who, in the garden-pony carry skeps
Of grass or fallen leaves, his knees gone slack,
Round belly, hollow back,
Sees the Mongolian Tarpan of the Steppes?
Or, the Shire with plaits and feathered feet,
The war-horse like the wind the Tartar knew?
Or, in the Suffolk Punch, spells out anew
The wild grey asses fleet
With stripe from head to tail, and moderate ears?
In cross sea-donkeys, sheltering as storm gathers,
The mountain zebras maned upon the withers,
With round enormous ears?

And who in thoroughbreds in stable garb
Of blazoned rug, ranged orderly, will mark
The wistful eyelashes so long and dark
And call to mind the old blood of the Barb?
And that slim island on whose bare campaigns
Galloped with flying manes
For a king's pleasure, churning surf and scud,
A white Arabian stud?

That stallion, teazer to Hobgoblin, free
And foaled upon a plain of Barbary:
Godolphin Barb, who dragged a cart for hire
In Paris, but became a famous sire,
Covering all lovely mares, and she who threw
Rataplan to the Baron, loveliest shrew;
King Charles's royal mares; the Dodsworth Dam;
And the descendants: Yellow Turk, King Tom;
And Lath out of Roxana, famous foal;
Careless; Eclipse, unbeaten in the race,
With white blaze on his face;
Prunella who was dam to Parasol.

Blood Arab, pony, pedigree, no name,
All horses are the same:
The Shetland stallion stunted by the damp,
Yet filled with self-importance, stout and small;
The Cleveland slow and tall;
New Forests that may ramp
Their lives out, being branded, breeding free
When bluebells turn the Forest to a sea,
When mares with foal at foot flee down the glades,
Sheltering in bramble coverts
From mobs of corn-fed lovers;
Or, at the acorn harvest, in stockades
A round-up being afoot, will stand at bay,
Or, making for the heather clearings, splay
Wide-spread towards the bogs by gorse and whin,
Roped as they flounder in
By foresters.

But hunters as day fails
Will take the short-cut home across the fields;
With slackening rein will stoop through darkening wealds;
With creaking leathers skirt the swedes and kales;
Patient, adventurous still,
A horse's ears bob on the distant hill;
He starts to hear
A pheasant chuck or whirr, having the fear
In him of ages filled with war and raid,
Night gallop, ambuscade;
Remembering adventures of his kin
With giant winged worms that coiled round mountain bases,
And Nordic tales of young gods riding races
Up courses of the rainbow; here, within
The depth of Hampshire hedges, does he dream

How Athens woke, to hear above her roofs
The welkin flash and thunder to the hoofs
Of Dawn's tremendous team?

NOBILITY

Ronald Duncan

1970

This Cavalcade of Grace now stands, it speaks in silence.
Its story is the story of this land.
    Where in this wide world can man find nobility
without pride, friendship without envy or beauty without
vanity? Here, where grace is laced with muscle, and
strength by gentleness confined.
    He serves without servility; he has fought
without enmity. There is nothing so powerful, nothing less
violent; there is nothing so quick, nothing more patient.
    England's past has been borne on his back. All
our history is his industry: we are his heirs, he our
inheritance.
    Ladies and Gentlemen:
    THE HORSE!

BLACK BEAUTY'S LAST HOME

Anna Sewell

1877

ONE DAY DURING THIS summer the groom cleaned and dressed me with such extraordinary care that I thought some new change must be at hand. He trimmed my fetlocks and legs, passed the tarbrush over my hoofs, and even parted my forelock. I think the harness also had an extra polish. Willie seemed half anxious, half merry, and he got into the chaise with his grandfather.

"If the ladies take to him," said the old gentleman, "they'll be suited, and he'll be suited: we can but try."

At the distance of a mile or two from the village we came to a pretty, low house with a lawn and shrubbery at the front and a drive up to the door.

Willie rang the bell, and asked if Miss Blomefield or Miss Ellen was at home. Yes, they both were. So whilst Willie stayed with me, Mr. Thoroughgood went into the house.

In about ten minutes, he returned, followed by three ladies. One tall, pale lady, wrapped in a white shawl, leaned on a younger lady with dark eyes and a merry face; the third, a very stately-looking person, was Miss Blomefield. They all came to look at me and ask questions. The younger lady – this was Miss Ellen – took to me very much; she said she was sure she would like me, for I had such a good face. The tall, pale lady said that she should always be nervous in riding behind a horse that had once been down, as I might come down again; and if I did, she should never get over the fright.

"You see, ladies," said Mr. Thoroughgood, "many first-rate horses have had their knees broken through the carelessness of their drivers, without any fault of their own; and from what I see of this horse, I should say that is his case: but of course I do not wish to influence you. If you wish, you can have him on trial, and then your coachman will see what he thinks of him."

"You have always been such a good adviser to us about our horses," said the stately lady, "that your recommendation would go a long way with me, and if my sister Lavinia sees no objection, we will accept with thanks your offer of a trial."

It was then arranged that I should be sent for the next day.

In the morning a smart-looking young man came for me. At first he looked pleased, but when he saw my knees, he said in a disappointed voice: "I didn't think, sir, you would have recommended my ladies a blemished horse like this."

"Handsome is that handsome does," said my master. "You are only

taking him on trial, and I am sure you will do fairly by him, young man; and if he is not as safe as any horse you ever drove, send him back."

I was led home, placed in a comfortable stable, fed, and left to myself. The next day, when my groom was cleaning my face, he said: "That is just like the star that Black Beauty had, and he is much the same height, too; I wonder where he is now."

A little farther on he came to the place in my neck where I was bled, and where a little knot was left in the skin. He almost started, and began to look me over carefully, talking to himself.

"White star in the forehead, one white foot on the off side, this little knot just in that place"; then, looking at the middle of my back – "and as I am alive, there is that little patch of white hair that John used to call 'Beauty's threepenny-bit.' It *must* be Black Beauty! Why, Beauty! Beauty! do you know me, little Joe Green that almost killed you?" And he began patting and patting me as if he was quite overjoyed.

I could not say that I remembered him, for now he was a fine grown young fellow with black whiskers and a man's voice, but I was sure he knew me, and that he was Joe Green; so I was very glad. I put my nose up to him, and tried to say that we were friends. I never saw a man so pleased.

"Give him a fair trial! I should think so indeed! I wonder who the rascal was that broke your knees, my old Beauty! You must have been badly served out somewhere. Well, well, it won't be my fault if you haven't good times of it now. I wish John Manly were here to see you."

In the afternoon I was put into a low park chair and brought to the door. Miss Ellen was going to try me, and Green went with her. I soon found that she was a good driver, and she seemed pleased with my paces. I heard Joe telling her about me, and that he was sure I was Squire Gordon's old Black Beauty.

When we returned, the other sisters came out to hear how I had behaved myself. She told them what she had just heard, and said, "I shall certainly write to Mrs. Gordon to tell her that her favourite horse has come to us. How pleased she will be!"

After this I was driven every day for a week or so, and as I appeared to be quite safe, Miss Lavinia at last ventured out in the small close carriage. After this, it was quite decided to keep me and to call me by my old name of "Black Beauty."

I have now lived in this happy place a whole year. Joe is the best and kindest of grooms. My work is easy and pleasant, and I feel my strength and spirits all coming back again. Mr. Thoroughgood said to Joe the other day, "In your place he will last till he is twenty years old – perhaps more."

Willie always speaks to me when he can, and treats me as his special friend. My ladies have promised that I shall never be sold, and so I have nothing to fear; and here my story ends. My troubles are all over and I am at home; and often before I am quite awake, I fancy I am still in the orchard at Birtwick, standing with my old friends under the apple-trees.

GARGANTUA'S MARE

François Rabelais

1534

IN THE SAME SEASON, Fayolles, the fourth king of Numidia, sent out of the country of Africk, to Grangousier, the most hideously great mare that ever was seen, and of the strangest form; for you know well enough how it is said, that Africk always is productive of some new thing. She was as big as six elephants, and had her feet cloven into toes like Julius Caesar's horse, with clough-hanging ears, like the goats in Languedoc, and a little horn on her buttock. She was of a burnt-sorrel hue, with a little mixture of dapple-gray spots; but, above all, she had a horrible tail; for it was little more or less than every whit as great as the steeple of Saint Mark beside Langes, and squared as that is, with tuffs and hair-pleats, wrought within one another, no otherwise than as the beards are upon the ears of corn.

If you wonder at this, wonder rather at the tails of the Scythian rams, which weighed above thirty pounds each, and of the Syrian sheep, who need (if Tenaud says true) a little cart at their heels, to bear up their tails, they are so long and heavy. You country wenchers have no such tails. And she was brought by sea in three carricks and a brigantine unto the harbor of Olone in Thalmondois. When Grangousier saw her, "Here is," said he, "what is fit to carry my son to Paris. So now, in the name of God, all will be well; he will one day be a great scholar: were it not for dunces, we should all be doctors." The next morning (after they had drunk, you must understand) they took their journey; Gargantua, his pedagogue Ponocrates, and their equipage, and with them Eudemon, the young page; and because the weather was fair and temperate, his father caused to be made him a pair of dun-colored boots; Babin calls them buskings. Thus did they merrily pass their time in traveling on the highway, always making good cheer, and were very pleasant till they came a little above Orleans, in which place there was a forest of five and thirty leagues long, and seventeen in breadth, or thereabouts. This forest was most horribly fertile and copious in dorflies, hornets, and wasps, so that it was a very purgatory for the poor mares, asses, and horses: but Gargantua's mare did avenge herself handsomely of all the outrages therein committed upon beasts of her quality, and that by a trick whereof they had no suspicion; for as soon as ever they were entered into the said forest, and that the wasps had given the assault, she drew out her tail, and therewith skirmishing, did so sweep them, that she overthrew all the wood along and athwart, here and there, this way and that, longwise and sidewise, over and under, and felled everywhere the wood with as much ease as a mower doth the grass, in such sort, that never since hath there been either wood or wasp;

for all the country was hereby reduced to a plain champaign field – which Gargantua took great pleasure to behold, and said to his company no more but this: "*Je trouve beau ce*," I find this pretty; whereupon that country hath been ever since that time called Beauce. But all the breakfast the mare got that day was but a little yawning and gaping, in memory whereof, the gentlemen of Beauce do as yet, to this day, break their fast with gaping, which they find to be very good, and do spit the better for it. At last they came to Paris, where Gargantua refreshed himself two or three days, making very merry with his folks, and inquiring what men of learning there were then in the city, and what wine they drunk there.

DRUMMER IN LOVE

Betty Smith

1947

TWO VERY IMPORTANT things happened in the year that Francie was thirteen. War broke out in Europe and a horse fell in love with Aunt Evy.

Evy's husband and his horse, Drummer, had been bitter enemies for eight years. He was mean to the horse; he kicked him and punched him and cursed at him and pulled too hard on the bit. The horse was mean to Uncle Willie Flittman. The horse knew the route and stopped automatically at each delivery. It had been his habit to start up again as soon as Flittman mounted the wagon. Lately, he had taken to starting up the instant Flittman got off to deliver milk. He'd break into a trot and often Flittman had to run more than half a block to catch up with him.

Flittman was through delivering at noon. He'd go home to eat dinner, then bring the horse and wagon back to the stable where he was supposed to wash Drummer and the wagon. The horse had a mean trick. Often when Flittman was washing under his belly, he'd wet on him. The other fellows would stand around waiting for this to happen so that they could have a good laugh. Flittman couldn't stand it so he got in the habit of washing the horse in front of his house. That was all right in the summer but it was a little hard on the horse in the winter. Often, on a bitterly cold day, Evy would go down and tell Willie that it was a mean thing to wash Drummer in the cold and with cold water, too. The horse seemed to know that Evy was taking his part. As she argued with her husband, Drummer would whinny pitifully and lay his head on her shoulder.

One cold day, Drummer took matters into his own hands – or as Aunt Evy said it, into his own feet. Francie listened enchanted while Aunt Evy told the story to the Nolans. No one could tell a story like Evy. She acted out all the parts – even the horse and, in a funny way, she'd put in what she thought each one was secretly thinking at the time. It happened like this according to Evy:

Willie was down on the street washing the shivering horse with cold water and hard yellow soap. Evy was standing at the window watching. He leaned under to wash the horse's belly and the horse tensed. Flittman thought that Drummer was going to wet on him again and it was more than the harassed and futile little man could stand. He hauled off and punched the horse in the belly. The horse lifted a leg and kicked him decisively in the head. Flittman rolled under the horse and lay unconscious.

Evy ran down. The horse whinnied happily when he saw her but she paid no attention to him. When he looked over his shoulder and saw that Evy was trying to drag Flittman out from under, he started to walk. Maybe he wanted to help Evy by pulling the wagon clear of the unconscious man or maybe he wanted to finish the job by rolling the wagon over him. Evy hollered out, "Whoa there, boy," and Drummer stopped just in time.

A little boy had gone for a policeman who had gone for the ambulance. The ambulance doctor couldn't make out whether Flittman had a fracture or a concussion. He took him to a Greenpoint hospital.

Well, there was the horse and a wagon full of empty milk bottles to be gotten back to the stables. Evy had never driven a horse but that was no reason why she couldn't. She put on one of her husband's old overcoats, wrapped a shawl around her head, climbed up into the seat, picked up the reins and called out, "Git for home, Drummer." The horse swung his head back to give her a loving look, then set off at a cheerful trot.

It was lucky he knew the way. Evy hadn't the slightest idea where the stables were. He was a smart horse. He stopped at each intersection and waited while Evy looked up and down the cross street. If all was clear, she'd say, "Giddy-yap, boy." If another vehicle was coming, she'd say, "Just a minute, boy." In this way they reached the stables without any mishap and the horse cantered in proudly to his usual place in the row. Other drivers, washing their wagons, were surprised to see a lady driver. They made such a commotion that the stable boss came running and Evy told him what had happened.

"I saw it coming," the boss said. "Flittman never did like that horse and the horse never liked him. Well, we'll have to take on another man."

Evy, fearful lest her husband lose his job, asked whether she couldn't take his route while he was in the hospital. She argued that the milk was delivered in the dark and no one would ever know. The boss laughed at her. She told him how much they needed that twenty-two-fifty a week. She pleaded so hard, and looked so little and pretty and spunky, that he gave in at last. He gave her the list of customers and told her the boys would load the wagon for her. The horse knew the route, he said, and it wouldn't be too hard. One of the drivers suggested that she take the stable dog along for company and protection against milk thieves. The boss agreed to that. He told her to report to the stables at 2 a.m. Evy was the first milk woman on the route.

She got along fine. The fellows at the stable liked her and said that she was a better worker than Flittman. In spite of her practicalness, she was soft and feminine and the men loved the low and breathless way she had of talking. And the horse was very happy and co-operated as much as he could. He stopped automatically before each house where milk was to be left and never started up again until she was safely in the seat.

Like Flittman, she brought him to her house while she ate her dinner. Because the weather was so cold, she took an old quilt from her bed and threw it over him so that he wouldn't catch cold while he waited for her. She took his oats upstairs and heated them for a few minutes in the oven before she fed him. She didn't think ice-cold oats were appetising. The horse enjoyed the warmed oats. After he finished munching, she treated him to half an apple or a lump of sugar.

She thought it was too cold to wash him on the street. She took him back to the stable for that. She thought the yellow soap was too biting, so she brought along a cake of Sweetheart Soap and a big old bath towel to dry him with. The men at the stable offered to wash the horse and wagon for her but she insisted on washing the horse herself. Two men got into a fight over who should wash the wagon. Evy settled it by saying one could wash it one day and the other, the next day.

She heated Drummer's wash water on a gas plate in the boss's office. She'd never think of washing him in cold water. She washed him with the water and the sweet-scented soap and dried him carefully bit by bit with the towel. He never committed an indignity on her while she washed him. He snorted and whinnied happily throughout the washing. His skin rippled in voluptuous delight when Evy rubbed him dry. When she worked around his chest, he rested his tremendous head on her small shoulder. There was no doubt about it. The horse was madly in love with Evy.

When Flittman recovered and reported back for work, the horse refused to leave the stable with him on the wagon seat. They had to give Flittman another route and another horse. But Drummer wouldn't go out with any other driver either. The boss had just about made up his mind to have him sold, when he got an idea. Among the drivers, there was an effeminate young man who talked with a lisp. They put him on Flittman's wagon. Drummer seemed satisfied and consented to go out with the lady-like driver on the seat.

So Drummer took up his regular duties again. But every day at noon, he turned into the street where Evy lived and stood in front of her door. He wouldn't go back to the stables until Evy had come down, given him a bit of apple or some sugar, stroked his nose and called him a good boy.

"He was a funny horse," said Francie after she heard the story.

"He may have been funny," said Aunt Evy, "but he sure knew what he wanted."

A DONKEY CALLED MODESTINE

R.L. Stevenson

1879

NOW, A HORSE IS a fine lady among animals – flighty, timid, delicate in eating, of tender health; he is too valuable and too restive to be left alone, so that you are chained to your brute as to a fellow galley-slave; a dangerous road puts him out of his wits; in short, he's an uncertain and exacting ally, and adds thirty-fold to the troubles of the voyager. What I required was something cheap and small and hardy, and of a stolid and peaceful temper; and all these requisites pointed to a donkey.

There dwelt an old man in Monastier, of rather unsound intellect according to some, much followed by street-boys, and known to fame as Father Adam. Father Adam had a cart, and to draw the cart a diminutive she-ass, not much bigger than a dog, the colour of a mouse, with a kindly eye and a determined under-jaw. There was something neat and high-bred, a quakerish elegance about the rogue that hit my fancy on the spot. Our first interview was in Monastier market-place. To prove her good temper, one child after another was set upon her back to ride, and one after another went head over heels into the air; until a want of confidence began to reign in youthful bosoms, and the experiment was discontinued from a dearth of subjects. I was already backed by a deputation of my friends; but as if this were not enough, all the buyers and sellers came round and helped me in the bargain; and the ass and I and Father Adam were the centre of a hubbub for near half an hour. At length she passed into my service for the consideration of sixty-five francs and a glass of brandy. The sack had already cost eighty francs and two glasses of beer; so that Modestine, as I instantly baptised her, was upon all accounts the cheaper article. Indeed, that was as it should be; for she was only an appurtenance of my mattress, or self-acting bedstead on four castors.

I had a last interview with Father Adam in a billiard-room at the witching hour of dawn, when I administered the brandy. He professed himself greatly touched by the separation, and declared he had often bought white bread for the donkey when he had been content with black bread for himself; but this, according to the best authorities, must have been a flight of fancy. He had a name in the village for brutally misusing the ass; yet it is certain that he shed a tear, and the tear made a clean mark down one cheek.

PRINCE HARRY

William Shakespeare

1598

SIR RICHARD VERNON All furnish'd, all in arms;
    All plum'd like estridges, that with the wind
    Bated like eagles having lately bath'd;
    Glittering in golden coats, like images;
    As full of spirit as the month of May
    And gorgeous as the sun at midsummer;
    Wanton as youthful goats, wild as young bulls.
    I saw young Harry with his beaver on,
    His cushes on his thighs, gallantly arm'd,
    Rise from the ground like feathered Mercury,
    And vaulted with such ease into his seat
    As if an angel dropp'd down from the clouds
    To turn and wind a fiery Pegasus,
    And witch the world with noble horsemanship. . .

GULLIVER EXPLAINS TO THE HOUYHNHNMS

Jonathan Swift

1726

I ASSERTED THAT the Yahoos were the only governing animals in my country, which, my master said, was altogether past his conception, he desired to know whether we had Houyhnhnms among us, and what was their employment. I told him we had great numbers; that in summer they grazed in the fields and in winter were kept in houses, with hay and oats, where Yahoo servants were employed to rub their skins smooth, comb their manes, pick their feet, serve them with food, and make their beds. "I understand you well," said my master; "it is now very plain, from all you have spoken, that, whatever share of reason the Yahoos pretend to, the Houyhnhnms are your masters; I heartily wish our Yahoos would be so tractable." I begged his honour would please to excuse me from proceeding any further, because I was very certain that the account he expected from me would be highly displeasing. But he insisted in commanding me to let him know the best and the worst: I told him, he should be obeyed. I owned that the Houyhnhnms among us, whom we called horses, were the most generous and comely animal we had; that they excelled in strength and swiftness; and when they belonged to persons of quality, employed in travelling, racing, or drawing chariots, they were treated with much kindness and care, till they fell into diseases, or became foundered in the feet; but then they were sold, and used to all kind of drudgery, till they died; after which their skins were stripped, and sold for what they were worth, and their bodies left to be devoured by dogs and birds of prey. But the common race of horses had not so good fortune, being kept by farmers and carriers, and other mean people, who put them to greater labour, and fed them worse. I described, as well as I could, our way of riding; the shape and use of a bridle, a saddle, a spur and a whip; of harness and wheels. I added, that we fastened plates of a certain hard substance, called iron, at the bottom of their feet, to preserve their hoofs from being broken by the stony ways on which we often travelled.

My master, after some expressions of great indignation, wondered how we dared to venture upon a Houyhnhnm's back; for he was sure, that the weakest servant in his house would be able to shake off the strongest Yahoo; or by lying down, and rolling on his back, squeeze the brute to death. I answered, that our horses were trained up from three or four years old, to the several uses we intended them for; that, if any of them proved intolerably vicious, they were employed for carriages; that they were

severely beaten, while they were young, for any michievous tricks; that they were, indeed, sensible of rewards and punishments: but his honour would please to consider, that they had not the least tincture of reason, any more than the Yahoos in this country.

THE REMARKABLE CHARGER OF BARON MUNCHAUSEN

Rudolph Eric Raspe

1792

MY SUPERB LITHUANIAN horse became mine by accident, which gave me an opportunity of showing my horsemanship to great advantage. I was at Count Przobossky's noble country seat in Lithuania, and remained with the ladies at tea in the drawing-room, while the gentlemen were down in the yard, to see a young horse of blood which had just arrived from the stud. We suddenly heard a noise of distress; I hastened downstairs and found the horse so unruly, that nobody durst approach or mount him. The most resolute horsemen stood dismayed and aghast; despondency was

expressed in every countenance, when in one leap, I was on his back, took him by surprise, and worked him quite into gentleness and obedience with the best display of horsemanship I was master of. Fully to show this to the ladies, and save them unnecessary trouble, I forced him to leap at one of the open windows of the tea-room, walked round several times, pace, trot, and gallop, and at last made him mount the tea-table, there to repeat his lessons in a pretty style of miniature which was exceedingly pleasing to the ladies, for he performed them amazingly well, and did not break either cup or saucer. It placed me so high in their opinion, and so well in that of the noble lord, that, with his usual politeness, he begged I would accept of the young horse, and ride him full career to conquest and honour in the campaign against the Turks.

The swiftness of my Lithuanian enabled me to be foremost in the pursuit; and seeing the enemy fairly flying through the opposite gate, I thought it would be prudent to stop in the market-place, to order the men to rendezvous; but judge of my astonishment when in this market-place I saw not one of my hussars about me! Are they scouring the streets? They could not be far off, and must, at all events, soon join me. In that expectation I walked my panting Lithuanian to a spring in this market-place, and let him drink. He drank uncommonly, with an eagerness not to be satisfied, but natural enough; for when I looked round for my men, what should I see, gentlemen! the hind part of the poor creature – croups and legs were missing, as if he had been cut in two, and the water ran out as it came in, without refreshing or doing him any good! How it could have happened was quite a mystery to me, till I returned with him to the town gate, There I saw, that when I rushed in pell-mell with the flying enemy, they had dropped the portcullis (a heavy falling door, with sharp spikes at the bottom, let down suddenly to prevent the entrance of an enemy into a fortified town) unperceived by me, which had totally cut off his hind part, that still lay quivering on the outside of the gate. It would have been an irreparable loss, had not our farrier contrived to bring both parts together while hot. He sewed them with sprigs and young shoots of laurel that were at hand; the wound healed, and, what could not have happened but to so glorious a horse, the sprigs took root in his body, grew up, and formed a bower over me; so that afterwards I could go upon many other expeditions in the shade of my own and my horse's laurels.

PETER DONOVAN, HORSE-BREAKER

Somerville and Ross

1923

I ONLY REMEMBER two or three falls. I was kicked off, cantering in a field (and was congratulated by Papa on becoming a "field-officer," a very old joke, and, as I thought, a poor one), and I was dragged once, for a short distance, on the road, after which I was given a safety-stirrup (and never had occasion to prove it); but my first noteworthy tumble was when I was about eleven. I had asked to be allowed to gallop a young mare round a field; the mare, whose name was Tidy, had been led about by my father, with one of my mother's cousins, a nervous lady of very ample proportions, on her back. I was put up on an enormous old-fashioned, two-crutch saddle (such a construction as I have heard defined as "The Divil's own howdah of an old side-saddle!") and, in about one minute, Tidy, who was very cold and much bored, had bucked me out of it on to the top of my head. I had slight concussion with the pleasurable result that I was allowed to do no lessons except music for the rest of the winter. It was unfortunate, however, that my mother had witnessed the disaster, as it intensified her already vigorous distrust of horses, and more especially of mares, a distrust in which she was ardently encouraged by her sister-in-law. My father had bought at a Bantry horse-fair a small chestnut mare, whose native mildness had been intensified by a life of what had obviously been semi-starvation. He exhibited her to my mother and my Aunt Katie. The little creature stood with a drooping head to be inspected. The ladies eyed her with dislike and suspicion, and then Aunt Katie said darkly:

"She may *seem* very gentle, Henry, *but she has a mare-y eye!*"

It was this same aunt of whom Peter Donovan said:

"Ah, Lady Coghill's a very frightful lady!" (which was less rude than it sounds, being merely a reflection upon her want of nerve).

Peter was a horse-breaker, and, in order to show that the colt he was training could, as he put it, "be said by his loodheen," i.e. be controlled by his little finger, he had galloped him directly at my aunt and some of her progeny, only swerving at the last moment from the path leading to destruction. He was both surprised and mortified that the feat was far from being appreciated by the lady in whose honour it was performed, but he said, forgivingly, to my father:

"Sure, the mother o' childhren has no courage!"

When I first knew Peter I was about thirteen, and he must have been well over sixty; he was a little fellow, of hardly five feet in height, without "as much meat on him as'd bait a rat-trap"; a beautiful rider, and with a gift for "gentle-ing" a young horse, rather than "breaking" him, that is rare in his class. In those days his opinions ranked for me above the Law and the Prophets. As a special treat I was now and then allowed to go out "schooling" with him, and I can truly say I have never been so gratified as when, in the course of a talk about horsemanship, he told me:

"'Twas the Grandfather gave you the sate, but 'twas the Lord Almighty that gave you the Hands!" (a beautiful compliment that we passed on to "Christian" in *Mount Music*).

I suppose I responded in kind, as well as I could, because I remember that Peter said:

"Ah, what good am I now? It brings the tears to my eyes and the grief to my heart that I cannot do now with a horse what I done in my bloom!"

Peter, in his bloom, must have broken hearts as well as horses. As I recollect him, he was like a little elderly Dresden china shepherd, with long silver ringlets over his ears and bright blue eyes, and cheeks as pink as a baby's. He was thrown and killed while showing-off a young horse at a fair, and it was said, in apology for his overthrow, that he had "drink taken." He must have been over seventy, and, after all, it was a good way of escape from old age and its limitations, and of getting back – as we may believe – to the days of his "bloom."

"SURE, THE MOTHER 'O CHILDHREN HAS NO COURAGE!"

THE MONK

Geoffrey Chaucer

c. 1380

A Monk there was, a fair for the mastery;
An out-ridér that lovèd venerie;
Greyhounds he had, as swift as fowl in flight.
A manly man, to be an abbot able.
Full many a dainty horse had he in stable;
And when he rode, men might his bridle hear

Gingle in a whistling wind so clear,
And eke as loud, as doth the chapel bell.
There as this lord was keeper of the cell,
The rule of saint Maure and of saint Beneit,
Because that it was old, and somdel strait,
This ilkè monk let oldè thingès pace;
And held aftér the newè world the trace.
He has not of that text a pulled hen
That saith, that hunters be none holy men;
Ne that a monk when he is cloisterless
Is likned to a fish that's waterless;
This is to say, a monk out of his cloister: —
But thilkè text held he not worth an oyster...

THE MONK AND HIS GREYHOUNDS.
(FROM THE ELLESMERE MS.)

STUBBS

Basil Taylor

1971

GEORGE STUBBS WAS BORN in Liverpool in 1724, the son of a well-established currier. He came therefore from the same social stratum as Constable. At the age of 15 he was apprenticed by his father to an undistinguished artist, Hamlet Winstanley, then employed at Knowsley Hall as a copyist; as the boy remained with him for only a few weeks, we must assume that he was essentially self-taught. Stubbs practised first as a portrait painter from various centres in the north, and by the age of 26 had come to York, where an interest in anatomy, reputedly formed when very young, led him to give private teaching in the subject to medical students.

In 1754, perhaps through the patronage of Lady Nelthorpe of Scawby, Lincolnshire, he travelled to Rome; Richard Wilson was one of the British artists then working in the city, Reynolds had been there two years earlier, and by an odd, if not very significant, coincidence, living in the same apartment house in the Piazza di Spagna was a French nobleman, le

Comte de Lauraguais who, a dozen years later, was to acquire from Lord Bolingbroke the racehorse Gimcrack, just after Stubbs had painted the animal in one of his most beautiful pictures. Having returned to England and spent a further period in Liverpool, he began, about 1758, the studies which were to result in *The Anatomy of the Horse*.

The preliminary work for this book, the dissection and the drawing, was done in the isolated village of Horkstow, near the south shore of the Humber, presumably in order to escape the hostile attention this undertaking might have attracted in a more populous place, for in York Stubbs had, according to a contemporary, won a 'vile renown', on account of his anatomical researches. He devised a tackle for hoisting horses into life-like postures, and then, without skilled assistance, anatomized a number of carcasses. By their fastidious clarity of structure and detail, the drawings prove that he had mastered those techniques which enabled parts such as veins, arteries and ligaments to be kept for investigation in a natural state and position, techniques developed in the seventeenth century by Jan Swammerdam and other workers. The preliminaries completed, he came to London about 1757, if for no other reason than to find a reproductive engraver willing to translate his studies into the plates for the book. In that purpose he failed, but by his immediate success in establishing an artistic practice, at this date he enters the history of English painting, as richly charged with talent and creative energy as any London immigrant of that calling has ever been.

THE WHITE KNIGHT

Lewis Carroll

1872

"Have you invented a plan for keeping the hair from being blown off?" Alice enquired.

"Not yet," said the Knight. "But I've got a plan for keeping it from *falling* off."

"I should like to hear it, very much."

"First you take an upright stick," said the Knight. "Then you make your hair creep up it, like a fruit-tree. Now the reason hair falls off is because it hangs *down* – things never fall *upwards*, you know. It's a plan of my own invention. You may try it if you like."

It didn't sound a comfortable plan, Alice thought, and for a few minutes she walked on in silence, puzzling over the idea, and every now and then stopping to help the poor Knight, who certainly was *not* a good rider.

Whenever the horse stopped (which it did very often), he fell off in front;

and, whenever it went on again (which it generally did rather suddenly), he fell off behind. Otherwise he kept on pretty well, except that he had a habit of now and then falling off sideways; and, as he generally did this on the side on which Alice was walking, she soon found that it was the best plan not to walk *quite* close to the horse.

"I'm afraid you've not had much practice in riding," she ventured to say, as she was helping him up from his fifth tumble.

The Knight looked very much surprised, and a little offended at the remark. "What makes you say that?" he asked, as he scrambled back into the saddle, keeping hold of Alice's hair with one hand, to save himself from falling over on the other side.

"Because people don't fall off quite so often, when they've had much practice."

"I've had plenty of practice," the Knight said very gravely: "plenty of practice!"

Alice could think of nothing better to say than "Indeed?" but she said it as heartily as she could. They went on a little way in silence after this, the Knight with his eyes shut, muttering to himself, and Alice watching anxiously for the next tumble.

"The great art of riding," the Knight suddenly began in a loud voice, waving his right arm as he spoke, "is to keep ——". Here the sentence ended as suddenly as it had begun, as the Knight fell heavily on the top of his head exactly in the path where Alice was walking. She was quite frightened this time, and said in an anxious tone, as she picked him up, "I hope no bones are broken?"

"None to speak of," the Knight said, as if he didn't mind breaking two or three of them. "The great art of riding, as I was saying is – to keep your balance properly. Like this, you know ——."

He let go the bridle, and stretched out both his arms to show Alice what he meant, and this time he fell flat on his back, right under the horse's feet.

"Plenty of practice!" he went on repeating, all the time that Alice was getting him on his feet again. "Plenty of practice!"

"It's too ridiculous!" cried Alice, losing all her patience this time. "You ought to have a wooden horse on wheels, that you ought!"

"Does that kind go smoothly?" the Knight asked in a tone of great interest, clasping his arms round the horse's neck as he spoke, just in time to save himself from tumbling off again.

"Much more smoothly than a live horse," Alice said, with a little scream of laughter, in spite of all she could do to prevent it.

"I'll get one," the Knight said thoughtfully to himself. "One or two – several."

THE FUSSY COLONEL

Siegfried Sassoon

1928

THE SUN WAS SHINING when we emerged from the musty smelling interior. The Colonel, with his nattily rolled umbrella, perfectly brushed bowler hat, and nervously blinking eyes, paid his respects to Mr. Colwood with punctilious affability; then he shepherded Stephen and myself away to have a look round his stables before lunch. We were there in less than five minutes, the Colonel chatting so gaily all the way that I could scarcely have got a word in edgeways even if I had felt sufficient confidence in myself to try.

The Colonel had been a widower for many years, and like most lonely living people he easily became talkative. Everything in his establishment was arranged and conducted with elaborate nicety and routine, and he took an intense pride in his stable, which contained half a dozen hunters who stood in well-aired and roomy loose-boxes, surrounded by every luxury which the Colonel's care could contrive: the name of each horse was on a tablet suspended above the manger. Elegant green stable-buckets (with the Colonel's numerous initials painted on them in white) were arranged at regular intervals along the walls, and the harness-room was hung with enough bits and bridles to stock a saddler's shop. It was, as Stephen pointed out to me afterwards, "a regular museum of mouth-gear". For the Colonel was one of those fussy riders with indifferent hands who are always trying their horses with a new bit.

"I haven't found the key to this mare's mouth yet," he would say, as the irritated animal shook its head and showered everyone within range with flecks of froth. And when he got home from hunting he would say to his confidential old head-groom: "I think this mare's still a bit under-bitted, Dumbrell," and they would debate over half the bits in the harness room before he rode the mare again.

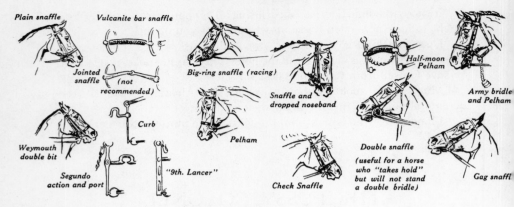

Plain snaffle

Vulcanite bar snaffle

Jointed snaffle (not recommended)

Big-ring snaffle (racing)

Snaffle and dropped noseband

Half-moon Pelham

Army bridle and Pelham

Weymouth double bit

Curb

Pelham

Double snaffle (useful for a horse who "takes hold" but will not stand a double bridle)

Gag snaffl

Segundo action and port

"9th. Lancer"

Check Snaffle

"Sunday morning stables" being one of his favourite ceremonies, the Colonel now led us from one loose-box to another, commenting affectionately on each inmate, and stimulated by the fact that one of his audience was a stranger. Each of them, apparently, was a compendium of unique equine qualities, on which I gazed with unaffected admiration, while Stephen chimed in with "Never seen the old chestnut look so fit, Colonel", or "Looking an absolute picture", while Dumbrell was deferentially at hand all the time to share the encomiums offered to his charges. The Colonel, of course, had a stock repertory of remarks about each one of them, including how they had won a certain point-to-point or (more frequently) why they hadn't. The last one we looked at was a big well-bred brown horse who stood very much "over at the knees". The Colonel had hunted him twelve seasons and he had an equivalently long rigmarole to recite about him, beginning with "I remember Sam Hames saying to me (I bought him off old Hames of Leicester, you know) – that horse is the most natural jumper I've ever had in my stable. And he was right, for the old horse has only given me one bad toss in twelve years, and that was no fault of his own, for he landed on the stump of a willow tree; it was at that rough fence just outside Clout's Wood – nasty place, too – you remember I showed it you the other day, Steve"; all of which Stephen had probably heard fifty times before, and had been shown the "nasty place" half a dozen times into the bargain. It was only when he heard the distant booming of the luncheon-gong that the Colonel was able to tear himself away from the brown horse's loose-box.

While going into the house we passed through what he called "the cleaning room", which was a sort of wide corridor with a skylight to it. Along the wall stood an astonishing array of hunting boots. These struck me as being so numerous that I had the presence of mind to count them. There were twenty-seven pairs. Now a good pair of top-boots, if properly looked after and repaired, will last the owner a good many years; and a new pair once in three years might be considered a liberal allowance for a man who has started with two or three pairs. But the Colonel was nothing if not regular in his habits; every autumn he visited, with the utmost solemnity, an illustrious bootmaker in Oxford Street; and each impeccable little pair of boots had signalized the advent of yet another opening meet. And, since they had been impeccably cared for and the Colonel seldom hunted more than three days a week, they had consequently accumulated. As we walked past them it was as though Lord Roberts were inspecting the local Territorials, and the Colonel would have been gratified by the comparison to the gallant Field-Marshal.

YOUTH

. . . And here I say to parents, especially to wealthy parents, "Don't give your son money. As far as you can afford it, give him horses."

No one ever came to grief – except honourable grief – through riding horses. No hour of life is lost that is spent in the saddle. Young men have often been ruined through owning horses, or through backing horses, but never through riding them; unless of course they break their necks, which, taken at a gallop, is a very good death to die.

WINSTON S. CHURCHILL,
My Early Life

TO MANY YOUNG PEOPLE the horse is the great symbol of adventure, the romantic conveyance of the hero – the cowboy and the cavalier, the hunter and the highwayman – in the stories they have read, or viewed. The ponies they beg, borrow or own, help them, if only in imagination, to share their heroes' exploits and to stimulate a desire for the adventurous life.

Such children may, like Velvet, in Enid Bagnold's classic, dream of owning a myriad of beautiful horses – "her room seemed full of the shape of horses . . . there was almost a dream-smell of stables. As she dressed they were stirring, shifting or tossing beneath their cotton bedspreads . . ." Or, like Mary O'Hara's Ken, they may yearn for a colt of the stamp of Flicka. Like the boy Cid, who was to become the greatest of all the Spanish national heroes, they may feel an impulsive empathy with a plain horse like Babieca, which was to carry him gallantly through all his campaigns. Or aspire to control one with the fiery reputation of a Bucephalus, which the future Alexander the Great, to the amazement of his elders, controlled. Or, like John O'Hara's hero in *It must have been Spring* there may be simply an acute self-consciousness to be overcome.

Maybe they have no real physical fear, but only a superstition, similar to that of bold young John Ridd in *Lorna Doone*, when he was faced with the offer of a ride on the highwayman's notorious strawberry: "not that I had the smallest fear of what the mare could do to me, by fair play or horse trickery; but that the glory of sitting upon her seemed to be too great to me; especially as there were rumours abroad that she was not a mare after all, but a witch." Or being deeply afraid, but overcoming their fear, like Borrow's hero in *Lavengro*, the exhilaration of the first ride is the most wonderful memory of their lives.

Every boy and girl should read *The Long Journey*, by the Danish Nobel Prize winner, Johannes V. Jensen. It was first published in 1908 as *The Glacier* and translated into English fourteen years later by Arthur Chater under the title given. Set among the steppes of prehistoric Sealand – in the days when horses were valued primarily for food, or, if broken, only broken to the sledge – it relates, among other legends, the one presented here, of *Wolf the Horsebreaker*, the youth who becomes the first in the world to break a horse as his steed. It is indeed the story – a story continually repeated ever since – of youth kindly, if firmly, harnessing Nature to its use.

Perhaps it is as well to end on a realistic note. For, basically, there is only one way for children and ponies to be brought together and that way has an arduous and unglamorous element in it, as "Crascredo" advised, in *Horse Sense and Sensibility*, sixty years ago. And how we smile, reading his account, to think of that groom in the background doubtless doing all the dirty work. Now (as Wolf was) youth is its own groom.

Churchill's advice that, although the young may have been ruined often enough by backing horses, they were never ruined through riding them –

"unless of course they break their necks, which is a very good death to die" – is an echo of the last piece, which is from Washington Irving's *Bracebridge Hall*. In this the squire has all his children " . . . on horseback at an early age, and made them ride, slap dash, about the country, without flinching at hedge, or ditch, or stone wall, to the imminent danger of their necks."

VELVET'S DREAMS

Enid Bagnold

1935

VELVET'S DREAMS WERE blowing about the bed. They were made of cloud but had the shapes of horses. Sometimes she dreamt of bits as women dream of jewellery. Snaffles and straights and pelhams and twisted pelhams were hanging, jointed and still in the shadows of a stable, and above them went up the straight damp oiled lines of leathers and cheek straps. The weight of a shining bit and the delicacy of the leathery above it was what she adored. Sometimes she walked down an endless cool alley in summer, by the side of the gutter in the old red-brick floor. On her left and right were open stalls made of dark wood and the buttocks of the bay horses shone like mahogany all the way down. The horses turned their heads to look at her as she walked. They had black manes hanging like silk as the thick necks turned. These dreams blew and played round her bed in the night and the early hours of the morning.

She got up while the sisters were sleeping and all the room was full of book-muslin and canaries singing. "How they can sleep! . . . " she said wonderingly when she became aware of the canaries singing so madly. All the sisters lay dreaming of horses. The room seemed full of the shapes of horses. There was almost a dream-smell of stables. As she dressed they were stirring, shifting and tossing in white heaps beneath their cotton bedspreads. The canaries screamed in a long yellow scream and grew madder. Then Velvet left the room and softly shut the door and passed down into the silence of the cupboard-stairway.

In her striped cotton dress with a cardigan over it she picked up the parcel of steak that had been left on the kitchen table and drank the glass of milk with a playing card on the top of it that Mrs. Brown had left her over-night. Then she got a half packet of milk chocolate from the string drawer, and went out to saddle Miss Ada.

In the brilliance of a very early summer morning they went off together, Miss Ada's stomach rumbling with hunger. Velvet fed her from a bag of oats she had brought with her up on the top of the hill. There were spiders' webs stretched everywhere across the gorse bushes.

Coming down over the rolling grass above Kingsworthy, Velvet could see the feathery garden looking like tropics asleep down below. Old Mr. Cellini by a miracle grew palms and bananas and mimosa in his. Miss Ada went stabbing and sliding down the steep hillside, hating the descent, switching her tail with vexation.

Velvet tied Miss Ada to the fence, climbed it and crept through the spiny undergrowth into the foreign garden. There was not a sound. Not a gardener was about. The grass squelched like moss, spongy with dew, so that each foot sank in and made a black print which filled with water. Then she looked up and saw that the old gentleman had been looking at her all the time.

He had on a squarish hat and never took his eyes off her. He was standing by a tree. Velvet's feet went down in the moss as she stood. His queer hat was wet, and there was dew on the shoulders of his ancient black frock-coat which buttoned up to the neck; he looked like someone who had been out all the night.

Raising one black-coated arm he rubbed his lips as though they were stiff, and she could see how frail he was, unsteady, wet.

"What have you come to do?" he said in a very low voice.

"Sir?"

He moved a step forwards and stumbled.

"Are you staying? Going up to the house?"

"The House."

"Stay here," he said, in an urgent tone which broke.

Velvet dropped her own eyes to her parcel, for she knew he was looking at her. And how his eyeballs shone round his eyes.

"How did you come?" (at last). She looked up. There was something transparent about his trembling face.

"On our pony," she said. "I rode. She's tied to the fence. There's some meat here for the cook, to leave at the back door."

"Do you like ponies?" said the rusty voice.

"Oh . . . yes. We've only the one."

"Better see mine," said the old gentleman in a different tone.

He moved towards her, and as they walked he rested one hand on her shoulder. They walked till they came to the open lawns and passed below some fancy bushes.

He stopped. And Velvet stopped.

" . . . if there was anything you wanted very much," he said, as though to himself.

Velvet said nothing. She did not think it was a question.

"I'm very much too old," said the old gentleman. "Too old. What did you say you'd brought?"

"Meat," said Velvet. "Rump."

"Meat, " said the old gentleman. "I shan't want it. Let's see it."

Velvet pulled the dank parcel out of her bag.

"Throw it away," said the old gentleman, and threw it into a bush. They walked on a few paces.

Something struck her on the hip as she walked. It was when his coat swung out. He looked down too, and unbuttoned his coat and slowly took it off. Without a word he hung it over his arm, and they walked on again, he in his black hat and black waistcoat and shirt-sleeves.

"Going to the stables," said he. "Why, are you fond of horses?"

There was something about him that made Velvet feel he was going to say goodbye to her. She fancied he was going to be carried up to Heaven like Elisha.

"Horses," he said. "Did you say you had horses?"

"Only an old pony, sir."

"All my life I've had horses. Stables full of them. You like 'em?"

"I've seen your chestnut," said Velvet. "Sir Pericles. I seen him jump."

"I wish he was yours, then," said the old gentleman, suddenly and heartily. "You said you rode?"

"We've on'y got Miss Ada. The pony. She's old."

"Huh!"

"Not so much *old*," said Velvet hurriedly. "She's obstinate."

He stopped again.

"Would you tell me what you want most in the world? . . . would you tell me that?"

He was looking at her.

"Horses," she said. "Sir."

"To ride on? To own for yourself?"

He was still looking at her, as though he expected more.

"I tell myself stories about horses," she went on, desperately fishing at her shy desires. "Then I can dream about them. Now I dream about them every night. I want to be a famous rider, I should like to carry despatches; I should like to get a first at Olympia, I should like to ride in a great race, I should like to have so many horses that I could walk down between the two rows of loose boxes and ride what I chose. I would have them all under fifteen hands, I like chestnuts best, but bays are lovely too, but I don't like blacks."

She ran out the words and caught her breath and stopped.

At the other end of the golden bushes the gardener's lad passed in the lit, green gap between two rhododendron clumps with a bodge on his arm. The old gentleman called to him. Then he walked onwards across the grass and Velvet and the gardener's boy followed after. They neared a low building of old brick with a square cobbled yard outside it. The three passed in under the arched doorway.

"Five," said the old gentleman. "These are my little horses. I like little ones too." He opened the gate of the first loose-box and a slender chestnut turned slowly towards him. It had a fine, artistic head, like horses which snort in ancient battles in Greece.

"Shake hands, Sir Pericles," said the old gentleman, and the little chestnut bent its knee and lifted a slender foreleg a few inches from the ground.

"But I've no sugar," said the old gentleman. "You must do your tricks for love today."

He closed the door of the loose-box.

In the next box was a grey mare.

"She was a polo pony" he said, "belonged to my son." He still wore his hat, black waistcoat, and shirt-sleeves. He looked at the gardener's boy. "I need not have bothered you," he said. "Of course the grooms are up." But the gardener's boy, not getting a direct order, followed them gently in the shadow of the stables.

The grey mare had the snowy grey coat of the brink of age. All the blue and dapple had gone out of her, and her eyes burnt black and kind in her white face. When she had sniffed the old gentleman she turned her back on him. She did not care for stable-talk.

In the next loose box was a small pony, slim and strong, like a miniature horse. He had a sour, suspicious pony face. There were two more loose-boxes to come and after that a gap in the stables. Far down the corridor between the boxes Velvet could see where the big horses stood. Hunters and carriage-horses and cart-horses.

The gardener's boy never stirred. The old gentleman seemed suddenly tired and still.

He moved and pulled a piece of paper from the pocket of his waistcoat. "Get me a chair," he said very loud. But before the boy could move a groom came running swiftly with a stable chair.

The old gentleman sat down and wrote. Then he looked up.

"What's your name?" he said and looked at Velvet.

"Velvet Brown," said Velvet.

"Velvet Brown," he said and tapped his pencil on his blue cheek. Then wrote it down. "Sign at the bottom, boy," he said to the gardener's boy, and the boy knelt down and wrote his careful name. "Now you sign too," he said to the groom.

The old gentleman rose and Velvet followed him out into the sunlight of the yard. "Take that paper," he said to her, "and you stay there," and he walked from her with his coat on his arm.

He blew himself to smithereens just round the corner. Velvet never went to look. The grooms came running.

The warm of the brick in the yard was all she had to hold on to. She sat on it and listened to the calls and exclamations. "Gone up to Heaven, Elisha," she thought, and looked up into the sky. She would like to have seen him rising, sweet and sound and happy.

In the paper in her hand she read that five of his horses belonged to her.

Taking the paper, avoiding the running and the calling of the household, she crept back through the garden to Miss Ada. When she got home she could not say what had happened, but cried and trembled and was put to bed and slept for hours under the golden screams of the canaries. At four o'clock Mally burst in and cried:

"They've drawn! They've drawn! We've got the piebald!"

"Whose ticket?" said Velvet faintly.

"Yours, oh yours. Are you ill?"

"Mr. Cellini's dead," whispered Velvet. "Just round the corner!"

Mally stood transfixed to the floor. "They're bringing the piebald home," she said staring. She could not be bothered by the death of Mr. Cellini.

Hearing a sound she ran to the window.

"It's here, it's down at the very door!" she called.

"Get mother," said Velvet, who could not move because the room was swaying.

FLICKA GOES DOWN

Mary O'Hara

1943

FLICKA HAD STOPPED chewing. There were still stalks of clover sticking out between her jaws, but her head was up and her ears pricked, listening, and there was a tautness and tension in her whole body.

Ken found himself trembling too.

"How're you going to catch her, Dad?" he asked in a low voice.

"I kin snag her from here," said Ross, and in the same breath McLaughlin answered, "Ross can rope her. Might as well rope her here as in the corral. We'll spread out in a semi-circle above this bank. She can't get up past us, and she can't get down."

They took their positions and Ross lifted his rope off the horn of his saddle.

Ahead of them, far down below the pocket, the yearlings were running. A whinny or two drifted up, and the sound of their hoofs, muffled by the fog.

Flicka heard them too. Suddenly she was aware of danger. She leaped out of the clover to the edge of the precipice which fell away down the mountainside toward where the yearlings were running. But it was too steep and too high. She came straight up on her hind legs with a neigh of terror, and whirled back toward the bank down which she had slid to reach the pocket. But on the crest of it, looming uncannily in the fog, were four black figures – she screamed, and ran around the base of the bank.

Ken heard Ross's rope sing. It snaked out just as Flicka dived into the bank of clover. Stumbling she went down and for a moment was lost to view.

"Goldarn———" said Ross, hauling in his rope, while Flicka floundered up and again circled her small prison, hurling herself at every point, only to realize that there was no way out.

She stood over the precipice, poised in despair and frantic longing. There drifted up the sound of the colts running below. Flicka trembled and strained over the brink – a perfect target for Ross, and he whirled his lariat again. It made a vicious whine.

Ken longed for the filly to escape the noose – yet he longed for her capture. Flicka reared up, her delicate forefeet beat the air, then she leaped out; and Ross's rope fell short again as McLaughlin said, "I expected that. She's like all the rest of them."

Flicka went down like a diver. She hit the ground with her legs folded under her, then rolled and bounced the rest of the way. It was exactly like the bronco that had climbed over the side of the truck and rolled down the forty-foot bank; and in silence the four watchers sat in their saddles waiting to see what would happen when she hit bottom – Ken already thinking of the Winchester, and the way the crack of it had echoed back from the hills.

Flicka lit, it seemed, on four steel springs that tossed her up and sent her flying down the mountainside – perfection of speed and power and action. A hot sweat bathed Ken from head to foot, and he began to laugh, half choking –

The wind roared down and swept up the fog, and it went bounding away over the hills, leaving trailing streamers of white in the gullies, and coverlets of cotton around the bushes. Way below, they could see Flicka galloping toward the yearlings. In a moment she joined them, and then there was just a many colored blur of moving shapes, with a fierce sun blazing down, striking sparks of light off their glossy coats.

"Get going!" shouted McLaughlin. "Get around behind them. They're on the run now, and it's cleared – keep them running, and we may get them all in together, before they stop. Tim, you take the short way back to the gate and help Howard turn them and get them through."

Tim shot off toward the County Road and the other three riders galloped down and around the mountain until they were at the back of the band of yearlings. Shouting and yelling and spurring their mounts, they kept the colts running, circling them around toward the ranch until they had them on the County Road.

Way ahead, Ken could see Tim and Howard at the gate, blocking the road. The yearlings were bearing down on them. Now McLaughlin slowed up, and began to call, "Whoa, whoa ――" and the pace decreased. Often enough the yearlings had swept down that road and through the gate and down to the corrals. It was the pathway to oats, and hay, and shelter from winter storms – would they take it now? Flicka was with them – right in the middle – if they went, would she go too?

It was all over almost before Ken could draw a breath. The yearlings turned at the gate, swept through, went down to the corrals on a dead run, and through the gates that Gus had opened.

Flicka was caught again.

Mindful that she had clawed her way out when she was corralled before, McLaughlin determined to keep her in the main corral into which the stable door opened. It had eight-foot walls of aspen poles. The rest of the yearlings must be maneuvered away from her.

Now that the fog had gone, the sun was scorching, and horses and men alike were soaked with sweat before the chasing was over and, one after the other, the yearlings had been driven into the other corral, and Flicka was alone.

She knew that her solitude meant danger, and that she was singled out for some special disaster. She ran frantically to the high fence through which she could see the other ponies standing, and reared and clawed at the poles; she screamed, whirled, circled the corral first in one direction, and then the other. And while McLaughlin and Ross were discussing the advisability of roping her, she suddenly espied the dark hole which was the open upper half of the stable door, and dived through it. McLaughlin rushed to close it, and she was caught – safely imprisoned in the stable.

The rest of the colts were driven away, and Ken stood outside the stable, listening to the wild hoofs beating, the screams, the crashes. His Flicka within there – close at hand – imprisoned. He was shaking. He felt a desperate desire to quiet her somehow, to tell her. If she only knew how he loved her, that there was nothing to be afraid of, that they were going to be friends –

Ross shook his head with a one-sided grin. "Sure a wild one," he said, coiling his lariat.

"Plumb loco," said Tim briefly.

McLaughlin said, "We'll leave her to think it over. After dinner we'll come up and feed and water her and do a little work with her."

But when they went up after dinner there was no Flicka in the barn. One of the windows above the manger was broken, and the manger was full of pieces of glass.

Staring at it, McLaughlin gave a short laugh. He looked at Ken. "She climbed into the manger – see? Stood on the feed box, beat the glass out with her front hoofs and climbed through."

The window opened into the Six Foot Pasture. Near it was a wagonload of hay. When they went around the back of the stable to see where she had gone they found her between the stable and the haywagon, eating.

At their approach, she leaped away, then headed east across the pasture.

"If she's like her mother," said Rob, "she'll go right through the wire."

"Ay bet she'll go over," said Gus. "She jumps like a deer."

"No horse can jump that," said McLaughlin.

Ken said nothing because he could not speak. It was the most terrible moment of his life. He watched Flicka racing toward the eastern wire.

A few rods from it, she swerved, turned and raced diagonally south.

"It turned her! it turned her!" cried Ken, almost sobbing. It was the first sign of hope for Flicka. "Oh, Dad, she has got sense, she has! She has!"

Flicka turned again as she met the southern boundary of the pasture, again at the northern, she avoided the barn. Without abating anything of her whirlwind speed, following a precise, accurate calculation, and turning each time on a dime, she investigated every possibility. Then seeing that there was no hope, she raced south towards the range where she had spent her life, gathered herself, and rose to the impossible leap.

Each of the men watching had the impulse to cover his eyes, and Ken gave a howl of despair.

Twenty yards of fence came down with her as she hurled herself through. Caught on the upper strands, she turned a complete somersault, landing on her back, her four legs dragging the wires down on top of her, and tangling herself in them beyond hope of escape.

"Damn the wire!" cursed McLaughlin. "If I could afford decent fences – "

Ken followed the men miserably as they walked to the filly. They stood in a circle watching while she kicked and fought and thrashed until the wire was tightly wound and tangled about her, piercing and tearing her flesh and hide. At last she was unconscious, streams of blood running on her golden coat, and pools of crimson widening on the grass beneath her.

With the wire cutters which Gus always carried in the hip pocket of his overalls, he cut the wire away; and they drew her into the pasture, repaired the fence, placed hay, a box of oats, and a tub of water near her, and called it a day.

"I doubt if she pulls out of it," said McLaughlin briefly. "But it's just as well. If it hadn't been this way it would have been another. A loco horse isn't worth a damn."

AD 1060: HOW CID CAMPEADOR FOUND HIS CHARGER

H. Butler Cooke

1897

ALMOST AS WELL KNOWN as the name of Cid is that of the famous steed Babieca which bore him in all his battles. Babieca is supposed to have lived more than fifty years and to have carried his master's dead body from Valencia to Burgos. How the Cid became possessed of this extraordinary horse, and the horse of his extraordinary name, is told as follows: The Cid's godfather was Don Pedro de Burgos or Peyre Pringos (Peter Fat), a priest of Burgos. From him the Cid, whilst still a boy, begged a colt. The good priest led his godson to a paddock where the mares were running with their colts at foot, and bade him choose the best. The boy stood by the gate of the paddock while the herd was driven past him. The best looking of the colts passed him unheeded, till at last a mare came by with a very ugly and mangy colt running by her side. Suddenly he called out, "This is the one for me." His godfather, angry at so apparently foolish a choice, exclaimed, "Booby (Babieca)! thou hast chosen ill." But the young Cid, no whit abashed, answered, "This will be a good horse, and Booby (Babieca) shall be his name."

ALEXANDER AND BUCEPHALUS

Plutarch

AD 100

WHEN PHILONEIKUS the Thessalian brought the horse Bucephalus and offered it to Philip for the sum of thirteen talents, the king and his friends proceeded to some level ground to try the horse's paces. They found that he was very savage and unmanageable, for he allowed no one to mount him, and paid no attention to any man's voice, but refused to allow any one to approach him. On this Philip became angry, and bade them take the vicious intractable brute away. Alexander, who was present, said, "What a fine horse they are ruining because they are too ignorant and cowardly to manage him." Philip at first was silent, but when Alexander repeated this remark several times, and seemed greatly distressed, he said, "Do you blame your elders, as if you knew more than they, or were better able to manage a horse?" "This horse, at any rate," answered Alexander, "I could manage better than any one else." "And if you cannot manage him," retorted his father, "what penalty will you pay for your forwardness?" "I will pay," said Alexander, "the price of the horse."

While the others were laughing and settling the terms of the wager, Alexander ran straight up to the horse, took him by the bridle and turned him to the sun as it seems he had noticed that the horse's shadow dancing before his eyes alarmed him and made him restive. He then spoke gently to the horse, and patted him on the back with his hand, until he perceived that he no longer snorted so wildly, when, dropping his cloak, he lightly leaped upon his back. He now steadily reined him in, without violence or blows, and as he saw that the horse was no longer ill-tempered, but only eager to gallop, he let him go, boldly urging him to full speed with his voice and heel.

Philip and his friends were at first silent with terror; but when he wheeled the horse round, and rode up to them exulting in his success, they burst into a loud shout. It is said that his father wept for joy, and, when he dismounted, kissed him, saying, "My son, seek for a kingdom worthy of yourself; for Macedonia will not hold you."

IT MUST HAVE BEEN SPRING

John O'Hara

1938

IT MUST HAVE BEEN one of the very first days of spring. I was wearing my boots and my new corduroy habit, and carrying my spurs in my pocket. I always carried my spurs on the way to the stable, because it was eight squares from home to the stable, and I usually had to pass a group of newsboys on the way, and when I wore the spurs they would yell at me, even my friends among them. The spurs seemed to make a difference. The newsboys were used to seeing me in riding breeches and boots or leather puttees, but when I wore the spurs they always seemed to notice it, and they would yell "Cowboy crazy!" and once I got in a fight about it and got a tooth knocked out. It was not only because I hated what they called me. I hated their ignorance; I could not stop and explain to them that I was not cowboy-crazy, that I rode an English saddle and posted to the trot. I could not explain to a bunch of newsboys that Julia was a five-gaited mare, a full sister to Golden Firefly, and that she herself could have been shown if she hadn't had a blanket scald.

This day that I remember, which must have been one of the very first days of spring, becomes clearer in my memory. I remember the sounds: the woop-woop of my new breeches each time I took a step, and the clop sound of the draught horses' hooves in the thawed ground of the streets. The draught horses were pulling wagon-loads of coal from the near-by mines up the hill, and when they got half-way up the driver would give them a rest; there would be a ratchety noise as he pulled on the brake, and then the sound of the breast chains and trace chains loosening up while the horses rested. Then presently the loud slap of the brake handle against the iron guard, and the driver yelling "Gee opp!" and then the clop sound again as the horses' hooves sank into the sloppy roadway.

My father's office was on the way to the stable, and we must have been at peace that day. Oh, I know we were, because I remember it was the first time I wore the new breeches and jacket. They had come from Philadelphia that day. At school, which was across the street from our house, I had looked out the window and there was Wanamaker's truck in front of our house, and I knew that The Things had come. Probably crates and burlap rolls containing furniture and rugs and other things that did not concern me; but also a box in which I knew would be my breeches and jacket. I went home for dinner, at noon, but there was no time for me to try on the new things until after school. Then I did hurry home and changed, because I thought I might find my father in his office if I hurried, although it would be after office hours, and I wanted him to see me in the new things.

Now, I guess my mother had telephoned him to wait, but then I only knew that when I got within two squares of the office, he came out and stood on the porch. He was standing with his legs spread apart, with his hands dug deep in his pockets and the skirt of his tweed coat stuck out behind like a sparrow's tail. He was wearing a grey soft hat with a black ribbon and with white piping around the edge of the brim. He was talking across the street to Mr. George McRoberts, the lawyer, and his teeth gleamed under his black moustache. He glanced in my direction and saw me and nodded, and put one foot up on the porch seat and went on talking until I got there.

I moved towards him, as always, with my eyes cast down, and I felt my riding crop getting sticky in my hand and I changed my grip on it and held the bone handle. I never could tell anything by my father's nod, whether he was pleased with me or otherwise. As I approached him, I had no way of telling whether he was pleased with me for something or annoyed because someone might have told him they had seen me smoking. I had a package of Melachrinos in my pocket, and I wanted to throw them in the Johnstons' garden, but it was too late now; I was in plain sight. He would wait until I got there, even though he might only nod again when I did, as he sometimes did.

I stood at the foot of the porch. "Hello," I said.

He did not answer me for a few seconds. Then he said, "Come up here till I have a look at you."

I went up on the porch. He looked at my boots. "Well," he said. "Did you polish them?"

"No. I had Mike do it. I charged it. It was a quarter, but you said–"

"I know. Well, you look all right. How are the breeches? You don't want to get them too tight across the knee or they'll hurt you."

I raised my knees to show him that the breeches felt all right.

"Mm-hmm," he said. And then, "Good Lord!" He took off his hat and laid it on the porch seat, and then began to tie my stock over again. I never did learn to tie it the way he wanted it, the way it should have been. Now I was terribly afraid, because he could always smell smoke – he didn't smoke himself – and I remembered I had had a cigarette at recess. But he finished tying the stock and then drew away and commenced to smile.

He called across the street to Mr. McRoberts. "Well, George. How does he look?"

"Like a million, Doctor. Regular English country squire, eh?"

"English, hell!"

"Going horseback riding?" said Mr. McRoberts to me.

"Yes," I said.

"Wonderful exercise. How about you, Doctor? You ought to be going, too."

"Me? I'm a working man. I'm going to trephine a man at four-thirty. No, this the horseman in my family. Best horseman in Eastern Pennsylvania," said my father. He turned to me. "Where to this afternoon? See that the mare's hooves are clean and see if that nigger is bedding her the way I told him. Give her a good five-mile exercise out to Indian Run and then back the Old Road. All right."

I started to go. I went down the porch steps and we both said good-bye, and then, when I was a few steps away, he called to me to wait.

"You look fine," he said. "You really look like something. Here." He gave me a five-dollar bill. "Save it. Give it to your mother to put in the bank for you."

"Thank you," I said, and turned away, because suddenly I was crying. I went up the street to the stable with my head bent down, because I could let the tears roll right out of my eyes and down to the ground without putting my hand up to my face. I knew he was still looking.

c. 1680: EXMOOR

R.D. Blackmore

1869

"Your mare," said I, standing stoutly up, being a tall boy now; "I never saw such a beauty, sir. Will you let me have a ride on her?"

"Think thou couldst ride her, lad? She will have no burden but mine. Thou couldst never ride her. Tut! I would be loth to kill thee."

"Ride her!" I cried with the bravest scorn, for she looked so kind and gentle; "there never was horse upon Exmoor foaled, but I could tackle in half-an-hour. Only I never ride upon saddle. Take them leathers off of her."

He looked at me, with a dry little whistle, and thrust his hands into his breeches-pockets, and so grinned that I could not stand it. And Annie laid hold of me, in such a way, that I was almost mad with her. And he laughed, and approved her for doing so. And the worst of all was – he said nothing.

"Get away, Annie, will you? Do you think I am a fool, good sir? Only trust me with her, and I will not over-ride her."

"For that I will go bail, my son. She is liker to over-ride thee. But the ground is soft to fall upon, after all this rain. Now come out into the yard, young man, for the sake of your mother's cabbages. And the mellow straw-bed will be softer for thee, since pride must have its fall. I am thy mother's cousin, boy, and am going up to house. Tom Faggus is my name, as everybody knows; and this is my young mare, Winnie."

What a fool I must have been not to know it at once! Tom Faggus, the great highwayman, and his young blood-mare, the strawberry! Already her fame was noised abroad, nearly as much as her master's; and my longing to ride her grew tenfold, but fear came at the back of it. Not that I had the smallest fear of what the mare could do to me, by fair play or horse-trickery; but that the glory of sitting upon her seemed to be too great to me; especially as there were rumours abroad that she was not a mare after all, but a witch. However, she looked like a filly all over, and wonderfully beautiful, with her supple stride, and soft slope of shoulder, and glossy coat beaded with water, and prominent eyes, full of love or fire. Whether this came from her Eastern blood of the Arabs newly imported, and whether the cream-colour, mixed with our bay, led to that bright strawberry tint, is certainly more than I can decide, being chiefly acquainted with farm-horses. And these come of any colour and form; you never can count what they will be, and are lucky to get four legs to them.

Mr. Faggus gave his mare a wink, and she walked demurely after him, a bright young thing, flowing over with life, yet dropping her soul to a higher one, and led by love to anything; as the manner is of females, when they know what is best for them. Then Winnie trod lightly upon the straw, because it had soft muck under it, and her delicate feet came back again.

"Up for it still, boy, be ye?" Tom Faggus stopped, and the mare stopped there; and they looked at me provokingly.

"Is she able to leap, sir? There is good take-off on this side of the brook."

Mr. Faggus laughed very quietly, turning round to Winnie, so that she might enter into it. And she, for her part, seemed to know exactly where the joke was.

"Good tumble-off, you mean, my boy. Well there can be small harm to thee. I am akin to thy family, and know the substance of their skulls."

"Let me get up," said I, waxing wroth, for reasons I cannot tell you, because they are too manifold; "take off your saddle-bag things. I will try not to squeeze her ribs in, unless she plays nonsense with me."

Then Mr. Faggus was up on his mettle, at this proud speech of mine; and John Fry was running up all the while, and Bill Dadds, and a half-a-dozen. Tom Faggus gave one glance around and then dropped all regard for me. The high repute of his mare was at stake, and what was my life compared to it? Through my defiance, and stupid ways, here was I in a duello, and my legs not come to their strength yet, and my arms as limp as a herring.

Something of this occurred to him, even in his wrath with me, for he spoke very softly to the filly, who now could scarce subdue herself; but she drew in her nostrils, and breathed to his breath, and did all she could to answer him.

"Not too hard, my dear," he said; "let him gently down on the mixen. That will be quite enough." Then he turned the saddle off, and I was up in a moment. She began at first so easily, and pricked her ears so lovingly, and minced about as if pleased to find so light a weight on her, that I thought she knew I could ride a little, and feared to show any capers. "Gee wugg, Polly!" cried I, for all the men were now looking on, being then at the leaving-off time; "Gee wugg, Polly, and show what thou be'est made of." With that I plugged my heels into her, and Billy Dadds flung his hat up.

Nevertheless, she outraged not, though her eyes were frightening Annie, and John Fry took a pick to keep him safe; but she curbed to and fro, with her strong fore-arms rising, like springs ingathered, waiting and quivering grievously, and beginning to sweat about it. Then her master gave a shrill clear whistle, when her ears were bent towards him, and I felt her form beneath me gathering up like whalebone, and her hind-legs coming under her, and I knew that I was in for it.

First she reared upright in the air, and struck me full on the nose with her comb, till I bled worse than Robin Snell made me; and then down with her fore-feet deep in the straw, and her hind-feet going to heaven. Finding me stick to her still like wax (for my mettle was up as hers was), away she flew with me, swifter than ever I went before, or since, I trow. She drove full-head at the cob-wall – "oh, Jack, slip off," screamed Annie – then she turned like light, when I thought to crush her, and ground my left knee against it. "Mux me," I cried, for my breeches were broken and short words went the furthest – "If you kill me, you shall die with me." Then she took the courtyard gate at a leap, knocking my words between my teeth, and then right over a quickset hedge, as if the sky were a breath to her; and away for the water-meadows, while I lay on her neck like a child at the breast, and wished I had never been born. Straight away, all in the front of the wind, and scattering clouds around her, all I knew of the speed we made was the frightful flash of her shoulders, and her mane like trees in a tempest. I felt the earth under us rushing away, and the air left far behind us, and my breath came and went, and I prayed to God, and was sorry to be so late of it.

All the long swift while, without power of thought, I clung to her crest and shoulders, and dug my nails into her creases, and my toes into her flank-part, and was proud of holding on so long, though sure of being beaten. Then in her fury at feeling me still, she rushed at another device for it, and leaped the wide water-trough sideways across, to and fro, till no breath was left in me. The hazel-boughs took me too hard in the face, and the tall dog-briars got hold of me, and the ache of my back was like crimping a fish; till I longed to give up and lay thoroughly beaten, and lie there and die in the cresses. But there came a shrill whistle from up the home-hill, where the people had hurried to watch us; and the mare stopped as if with a bullet; then set off for home with the speed of a swallow, and going as smoothly and silently. I had never had dreamed of such delicate motion, fluent, and graceful, and ambient, soft as the breeze flitting over the flowers, but swift as the summer lightning. I sat up again, but my strength was all spent, and no time left to recover it; and at last, as she rose at our gate like a bird, I tumbled off into the mixen.

FIRST RIDE

George Borrow

1851

AND IT CAME TO PASS that, as I was standing by the door of the barrack stable, one of the grooms came out to me, saying, "I say, young gentleman, I wish you would give the cob a breathing this fine morning."

"Why do you wish me to mount him?" said I; "you know he is dangerous. I saw him fling you off his back only a few days ago."

"Why, that's the very thing, master. I'd rather see anybody on his back than myself; he does not like me; but, to them he does, he can be as gentle as a lamb."

"But suppose," said I, "that he should not like me?"

"We shall soon see that, master," said the groom; "and, if so be he shows temper, I will be the first to tell you to get down. But there's no fear of that; you have never angered or insulted him, and to such as you, I say again, he'll be as gentle as a lamb."

"And how came you to insult him," said I, "knowing his temper as you do?"

"Merely through forgetfulness, master. I was riding him about a month ago, and having a stick in my hand, I struck him, thinking I was on another horse, or rather thinking of nothing at all. He has never forgiven me, though before that time he was the only friend I had in the world; I should like to see you on him, master."

"I should soon be off him; I can't ride."

"Then you are all right, master; there's no fear. Trust him for not hurting a young gentleman, an officer's son, who can't ride. If you were a blackguard dragoon, indeed, with long spurs, 'twere another thing; as it is, he'll treat you as if he were the elder brother that loves you. Ride! he'll soon teach you to ride, if you leave the matter with him. He's the best riding-master in all Ireland, and the gentlest."

The cob was led forth; what a tremendous creature! I had frequently seen him before, and wondered at him; he was barely fifteen hands, but he had the girth of a metropolitan dray-horse, his head was small in comparison with his immense neck, which curved down nobly to his wide back. His chest was broad and fine, and his shoulders models of symmetry and strength; he stood well and powerfully upon his legs, which were somewhat short. In a word, he was a gallant specimen of the genuine Irish cob, a species at one time not uncommon, but at the present day nearly extinct.

"There!" said the groom, as he looked at him, half admiringly, half sorrowfully, "with sixteen stone on his back, he'll trot fourteen miles in one hour; with your nine stone, some two-and-a-half more, ay, and clear a six-foot wall at the end of it."

"I'm half afraid," said I; "I had rather you would ride him."

"I'd rather so, too, if he would let me; but he remembers the blow. Now, don't be afraid, young master, he's longing to go out himself. He's been trampling with his feet these three days, and I know what that means; he'll let anybody ride him but myself, and thank them; but to me he says, 'No! you struck me.'"

"But," said I, "where's the saddle?"

"Never mind the saddle; if you are ever to be a frank rider, you must begin without a saddle; besides, if he felt a saddle, he would think you don't trust him, and leave you to yourself. Now, before you mount, make his acquaintance – see there, how he kisses you and licks your face, and see how he lifts his foot, that's to shake hands. You may trust him – now your are on his back at last; mind how you hold the bridle – gently, gently! It's not four pair of hands like yours can hold him if he wishes to be off. Mind what I tell you – leave it all to him."

Off went the cob at a slow and gentle trot, too fast and rough, however, for so inexperienced a rider. I soon felt myself sliding off, the animal perceived it too, and instantly stood stone still till I had righted myself; and now the groom came up: "When you feel yourself going," said he, "don't lay hold of the mane, that's no use; mane never yet saved man from falling, no more than stray from drowning; it's his sides you must cling to with your calves and feet, till you learn to balance yourself. That's it, now abroad with you; I'll bet my comrade a pot of beer that you'll be a regular rough-rider by the time you come back."

And so it proved; I followed the directions of the groom, and the cob gave me every assistance. How easy is riding, after the first timidity is got over, to supple and youthful limbs; and there is no second fear. The creature soon found that the nerves of his rider were in proper tone. Turning his head half round he made a kind of whining noise, flung out a little foam, and set off.

In less than two hours I had made the circuit of the Devil's Mountain, and was returning along the road, bathed with perspiration, but screaming with delight; the cob laughing in his equine way, scattering foam and pebbles to the left and right, and trotting at the rate of sixteen miles an hour.

Oh, that ride! that first ride! – most truly it was an epoch in my existence; and I still look back to it with feelings of longing and regret. People may talk of first love – it is a very agreeable event, I dare say – but give me the flush, and triumph, and glorious sweat of a first ride, like mine on the mighty cob! My whole frame was shaken, it is true; and during one long week I could hardly move foot or hand; but what of that? By that one trial I had become free, as I may say, of the whole equine species. No more fatigue, no more stiffness of joints, after that first ride round the Devil's Hill on the cob.

Oh, that cob! that Irish cob! – may the sod lie lightly over the bones of the strongest, speediest, and most gallant of its kind! Oh! the days when, issuing from the barrack-gate of Templemore, we commenced our hurry-scurry just as inclination led – now across the fields – direct over stone walls and running brooks – mere pastime for the cob! – sometimes along the road to Thurles and Holy Cross, even to distant Cahir! – what was distance to the cob?

It was thus that the passion for the equine race was first awakened within me – a passion which, up to the present time, has been rather on the increase than diminishing. It is no blind passion; the horse being a noble and generous creature, intended by the All-Wise to be the helper and friend of man, to whom he stands next in the order of creation. On many occasions of my life I have been much indebted to the horse, and have found in him a friend and coadjutor, when human help and sympathy were not to be obtained. It is therefore natural enough that I should love the horse; but the love which I entertain for him has always been blended with respect; for I soon perceived that, though disposed to be the friend and helper of man, he is by no means inclined to be his slave; in which respect he differs from the dog, who will crouch when beaten; whereas the horse spurns, for he is aware of his own worth, and that he carries death within the horn of his heel. If, therefore, I found it easy to love the horse, I found it equally natural to respect him.

WOLF THE HORSEBREAKER –
Prehistoric

Johannes V. Jensen

1922

WHITE BEAR WAS the first to sail on the water in a ship, he tamed horses and invented the chariot but . . . White Bear's adventurous boys were the first on earth to *ride*.

It was not for the old man to trust his heavy frame to the bucking wild horse to the extent of climbing on its back; there was a certain fatherly dignity to be thought of, too. White Bear was content to develop his powers as a charioteer. Nor, though a mighty skipper, had he learnt to swim, whereas the boys had taken to the water from sheer curiosity and daring, and had risked drowning so often that at last they swam like seals. The fact was they were restless creatures and had to be on the go, up and down, in and out, wherever there was a chance. Many things that they started as purely thoughtless pranks afterwards stuck and became permanent acquirements, part of the everyday life both of themselves and their successors. They learned horsemanship in the same way, through play and passion for novelty, and above all through the necessity of constantly risking their necks, which seems to be essential to every boy. It came about in this way:

Behind White Bear's settlement on the coast of Lifeland the steppes began and stretched eastward to infinity, so far that nobody had ever seen their boundary, right away to the place of the sun's rising. The country was fairly level and clothed league after league with high grass, but in the coastal district and many other places inland there were young forests of birch and stretches of thick scrub, besides bogs with bushes and reeds. Game roamed everywhere, bears and deer, aurochs, wolves and wild cattle living as neighbours; the sea was full of fish, and farther north, where the steppe passed into endless frozen marshes and hills, the reindeer dwelt in countless herds; in winter they came south, and at that season supplied all the needs of White Bear and his household. But in summer the wild horses came in from the warm pastures in the south and roamed over the open steppes and in the glades of the bush; then *they* were the quarry and daily fattened the smoke of May's kitchen fire with their sweet flesh. The wild horse tasted so good that White Bear preferred it to all other animals as an offering to the distant Powers he honoured; every year he had his days of mark when more than one of the handsome, refractory animals was led to the pyre and sacrificed.

But he also domesticated the wild horse, partly as a good food reserve which might be left alive against a shortage of game, partly of course for use in his car and sledge. This latter the horses did not seem to object to, and thus a mutual confidence soon grew up between them and White Bear.

But the boys especially had more and more to do with the spirited animals. Wolf, the eldest, was quite irresistibly attracted by them, and it looked as if they on their side were willing to make a special friend of him.

A secret sympathy arose between horse and man, a feeling of kinship that seemed to belong to a very distant past, forgotten on both sides. Perhaps it was due to the horse having once been a primitive animal in the same period when man's ancestors still lived in the trees, so that the obscure memory that linked them together dated from the Lost Country.

While the jungle man, in the days before Time came into the world, hooked himself from branch to branch in the tropical forests of Northern Europe, the primitive horse padded about down below on the hot, swampy ground as a beast just about the size of a rabbit, with four well-developed toes adapted for spreading themselves over the mud and with a mouthpiece that craved for waterplants and fruit; a plump little mammal that might be something between a rodent and a ruminant, half-way to becoming a lazy tapir but possessed by an ambition to follow the distinguished career of the okapi and peaceful enough to join the herds of antelopes. Here in Paradise, the eternal spring-time of the forests, the jungle man must often have dropped a juicy fruit to the beast in the swamp below, which devoured it in good faith as a gift from on high. Coconuts on the head it received from those above, but also the goodly breadfruit – the primeval horse was fond of that. Later on, when the tree-dwellers found themselves entitled to descend to earth and in that connection took to eating flesh, the little, wide-spread, easily caught swamp horse became their favourite food; that was the origin of *their* warm feelings.

Afterwards, when the ice came and overwhelmed the forests, they parted; the jungle man entered upon the inclement existence, under the law of the icefield, which made him human, and the horse went his way, which in course of time and in a literal sense was not without influence on his toes. Instead of the soft forest floor and the secure hiding-places of the jungle, he came out upon dry steppes, where there was no need to spread his toes to prevent sinking in, but where, on the contrary, they were a hindrance, when for thousands of years he had to run for his life with packs of wolves and other hungry beasts of prey at his heels. Instead of plantain and young bamboo shoots he had nothing to live on but grass. But better to change little by little than give way to bad times. The horse had to travel long distances every day, and that quickly, so he raised himself on his middle toe and it gave him a feeling of greater freedom, of being more in alliance with the wind; and as the other side toes were not used, they shrank and became superfluous, while the nail hardened into a hoof; thus time and the road turned a fugitive beast into a horse. And it thrived so well that the puny creature of the forest floor gradually rose into an animal of size, one of those that are seen at a distance.

Its youthful dreams of subsiding into a tapir or a ruminant vanished, of course, together with the Lost Country. This beast of many possibilities, then, had now become a horse with no chance of retreat nor any desire of it; no more rabbit existence for him; he was a horse right through. And now it had met man again and felt strangely affected by an ancient memory, inexplicably attracted – but at the same time instinctively warned. There was something in man's gestures which promised fairly, and then the horse through all its trials had preserved the sweetness of Paradise in its blood, the great curiosity, it was so ready to come on. But a rather uncanny light in man's eye, something like the taste of an old and much-loved friend and a newly awakened appetite, could but induce the horse to keep at a suitable distance.

Such was the position when the boys made the acquaintance of the wild horse. Their closer relations began in the neighbourhood of the settlement, where White Bear kept the half-tamed horses he had caught for driving. They ran loose in a big paddock, a sort of island that White Bear had contrived by digging a ditch on the fourth side of a pasture which was naturally surrounded on three sides by water. Here the horses lived just as in a free state; there was open ground and trees where they could roam about or stand in shelter as they pleased. Every time they had to be brought to the settlement to be harnessed it was a case of catching them over again, and as the enclosure was so big this gave rise to many skirmishes and much strategy on both sides.

It was the boys' task to fetch the horses, and if they could not succeed in any other way in getting near enough to throw the leather noose about their neck, they would entice them with a bunch of tempt-grass or a particularly succulent root, or perhaps even a bit of bread Mother had given them for the dear horses, and when they couldn't resist any longer and let the boys come near – then hey! catch hold of his forelock, out with the halter and slip it over his head, and the dainty one was caught.

Now it was no little way from the paddock home to the settlement, and

the boys, who naturally wanted to get out of the tramp when there were others to do it for them, often coolly tried to jump up on the horses so as to be carried home instead of trudging by their side. This the horses invariably took in very bad part. The halter one could put up with, if there was no way out of it, and a good-natured pat on the muzzle might also pass; nor need one object to snuffling up to one of these humans now and then and tripping a dance round him, for company's sake and three paces off – but to be clawed by the mane and mounted like a tree, to have this biped on one's back! Every time the boys attempted it you could see the offended horse spring straight up into the air with all four feet to send him to the stars, and if he actually kept his seat, then a vertical rear with the hindquarters and the next instant up with the forelegs the same way, and if this pitching didn't make him seasick, then a wild jump to one side and up with the back in an arch that nobody *could* hang on to; but if he stuck on all the same, as Wolf did more and more often, why then there was nothing for it but to fling yourself down like a dog and roll on the ground, or a heap of stones for choice, with all four legs in the air, to get rid of the vermin; or it might be necessary to rush at full gallop for a tree with a low bough that would scrape him off – in short, it was not to be thought of that the horse would tolerate a man on his inviolable back. The inherited experience of generations, the bloody consequences of getting anything on one's back – the *lynx*, the *wolverine* – made the horse blindly resist the slightest advances of that kind.

And then, in spite of this, May witnessed one day from the door of her house a half-terrifying, half-ridiculous performance in which Wolf played the chief part, sitting red-haired and glorious on the back of one of the horses on the way home from the paddock – dreadful boy! The other brothers were decorously leading theirs by the halter, but Wolf sat astride his horse with his legs proudly dangling in the air, and guided it with a strap on its neck. And the horse seemed to submit with a good grace; it walked with its head down, pondering deeply, as though it had an inkling of the bearing of this first complaisance, but without any attempt at revolt. Cheers and great reception of the boys! Even White Bear, who was ardently engaged on his new ship, looked up from his flint wedge and cast a fatherly eye upon his offspring, shook his head in thoughtful approval;

he knew what might result from heresies. He himself had made his way by doing the impossible. The boys might well behave a little differently from just what one had expected of them.

Wolf had at last achieved it. The stallion he rode had been his friend from a foal. It was born in captivity and reared in the paddock, looked after and petted by Wolf with all the good things he could get hold of and spare for it; it knew him from any of the others and liked being taken round the neck and patted by him, even after it was grown up. True, its innate shyness lay so deep in its blood that it was ready to start off all the time as though possessed by a thousand promptings of flight, quivering in every joint and with wide, fleeting eyes; its ears twitched nervously, lay back flat while its teeth showed in an ugly grin; its nostrils stretched so that the daylight gleamed through the rosy cartilage between them; it wanted to be patted and yet did not want it, swung its flank forward and drew back ticklishly, as though it was fire it felt and not a human hand; its mood shifted like a breeze on the water; only after a long, long time of tireless overtures would it accept the relationship, but really *tame* it never was.

Only Wolf could approach it. He came so calmly, controlling every single step, and put out his hand so cautiously, lest its limbs should be seized with instinctive flight; and when he had once come up to it he took care never to make the slightest unexpected movement or do anything suddenly, which would have sent it off with stones and turf flying from its hoofs. The wild horse itself always stood perfectly still when it was not grazing or actually on the move; when at rest it stood straight up with its head out without moving so much as an ear; even at a short distance it was not easily sighted in the field before it moved; that was its protection against pursuit; moreover, it is only ignoble animals that always have to be fidgeting and cannot be restful in themselves when there is no real need for exertion.

When the horse stood like this, probably under a birch if the sun was shining, Wolf would approach it with every sign of profound calm in his gait, and then it stood still and awaited his coming. Wolf might then take it round the neck and stay talking to it a long while, with his head laid against its fine skin; and the horse did not move a hoof, nor tremble, only now and again it threw up its head as though it didn't want to hear a word more; but it stayed with Wolf, and he patted it here and there, stroked it and made it feel safe all over, until every fidre, every hair of its body, which had been timid at first, was calmed down by gradually being accustomed to the strange touch.

And Wolf was clever. With his experience of the others which had never allowed themselves to be tamed, because he had taken them by surprise, and had only become more unmanageable, he was wary of attempting to jump on the back of his friend; it was not to know *when* he sat there. He began by leaning against the horse's flank and laying an arm across the handsome, faintly striped back, just casually, as it were, and yet the first few times the horse received his arm with a tremble. Later, when after long and patient repetition it learned to bear his arm and allowed him to lay his whole weight on it, he proceeded as though in play to hoist a leg now and then on to its side, and he kept on at that until it found nothing odd in his pulling up his body after it little by little and hanging over its back for longer and longer at a time.

Then the day actually arrived when the horse without noticing any difference allowed him to sit right up and stay there; but then it is true he had talked to it as long and as sweetly as the south wind and summer days. But when he *sat* there and the horse still stood quietly under him, Wolf laughed, laughed only too well; his heart leapt in his breast for happiness.

Now the horse was to begin to walk with him, and he had to be very careful not to do anything to scare it. Afterwards, when besides walking it came to trotting and galloping, some of the difficulties were indeed transferred to himself; it was not directly in accordance with human nature to sit a horse in *all* dispensations; it had to be learnt. But as Wolf was very willing, and the horse had no objection, and there was time enough, it came quicker than he knew, and soon his younger brothers, yelling with admiration, could see the pair dashing at full gallop round the paddock and then out on the steppe.

The first horseman, with a scrap of wolf's skin tied about his middle and his fiery hair flying about his ears, Wolf's red elf-locks that he used to dry his fingers in, always full of last year's burrs and affording shelter to all kinds of crawling things up to the size of a grasshopper; Wolf moulded in one with the wild horse, still half striped like a zebra, its shoulders marked with the lightning, with a dumpy head like a foal all its days, and with the thunderbolt under each of its heart-shaped hoofs!

When Wolf had won the first victory, his brothers gradually followed his lead; each of them chose a pet among the foals and caressed it and hung upon its neck so long that they became confidential friends and united as one figure in the landscape, to the stupefaction, terror and disturbance of all other creatures. And this somewhat strained but never-changing friendship, half based on deceit, half with the character of a providence, has since persisted between horse and man.

FIRST TAKE YOUR BOY . . .

"Crascredo"

1925

"First take your boy" – you can almost do the thing on the principle of a cooking recipe – or, preferably, take someone else's boy. In the latter case, you will neither be so annoyed when he shows himself to be frightened, stupid and forgetful, nor will you be so extravagantly proud when he proves himself courageous, quick-witted and apt to learn. Being a normal boy, he will inevitably be all these in turn; but on your intelligent, as well as sympathetic, reading of all the outstanding traits in his character, depends your whole chance of success.

Of course, if you are satisfied that the boy is a hopeless fool, you will at once set him, bare-back, on a very large, fast and broad pony with a mouth of iron, and attach a lighted rocket to the pony's tail. You can then, with a perfectly clear conscience, go home and tell his mother.

But, while few boys want to learn to ride, all boys would like to be able to ride: there can, therefore, be no boys who are either hopeless or fools, and this is an encouraging truth which their teacher will find it comforting to keep constantly before him.

He must, therefore, persuade himself to take boys as he finds them, and it is equally important to be prepared to take ponies as they are made (or spoilt). The proper pony on which to teach a boy to ride is, of course, one with perfect manners; a narrow pony with a light mouth, and one which is both fast and temperate, and a safe and confident jumper: a pony that does not mind being kicked in the ribs for no reason, or jabbed in the mouth for a bad reason. It will save time if we allow that such a pony does not exist.

On the other hand, so far as horsemanship is concerned, it is a waste of both time and money to set a boy a on a fussy Shetland; while the practice of putting a man and his sister (both being of tender years) back to back in badly balancing baskets on a donkey is simply silly. It probably gives rise to a false complex on saddle-fitting in the boy's mind, and certainly prevents his sister from pulling his hair. Which must be wrong.

Take both ponies and boys as you find them; but if you can find an Exmoor pony for the small boy and a Welsh pony for his bigger brother you won't go far wrong – especially if you can keep both boys and ponies out of the hands of a groom in their days of early instruction. For, while opinions about horsemanship and horsemastership may differ, in one respect there are are no differences – every horseman and horsewoman will unite in raining curses on the devoted heads of grooms as a class, on their love of blistering, their total incompetence.

One wonders how they have managed to survive this general "hate" – probably, so far as children are concerned, it is because their heads *are* devoted. Many a man connects his first enthusiasm for horses with the round, red, smiling face of an old groom or the spidery legs and hissing noises of a young one. And the most mutton-fisted groom in the world has always got a fund of tremendous tales of horsemanship to share with a small boy.

Having got his boy and his pony, and having left the groom (much to his annoyance) at home, the teacher can now sally forth. He will do so on foot, and he may as well make up his mind that the first few lessons will certainly be exhausting, and probably be painful – for himself. They will consist of a series of short rushes down secluded lanes, throughout which his pupil will clasp him round the neck with one or more arms.

It is the teacher's duty to proceed in this manner, come what may; and whether it is cows or cars that come, the teacher will steadfastly refuse to allow the small boy to dismount. He will not do so brutally, but will exclaim "Oh *no!*" or "That would be absurd," and be prepared, if necessary, to elaborate on the absurdity until the cars or cows have passed. It is, of course, understood that he will maintain his attitude of *non possumus* in spite of the fact that his pupil is half throttling him, and the pony is standing on his toes.

On the other hand he will *encourage* the boy to dismount at frequent intervals, so long as fear is not the motive! At such times he will get the boy to lift the pony's fore legs (hind legs come later) or to loosen and tighten the girths, and he may even venture on a casual remark to the effect that "these" are the withers and "this" is what they call the hock. If all this is done casually, there is at least a fifty-fifty chance that the boy may take a real interest: if it is done, as some men do it, with the pugnacity of an old-fashioned drill-sergeant, there is the certainty that, when next a ride is suggested, the small boy will prefer to spend the afternoon making this rabbit's life a misery.

Indeed, all through the training, you and the rabbit will always be up against the fact that, if teaching is conducted in such a way that the small boy is either bored or frightened, he will plump for more peaceful pursuits – in which he gets peace, even if other people and his rabbit are frightened or bored. And his mother will support him!

BETTER THE SADDLE THAN THE COACH

Washington Irving

1822

I HAVE MADE casual mention, more than once, of one of the Squire's anti-quated retainers, old Christy, the huntsman. I find that his crabbed humour is a source of much entertainment among the young men of the family; the Oxonian, particularly, takes a michievous pleasure now and then in slyly rubbing the old man against the grain; and then smoothing him down again; for the old fellow is as ready to bristle up his back as a porcupine. He rides a venerable hunter called Pepper, which is a counterpart of himself; a heady, cross-grained animal, that frets the flesh off its bones; bites, kicks, and plays all manner of villainous tricks. He is as tough, and nearly as old as his rider, who has ridden him time out of mind, and is, indeed, the only one that can do anything with him. Sometimes, however, they have a complete quarrel, and a dispute for mastery, and then, I am told, it is as good as a farce to see the heat they both get into, and the wrong-headed contest that ensues; for they are quite knowing in each other's ways, and in the art of teasing and fretting each other. Notwithstanding these doughty brawls, however, there is nothing that nettles old Christy sooner than to question the merits of his horse; which he upholds as tenaciously as a faithful husband will vindicate the virtues of the termagant spouse, that gives him a curtain lecture every night of his life.

The young men call old Christy their "professor of equitation," and in accounting for the appellation, they let me into some particulars of the Squire's mode of bringing up his children. There is an odd mixture of eccentricity and good sense in all the opinions of my worthy host. His mind is like modern Gothic, where plain brickwork is set off with pointed arches and quaint tracery. Though the main ground-work of his opinions is correct, yet he has a thousand little notions, picked up from old books, which stand out whimsically on the surface of his mind.

Thus, in educating his boys, he chose Peachem, Markham, and suchlike old English writers, for his manuals. At an early age he took the lads out of their mother's hands, who was disposed, as mothers are apt to be, to make fine, orderly children of them, that they should keep out of sun and rain, and never soil their hands, nor tear their clothes.

In place of this, the Squire turned them loose to run free and wild about the park, without heeding wind or weather. He was also particularly attentive in making them bold and expert horsemen; and these were the days when old Christy, the huntsman, enjoyed great importance, as the lads were put under his care to practice them at the leaping-bars, and to keep an eye on them in the chase.

The Squire always objected to their riding in carriages of any kind, and is still a little tenacious on this point. He often rails against the universal use of carriages, and quotes the words of honest Nashe, in his "Quaternio", – "a kind of solecism, and to savour of effeminacy, for a young gentleman in the flourishing time of his age to creep into a coach, and to shroud himself from wind and weather: our great delight was to outbrave the blustering Boreas upon a great horse; to arm and prepare ourselves to go with Mars and Bellona into a field was our sport and pastime; coaches and caroches we left unto them for whom they were first invented, for ladies and gentlemen, and decrepit age and impotent people."

The Squire insists that the English gentlemen have lost much of their hardiness and manhood since the introduction of carriages, "Compare," he will say, "the fine gentleman of former times, ever on horseback, booted and spurred, and travel-stained, but open, frank, manly and chivalrous, with the fine gentleman of the present day, full of affectation and effeminacy, rolling along a turnpike in his voluptuous vehicle. The young men of those days were rendered brave, and lofty, and generous in their notions, by almost living in their saddles, and having their foaming steeds 'like proud seas under them.' There is something," he adds, "in bestriding a fine horse that makes a man feel more than mortal. He seems to have doubled his nature, and to have added to his own courage and sagacity the power, the speed, and stateliness of the superb animal on which he is mounted."

"It is a great delight," says old Nashe, "to see a young gentleman with his skill and cunning, by his voice, rod, and spur, better to manage and to command the great Bucephalus, than the strongest Milo, with all his strength; one before to see him make tread, trot and gallop the ring; and one after to see him make him gather up roundly; to bear his head steadily; to run a full career swiftly; to stop a sudden lightly: anon after to see him make him advance, to yorke, to go back, and side long, to turn on either hand; to gallop the gallop galliard; to do the capriole, the cham-betta, and dance the curvetty."

In conformity to these ideas, the Squire had them all on horseback at an early age, and made them ride, slap dash, about the country, without flinching at hedge, or ditch, or stone wall, to the imminent danger of their necks.

Even the fair Julia was partially included in this system; and, under the instructions of old Christy, has become one of the best horsewomen in the county. The Squire says it is better than all the cosmetics and sweeteners of the breath that ever were invented. He extols the horsemanship of the ladies in former times, when Queen Elizabeth would scarcely suffer the rain to stop her accustomed ride. "And then think," he will say, "what nobler and sweeter beings it made them. What a difference must there be, both in mind and body, between a joyous high-spirited dame of those days, glowing with health and exercise, freshened by every breeze, seated loftily and gracefully on her saddle, with plume on head, and hawk on hand, and her descendant of the present day, the pale victim of routs and ballrooms, sunk languidly in one corner of an enervating carriage."

The Squire's equestrian system had been attended with great success, for his sons, having passed through the whole course of instruction without breaking neck or limb, are now healthful, spirited, and active, and have the true Englishman's love for a horse. If their manliness and frankness are praised in their father's hearing, he quotes the old Persian maxim, and says, they have been taught "to ride, to shoot, and to speak the truth."

It is true the Oxonian has now and then practised the old gentleman's doctrines a little in the extreme. He is a gay youngster, rather fonder of his horse than his book, with a little dash of the dandy; though the ladies all declare that he is "the flower of the flock." The first year that he was sent to Oxford, he had a tutor appointed to overlook him, a dry chip of the university. When he returned home in the vacation, the Squire made many inquiries about how he liked his college, his studies, and his tutor.

"Oh, as to my tutor, sir, I've parted with him some time since."

"You have; and, pray, why so?"

"Oh, sir, hunting was all the go at our college, and I was a little short of funds; so I discharged my tutor, and took a horse you know."

"Ah, I was not aware of that, Tom," said the Squire, mildly.

When Tom returned to college his allowance was doubled, that he might be enabled to keep both horse and tutor.

EQUITATION

~~~~~~

There is many a rider in full paraphernalia, who has his horses trained by somebody else, who mounts them for horse shows only, who has never trained a horse himself, and who therefore will never understand that it is he himself who has to learn from the horse if he strives to reach the highest level of equitation.

COLONEL ALOIS PODHAJSKY,
My Horses, My Teachers

THE ATHENIAN, Xenophon, who was born around 430 BC, wrote the first comprehensive treatise on equitation still on record. A pupil and friend of Socrates he went on to command a wing of the Greek army, and, following the Persian treachery after the Battle of Cunaxa, led the skillful "Retreat of the Ten Thousand." Afterward he held a command in the Spartan army, and was regarded as the greatest cavalry general and tactician of his day. For his retirement he settled at Corinth, where he wrote prolifically until he died in 356 BC. Since all the great masters of equitation have extolled his wisdom it seems fitting that this brief anthology in equitation should open with an extract from Xenophon's *On Horsemanship*.

I have next quoted from the treatise of William Cavendish, Duke of Newcastle, who was the principal English authority on horsemanship in the seventeenth century. He it was who made the French school of riding

COMPARATIVE SKELETONS OF MAN & HORSE IN ACTION

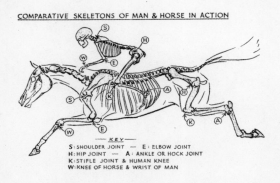

KEY
S: SHOULDER JOINT — E: ELBOW JOINT
H: HIP JOINT — A: ANKLE OR HOCK JOINT
K: STIFLE JOINT & HUMAN KNEE
W: KNEE OF HORSE & WRIST OF MAN

popular at the court of Charles I – hence the adoption of the French word for horseman, *cavalier*, as the name for adherents to the Royal cause. Newcastle was one of the ablest commanders on the Royalist side during the Civil War, and was subsequently governor and tutor to the young prince who became Charles II. With his reputation for gallantry, considerateness and courtesy, the Duke's name became synonymous with all that was best in the "cavalier" ideals.

Writing two centuries later, George Borrow, that inveterate traveler and author of *The Bible in Spain*, *Romany Rye* and the already quoted *Lavengro* advises on horsemastership on a journey. Then a passage from the opening pages of the splendid *My Horses, My Teachers*, by Colonel Alois Podhajsky, sometime Director of the Spanish Riding School at Vienna, is followed by a piece by Podhajsky's colleague, Waldemar Seunig (whom we have already met in the section entitled "Handsome Is . . . ") on the horseman's conformation, a subject which has been a little neglected, perhaps because we are ashamed at how often good-looking horses are handicapped by ungainly, ill-proportioned riders.

ADVICE FROM GREECE
Xenophon

400 BC

THE MASTER, let us suppose, has received his horse and is ready to mount. We will now prescribe certain rules to be observed in the interests not only of the horseman but of the animal which he bestrides. First, then, he should take the leading rein, which hangs from the chin-strap or noseband, conveniently in his left hand, held slack so as not to jerk the horse's mouth, whether he means to mount by hoisting himself up, catching hold of the mane beside the ears, or to vault on to horseback by help of his spear. With the right hand he should grip the reins along with a tuft of hair beside the shoulder joint, so that he may not in any way wrench the horse's mouth with the bit while mounting. In the act of taking the spring off the ground for mounting, he should hoist his body by help of the left hand, and with the right at full stretch assist the upward movement (a position in mounting which will present a graceful spectacle also from behind); at the same time with the leg well bent, and taking care not to place his knee on the horse's back, he must pass his leg clean over to the off side; and so having brought his foot well round, plant himself firmly on his seat.

To meet the case in which the horseman may chance to be leading his horse with the left hand and carrying his spear in the right, it would be good, we think, for every one to practise vaulting on to his seat from the right side also. In fact, he has nothing else to learn except to do with his right limbs what he has previously done with the left, and *vice versa*. And the reason we approve of this method of mounting is that it enables the soldier at one and the same instant to get astride of his horse and to find himself prepared at all points, supposing he should have to enter the lists of battle on a sudden.

But now, supposing the rider fairly seated, whether bareback or on a saddle-cloth, a good seat is not that of a man seated on a chair, but rather the pose of a man standing upright with his legs apart. In this way he will be able to hold on to the horse more firmly by his thighs; and this erect attitude will enable him to hurl a javelin or to strike a blow from horseback, if occasion calls, with more vigorous effect. The leg and foot should hang loosely from the knee; by keeping the leg stiff, the rider is apt to have it broken in collision with some obstacle; whereas a flexible leg will yield to the impact, and at the same time not shift the thigh from its position. The rider should also accustom the whole of his body above the hips to be as supple as possible; for thus he will enlarge his scope of action, and in case of a tug or shove be less liable to be unseated. Next, when the rider is seated, he must, in the first place, teach his horse to stand quiet, until he has drawn his skirts from under him, if need be, and got the reins an equal length and grasped his spear in the handiest fashion; and, in the next place, he should keep his left arm close to his side. This position will give the rider absolute ease and freedom, and his hand the firmest hold.

As to reins, we recommend those which are well balanced, without being weak or slippery or thick, so that when necessary the hand which holds them can also grasp a spear.

As soon as the rider gives the signal to the horse to start, he should begin at a walking pace, which will tend to allay his excitement. If the horse is inclined to droop his head, the reins should be held pretty high; or somewhat low, if he is disposed to carry his head high. This will set off the horse's bearing to the best advantage. Presently, as he falls into a natural trot, he will gradually relax his limbs without the slightest suffering, and so come more agreeably to the gallop. Since, too, the preference is given to starting on the left foot, it will best conduce to that lead if, while the horse is still trotting, the signal to gallop should be given at the instant of making a step with his right foot. As he is on the point of lifting his left foot he will start upon it, and while turning left simultaneously make the first bound of the gallop; since, as a matter of instinct, a horse, on being turned to the right, leads off with his right limbs, and to the left with his left.

As an exercise, we recommend what is called the volte, since it habituates the animal to turn to either hand; while a variation in the order of the turn is good as involving an equalisation of both sides of the mouth, in first one, and the other half of the exercise. But of the two we commend the oval form of volte rather than the circular; for the horse, being already sated with the straight course, will be all the more ready to turn, and will be practised at once in the straight course and in wheeling. At the curve, he should be held up, because it is neither easy nor indeed safe when the horse is at full speed to turn sharp, especially if the ground is broken or slippery.

But in collecting him, the rider should as little as possible sway the horse obliquely with the bit, and as little as possible incline his own body; or, he may rest assured, a trifle will suffice to stretch him and his horse full length upon the ground. The moment the horse has his eyes fixed on the straight course after making a turn, is the time to urge him to full speed.

SEVENTEENTH-CENTURY SEAT

William Cavendish, Duke of Newcastle (1592–1676)

1640

BEFORE A HORSEMAN MOUNTS, he ought first to take care that his horse's furniture is in order, which is done without prying into every minute circumstance to show himself an affected connoisseur in the art. . . . He ought to sit upright upon the twist, and not upon the buttocks. . . . When he is thus placed upon his twist in the middle of the saddle, he ought to advance as much as he can towards the pommel, leaving a handsbreadth between his backside and the arch of the saddle, holding his legs perpendicular as when he stands upon the ground, and his knees and thighs turned inwards towards the saddle, keeping as close as if they were glued to the saddle. . . . He ought to fix himself firm upon his stirrup, with his heels a little lower than the toes, so that the end of his toes may pass about half-an-inch beyond the stirrup, or somewhat more. He should keep his hams stiff, having his legs neither too near nor too far distant from his horse. . . . He ought to hold the reins in his left hand. . . . His arm bent and close to the body in an easy posture. . . . The bridle hand ought to be held three inches above the pommel and two inches beyond it. . . . He should have a slender switch in his right hand, not too long like a fishing-rod, nor too short like a bodkin. . . . The rider's breast ought to be in some measure advanced, his countenance pleasant and gay, but without a laugh.

HOW TO MANAGE A HORSE ON A JOURNEY

George Borrow

c. 1850

OF ONE THING I AM CERTAIN, that the reader must be much delighted with the wholesome smell of the stable of these pages . . . What a contrast to the sickly odours exhaled from those of some of my contemporaries, especially of those who pretend to be of the highly fashionable class, and who treat of reception-rooms, well may they be styled so, in which dukes, duchesses, earls, countesses, archbishops, bishops, mayors, mayoresses – not forgetting the writers themselves, both male and female – congregate and press upon one another; how cheering, how refreshing, after having been nearly knocked down with such an atmosphere, to come in contact with genuine stable hartshorn. Oh! the reader shall have yet more of the stable, and of that old ostler, for which he or she will doubtless exclaim, "Much obliged!" – and lest I should forget to perform my promise, the reader shall have it now.

I shall never forget an harangue from the mouth of the old man, which I listened to one warm evening as he and I sat on the threshold of the stable, after having attended to some of the wants of a batch of coach-horses. It

related to the manner in which a gentleman should take care of his horse and self, whilst engaged in a journey on horseback, and was addressed to myself, on the supposition of my one day coming to an estate, and of course becoming a gentleman.

"When you are a gentleman," said he, "should you ever wish to take a journey on a horse of your own and you could not have a much better one than the one you have here eating its fill in the box yonder – I wonder by the by, how you ever came by it – you can't do better than follow the advice I am about to give you, both with respect to your animal and yourself. Before you start, merely give your horse a couple of handfuls of corn, and a little water somewhat under a quart, and if you drink a pint of water yourself out of the pail, you will feel all the better during the whole day; then you may walk and trot your animal for about ten miles, till you come to some nice inn, where you may get down and see your horse led into a nice stall, telling the ostler not to feed him till you come. If the ostler happens to be a dog-fancier, and has an English terrier dog like that of mine there, say what a nice dog it is, and praise its black and tawn; and if he does not happen to be a dog-fancier, ask him how he's getting on, and whether he ever knew worse times; that kind of thing will please the ostler, and he will let you do just what you please with your own horse, and when your back is turned, he'll say to his comrades what a nice gentleman you are, and how he thinks he has seen you before; then go and sit down to breakfast, and before you have finished breakfast, get up and go and give your horse a feed of corn; chat with the ostler two or three minutes till your horse has taken the shine out of his corn, which will prevent the ostler taking any of it away when your back is turned, for such things are some-times done – not that I ever did such a thing myself when I was at the inn at Hounslow. Oh, dear me, no! Then go and finish your breakfast, and when you have finished your breakfast and called for the newspaper, go and water your horse, letting him have about one pailful, then give him another feed of corn, and enter into discourse with the ostler about bull-baiting, the prime minister, and the like; and when your horse has once more taken the shine out of his corn, go back to your room and your newspaper – and I hope for your sake it may be the *Globe*, for that's the best paper going – then pull the bell-rope and order in your bill, which you will pay without counting it up – supposing you to be a gentleman. Give the waiter sixpence, and order out your horse, and when your horse is out, pay for the corn, and give the ostler a shilling, then mount your horse and walk him gently for five miles; and whilst you are walking him in this manner, it may be as well to tell you to take care that you do not let him down and smash his knees, more especially if the road be a particularly good one, for it is not at a desperate hiverman pace, and over very bad roads, that a horse tumbles and smashes his knees, but on your particularly nice road, when the horse is going gently and lazily, and is half asleep, like the gemman on his back; well, at the end of the five miles, when the horse has digested his food, and is all right, you may begin to push your horse on, trotting him a mile at a heat, and then walking him a quarter of a one, that his wind may be not distressed; and you may go on in that manner for thirty miles, never galloping of course, for none but fools or hivermen ever gallop horses on roads; and at the end of that distance you may stop at some other nice inn for dinner. I say, when your horse is led into the stable, after that same thirty miles trotting and walking, don't let the saddle be whisked off at once, for if you do your horse will have such a sore back as will frighten you, but let your saddle remain on your horse's back, with the girths loosened, till after his next feed of corn, and be sure that he has no corn, much less water, till after a long hour and more; after he is fed he may be watered to the tune of half a pail, and then the ostler can give him a regular rub down; you may then sit down to dinner, and when you have dined get up and see to your horse as you did after breakfast, in fact you must do much after the same fashion you did at t'other inn; see to your horse, and by no means disoblige the ostler. So when you have seen to your horse a second time, you will sit down to your bottle of wine – supposing you to be a gentleman – and after you have finished it, and your argument about the corn-laws with any commercial gentleman who happens to be in the room, you may mount your horse again – not forgetting to do the proper thing to the waiter and ostler; you may mount your horse again and ride him, as you did before, for about five and twenty miles, at the end of which you may put up for the night after a very fair day's journey, for no gentleman – supposing he weighs sixteen stone, as I suppose you will be the time you become a gentleman – ought to ride a horse more than sixty-five miles in one day, provided he has any regard for his horse's back, or his own either. See to your horse at night and have him well rubbed down. The next day you may ride your horse forty miles just as you please, but never foolishly, and those forty miles will bring you to your journey's end, unless your journey be a plaguey long one, and if so, never ride your horse more than five and thirty miles a day, always, however, seeing him well fed, and taking more care of him than yourself; which is but right and reasonable, seeing as how the horse is the best animal of the two.

A SPANISH RIDING SCHOOL DIRECTOR LOOKS BACK

Colonel Alois Podhajsky

1967

FROM MY EARLIEST CHILDHOOD it was my most ardent desire to ride, and I dreamed about it night and day. I wanted to ride and believed I would experience the greatest happiness of this world on the back of a horse. I wanted to ride and develop the horse's movements into dance and music . . . to ride and feel and learn from the smallest signs of the mute creature how to communicate with him, how to understand him and to create a

Colonel Podhajsky at the White City.

language between horse and rider which would always remain simple, distinct, and constant. This attitude means thinking from the point of view of the horse, knowing what the horse feels, what he likes, what difficulties he has to overcome, and how he, too, is influenced by moods or the surrounding atmosphere.

It is the long way of learning, and looking back, I understand now that the process never really comes to an end. The apprenticeship may be roughly divided into three phases. In the first, the rider must learn to maintain his balance in all movements of the horse and to remain "on top." Some are content with this modest result and may feel they are already great riders at this stage. But soon the student must realise that he has not reached the summit with these simple achievements. The aim from now on is to set the programme of work for the horse, to strengthen him by physical training, and to develop his mental abilities. This is the beginning of the second phase, and in the course of it the rider often despairs of ever learning this art. If the rider has succeeded in penetrating into the sphere of the art of riding and has trained a horse up to the standards of high school, he has overcome the second phase and progressed to the third, but he has not gone all the way to the ultimate of learning. For a single horse trained to this degree does not yet make a perfect rider. There are quite a number of horsemen, however, who have to content themselves with this sole achievement. There is many a "rider" in full paraphernalia, who has his horses trained by somebody else, who mounts them for horse shows only, who has never trained a horse himself, and who therefore will never understand that it is he himself who has to learn from the horse if he strives to reach the highest level of equitation.

THE WELL-MADE RIDER

Waldemar Seunig

1956

THE RIDER WHOSE *figure* facilitates balance and control is at a great advantage. In general a slender figure of medium build (the asthenic-leptosomic figure) is to be desired because such a figure makes it very much easier for the rider to select a horse that fits him well, that is, "tailored" to his figure. If we were to make comparisons with daily life, the figure of a runner or dancer is similar to that of the "rider's figure". The short-legged rider, with an athletically developed upper body, whose knotty wrestler's musculature has a tendency to cramped contraction, will find it hard to keep his balance, and even harder to moderate the control exercised by his hand. The layman, to be sure, considers either the lightweight jockey or the martial guardsman the ideal figure of a rider, though both of these types really find it very hard to control horses that are not "tailored" to their figures.

Since it receives the impulses of the moving horse, on the one hand, and transmits the riding controls originating in the small of the back, on the other, *the base of support* plays a dominant role, together with the legs and the hands.

It consists of the *thighs* and *pelvis*, which are connected together in the hip joint.

If the pelvis is low and narrow (that is, if the distance from the ilium to the lower edge of the ischium is small and the distance between the two ilia themselves is relatively small), the centre of gravity is low and more stable, even when the upper body is sitting straight and unconstrained, as in the normal seat. This increases the rider's ability to urge the horse onward, unless the lower end of the spinal column – the pelvic vertebrae – slopes too much to the rear and thus affords only slight support to the ischia when it is thrown forward. And if the buttocks are too fleshy, we get an even greater impression of a base of support slipping to the rear. As a matter of fact, the surplus flesh that sticks out behind interferes greatly with the pushing forward of the buttocks, which can act as an impelling force without the assistance of other parts of the body only if the rider's weight acts upon the dorsal processes of the horse's spinal column (which are vertical in this region) at an angle that is at least 90 degrees.

The principle that only an extended surface of contact affords stability,

"*The Levade.*"

107

plus breathing and swinging in time with the mechanism of the horse, is satisfied by a thigh that is flat on its inner surface. Anyone who is not born with this fortunate configuration, which is a great advantage for a solid seat in the saddle – and in this respect we men have an advantage over the fair sex – will have to spend years massaging the disturbing, round fleshy muscles to the rear until he obtains the desired "flat thigh". The best cure is riding without stirrups and often pulling one's body forward.

Well-shaped thighs afford still another advantage. When turned inwards from the hip joint and lying flat with relaxed, opened buttocks, they naturally cause the *knee* to take the right position – "slapped on the saddle like a hunk of raw meat", as a chief riding instructor of the Spanish Riding School of Vienna used to put it.

The proper position of the knee, about which so much has been said and for which so many remedies have been offered, is a result of just placing the base of support correctly and throwing the small of the back forward. This must precede every control, and it will make the rider "grow longer from the hip joints downward" and "grow taller from the hips upward".

Anyone who is master of his seat and his controls will be able to do without the pampering knee pads sewn underneath the saddle flaps.

A good knee position never becomes a problem for the well-set-up rider if he is properly instructed, though it costs the rider not so well favoured by nature considerable sweat. He must undergo wearisome massage, for a steady, absolutely fixed knee is an indispensable prerequisite for success, both for the dressage rider and for the rider who hopes to pluck the laurels that hang somewhat lower over tournament jumps. He will jump his horse satisfactorily only if his knee, now justifiably supported by those beloved pads, constitutes the sole stationary pole for the other parts of the body, some oscillating downward and others upward and forward.

CAVALRY

~~~~~~

Soldiers are the noblest estate of mankind, and horsemen the noblest of soldiers.

SIR PHILIP SIDNEY,
An Apologie for Poetrie

ALTHOUGH, SINCE the First World War, the horsed cavalryman has reappeared here and there around the globe – in the guise of a scout or policeman – he virtually expired where the machine-gun bullets, high-explosive shells and barbed-wire ruled across the mud of Flanders. While he lasted as a warrior he took pride of place on the battlefield as well as the parade-ground. Surviving as a ceremonial asset he now reminds us of the reputation for quick-thinking and resourcefulness, élan and esprit de corps of the fighting cavalry, qualities now enshrined in the character of the tank and armoured car units.

I begin my cavalry anthology with Job on the courage of the war-horse, then a little of Caesar's clipped style, giving the flavor of mounted troops under firm command 2,000 years ago, accompanied by a vignette of personal courage. This is followed by an account of the Mongols under Genghis Khan; then the effect of Cortez's cavalry in Mexico, in 1519, against Aztec troops, who had never seen a horse before, is well portrayed in an incident from Prescott's history.

Few can have appreciated the preeminence of the horse on the battlefield more than Shakespeare, and to represent him I have quoted the scene at the end of the Battle of Bosworth when Richard III offers his "kingdom for a horse," and, from *Henry V*, the dialogue at the French headquarters on the eve of Agincourt, in which the English horsemen and their mounts are severely scorned. These cameos are followed by an anecdote from the pen of Shakespeare's contemporary, the poet, courtier and soldier, Sir Philip Sidney, of his visit to Italy with his friend Edward Wootton, to learn military horsemanship under the renowned John Pietro Pugliano (who vows that "soldiers are the noblest estate of mankinde, and horsemen the noblest of soldiers").

About a century later one of the strangest forces of cavalry ever raised appeared in England's West Country. It was largely composed of marsh-mares, hunters and coach- and cart-horses, mounted by peasants with rusty swords stuck in their belts. The 8,000-strong army, to which this force belonged, was under command of the son of Charles II, by Lucy Walter, James, Duke of Monmouth, a former Captain-General of the English Army, who, four months after his father's death, in 1685, landed on the Dorset coast from Holland, to claim the throne occupied by his uncle, James II. From my own biography of Monmouth, *Captain-General and Rebel Chief*, I have taken the narrative of the rebel army's night march from Bridgewater, which ended in its defeat at the Battle of Sedgemoor, the last encounter to be fought on British soil.

Primarily officered by its squirearchy and recruited from its yeomanry and tenantry, the cavalry of civilized Europe was the military élite. "Dash," "glamor" and "style" were the words associated with lancers, hussars, cuirassiers and dragoons, and I think their color and style are well portrayed in my choice from Hardy's *Trumpet-Major*, when the York Hussars ride into camp. I remember feeling the same thrill when I saw my father's yeomanry squadron, albeit in khaki, riding to and from their lines during their summer maneuvers in the 1930s.

But, recalling the times when the cavalry was not always entirely fit for service or was not competently or suitably employed by their commanders, one's mind turns to the Crimea. Most people think of Captain Louis Edward Nolan as the officer who carried the order from Raglan to Cardigan for the Light Brigade to charge at Balaclava, and who lost his life in the execution of this duty. Few know him now as the author of an important military manual, *Cavalry: Its History and Tactics*, which was published a year before he died. I have selected his interesting survey of the excellent mounts provided for the army in India and the superior training they were given, and his exhortation to the British cavalry commanders to follow the example of their counterparts in the *Raj*. If only briefly, Nolan saw his strictures justified in the Crimea.

But at least "Captain," the old charger in *Black Beauty* had, as we see, a thoughtful as well as a gallant cavalryman to ride him toward the guns at Balaclava. Nor did Tennyson underestimate the overall courage of the affair.

The horsed cavalryman received a comparatively long and thorough training. Since he was required to scout, deploy and fight, without being preoccupied with his riding, his equitation and horsemastership had to be as second nature. Riding school was tough and thorough. In *My Early Life*, Winston Churchill gives us a taste of what it was like for a young officer in the 1890s, and Howard Marshall, the old nagsman, whose voice George Millar put on tape, for *Horseman*, and who was Geoffrey Brooke's groom in the 16th Lancers, tells us how he fared ten years later. Those of us who have, since the days of the fighting cavalry been through the full course, will identify closely with both these experiences, and so will the young horsed cavalryman and horse gunner of today.

In 1898 Churchill was fighting with the 21st Lancers against the forces of the Khalifa in the Sudan, and that September, at Omdurman, took part in the world's last full scale cavalry charge, which he recorded in both *The River War* and *My Early Life*. In 1895 he had served with the Spanish forces during their conflict in Cuba. Three years later the Americans intervened on behalf of the Cubans, and Theodore Roosevelt, who was to become 26th President of the United States, was soon heavily involved in the commitment. In the year that the young Churchill was in the Sudan, Roosevelt was Assistant Secretary to the United States Navy, a post he then resigned, because, as he explains in *Rough Riders*: "While my party was in opposition I had preached, with all the fervor and zeal I possessed, our duty to . . . take this opportunity of driving the Spaniard from the Western World. Now that my party had come to power, I felt it incumbent on me . . . to do all I could to secure the carrying out of a policy in which I so heartily believed; and, from the beginning, I had determined that . . . I was going to the front." The energy, imagination and strength of character applied by Roosevelt in raising and training the regiment, which became famous as *The Rough Riders*, shines powerfully through in the excerpt given here.

Although the weaponry and tactical conditions which the British encountered in their campaign against the Boers were not too inhibiting for cavalry, those of the Great War certainly were – as the quotation from Jack Fairfax-Blakeborough's autobiography well illustrates. The days of the horsed cavalryman were almost over. But here we have just one last glimpse of him seen in retrospect through the eyes of the Commanding Officer of the Ist Household Cavalry Regiment in the Middle East, in 1940. "We may, before leaving the subject of the horses," wrote Colonel Wyndham – relating the mechanization of the Regiment – "reflect for a moment on one military advantage which they gave, and to which the machine can offer no parallel. Every man, however humble, who rode in the ranks of a cavalry regiment, had an independent command, consisting of one living creature, his horse. The successful command of any living creature depends largely upon sympathy, an emotion which plays no part in the control of a machine. It is in great measure due to this advantage that the mounted soldier has always been very adaptable. . . . "

CHARACTER OF THE WAR-HORSE

Job

HAST THOU GIVEN the horse strength? Hast thou clothed his neck with thunder? Canst thou make him afraid as a grasshopper? The glory of his nostrils is terrible. He paweth in the valley, and rejoiceth in his strength: he goeth on to meet the armed men. He mocketh at fear, and is not affrighted; neither turneth he back from the sword. The quiver rattleth against him, the glittering spear and the shield. He swalloweth the ground with fierceness and rage: neither believeth he that it is the sound of the trumpet. He saith among the trumpets, Ha, ha; and he smelleth the battle afar off, the thunder of the captains, and the shouting.

THE AQUITANIAN BROTHERS

Julius Caesar

56 BC

WHEN CAESAR WAS NOT more than twelve miles from the Germans their envoys returned according to agreement, and meeting him on the march earnestly begged him to advance no farther. On Caesar's refusing to comply, they asked him to send word to the cavalry which had gone in advance of the column, forbidding them to engage in battle, and also requested leave to send an embassy to the Ubii. They said that if the Ubian chiefs and council would swear to keep faith with them, they would avail themselves of the offer that Caesar had made, and asked for three days to complete the necessary negotiations. Caesar believed that all these suggestions had the same object as their previous manoeuvre – to obtain a further three days' delay to give time for the return of the German cavalry from their foray. However, he said that he would restrict his advance that day to four miles – the distance that was necessary to get water. On the next day, if as many of them as possible would assemble at his halting-place, he would give their requests a formal hearing. In the meantime he sent orders to the officers who had gone on in front with the whole cavalry force that they were not to attack the enemy, and, if attacked themselves, were to remain on the defensive until he approached with the main army. But when the enemy caught sight of our cavalry, five thousand strong, although they themselves had not more than eight hundred horse – those who had crossed the Meuse to get corn having not yet returned – they immediately charged. Our men, who thought themselves safe from attack because the enemy's envoys had only just left Caesar and had asked for a truce for that day, were at first thrown into disorder. When they rallied, the German horsemen, following their usual practice, jumped down, unhorsed a number of our men by stabbing their horses in the belly, put the rest to flight, and kept them on the run in such a panic that they did not stop until they came in sight of the marching column of infantry. In this engagement seventy-four of our cavalrymen were killed, including Piso, a gallant Aquitanian of very good family, whose grandfather had been king of his tribe and had been granted the title of "Friend" by the Roman Senate. He went to the assistance of his brother, who was cut off by some of the Germans, and succeeded in rescuing him; but his own horse was wounded and threw him. As long as he could, he resisted with the utmost bravery, but eventually was surrounded and fell covered with wounds. When his brother, who by this time had got well away from the fight, saw what had happened, he galloped straight up to the enemy and let them kill him too.

THE MONGOLS – *c.* 1200

J.M. Brereton

1976

IN THE EARLY THIRTEENTH century a tidal wave of mounted warriors burst out of the high plateaux of Central Asia and, sweeping all before it, ravaged the whole of the Middle East and pounded against the gates of Europe. The name Genghis Khan has become synonymous with death and destruction; while his savage hordes have been likened to a devastating typhoon. However posterity may have judged him, there is no denying his military genius as a cavalry general, and his troops were amongst the finest light horsemen the world has ever seen. The very antithesis of Muhammad, whose Islamic legacy he was to shatter, the Great Khan was a man of deeds, not words. Born an illiterate nomad of the cruel Gobi desert, he founded within his own lifetime an empire that stretched from the China Sea to the Baltic – some two-thirds of the then known world. His astonishing conquests were achieved entirely on the backs of the shaggy Mongolian ponies that were the direct descendants of the wild Przevalski horse.

For centuries before Genghis Khan's time the horse had been the fulcrum of the nomad's very existence; it defeated the limitations of vast distances, and made possible far-ranging pastoral movements and raids. Almost from birth, the Mongolian boy was brought up as a horseman. Before he could toddle, his first riding lessons were on the back of a sheep, and by the age of sixteen, when he was enlisted as a warrior, he was virtually living in the saddle. He ate and drank, even slept, on the back of a horse, and did not bother to dismount to answer the calls of nature. Sent on an errand of few hundred yards, he would leap on the nearest pony rather than use his own legs. He was weaned on mares' milk, and sheltering in his *yurt*, created some semblance of warmth by burning horse dung. When rations ran out on a forced march, he stuck a knife into a horse's vein, sucked a pint or so of blood and sewed up the wound. Sometimes the blood was stored in gut bags made from the horses' intestines; heated over a fire, this served as a sort of black pudding emergency ration. On the march, slabs of raw beef or mutton were rendered chewable by the simple process of clapping them on the horse's back underneath the saddle and riding on them.

As a babe, the Mongolian was doused daily in cold water to toughen him up, thus effectively putting him off bodily hygiene for the rest of his life, for he seldom washed again. The trooper's garments were worn continuously, day and night, and only when they became threadbare were they renewed. He tore his greasy meat with his hands then wiped them on his boots, to keep the leather supple. Rancid butter was stored away in hairy pockets, and any unconsumed portions of the day's rations were stuffed down the rider's trousers and sat upon in the saddle. It was said that a Mongol army on the march could be scented by the enemy up to a distance of twenty miles, if the wind was right.

The all-conquering hordes were exclusively cavalry and the horse was their sole means of mobility. Bred to incredible hardship, the native Mongolian pony was not a handsome beast, but he was as tough as his rider. Standing about 13 hands, he had a coarse Roman-nosed head and a thickset deep-barrelled body with long mane and tail. His shaggy coat was usually dun in colour – ideal as camouflage in his native environment – but bays, chestnuts and greys were not uncommon.

The stamina of these ponies is legendary yet they subsisted entirely on the sparse herbiage of the steppe, for the Mongols grew no cereals. Marches of 80 miles a day for days on end were nothing unusual for the advancing hordes . . . forced marches of 120 miles in one day – probably of 24 hours – were recorded. A man did not ride a single horse throughout; as one tired, he switched to a fresh mount, perhaps using ten or more in a day.

One might suppose that the herds of reserve horses would have created problems, but each group of these docile little beasts followed a bell-mare, which was either ridden or led in hand. When action was imminent, they were dropped behind with an escort. Sometimes superior numbers of the enemy might be overawed by the Mongolian ruse of mounting dummies on the spare horses. And the ponies had other uses: in the last resort, they served as emergency rations; unlike most other cavalrymen, the Mongol was not averse to eating his mount. With so many horses, casualties were less of a problem and, as grazing was always available, the vast self-sufficient mounted hosts could easily cover distances impossible for more conventional forces.

Marco Polo recorded that: "Their horses are fed upon grass alone, and do not require barley or other grain. The men are habituated to remain on horseback during two days and two nights, without dismounting; sleeping in that situation whilst their horses graze . . . Their horses are so well broken-in to quick changes of movement, that, upon the signal given, they instantly turn in every direction; and by these rapid manoeuvres many victories have been obtained."

The popular conception of a Mongol horde as a wild, undisciplined rabble riding hell-for-leather, with no command structure and little thought for horseflesh, seems very far from the truth. In Genghis Khan's day the army was properly organised on a decimal system of units: a troop comprised ten men, a squadron ten troops, a regiment ten squadrons. At formation level was the division, or *touman*, of ten regiments – 10,000 men, with perhaps 100,000 horses. A formidable command; and certainly no other army had ever fielded such a vast array of horseflesh. Discipline was strict. The Khan's standing orders, quoted in the *Secret History*, laid down that any trooper disobeying an order was to be flogged and put under arrest, while those who failed to carry out a personal order from the Khan himself were to be beheaded on the spot. Good horsemastership was not overlooked: "Take care of the spare horses in your troop before they lose condition. For once they have lost it, you may spare them as much as you will, they will never recover it on campaign." On the march, the men were not to tire their horses by galloping about after game – an understandable temptation for these natural hunters – and the pace of the march was to be a steady jog-trot. Bridles were not to be worn: " . . . if this is done, the men cannot march at a gallop" – and no unauthorised personal baggage was to be carried on the saddle.

The tactics of the Mongol cavalry were similar to those of other mounted nomad peoples: lightning attacks on the flanks of an enemy, ambushes and feigned withdrawals. Often a horde would lure pursuers on for two or three days; then, mounting their spare horses, they would turn and deliver a ferocious assault on the exhausted enemy column. All planned attacks were preceded by thorough reconnaissance.

The main assault troops were the mounted archers armed with fearsome bows of 170-lb draw-weight, with which they could pour in showers of arrows at full gallop. It is odd that, although the mounted bowman was an essential arm of most Asiatic armies, he was never adopted in Europe. Perhaps the standard of horsemanship was not high enough, for handling a bow in the saddle obviously demands a secureness of seat and agility not easily acquired – and an unusually well-schooled horse. The swordsman and lancer needed only one hand to use his weapon, the other being free to control his mount – hence, the left has always been known as the "bridle hand" – but in action the archer must drop his reins and rely on legs alone.

1519: MEXICO

W. H. Prescott

1843

THE TROOPS ADVANCED more than a league on their laborious march, without descrying the enemy. The weather was sultry, but few of them were embarrassed by the heavy mail worn by the European cavaliers at that period. Their cotton jackets, thickly quilted, afforded a tolerable protection against the arrows of the Indians, and allowed room for the freedom and activity of movement essential to a life of rambling adventure in the wilderness.

At length they came in sight of the broad plains of Ceutla, and beheld the dusky lines of the enemy stretching, as far as the eye could reach, along the edge of the horizon. The Indians had shown some sagacity in the

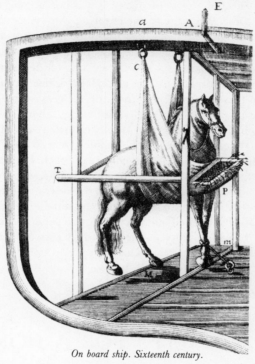

On board ship. Sixteenth century.

choice of their position; and, as the weary Spaniards came slowly on, floundering through the morass, the Tabascans set up their hideous battle-cries, and discharged volleys of arrows, stones, and other missiles, which rattled like hail on the shields and helmets of the assailants. Many were severely wounded before they could gain the firm ground, where they soon cleared a space for themselves, and opened a heavy fire of artillery and musketry on the dense columns of the enemy, which presented a fatal mark for the balls. Numbers were swept down at every discharge; but the bold barbarians, far from being dismayed, threw up dust and leaves to hide their losses, and, sounding their war-instruments, shot off fresh flights of arrows in return.

They even pressed closer on the Spaniards, and, when driven off by a vigorous charge, soon turned again, and, rolling back like the waves of the ocean, seemed ready to overwhelm the little band by weight of numbers.

Thus cramped, the latter had scarcely room to perform their necessary evolutions, or even to work their guns with effect.

The engagement had now lasted more than an hour, and the Spaniards, sorely pressed, looked with great anxiety on the arrival of the horse – which some unaccountable impediments must have detained – to relieve them from their perilous position. At this crisis, the farthest columns of the Indian army were seen to be agitated and thrown into a disorder that rapidly spread through the whole mass. It was not long before the ears of the Christians were saluted with the cheering war-cry of "San Jago and San Pedro!" and they beheld the bright helmets and swords of the Castilian chivalry flashing back the rays of the morning sun, as they dashed through the ranks of the enemy, striking to the right and left, and scattering dismay around them. The eye of faith, indeed, could discern the patron saint of Spain, himself, mounted on his gray war-horse, heading the rescue and trampling over the bodies of the fallen infidels!

The approach of Cortès had been greatly retarded by the broken nature of the ground. When he came up, the Indians were so hotly engaged that he was upon them before they observed his approach. He ordered his men to direct their lances at the faces of their opponents, who, terrified at the monstrous apparition, – for they supposed the rider and the horse, which they had never before seen, to be one and the same, – were seized with a panic. Ordaz availed himself of it to command a general charge along the line, and the Indians, many of them throwing away their arms, fled without attempting further resistance.

MY KINGDOM FOR A HORSE!

William Shakespeare

1597

. . . ANOTHER PART OF THE FIELD.
Alarum; excursions. Enter NORFOLK and Forces; to him CATESBY.
CATESBY. Rescue, my Lord of Norfolk, rescue, rescue!
      The King enacts more wonders than a man,
      Daring an opposite to every danger.
      His horse is slain, and all on foot he fights,
      Seeking for Richmond in the throat of death.
      Rescue, fair lord, or else the day is lost.
    Alarums. Enter KING RICHARD.
KING RICHARD. A horse! a horse! my kingdom for a horse!

CATESBY. Withdraw my lord; I'll help you to a horse.
KING RICHARD. Slave, I have set my life upon a cast
> And I will stand the hazard of the die.
> I think there be six Richmonds in the field;
> Five have I slain to-day instead of him.
> A horse! a horse! my kingdom for a horse!

> *(Exeunt)*

1415: FRENCH MORALE BEFORE AGINCOURT

William Shakespeare

1600

THE FRENCH CAMP
Enter The Dauphin, Orleans, Rambures and others.
ORL. The sun doth gild our armour; Up, my lords!
DAU. Montez à cheval! My horse! Varlet, laquais! Ha!
ORL. O brave spirit!
DAU. Via! Les eaux et la terre –
ORL. Rien puis? L'air et le feu.
DAU. Ciel! cousin Orleans.
> *Enter Constable*
Now, my Lord Constable!
CON. Hark how our steeds for present service neigh!
DAU. Mount them, and make incision in their hides,
> That their hot blood may spin in English eyes,
> And dout them with superfluous courage, ha!
RAM. What, will you have them weep our horses' blood?
> How shall we then behold their natural tears?
> *Enter a Messenger*
MESS. The English are embattl'd, you French peers.
CON. To horse, you gallant Princes! straight to horse!
> Do but behold yon poor and starved band
> And your fair show shall suck away their souls,
> Leaving them but the shales and husks of men.
> There is not work enough for all our hands;
> Scarce blood enough in all their sickly veins
> To give each naked curtle-axe a stain
> That our French gallants shall to-day draw out,
> And sheathe for lack of sport. Let us but blow on them,

The vapour of our valour will o'erturn them.
'Tis positive 'gainst all exceptions, lords
That our superfluous lackeys and our peasants –
Who in unnecessary action swarm
About our squares of battle – were enow
To purge this field of such a hilding foe;
Though we upon this mountain's basis by
Took stand for idle speculation –
But that our honours must not. What's to say?
A very little let us do.
And all is done. Then let the trumpets sound
The tucket sonance and the note to mount;
For our approach shall so much dare the field
That England shall couch down in fear and yield.

Enter Grandpré

GRAND. Why do you stay so long, my lords of France?
Yond island carrions, desperate of their bones,
Ill-favouredly become the morning field;
Their ragged curtains poorly are let loose,
And our air shakes them passing scornfully;
Big Mars seems bankrupt in their beggar'd host,
And faintly through a rusty beaver peeps.
The horsemen sit like fixed candlesticks
With torch-staves in their hand; and their poor jades
Lob down their heads, dropping the hides and hips,
The gum down-roping from their pale-dead eyes,
And in their pale dull mouths the gimmal'd bit
Lies foul with chaw'd grass, still and motionless;
And their executors, the knavish crows,
Fly o'er them, all impatient for their hour.
Description cannot suit itself in words
To demonstrate the life of such a battle
In life so lifeless as it shows itself.

CON. They have said their prayers and they stay for death.

DAU. Shall we go send them dinners and fresh suits,
And give their fasting horses provender,
And after fight with them?

CON. I stay but for my guidon. To the field!
I will the banner from a trumpet take,
And use it for my haste. Come, come, away!
The sun is high, and we outwear the day.

(Exeunt)

HORSEMEN – THE NOBLEST OF SOLDIERS

Sir Philip Sidney

1595

WHEN THE RIGHT vertuous *Edward Wotton*, and I, were at the Emperors Court together, wee gave our selves to learne horsemanship of *John Pietro Pugliano*: one that with great commendation had the place of an Esquire in his stable. And hee, according to the fertilnes of the Italian wit, did not onely afoord us the demonstration of his practise, but sought to enrich our mindes with the contemplations therein, which he thought most precious. But with none I remember mine eares were at any time more loden, then when (either angred with slowe paiment, or mooved with our learner-like admiration,) he exercised his speech in the prayse of his facultie. Hee sayd, Souldiours were the noblest estate of mankinde, and horsemen, the noblest of Souldiours. Hee sayde, they were the Maisters of warre, and ornaments of peace: speedy goers, and strong abiders, triumphers both in Camps and Courts. Nay, to so unbeleeved a poynt he proceeded, as that no earthly thing bred such wonder to a Prince, as to be a good horseman. Skill of government was but a Pedanteria in comparison: then would hee adde certaine prayses, by telling what a peerlesse beast a horse was. The onely servicable Courtier without flattery, the beast of most beutie, faithfulnes, courage, and such more, that if I had not beene a peece of a Logician before I came to him, I think he would have perswaded mee to have wished my selfe a horse.

1685: NIGHT MARCH TO SEDGEMOOR

J.N.P. Watson

1979

BRIDGEWATER JULY 4, 1685. After attending the Reverend Ferguson's Matins, James, Duke of Monmouth, resplendent still in princely purple, Garter star and neatly-combed periwig, climbed the stumpy tower supporting St Mary's Church spire – as you can still climb it today – and pointed his glass eastwards. The view – now obstructed by industrial chimneys, trees and houses – then opened clear across the King's Sedgemoor to Weston. To see the white tents and, around them, the scarlet dots of the men he had once commanded, and to know his half-brother, Grafton, and the deputy commanders who had been the companions of his youth – Feversham, the two Churchills, Kirke, Douglas, Sackville and Compton – were at their head, must have roused some strange sensations in him. There, three miles away, was the memory of his illustrious Captain-Generalcy, while here below, in Castlefield, was all he represented now, a ragged, ill-armed host of revolutionaries with their backs to the wall, a host which had marched all of 200 miles with him, which had lured him, with loving respect, to this fatal Bridgewater.

Ranging his spyglass along the Royalist lines, he noted that the horse were widely separated from the foot, and an idea began to form in his mind. It might be possible to circumvent their artillery, to infiltrate the enemy lines in strength by night, take the cavalry and infantry by two distinct and simultaneous assaults, and so "prevent their arms coming together". Why not attack Feversham by stealth, before further reinforcements reach him, then, having routed him, proceed with the current plan and ride to Cheshire? He had climbed that church tower in a state of utter despair. For everything had gone against him during the past week. He had been forced into ignominious retreat, his ally, Argyle, had been defeated in the Lowlands, William of Orange was poised to support the enemy, while James's own army, dishevelled and ill-equipped, was reduced to 4,000, and there were desertions on every hand.

But now! . . . now he was warmed by this splendid chance to defeat his uncle and seize the throne vacated by his father of beloved memory, and fulfil the wish of England's common people, who loved him.

When he climbed down from the Tower, he was told that a Sedgemoor peasant sought an interview. He listened eagerly to Godfrey. The Royalists appeared to have posted no guards or picquets, the herdsman reported excitedly, and many of them were drunk, or sleeping, their scarlet coats laid out as blankets. The horse were indeed some distance from the foot. Oh yes, Godfrey knew the way across Sedgemoor like the back of his rustic hand, *and* the paths to Weston. James called a council of war and put his plan to them. Let us surprise the enemy in dead of night. We can avoid the guns on the Bridgewater road, and any standing patrols that might be watching in this direction, by making a detour north of Chedzoy. This good fellow Godfrey will guide us across Sedgemoor . . .

11.00 p.m. With Wade's vanguard to set the pace, and his own lifeguard of horse riding closely fore and aft of him, James gave the signal for his army to begin its furtive march north-east.

These unschooled horses were his worst liability; the eerie darkness, the nerviness of their inexperienced riders, straining to hear whispered orders from tense lips, the swirling march mist, and the inevitable, continuous concertinaing of the column, would have all contributed to shake the temper of the ill-broken, ill-assorted nags, kicking and shying, often stopping dead in their tracks, and transmitting fear to the troopers, who relayed back their own nervousness. But, considering, the whole force numbered more than 600 horses and 3,000 men, all raw levies in a single force, their order and discipline spoke much for their leadership.

Strange, inopportune thoughts come into men's minds during periods of silent tension and crisis. Riding onto the King's Sedgemoor that night did James, Duke of Monmouth's thoughts return fleetingly to his early boyhood in the Netherlands, and his beautiful Welsh mother, Lucy Barlow, who had told him over and over that he should be Prince of Wales ("for I was married to your father by a bishop at Liege"). Or did he remember for a moment his father's oft-repeated account of the Battle of Worcester in '51; how he had climbed the Cathedral tower to observe the enemy's movements; and how, when Cromwell began to deploy, Charles had taken command of the Royalist Horse and attacked uphill under artillery cover; and how the Foot, coming up behind, ran out of ammunition, but stood their ground with pike and sword, and after a long, brave struggle, were inched back into the City. His father had quit his horse by then, and only when Worcester's walls were stormed, did he fly.

But memories of his father's defeat were not appropriate to this inspired midnight of July 4, 1685 . . .

Well on to the open moor now, the smell of peat marsh in their nostrils, the silent army came to another channel called the Langmoor Rhine, whose best crossing was marked by a great boulder, the Devil's Upping Stock, or Langmoor Stone. That night the rock was hidden by fog, and Godfrey steered too far east of it. But, after a long agony of suspense, with much blind casting up and down (any moment one of Compton's outposts might have tumbled on the great column), eventually the plungeon was found, and over they tramped. They were only three-quarters of a mile from the Royalist camp now, and the clock on Chedzoy steeple struck one. James sent Grey, accompanied by Godfrey, to the front of the column with the eight troops of cavalry. But no sooner was the march resumed than the stillness of Sedgemoor was broken by a single shot. One of Compton's blue-coated troopers, glimpsing them through the fog, had raised the alarm.

From now on, in the vicinity of the Royalists' camp at Western Zoyland, all was bustle. Spurs hard on, Compton's men galloped back across the Bussex upper plungeon, then down the Royalist battalions' front with a breathless "beat the drums, the enemy is come! For the Lord's sake, beat the drums!" Moments later came the drummers' *rat-tat-tat* . . .

Monmouth must take advantage of such surprise as he had gained . . .

c. 1840: RIDING INTO CAMP

Thomas Hardy

1880

THE SOLDIERS MUST HAVE come there to camp: those men they had seen first were the markers: they had come on before the rest to measure out the ground. He who had accompanied them was the quartermaster. "And so you see they have got all the lines marked out by the time the regiment have come up," he added. "And then they will – well-a-deary! who'd ha' supposed that Overcombe would see such a day as this!"

"And then they will –"

"Then – Ah, it's gone from me again!" said Simon. "O, and then they will raise their tents you know, and picket their horses. That was it; so it was."

By this time the column of horse had ascended into full view, and they formed a lively spectacle as they rode along the high ground in marching order, backed by the pale blue sky, and lit by the southerly sun. Their uniform was bright and attractive; white buckskin pantaloons, three-quarter boots, scarlet shakos set off with lace, mustachios waxed to a needle point; and above all, those richly ornamented blue jackets mantled with the historic pelisse – that fascination to women, and encumbrance to the wearers themselves.

"'Tis the York Hussars!" said Simon Burden, brightening like a dying ember fanned. "Foreigners to a man, and enrolled long since my time. But as good hearty comrades, they say, as you'll find in the King's service."

"Here are more and different ones," said Mrs. Garland.

Other troops had, during the last few minutes been ascending the down at a remoter point, and now drew near. These were of different weight and build from the others; lighter men, in helmet hats, with white plumes.

"I don't know which I like best," said Anne. "These, I think, after all."

Simon, who had been looking hard at the latter, now said that they were the —th Dragoons.

"All Englishmen they," said the old man. "They lay at Budmouth barracks a few years ago."

"They did. I remember it," said Mrs. Garland.

"And lots of the chaps about here 'listed at the time," said Simon. "I can call to mind that there was – ah, 'tis gone from me again! However, all that's of little account now."

The dragoons passed in front of the lookers-on as the others had done, and their gay plumes, which had hung lazily during the ascent, swung to northward as they reached the top, showing that on the summit a fresh breeze blew. "But look across there," said Anne. There had entered upon the down from another direction several battalions of foot, in white kerseymere breeches and cloth gaiters. They seemed to be weary from a long march, the original black of their gaiters and shoes being whitey-brown with dust. Presently came regimental waggons, and the private canteen carts which followed at the end of a convoy.

The space in front of the mill-pond was now occupied by nearly all the inhabitants of the village, who had turned out in alarm, and remained for pleasure, their eyes lighted up with interest in what they saw; for trappings and regimentals, war horses and men, in towns an attraction, were here almost a sublimity.

The troops filed to their lines, dismounted, and in quick time took off their accoutrements, rolled up their sheep-skins, picketed and unbitted their horses, and made ready to erect the tents as soon as they could be taken from the waggons and brought forward. When this was done, at a given signal the canvases flew up from the sod; and thenceforth every man had a place in which to lay his head.

c. 1850: THE ENGLISH REGIMENTS POORLY MOUNTED

Captain L.E. Nolan

1853

BEFORE I LEFT INDIA, some very interesting trials were made at Madras, by order of the Commander-in-Chief, General Sir George Berkeley, the object of which was to test the capabilities of the troop-horses, as well as the relative merits of entire horses and geldings for the purposes of war.

Three trials were made.

The first with two regiments of Native Regular cavalry, one of stallions, one of geldings.

The next with two troops of Horse Artillery.

The third, and last, with two hundred English dragoons (15th Hussars); one hundred riding stallions, and one hundred mounted on geldings. This squadron marched upwards of eight hundred miles – namely, from Bangalore to Hyderabad, where they remained a short time to take part in the field-days, pageants, etc. They then returned to Bangalore, four hundred miles, by forced marches: only one rest-day was allowed them, and the last six marches in were made at the rate of thirty miles a day. They brought in but one led horse; stallions and geldings did their work equally well, and were in equally good condition on their return. The question was, however, decided in favour of the latter, because they had been cut without reference to age, and only six months before the trial took place.

The English cavalry in India is well mounted. On an emergency any one of these Indian regiments would gallop fifty miles in a pursuit, leave few horses behind, and suffer but little from the effects of such exertion. The horses on which they are mounted are small but powerful. The Arab, the Persian, the Turcoman, the horses from the banks of the Araxes, are all unrivalled as war-horses. I have seen a Persian horse fourteen hands three inches carrying a man of our regiment of gigantic proportions, and weighing in marching order twenty-two-and-a-half stone: I have seen this horse on the march above alluded to, of eight hundred miles, carrying this enormous weight with ease, and keeping his condition well; at the crossing of the Kistnas, a broad, rapid, and dangerous river, the owner of this horse (Private Herne, of C troop) refused to lead the animal into the ferry-boat to cross, but, saying "An hussar and his horse should never part company," he took the water in complete marching order, and the gallant little horse nobly stemmed the tide, and landed his rider safely on the opposite bank.

An officer in India made a bet that he would himself ride his charger (an

126

Arab, little more than fourteen hands high) four hundred measured miles in five consecutive days, and he won the match; the horse performed his task with ease, and did not even throw out a wind-gall. The owner, an officer of the Madras Artillery, died shortly afterwards.

General Daumas relates that the horses of the Sahara will travel during five or six days from seventy-five to ninety miles a day, and that in twenty-four hours they will go over from one hundred and fifty to one hundred and eighty miles, and this over a stony desert. Diseases of the feet and broken wind are almost unknown amongst them.

What would become of an English cavalry regiment if suddenly required to make a few forced marches, or to keep up a pursuit for a few hundred miles!! Their want of power to carry *the* weight, and want of breeding, makes them tire after trotting a few miles on the line of march.

Our cavalry horses are feeble; they measure high, but they do so from length of limb, which is weakness, not power. The blood they require is not that of our weedy race-horse (an animal more akin to the greyhound, and bred for speed alone), but it is the blood of the Arab and Persian, to give them that compact form and wiry limb in which they are wanting.

The fine Irish troop-horses, formerly so sought for, are not now to be procured in the market. Instead of the long, low, deep-chested, short-backed, strong-loined horse of former dàys, you find nothing now but long-legged, straight-shouldered animals, prone to disease from the time they are foaled, and whose legs grease after a common field-day. These animals form the staple of our remount horses.

Decked out in showy trappings, their riders decorated with feathers and plumes, they look well to the superficial observer; but the English cavalry are not what they should be. If brought fresh into the field of battle, the speed of the horses, and the pluck of the men, would doubtless achieve great things for the moment; but they could not *endure*, they could not follow up, they could not *come again*.

All other reforms in our cavalry would be useless unless this important point be looked to. It is building a house on the sand to organise cavalry without good horses. Government alone could work the necessary reform by importing stallions and mares of eastern blood, for the purpose of breeding troop-horses and chargers for the cavalry of England.

It is said that a government stud is opposed to the principle of competition. What competition can there be amongst breeders for the price of a troop-horse when by breeding cart-horses they obtain forty pounds for them when two years old? How could they possibly afford to rear animals with the necessary qualifications for a cavalry horse of the first class? To breed such horses a cross must first be obtained with our race-horses: this would entail a large outlay of capital; and when the good troop-horse was produced, the breeder could not obtain his price for him.

The rules of our Turf encourage speed only, and that for short distances. Horses are bred to meet these requirements, and from these weeds do our horses of the present day inherit their long legs, straight shoulders, weak constitutions, and want of all those qualities for which the English horse of former days was so justly renowned.

I had heard of fine horses in Russia, but I complacently said to myself, "Whatever they are, they cannot be as good as the English." However, I went to Russia – and seeing is believing. Their horse-artillery and cavalry are far better mounted than ours; and their horses are immeasurably superior in those qualities which constitute the true war-horse – namely, courage, constitution, vigour, strength of limb, and great power of endurance under fatigue and privation.

The excellent example set by Sir George Berkeley in India might be followed up at home with great advantage to the service; the capabilities of our cavalry horses of the present day should be severely tested, and the saddles should be tried and experiments made to ascertain how sore backs may be avoided.

VETERAN OF BALACLAVA

Anna Sewell

1877

CAPTAIN HAD BEEN broken in and trained for an army horse, his first owner being an officer of cavalry going out to the Crimean War. He said he quite enjoyed the training with all the other horses – trotting together, turning together to the right hand or the left, halting at the word of command, or dashing forward at full speed at the sound of the trumpet or signal of the officer. When young, he was a dark, dappled iron grey, and was considered very handsome. His master, a young, high-spirited gentleman, was very fond of him, and from the first treated him with the greatest care and kindness. He told me he thought the life of an army horse was very pleasant; but when it came to being sent abroad in a great ship over the sea, he almost changed his mind.

"That part of it," he said, "was dreadful! Of course we could not walk off the land into the ship; so they were obliged to put strong straps under our bodies, and then we were lifted off our legs in spite of our struggles, and were swung through the air, over the water, to the deck of the great vessel. There we were placed in small, close stalls, and never for a long time saw the sky, or were able to stretch our legs. The ship sometimes rolled about in high winds, and we were knocked about, and felt very ill. However, at last it came to an end, and we were hauled up, and swung over again to the land. We were very glad, and snorted and neighed for joy when we once more felt firm ground under our feet."

"We soon found that the country to which we had come was very different from our own, and that we had many hardships to endure besides the fighting; but many of the men were so fond of us that they did everything they could to make us comfortable, in spite of snow, wet, and the fact that all things were out of order."

"But what about that fighting?" said I; "was not that worse than anything else?"

"Well," said he, "I hardly know. We always liked to hear the trumpet sound, and to be called out, and were impatient to start off, though sometimes we had stand for hours, waiting for the word of command. But when the word was given, we used to spring forward as gaily and eagerly as if there were no cannonballs, bayonets, or bullets. I believe so long as we felt our rider firm in the saddle, and his hand steady on the bridle, not one of us gave way to fear, not even when the terrible bombshells whirled through the air and burst into a thousand pieces.

"With my noble master, I went into many actions without a wound; and though I saw horses shot down with bullets, others pierced through

with lances or gashed with fearful sabre-cuts, though I left them dead on the field, or dying in the agony of their wound, I don't think I feared for myself. My master's cheery voice as he encouraged his men made me feel as if he and I could not be killed. I had such perfect trust in him that whilst he was guiding me, I was ready to charge up to the very cannon's mouth.

"I saw many brave men cut down, and many fall from their saddles mortally wounded. I have heard the cries and groans of the dying, cantered over ground slippery with blood, and frequently had to turn aside to avoid trampling on wounded man or horse; but, until one dreadful day, I had never felt terror; that day I shall never forget."

Here old Captain paused for a while and drew a long breath; I waited, and he went on.

"It was one autumn morning, and, as usual, an hour before daybreak our cavalry had turned out, ready caparisoned for the day's work, whether fighting or waiting. The men stood waiting by their horses, ready for orders. As the light increased, there seemed to be some excitement among the officers; and before the day was well begun, we heard the firing of the enemy's guns.

"Then one of the officers rode up and gave the word for the men to mount, and in a second every man was in his saddle, and every horse stood expecting the touch of the rein, or the pressure of his rider's heels – all animated, all eager. But still we had been trained so well, that, except by the champing of our bits, and by the restive tossing of our heads from time to time, it could not be said that we stirred.

"My dear master and I were at the head of the line, and as all sat motionless and watchful, he took a little stray lock of my mane which had turned over the wrong side, laid it over on the right and smoothed it down with his hand; then, patting my neck, he said, 'We shall have a day of it to-day, Bayard, my beauty; but we'll do our duty as we always have done.'

"That morning he stroked my neck more, I think, than he had ever done before; quietly on and on, as if he were thinking of something else. I loved to feel his hand on my neck, and arched my crest proudly and happily; but I stood very still, for I knew all his moods, and when he liked me to be quiet and when gay.

"I cannot tell all that happened that day, but I will tell of the last charge that we made together; it was across a valley right in front of the enemy's cannon. By this time we were well used to the roar of heavy guns, the rattle of musket fire, and the flying of shot near us; but never had I been under such a fire as we rode through that day. From right, left, and front, shot and shell poured in upon us. Many a brave man went down, many a horse fell, flinging his rider to the earth; many a horse without a rider ran wildly out of the ranks; then, terrified at being alone with no hand to guide him, came pressing in amongst his old companions, to gallop with them to the charge.

"Fearful as it was, no one stopped, no one turned back. Every moment the ranks were thinned, but as our comrades fell we closed in to keep the others together; and instead of being shaken or staggered in our pace, our gallop became faster and faster as we neared the cannon, all clouded in white smoke, while the red fire flashed through it.

"My master, my dear master, was cheering on his comrades, with his right arm raised on high, when one of the balls whizzing close to my head, struck him. I felt him stagger with the shock, though he uttered no cry. I tried to check my speed, but the sword dropped from his right hand, the rein fell loose from the left, and sinking backward from the saddle, he fell to the earth; the other riders swept past us, and by the force of their charge I was driven from the spot where he fell.

"I wanted to keep my place at his side, and not to leave him under that rush of horses' feet, but it was in vain. And now, without a master or a friend, I was alone on that great slaughter-ground. Then fear took hold of me, and I trembled as I had never trembled before. Then I, too, as I had seen other horses do, tried to join in the ranks and to gallop with them; but

I was beaten off by the swords of the soldiers.

"Just then, a soldier whose horse had been killed under him caught at my bridle and mounted me, and with this new master I was again going forward. But our gallant company was cruelly overpowered, and those who remained alive after the fierce fight for the guns came galloping back over the same ground.

"Some of the horses had been so badly wounded that they could scarcely move from loss of blood; other noble creatures were trying on three legs to drag themselves along; and others were struggling to rise on their fore feet when their hind legs had been shattered by shot. Their groans were piteous to hear, and the beseeching look in their eyes as those who escaped passed by and left them to their fate I shall never forget. After the battle, the wounded men were brought in, and the dead were buried."

"And what about the wounded horses?" I said; "were they left to die?"

"No, the army farriers went over the field with their pistols, and shot all that were ruined. Some that had only slight wounds were brought back and attended to, but the greater part of the noble, willing creatures that went out that morning never came back! In our stables there was only about one in four that returned.

"I never saw my dear master again. I believe he fell dead from the saddle. Never did I love any other master so well. I went into many other engagements, but was only once wounded, and then not seriously; and when the war was over, I came back again to England, as sound and strong as when I went out."

I said, "I have heard people talk about war as if it was a very fine thing."

"Ah!" said he, "I should think they have never seen it. No doubt it is very fine when there is no enemy, only just exercise, parade, and sham-fight. Yes, it is very fine then; but when thousands of good, brave men and horses are killed or crippled for life, then it has a very different look."

"Do you know what they fought about?" said I.

"No," he said, "that is more than a horse can understand; but the enemy must have been awfully wicked people if it was right to go all that way over the sea on purpose to kill them."

SOMEONE HAD BLUNDERED

Alfred, Lord Tennyson

1854

Half a league, half a league,
Half a league onward,
All in the valley of death

Rode the six hundred.
"Forward, the Light Brigade!
Charge for the guns!" he said;
Into the valley of Death
Rode the six hundred.

"Forward, the Light Brigade!"
Was there a man dismay'd?
Not tho' the soldier knew
Some one had blunder'd:
Their's not to make reply,
Their's not to reason why,
Their's but to do and die:
Into the valley of Death
Rode the six hundred . . .

1895: AN OFFICER IN RIDING SCHOOL

Winston Churchill

1930

IN MARCH, 1895, I was gazetted to the 4th Hussars. I joined the Regiment six weeks earlier in anticipation, and was immediately set with several other subalterns to the stiff and arduous training of a Recruit Officer. Every day long hours were passed in the Riding-School, at Stables or on the Barrack Square. I was fairly well fitted for the riding-school by the two long courses through which I had already gone; but I must proclaim that the 4th Hussars exceeded in severity anything I had previously experienced in military equitation.

In those days the principle was that the newly-joined Officer was given a recruit's training for the first six months. He rode and drilled afoot with the troopers and received exactly the same instruction and training as they did. At the head of the file in the riding-school, or on the right of the squad on the Square, he had to try to set an example to the men. This was a task not always possible to discharge with conspicuous success. Mounting and dismounting from a bare-backed horse at the trot or canter; jumping a high bar without stirrups or even saddle, sometimes with hands clasped behind one's back; jogging at a fast trot with nothing but the horse's hide between your knees, brought their inevitable share of mishaps. Many a time did I pick myself up shaken and sore from the riding-school tan and don again my little gold braid pork-pie cap, fastened on the chin by a boot-lace strap, with what appearance of dignity I could command, while twenty recruits grinned furtively but delightedly to see their Officer suffering the same misfortunes which it was their lot so frequently to undergo. I had the ill-luck, at an early stage in these proceedings, to strain my tailor's muscle on which one's grip upon a horse depends. In consequence I suffered tortures. Galvanic treatment was then unknown; one simply had to go on tearing at a lacerated muscle with the awful penalty of being thought a booby, if one begged off even for a day.

1905: A TROOPER IN RIDING SCHOOL

J.H. Marshall

1970

"RIDING SCHOOL TOMORROW!"

When those words were barked at us by I cannot remember which performing tomcat of an N.C.O. I'd three months on the barrack square at foot drill with two hours' stables a day, but most of my squad had done much longer, some of them as long as a twelve-month without getting on a horse. The funny thing was that if I asked them why they'd offered their services to the cavalry arm the usual answer was that they disliked walking and hated or feared the sea. There was no air force in those days.

We were ordered to parade outside the riding school, ourselves in breeches and puttees, our horses in blankets with surcingles round them (no saddles) and plain bridoon bits.

Mr Jock Lang, the riding master, inspected us and then, in tones of facetious refinement, delivered a standard but by no means stupid description of the horse as a conveyance. He was a smart little fellow, immaculate in Kiwi-ed boots, and spurs, Sam Browne belt, moustaches. He wore an eye-glass. We'd been warned that he was an absolute so-and-so, and eyed him as though he were a poisonous snake. He had us lead round inside the riding school for a while, then halted us, facing him.

"Any of you fellows ever ridden befoah?" he asked.

No answer.

"Well, in your own time . . . Mmm-ount!" He had a good many minions and quite soon everybody had been hove up on top. Most of us looked scared and uncomfortable.

"Walk mm-arch!"

Clever as monkeys and schooled to death, the horses went trailing round at the word of command whether the blokes had them by the head or not.

"Trr-ot!"

The old horses jogged on round.

"Haaalt!"

Everyone fell off except me. I forgot to. The horses were quietly sniggering.

"Come out he-ah, young man, yes you, Lofty," Mr Lang said in tones from which kindness was conspicuously absent. "*You* have ridden befo-ah."

"Yes, sir."

"Did I not inqui-ah if any of you had ridden befo-ah?"

"Yes sir."

"Then are you a cheat or a li-ah?"

"Neither, sir. I feared you'd think I was showing off."

"Neith-ah, sir," he mimicked. "A barrackroom law-yah. Come he-ah." He put me through a few movements with the horse. I sat still and sat back, riding as well as I could, now that I was found out. My fellow recruits stood by their horses' heads, their eyes glassy, anguished.

"Fetch us three bah-rs," Mr Lang called to his assistants. They set up one decent obstacle, neither low nor high, the battered bars laid on pegs. "Come, Lofty. Canter your horse round and ov-ah." My dobbin went round as though he meant it, and sailed the bars almost handsomely. An intake of breath from the squad. "Round and ovah again," Mr Lang said to me. I could see him unreefing his whip and I knew his plan well enough. As we came into the fence his thong shot out and round my horse's forelegs. He put in two short ones, hit the bars hard, and came down with me in the peat beyond. "Now", said Mr Lang, "You must get that peat out of your eyes and your e-ahs and your neck, and brush down your clothes and report to the orderly sergeant, for you are to join the other squad tomorrow, so I understand." He'd known all along that I could ride.

While my recruits' squad was beginning its eighteen-month stint in the riding school, the other squad was to pass out (if judged worthy) the following day. It was to be a parade in full dress uniform, an event for which they had long been working.

"Draw your passing-out parade kit at the store," the orderly-sergeant said. "And if you know what's good for you, make haste and get your turnout clean and sparkling, or you'll know all about it."

From the time when I was seven years old I'd been cleaning tack, boning boots, burnishing bits and irons, doing things properly. I saw straight off that the stuff they pushed at me from the store was absolutely impossible. I spent half the night sweating at it in the passage under a gas jet. I finally crawled into bed sick with apprehension. I knew that nothing, NOTHING, was going to put suppleness and shine into that old, cracked, salty, discoloured leather and the heavily-vaselined dull metal. And that was only the start of it, since my weapons and my dress uniform as well as my person and that of my poor old dull-coated horse also had to be worked up to the peak of smartness. I was supposed to do in hours what the others had taken months over, and it just could not be done.

My appearance on parade next morning, the ugly one among all those smug ducklings, made Squadron Sergeant-Major Mullins howl like a seal. "You'd spoil any parade you heap! You'd disgrace any ride, you basket, you closet! Out! OUT! Go on, get out of it!" That was how he spoke to me.

Although I'd feared such a reaction, I put my horse away sadly and went up to the barrack-room to change into fatigue trousers and shirt. I joined my former squad of tyros at stables. But I hadn't been there long when I was suddenly engulfed in a wave of half-friendly, half-bullying sergeants and corporals. I couldn't imagine what they were trying to do to me.

CAVALRY HORSES
Rudyard Kipling

1894

By the brand on my withers, the finest of tunes
Is played by the Lancers, Hussars, and Dragoons,
And it's sweeter than "Stables" or "Water" to me,
The Cavalry Canter of "Bonnie Dundee!"

Then feed us and break us and handle and groom,
And give us good riders and plenty of room,
And launch us in column of squadron and see
The Way of the War-horse to "Bonnie Dundee!"

1898: A CHARGE BY THE LANCERS
Winston Churchill

1930

EVERYONE EXPECTED THAT we were going to make a charge. That was the one idea that had been in all minds since we had started from Cairo. Of course there would be a charge. In those days, before the Boer War,

British cavalry had been taught little else. Here was clearly the occasion for a charge. But against what body of enemy, over what ground, in which direction or with what purpose, were matters hidden from the rank and file. We continued to pace forward over the hard sand, peering into the mirage-twisted plain in a high state of suppressed excitement. Presently I noticed, 300 yards away on our flank and parallel to the line on which we were advancing, a long row of blue-black objects, two or three yards apart. I thought there were about a hundred and fifty. Then I became sure that these were men – enemy men – squatting on the ground. Almost at the same moment the trumpet sounded "Trot", and the whole long column of cavalry began to jingle and clatter across the front of these crouching figures. We were in the lull of the battle and there was perfect silence. Forthwith from every blue-black blob came a white puff of smoke, and a loud volley of musketry broke the odd stillness. Such a target at such a distance could scarcely be missed, and all along the column here and there horses bounded and a few men fell.

The intentions of our Colonel had no doubt been to move round the flank of the body of Dervishes he had now located, and who, concealed in a fold of the ground behind their riflemen, were invisible to us, and then to attack them from a more advantageous quarter; but once the fire was opened and losses began to grow, he must have judged it inexpedient to prolong his procession across the open plain. The trumpet sounded "Right wheel into line", and all the sixteen troops swung round towards the blue-black riflemen. Almost immediately the regiment broke into a gallop, and the 21st Lancers were committed to their first charge in war!

I propose to describe exactly what happened to me: what I saw and what I felt. I recalled it to my mind so frequently after the event that the impression is as clear and vivid as it was a quarter of a century ago. The troop I commanded was, when we wheeled into line, the second from the right of the regiment. I was riding a handy, sure-footed, grey Arab polo pony. Before we wheeled and began to gallop, the officers had been marching with drawn swords. On account of my shoulder I had always decided that if I were involved in hand-to-hand fighting, I must use a pistol and not a sword. I had purchased in London a Mauser automatic pistol, then the newest and the latest design. I had practised carefully with this during our march and journey up the river. This then was the weapon with which I determined to fight. I had then to draw my pistol from its wooden holster and bring it to full cock. This dual operation took an appreciable time, and until it was finished, apart from a few glances to my left to see what effect the fire was producing, I did not look up at the general scene.

Then I saw immediately before me, and now only half the length of a polo ground away, the row of crouching blue figures firing frantically, wreathed in white smoke. On my right and left my neighbouring troop leaders made a good line. Immediately behind was a long dancing row of lances crouched for the charge. We were going at a fast but steady gallop. There was too much trampling and rifle fire to hear any bullets. After this glance to the right and left and at my troop, I looked again towards the enemy. The scene appeared to be suddenly transformed. The blue-black men were still firing, but behind them there now came into view a depression like a shallow sunken road. This was crowded and crammed with men rising up from the ground where they had hidden. Bright flags appeared as if by magic, and I saw arriving from nowhere Emirs on horseback among and around the mass of the enemy. The Dervishes appeared to be ten or twelve deep at the thickest, a great grey mass gleaming with steel, filling the dry watercourse. In the same twinkling of an eye I saw also that our right over-lapped their left, that my troop would just strike the edge of their array, and that the troop on my right would charge into air. My subaltern comrade on the right, Wormald of the 7th Hussars, could see the situation too; and we both increased our speed to the very fastest gallop and curved inwards like the horns of the moon. One really had not time to be frightened or to think of anything else but these particular necessary actions which I have described. They completely occupied mind and senses.

The collision was now very near. I saw immediately before me, not ten yards away, the two blue men who lay in my path. They were perhaps a couple of yards apart. I rode at the interval between them. They both fired. I passed through the smoke conscious that I was unhurt. The trooper immediately behind me was killed at this place and at this moment, whether by these shots or not I do not know. I checked my pony as the ground began to fall away beneath his feet. The clever animal dropped like a cat four or five feet down on to the sandy bed of the watercourse, and in this sandy bed I found myself surrounded by what seemed to be dozens of men. They were not thickly-packed enough at this point for me to experience any actual collision with them. Whereas Grenfell's troop next but one on my left was brought to a complete standstill and suffered very heavy losses, we seemed to push our way through as one has sometimes seen mounted policemen break up a crowd. In less time than it takes to relate, my pony had scrambled up the other side of the ditch. I looked round.

Once again I was on the hard, crisp desert, my horse at a trot. I had the impression of scattered Dervishes running to and fro in all directions. Straight before me a man threw himself on the ground. The reader must remember that I had been trained as a cavalry soldier to believe that if ever cavalry broke into a mass of infantry, the latter would be at their mercy. My first idea therefore was that the man was terrified. But simultaneously I saw the gleam of his curved sword as he drew it back for a ham-stringing cut. I had room and time enough to turn my pony out of his reach, and leaning over on the off side I fired two shots into him at about three yards. As I straightened myself in the saddle, I saw before me another figure with uplifted sword. I raised my pistol and fired. So close were we that the pistol itself actually struck him. Man and sword disappeared below and behind me. On my left, ten yards away, was an Arab horseman in a bright-coloured tunic and steel helmet, with chain-mail hangings. I fired at him. He turned aside. I pulled my horse into a walk and looked around again.

In one respect a cavalry charge is very like ordinary life. So long as you are all right, firmly in your saddle, your horse in hand, and well armed, lots of enemies will give you a wide berth. But as soon as you have lost a stirrup, have a rein cut, have dropped your weapon, are wounded, or your horse is wounded, then is the moment when from all quarters enemies rush upon you. Such was the fate of not a few of my comrades in the troops immediately on my left. Brought to an actual standstill in the enemy's mass, clutched at from every side, stabbed at and hacked at by spear and sword, they were dragged from their horses and cut to pieces by the infuriated foe. But this I did not at the time see or understand. My impressions continued to be sanguine. I thought we were masters of the situation, riding the enemy down, scattering them and killing them. I pulled my horse up and looked about me. There was a mass of Dervishes about forty or fifty yards away on my left. They were huddling and clumping themselves together, rallying for mutual protection. They seemed wild with excitement, dancing about on their feet, shaking their spears up and down. The whole scene seemed to flicker. I have an impression, but it is too fleeting to define, of brown-clad Lancers mixed up here and there with this surging mob. The scattered individuals in my immediate neighbourhood made no attempt to molest me. Where was my troop? Where were the other troops of the squadron? Within a hundred yards of me I could not see a single officer or man. I looked back at the Dervish mass. I saw two or three riflemen crouching and aiming their rifles at me from the fringe of it. Then for the first time that morning I experienced a sudden sensation of fear. I felt myself absolutely alone. I thought these riflemen would hit me and the rest devour me like wolves. What a fool I was to loiter like this in the midst of the enemy! I crouched over the saddle, spurred my horse into a gallop and drew clear of the *mêlée*.

1898: TRAINING THE U.S. ROUGH RIDERS

Colonel Theodore Roosevelt

1899

RIGID GUARD DUTY was established at once, and everyone was impressed with the necessity for vigilance and watchfulness. The policing of the camp was likewise attended to with the utmost rigor. As always with new troops, they were at first indifferent to the necessity for cleanliness in camp arrangements; but on this point Colonel Wood brooked no laxity, and in a very little while the hygienic conditions of the camp were as good as those of any regular regiment. Meanwhile the men were being drilled, on foot at first, with the utmost assiduity. Every night we had officers' school, the non-commissioned officers of each troop being given similar schooling by

Colonel Theodore Roosevelt.

the Captain or one of the Lieutenants of the troop; and every day we practised hard, by squad, by troop, by squadron and battalion. The earnestness and intelligence with which the men went to work rendered the task of instruction much less difficult than would be supposed. It soon grew easy to handle the regiment in all the simpler forms of close and open order. When they had grown so that they could be handled with ease in marching, and in the ordinary manoeuvres of the drill-ground, we began to train them in open-order work, skirmishing and firing. Here their woodcraft and plains-craft, their knowledge of the rifle, helped us very much. Skirmishing they took to naturally, which was fortunate, as practically all our fighting was done in open order.

Meanwhile we were purchasing horses. Judging from what I saw I do not think that we got heavy enough animals, and of those purchased certainly a half were nearly unbroken. It was no easy matter to handle them on the picket-lines, and to provide for feeding and watering; and the efforts to shoe and ride them were at first productive of much vigorous excitement. Of course, those that were wild from the range had to be thrown and tied down before they could be shod. Half the horses of the regiment bucked, or possessed some other of the amiable weaknesses incident to horse life on the great ranches; but we had abundance of men who were utterly unmoved by any antic a horse might commit. Every animal was speedily mastered, though a large number remained to the end mounts upon which an ordinary rider would have felt very uncomfortable.

My own horses were purchased for me by a Texas friend, John Moore, with whom I had once hunted peccaries on the Nueces. I only paid fifty dollars apiece, and the animals were not showy; but they were tough and hardy, and answered my purpose well.

Mounted drill with such horses and men bade fair to offer opportunities for excitement; yet it usually went off smoothly enough. Before drilling the men on horseback they had all been drilled on foot, and having gone at their work with hearty zest, they knew well the simple movements to form any kind of line or column. Wood was busy from morning till night in hurrying the final details of the equipment, and he turned the drill of the men over to me. To drill perfectly needs long practice, but to drill roughly is a thing very easy to learn indeed. We were not always right about our intervals, our lines were somewhat irregular, and our more difficult movements were executed at times in rather a haphazard way; but the essential commands and the essential movements we learned without any difficulty, and the men performed them with great dash. When we put them on horseback, there was, of course, trouble with the horses; but the horsemanship of the riders was consummate. In fact, the men were immensely interested in making their horses perform each evolution with the upmost speed and accuracy, and in forcing each unquiet, vicious brute to get into line and stay in line, whether he would or not. The guidon-bearers held their plunging steeds true to the line, no matter what they tried to do; and each wild rider brought his wild horse into his proper place with a dash and ease which showed the natural cavalryman.

In short, from the very beginning the horseback drills were good fun, and everyone enjoyed them. We marched out through the adjoining country to drill wherever we found open ground, practising all the different column formations as we went. On the open ground we threw out the line to one side or the other, and in one position and the other, sometimes at the trot, sometimes at the gallop. As the men grew accustomed to the simple evolutions, we tried them more and more in skirmish drills, practising them so that they might get accustomed to advance in open order and to skirmish in any country, while the horses were held in the rear.

1916–1918

Major Jack Fairfax-Blakeborough

1978

WE WERE POSTED TO Fermoy in Ireland before going to France in March 1916. We all met at Southampton and embarked. We spent a few days at Rouen before setting off for Belle Eglise. At this stage of the war, when barbed-wire, trenches and shell-holes made cavalry useless, several hussar officers were drafted to artillery brigades to assist with horse management, with the official title of Horsemaster. It had been found that the majority of the younger artillery officers had had no experience of horses and that equine mortality was increasing.

Jim Barry and I were selected to be Horsemasters. Our posting came through. We were attached to the 223rd Brigade, R.F.A., who were part of the Royal Naval Division. Eventually a mule cart came for us after hours of weary waiting. We were taken to Varennes. It was knee deep in filth and we had to sleep in a room with three other officers. Although we were

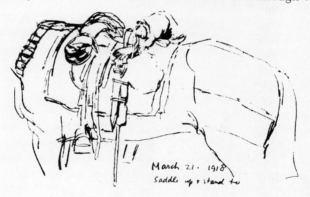

March 21. 1918
Saddle up & stand to

known as Horsemasters, in reality we were stud-grooms. I had the care of nearly 1,000 horses. Poor beggars! They were often standing hock-deep in slush and mud, with soaked rugs on their backs, never able to lie down. I think we were able to do a worthwhile job. I know I got a good deal of satisfaction out of what I did, apart from the fun I had in riding some of the Australian buck jumpers, of which we had a good many at the latter end of the war. Later I was posted North, and an hour after my arrival I rode up to the front line. This was my first introduction to the sounds of warfare and to dead lying about unburied. It was very cold and the ground was covered in snow and filth. I was in a tent in an orchard. The horses were mangy and stood belly deep in water and filth. We Horsemasters were not altogether welcome and had to tread very carefully at first. I never saw horses in such a state. Pack, pack, packing ammunition day and night, and waiting for hours at dumps for ammunition played havoc with them. My first direct job was to be in charge of 60 remounts, some of them mules with which I had never had any dealings before. I made horse-lines in a sunken road by the side of a wood and lost three of the mules the first night. I expected Courts of Inquiry and a rumpus, but it seemed quite a usual occurrence – some other unit had stolen them. To start with I hated and abominated the mules, but soon I came to have a very profound respect for them as they carried on under weather and forage conditions which caused horses to die like flies. I used to say that you could follow us when we "trekked" by our line of dead horses by the road side. Personally I was inclined to think that our veterinary sergeants were a little too handy with their pistols. Of course, it saved them a lot of trouble if a horse was dead beat to shoot it. They could always get sanction from an officer if that was necessary because most of the officers had never had anything to do with horses before the war. Goodness knows what effect this had on Britain's horse-breeding superiority in the long term though. Surely it must have been little short of disastrous. I continually tried to get watering conditions improved and extra forage, but soon found that the staff were helpless, though anxious to be helpful.

I wanted to get my horses strapped for a couple of hours at the end of each day and exercised as they had been used to, but you have got to have men born and trained among horses to do this. If I asked for men, Sergeant-Majors invariably detailed the most useless and notorious shirkers they could discover so that their own work would not suffer. Going to water each day the horses were belly-deep in mud, and often had to wait an hour or more for their turn.

Finally we left this base and had a trek in the snow with many hardships to a place near Vimy Ridge. We were camped in a wheat field which was soon a bog. We spent Easter Monday there in snow and indescribable filth. Some of the 15th/19th Hussars came up near us, and I went to see them. They had their horses in a wood and were under little better conditions than our own. Their horses had mange. Conditions for the horses were dreadful. My diary entry for March 15, 1917 was typical: "27 horses evacuated, 1 died, 3 destroyed." The following week: "42 horses were evacuated, 3 died, and 4 were destroyed." This sad story continued until April 11 when we moved in a blizzard to a site near the front. There we had not a particle of shelter or cover, and the next day: "160 Horses were evacuated, 6 died and 14 were destroyed because of exposure and exhaustion."

We had very short rations here owing to the difficulties of travel and, even on the roads, sank to the thighs in mud. If a horse went down with exhaustion it was drowned, and carts and gun-carriages would pass over it. After the successful Vimy Ridge attack we were supposed to have a rest. We pulled out, a tired, mudstained rabble, and after a cold march of a day or two, we arrived in a bitter snowstorm at Madagascar corner near Arras. There was not a stitch of canvas there for us and the site was just a mud heap, but eventually some tents arrived and we put them up in a blinding snowstorm. My neck was swollen up with the cold and the poor horses were standing shivering. The weather began to look up towards the end of March and beginning of April, 1917. After six weeks, during which time I replaced as many horses as possible, we went to Roclincourt which was the nicest camp that we were in all the time I was in France. Roclincourt was nearer the firing-line, and occasionally we got a shell. I saw Arras shelled regularly every morning. The weather was lovely. We had water troughs in the camp, good horse lines and any amount of excellent lucerne and beet growing on old trenches. This I had gathered and boiled up for the poor-conditioned horses. It was very hot in May, there was very little firing, and consequently there was little ammunition to take up to the line. I had old barbed-wire entanglements cleared so that the horses could graze, though the M.P.s continually warned me off because they said that I was in full view of the Germans and would draw fire. I really did see horses improve here and thoroughly enjoyed life. We had a little steeplechase course put up, and jumping competitions. We even began to build wooden stabling for the winter, and the men asked if they were booked for life in France. Bricks were obtained from ruined houses for standings. I often went up to headquarters. They had a snug place in a trench not far from Chanticleer Corner and it even had flowers outside the doorway. We went about without tunics and hardly knew that there was a war on. The summer really was lovely and I went on daily with grazing parties to improve the horses. In August, 1917, I got away for my first leave home – 10 days. I got into civilian clothes as soon as I could and at Norton was asked by an elderly woman: "Why are you not serving your country?"

1940: IN RETROSPECT

Colonel The Hon. Humphrey Wyndham

1952

EVERY MAN, HOWEVER HUMBLE, who rode in the ranks of a cavalry regiment had an independent command consisting of one living creature, his horse. The successful command of any living creature depends largely upon sympathy, an emotion which plays no part in the control of a machine. It is in great measure due to this advantage that the mounted soldier has always been very adaptable. When the next phase of operations appeared in the offing, some officers were perturbed at what might happen, because the Regiment would be taking part in them without having had the opportunity of doing troop and squadron training in the new role of motorized cavalry regiment. They need have had no such anxiety. There is no black magic about the tactics of any arm. All ranks of the Regiment had, throughout their service, been regularly trained on sound tactical principles. This, plus the advantage of mounted training . . . made the change-over easy.

THE WEST

So long as there are vast stretches of Western range land, so long as there are rodeos and parades and people who like to ride, there will remain thousands of horses — and those horses will be "Western."

PERS CROWELL,
A Cavalcade of American Horses

IN HOW MANY breasts have Western movies and books prompted the first yearnings to ride? And how many more young hearts will be set aflame by the galloping "Westerns" when the era of the romantic cowboys has been dead for a century and more?

Christopher Columbus introduced the European horse to the Americas, via the West Indies, and a little later Cortez did so, via Mexico, and Pizarro, via Peru; and I have introduced this assortment of adventure in the West with Pers Crowell's interesting essay on quarter horses from his *Cavalcade of American Horses*, a chapter which gives an absorbing

account of the fortunes of the horses introduced by the early settlers of North America.

T.C. Hinckle's *Pinto the Mustang* is a fast-moving tale of a very independent youngster, "foaled near the foot of Big Thunder Mountain, in Wyoming" and the property of one Joe Gunnison. As the end of my extract – in which Pinto escapes from horse-thieves to rejoin Joe – indicates, there's a great deal more trouble in store for both of them. But, needless to say, in the true Western tradition, they turn up trumps. *Smoky*, Will James's subject, is the story of another spirited "pardner," born in the wild, and falling into the hands of a good, straight cowboy. James, from long personal experience, was closely acquainted with the range, and his description of the fall round-up may be taken as impeccably authentic.

The first of two word-pictures on the subject of South American broncos, one factual, one fictional, comes from A.F. Tschiffely's account of his ride from Buenos Aires to New York with Gato and Mancha in 1925. His description of a horse-breaking, or *domada*, is very similar to the scene quoted from La Farge's *Sparks Fly Upward*, which follows.

Lastly, in a less voluntary fashion, we find Mark Twain (a pseudonym, incidentally, adopted from the leadsman's call, which had become familiar to him on the Mississippi) youthful and self-mocking on the frontiers of California and Mexico, being "taken for a ride" after buying a "Genuine Mexican Plug."

QUARTER HORSES

Pers Crowell

1951

"HE'S A SLEEPY little hoss that can unwind like lightnin'!" That is the Texan's laconic description of the Quarter Horse. Tremendous speed and even temperament are the factors that make this little animal valuable to those who need a "using" horse. From the standpoint of utility, no horse can lay greater claim to his right of being.

The Quarter Horse has always been found at the outermost fringe of the frontiers of America because he could be counted upon when the jobs were difficult.

For those who think that the Quarter-type horse is a "Johnny-come-lately", let us leave the great cow country of the Southwest and go back about three hundred years to the time of the early English colonists in Virginia and the Carolinas.

As early as 1611, Sir Thomas Dale brought seventeen horses from England. Other stock was undoubtedly brought into the English colonies from the Indian and Spanish settlements to the south, and even before there was sufficient timber cut from the land to form an oval race track, "short" horses were burning up the forest paths with their bursts of terrific speed. By 1656, quarter-mile races were popular, and in 1690, short races with substantial purses were offered for Colonial quarter-of-a-mile race horses.

It is interesting to picture the difficult living conditions of those times. It had only been eighty-four years since King James I had given to the Virginia Company, under the Royal charter of 1606, a map of the territory which included a 75– to 100–mile strip extending along the Atlantic seaboard from what is now the southern boundary of South Carolina to the Canadian border. So wild and impenetrable was this strip that it was believed the great Western ocean lay to its west. The task of hewing a livelihood out of such country was laborious and dangerous. The horses which served the colonists had to be of tough fiber and able to perform the most difficult equine tasks. It would be another eight-five years before Daniel Boone would be able to thrust open the old Wilderness Trail in Kentucky.

Perhaps many of the racecourses over which Colonial Quarter Horses ran were the old war trails of the Indians who, in the tragic year of 1622, had massacred at least one-third of the English settlers in Virginia. It is easy to imagine the reckless abandon with which the early Cavaliers grasped at, in fleeting moments, such sportive equine diversion.

"Where did these horses get their stamina," we may ask, "and where did they originally come from?"

The origin of the early horses along the Atlantic seaboard has never been fully established, but parts of the puzzle can be put together. There is much evidence to support the contention of Quarter Horse breeders and enthusiasts that this little horse is the oldest fixed type in America today. Let us consider some of the possible sources in the century before the English colonists started racing their Quarter Horses.

There is little doubt that the first horses to place a hoof on American soil in any number were the sixteen landed by Cortez in preparation for his conquests in Mexico. These horses – eleven stallions and five mares – were put ashore in the year 1519. They were of Spanish variety, two of them being of the famous Jennet breed. It is possible, but highly improbable, that of the horses that strayed and multiplied, one could have migrated to the eastern part of the continent in the one-hundred-year period before the landing of the first English colonists.

On August 1, 1539, De Soto and his party started northward from Florida with 200 horses. On this expedition he spent considerable time in the land of the Chickasaw Indians. When he was ready to depart from this section, he demanded native male carriers and women. This the Chickasaws considered an insult, and they fell upon the Spaniards at dawn. By the time those in the town were aware of what was happening, half the houses were in flames. The confusion that followed left the soldiers no time to arm or saddle their mounts. The terrorized horses snapped their halters and stampeded, a few being lost in the fire. This encounter would have been complete victory for the Chickasaws and would have put an end to the expedition if the Indians had not mistakenly believed the sound of running horses to mean that the cavalry had managed to mount and pursue them.

It is possible to believe that some of the horses that stampeded that March morning, remained at liberty until the Chickasaws later captured them. Perhaps these were the horses which the Chickasaw Indians are reported to have obtained from the Spanish settlers. Chickasaw horses were raced at quarter-mile distances, but aside from their more glamorous holiday-sports use, the animals were good at plain labor and for purposes of transportation. Writers of those times referred to the Chickasaw as a breed, and their descriptions give an excellent picture of the horse. He was small from the standpoint of height, averaging around 13 hands 2 inches; he was closely coupled and well muscled. At short distances, he showed great speed but was not noted for endurance in long races. It was conceded that the Chickasaw horse was the best all-round utility horse in Colonial America.

PINTO'S ESCAPE

T.C. Hinckle

1935

THE TWO MEN, thinking that Pinto was well tied, set about cooking their breakfast. One of them lifted some stones out of a hole and brought out something from a square tin box. This was "grub" the two men had cached there. A coffee-pot and frying-pan, among other things, was brought out, and it wasn't long until there was a small fire with the cheerful smell of coffee and frying bacon. This was all fine for the two strangers while they talked and laughed at what they supposed was their good luck. But Pinto didn't care anything about the smell of the bacon and coffee. He had other ideas about things. He stood there in the deep gloom of the rocky hills of the canyon, his eyes on the two men squatting before the fire. Their two saddle horses were tied to a pine tree a little farther up the canyon. All seemed to be going perfectly with the strangers, when all at once something happened they hadn't allowed for.

One of the ropes had been left on Pinto's neck, but was tied so that he could move about and drink when he wished. This rope had been fixed in such a way that it couldn't slip and choke him; it could do nothing more than hold him. All at once Pinto lunged backward with all his might and he put all of his twelve hundred pounds in that lunge. He made a noise in this struggle, and both men jumped up from the fire and looked. Pinto broke the rope, and in the mighty effort fell back hard with a short piece of the rope still dangling from his neck. Pinto was not hurt. He had had the wind half knocked out of him when he fell, but in a second he was up. The two men started for him. But the strangers were not quick enough. They ran forward just as the great sorrel horse got on his feet. A second only he looked at them with wild flashing eyes, then with a snort of contempt he whirled and raced away down the rocky canyon floor.

Swiftly the two men mounted their horses and, cursing their luck, spurred after the flying Pinto. For a time there was heard the loud, swift clatter of flying hoofs on the canyon floor, then out of the canyon burst the great sorrel, the short broken rope swinging from his neck, the two riders spurring hard after him. The two men tried to take advantage of Pinto, knowing the lay of the country as they did, but even though they cleverly made him run over the high ridges while they cut through to the lowland they were no match for him. They ran him for five miles before they saw it was no use. Pulling up their puffing horses, the men watched as the big sorrel faded out of sight in the distance. They held their horses here for a time and talked the matter over.

After a lot of arguing the man with the scar on his cheek said, "No use to try to get him at the ranch again. And he'll go back there, too. He'll go back there for that kid to feed him, that is, he'll go back if he's let alone. And," the man continued, "the fellers at that ranch don't know as much as we do about that seventeen-year-old Gunnison kid and that sorrel horse. Now, here's what I say: We'll keep away for a time and see what happens. Nobody knows we took that outlaw away. We'll keep away and be here and there and get the reports! That horse is so well known now that fellers everywhere on the ranches around here know what's going on about him. How's that!"

"That's a fact," said the other. "No use to chase that sorrel even with a dozen horses. We can get him, I'm agreed, but it'll take time, and we've somehow got to get the advantage of both him and that kid."

THE FALL ROUND-UP

Will James

1926

THE FIRST DAY of the fall round-up was to Smoky a whole lot like the first day of school to the kids of the settlement, only Smoky was full grown and his brain full developed. His eyes stayed wide open and worked with his ears so that nothing of interest would be missed.

There was so much that was strange and which kept his senses on the jump. The big wagons with the four and six horse teams done a lot of spooky rattling as they followed the pilot, sometimes on a high lope, across the rolling prairie, over benches and down draws. Then trailing along close behind the thumping of hoofs of many ponies, the remuda, made a sound which hinted everything to Smoky, everything from a stampede on up, and if it hadn't been for the hand that once in a while was felt on his neck, and the voice which he heard and knowed so well, the little horse would of sure left a streak of dust and shot away from all that confusion of wagons and men.

There was too many riders around him. They all kept too close, and once in a while as the outfit sashayed on towards the first camp grounds and some bronc would bust out a bucking and a trying to shed off a cowboy, Smoky felt a lot like doing the same. But always, and whenever he felt like "kettling" the most, Clint's hand and voice was there to quiet him down. That hand and voice worked the same as to prove to Smoky, that as long as Clint was around close, there was nothing for him to fear.

As the outfit rambled on, Clint gradually reined Smoky to one side till he was well away and where he would feel more at ease to watch without fear all what the layout had to show that was strange. Smoky's ears then perked up at a different angle, and as Clint talked to him that spooky looking outfit lining out across the range got to look less spooky and more interesting.

Smoky followed the outfit and watched it till the sun was well up in the middle of the sky, then the pilot raised his hand, made a circle and the wagons followed him to a standstill. A dry camp was made and the cook had the pots to working a few minutes after the outfit had come to a stop. The rope corrals was strung out in a wink of an eye and the remuda run in.

Smoky had watched the whole proceedings with a lot of interest, the many horses, men, and all had him to using his eyes and ears to the limit, and the low snorts he'd let out every once in a while as he turned to watch all that went on, was as plain as talk, that for excitement this sure had everything he'd ever seen before beat to a frazzle.

"Come and get it, you Rannies!" It was the cook's holler for the riders to come and eat. About then Smoky seen Clint headed towards him and where he'd been left picketed. A little rub back of the ear and Smoky was led to the rope corral, unsaddled, and turned in with the remuda.

"Have a good roll, Smoky horse," says Clint as he turned him loose, "and don't let no ornery pony get the best of you."

Smoky looked back at Clint for a spell the same as to ask him where *he* was going, and as the cowboy stood there watching the little horse moseyed on and disappeared amongst the saddle bunch.

The "round-up pan" was filling up with the tin cups and plates as the cowboys, thru eating, was making their way towards their saddles by the rope corrals. A hard twist catch rope was unbuckled from them saddles, loops was shook out, and pretty soon them same loops begin a sailing and a reaching out like a mighty long arm for the horse each cowboy picked out for that afternoon's ride.

Smoky seen and heard the hiss of them loops as they sailed on over past him to settle around some other pony's neck, and even tho' all was done quiet so none of the horses would start running too much, Smoky had a mighty restless feeling whenever them snaky ropes appeared. Clint hadn't roped him only once and that was when he was a raw bronc, but he hadn't forgotten the feeling that'd been his when that same rope had caught him, stretched him out, and left him plumb helpless.

Smoky was spooked up once more as he heard the ropes sing over his ears. He heard a familiar voice say "How's she going Smoky?" but the little horse was busy hunting a hole about that time and he was too excited to nicker an answer. Then, after what seemed an awful long time to Smoky, the ponies was left out of the corral once more and when the wrangler checked 'em all to graze, him and Pecos was in the lead.

The ponies was grazing on a low bench and on the opposite side of the creek from where the cattle herd was being worked. Many was cut out and started back on the same range from where they come, and pretty soon Smoky's sensitive nostrils smelled the smoke from the fire that kept the branding irons hot; then the smell of burnt hair followed, he heard the beller of the critters, and snorting sorta low and in wonder, the mouse colored pony watched.

He watched the riders at work, seen long ropes a swinging, and how them long ropes would stop the bunch-quitting steer; he was familiar with some of that and somehow there came in him a hunch that he'd like to be closer; there was something about the workings of that herd across the creek that had his blood racing above natural, and he felt a kind of a call for the whole of the goings on, a call of the kind he couldn't as yet understand, but it was there sure enough.

Finally, the smell of singed hair wasn't on the breeze no more, branding was over for that day, and the last rope was coiled up and fastened by the saddle horn. Smoky watched as all but a few riders left the herd and headed for camp, he went to grazing then, and neck and neck with Pecos he listed to the rattle of tin plates and the laugh of the cowboys as he nosed around for the tenderest stems of the blue joint.

Four riders on "cocktail" (hours between the last meal of the day and the first night guard) got on their horses and rode to "relieve" the riders holding the herd, and it wasn't long after that when the quiet of the evening settled on the range. Even the critters seemed to want to stop bellering for a spell at that time, most of the bells of the remuda was quiet and the ponies was dozing.

Smoky had been dozing too, but pretty soon his ears perked up at a sound the likes of which he'd never heard before, the sound came from the camp, and strange as it was there was something about it that wasn't at all aggravating.

Around a good size fire was gathered the cowboys – the cook, the flunky, the wrangler, Jeff the foreman and all was in the circle, all but the four riders on "cocktail" and the "nighthawk" who'd took the wrangler's place for the night's herding of the saddle horses. Most of the boys was setting on or leaning against a big roll of tarpaulin covered bedding, and one closest to the fire was a working away trying to get a tune on his mouth organ.

That was the sound which'd come to Smoky's ears; the older cowhorses all knowed that sound well, and if any of 'em could of packed a tune there'd been many in the remuda a humming.

The song that was being worked at just then had been heard at all the cow camps and round-up wagons of the cow country for many years, and handed down from the injun fighting cowboy to the son that took up the trail where he left it and when the horns on the critter wasn't so long no more. There was a lot of memories stirred up whenever them songs was heard and many a cowboy got sentimental at the sound of 'em, for most all cowboys can remember some quiet night when the time of such a song was spread around the herd; – then of a sudden and for no reason a stampede is in full swing, a dead cowboy is found under his horse at the bottom of a fifty foot jump, and leaves only the memory of the song he's been singing that night.

> *Oh, I'm a Texas cowbo-o-oy and far away from home,*
> *And if ever I get back again no more will I ever roam,*
> *Wyoming's too cold for me-e-e, the winters are too long,*
> *And when round up comes again, my money's all go-o-o-ne.*

Clint had got harmonious, and with the other cowboy a trying to keep up on the mouth organ was singing the song. He mixed in about ten verses and took in other songs as he went, the tunes changed some, but the "Texas whang" he carried with the tunes made 'em more or less alike and all appreciated the same.

The last verse had died down, some of the boys looked up expecting more, and others, hat brim pulled down, was star-gazing at the fire, and letting the memories the songs had brought lead 'em back to times and happenings that'd been stirred the most.

All was quiet, excepting for the crackling of the fire, and one of the boys was just about to speak the name of some other old song when off from the direction where the remuda was held, a snicker was heard.

Clint looked towards where the familiar nicker had come and smiled, – the cowboy's voice had carried to where Smoky had been grazing, and the little horse had stopped grinding on his feed soon as the first verse had hit his ears; he'd listened on thru to the end, nickered, and watched the fire on the creek bottom from where the voice had come.

He watched it long into the night till all was quiet and the fire had dwindled down to coals; time for first night guard to be relieved was near and Smoky was still watching; Pecos was dozing off a ways, and pretty soon Smoky begin to feel a little groggy too and he dozed with him.

ARGENTINA, 1925

A.F. Tschiffely

1952

AT ANOTHER ESTANCIA I had the opportunity of witnessing a *domada*, or horse-breaking. The *domador* (breaker) was occupied in taming a troop of *potros* (broncos), from three to four years old, some of them as wild as cats. He was a tall, slim young fellow, about twenty-four years of age, dark and handsome, and concerned himself solely with the riding. The catching and saddling were in the hands of two assistants. These entered the corral, lasso in hand, and with shouts and waving of the rope caused the horses to gallop wildly round and round until the object of their search was clear of the others, when the rope was dropped on his neck with unerring aim. It was almost uncanny the way in which the horse that was wanted divined their intentions. He would twist and turn about, always keeping two or three other horses between himself and the men, while the rest appeared to be helping him deliberately. However, in the long run he was caught and the lasso immediately whipped about a *palenque* (post) in the middle of the corral. As he kicked and struggled his legs were roped and he came to earth with a crash. While he was down the *bocado* was slipped into his mouth. This was used instead of a bit and is simply a strip of raw hide tied firmly round his lower jaw and to which the reins are attached. He was then allowed to rise, but his hind legs were roped together, one foreleg slung up and his head tied close to the palenque. Then one of the assistants saddled him while the other looked after the ropes. The cinches were tightened until the unfortunate animal looked like an early Victorian belle, and when all was ready he was dragged out cautiously on three legs, the foreleg still slung up, into the open field. Even with only three legs to walk on he could spare one to kick with, and the men were extremely careful.

Once in the open the *domador* mounted, the ropes were cast off and then the band began to play. Plunging, kicking, bucking, the maddened *potro* strove to rid himself of his rider, but each buck only resulted in a vicious whack from the broad raw-hide lash of the *rebenque* (whip). Changing his tactics he tore at full speed, and now found another horse on each side of him, whose riders frustrated any attempts he made to get to the fence where he might brush his burden from his back. Round and round the field they galloped, the *domador* occasionally forcing him to slow down by hauling with all his strength on the reins, at other times encouraging him to dash along with shouts and lashes. Finally he was brought to a stand-still; the first lesson was over. The rider dismounted and calmly lit a cigarette without – as far as I could see – the slightest sign of a tremor in his hand, and waited for the next animal to be saddled.

HOW TO TAME A MUSTANG

Oliver La Farge

1931

THE MEN MOVED EAGERLY, anticipating a show. Two of them got behind the corral, another threw down the bars, Marcos and Jesús stood ready with ropes. The men behind whooped and smote the logs. The horse trembled, hesitated, and shot out like an explosion. The ropes swung and fell, the horse went down; before the dust cleared it was hog-tied, and Esteban, sitting on its head, had it blindfolded. Then they saddled it, gingerly, avoiding heels. The mustang was shaking all over, and jerked convulsively as the crupper was slid on and the cinch tightened, and again at the feel of the hackamore around its nose and ears. Esteban threw away his sombrero, tightened his wide sash, and stood ready; he was pale and his heart beat violently, but his face, his quiet mouth looked indifferent, just very Indian.

"*Sta 'ueno,'*" he said quietly, "*suéltenlo.*"

They snatched away the blindfold and the horse rose under him. It was caught in some kind of a trap, things bound it, like the day it was roped and brought in, something heavy was on its back. It lunged forward, but the bindings and the weight came with it, offering no resistance. It could not brush past the ropes that bound its head, it twisted, and nothing happened. Then there was hot pain, spurs thrust into its flanks, the stinging quirt on its quarters, and yells from the men standing about. The thing on top was screeching and clawing like a wildcat, only the horse knew it was a man. It twisted itself once like a snake, then it leaped high into the air and came down stiff-legged. As it continued bucking, its fighting spirit returned, twisting on itself, lashing out forefeet and hind, leaping and turning in the air, all one wild passion of fury that was close kin to panic.

Esteban, scratching and pouring in leather, felt the blood return to his skin; he smiled broadly, loving the animal as he swung and adjusted to jolt after jolt; he forgot himself completely. As they moved leaping, now forward, now sideways, along the wide road, he heard the men yelling as though they were very far away. Really he did not hear them but saw something across the whirling confusion of sky and trees that he knew was sound, and recognized that Don Gerónimo was cheering him by name, and then a brighter, sharp sound that was Doña Favia. In mid-air at the height of an S-shaped pitch, where they seemed to hang for an eternity, he had time to be aware that she was there, and feel triumph because of it, but the split second was too short for him to turn his head to look.

He was astride a genius. The mustang produced new tricks in the rapid succession of a man dealing cards. Out of one distorted position it moved to the next as though the air supported it, its joints were all steel springs anointed with lightning. And always in an irregular rhythm it struck the ground with hard jolts, a series of recurrent dead stops out of flashing motion, from which motion took up instantly again.

Man was no wildcat to be shaken off; he was a creator of hell who could not be fought – ropes that caught and burned, corrals like strait-jackets, harness like a trap. The comparative reason of combat gave way to the one great horse instinct, flight. It straightened out, running, running, down the long, straight road, not seeing anything but automatically following the line of the road, running.

Esteban eased up on quirt and spur as he settled into the saddle. This was a horse, *por Dios*. He felt the quick succession of flying feet under him, the perfect smoothness, the powerful, steady play of the shoulder muscles. This was a horse.

Slowly the rush slackened to the more marked rhythm of a gallop, the gallop flagged, then picked up again irregularly as the horse drove itself forward with failing hope. At last it fell into a lope, trotted, stopped with head hanging low and flanks trembling, beaten.

Esteban patted its neck, thinking what a shame it was the mustang had not let itself be gentled. He lifted the reins and just gave a touch of spur, to which it responded with a quiver. Speaking to it, he brought its head round, and started back at a trot. Schooling was begun.

A GENUINE MEXICAN PLUG

Mark Twain

1875

I RESOLVED TO HAVE a horse to ride. I had never seen such wild, free magnificent horsemanship outside of a circus as these picturesquely-clad Mexicans, Californians and Mexicanized Americans displayed in Carson streets every day. How they rode! Leaning just gently forward out of the perpendicular, easy and nonchalant, with broad slough-hat brim blown square up in front, and long *riata* swinging above the head, they swept through the town like the wind! The next minute they were only a sailing puff of dust on the far desert. If they trotted, they sat up gallantly and gracefully, and seemed part of the horse; did not go jiggering up and down after the silly Miss-Nancy fashion of the riding-schools. I had quickly learned to tell a horse from a cow, and was full of anxiety to learn more. I was resolved to buy a horse.

While the thought was rankling in my mind, the auctioneer came scurrying through the plaza on a black beast that had as many humps and corners on him as a dromedary, and was necessarily uncomely; but he was "going, going, at twenty two! – horse, saddle and bridle at twenty-two dollars, gentlemen!" and I could hardly resist.

A man whom I did not know (he turned out to be the auctioneer's brother) noticed the wistful look in my eye, and observed that that was a very remarkable horse to be going at such a price; and added that the saddle alone was worth the money. It was a Spanish saddle, with ponderous *tapidoros*, and furnished with the ungainly sole-leather covering with the unspellable name. I said I had half a notion to bid. Then this keen-eyed person appeared to me to be "taking my measure"; but I dismissed the suspicion when he spoke, for his manner was full of guileless candor and truthfulness. Said he:

"I know that horse – know him well. You are a stranger, I take it, and so you might think he was an American horse, maybe, but I assure you he is not. He is nothing of the kind; but – excuse my speaking in a low voice, other people being near – he is, without the shadow of a doubt, a Genuine Mexican Plug!"

I did not know what a Genuine Mexican Plug was, but there was something about this man's way of saying it, that made me swear inwardly that I would own a Genuine Mexican Plug, or die.

"Has he any other – er – advantages?" I inquired, suppressing what eagerness I could.

He hooked his forefinger in the pocket of my army-shirt, led me to one side, and breathed in my ear impressively these words:

"He can out-buck anything in America!"

"Going, going, going – at *twent-ty*-four dollars and a half, gen-"

"Twenty-seven!" I shouted, in a frenzy.

"And sold!" said the auctioneer, and passed over the Genuine Mexican Plug to me.

I could scarcely contain my exultation. I paid the money, and put the animal in a neighboring livery-stable to dine and rest himself.

In the afternoon I brought the creature into the plaza, and certain citizens held him by the head, and others by the tail, while I mounted him.

As soon as they let go, he placed all his feet in a bunch together, lowered his back, and then suddenly arched it upward, and shot me straight into the air a matter of three or four feet! I came as straight down again, lit in the saddle, went instantly up again, came down almost on the high pommel, shot up again, and came down on the horse's neck – all in the space of three or four seconds. Then he rose and stood almost straight up on his hind feet, and I, clasping his lean neck desperately, slid back into the saddle, and held on. He came down, and immediately hoisted his heels into the air, delivering a vicious kick at the sky, and stood on his forefeet. And then down he came once more, and began the original exercise of shooting me straight up again. The third time I went up I heard a stranger say:

"Oh, *don't* he buck, though!"

While I was up, somebody struck the horse a sounding thwack with a leathern strap, and when I arrived again the Genuine Mexican Plug was not there. A Californian youth chased him up and caught him, and asked if he might have a ride. I granted him that luxury. He mounted the Genuine, got lifted into the air once, but sent his spurs home as he descended, and the horse darted away like a telegram. He soared over three fences like a bird, and disappeared down the road toward the Washoe Valley.

I sat down on a stone, with a sigh, and by a natural impulse one of my hands sought my forehead, and the other the base of my stomach. I believe I never appreciated, till then, the poverty of the human machinery – for I still needed a hand or two to place elsewhere. Pen cannot describe how I was jolted up. Imagination cannot conceive how disjointed I was – how internally, externally and universally I was unsettled, mixed up and ruptured. There was a sympathetic crowd around me, though.

One elderly-looking comforter said:

"Stranger, you've been taken in. Everybody in this camp knows that horse. Any child, any Injun, could have told you that he'd buck; his is the very worst devil to buck on the continent of America. You hear *me*. I'm Curry. *Old* Curry. Old *Abe* Curry. And moreover, he is a simon-pure, out-and-out, genuine d-d Mexican plug, and an uncommon mean one at that, too. Why, you turnip, if you had laid low and kept dark, there's chances to buy an *American* horse for mighty little more than you paid for that bloody old foreign relic."

SPAIN

~~~~~~

These sorts of independent expeditions are equally conducive to health of body: after the first few days of the new fatigue are got over, the frame becomes of iron, hecho de bronze, *and the rider a centaur not fabulous. The living in the pure air, the sustaining excitement of novelty, exercise and constant occupation are all sweetened by the willing heart, which renders even labour itself a pleasure.*

RICHARD FORD.
Gatherings in Spain

IF YOU HAVE EXPERIENCED the animation and excitement of an Andalucian horse-market, if you have seen what prestige the *rejoneador* holds, or the peacock pride with which the *caballeros* and their *señoritas* ride at the *feria,* you will agree that Spain is still one of the most horse-minded nations in the world. It is also, I believe, the only tract remaining in Europe where you can enjoy a prolonged riding expedition, being fairly sure, at the end of each day's journey, that you will find a place for yourself and stabling for your horse.

Richard Ford was the first to show us a comprehensive horseman's view of Spain. Born in Chelsea, in 1793, the elder son of Sir Richard Ford (an Undersecretary of State, close friend of Pitt and creator of London's mounted police), Ford married, in 1824, Lady Harriet Capel, a celebrated beauty, and daughter of the Earl of Essex. For the sake of her delicate health he gave up his legal career to live in the comparatively temperate climate of Andalusia, and from there began to make long riding excursions covering 2,000 miles, which resulted, after only three years in the country, in *A Handbook for Travellers in Spain* and *Gatherings in Spain.* It was said of him that "although he inherited the full-bodied social and religious prejudices of an English country gentleman of good family, he never exhibited these in his intercourse with Spaniards, who, being particularly sensitive to pride of race, were charmed with his easy grace of manner and infallible courtesy. He was equally welcomed by peasant, grandee, or insurgent chief . . . " Ford also knew his horses, as well, if not better, than he knew the Castilian language, and was, in fact, the ideal traveler in Spain.

Perhaps the best up-to-date book on seeing Spain from horseback is *The Road from Ronda*, by Alastair Boyd (Lord Kilmarnock). Some years ago I accompanied Alastair Boyd on a fortnight's ride through the *sierras*, from Ronda to Arcos de la Frontera and Jerez, returning by a southerly route, above Algeciras. The weather was kind, the cork woods silent, the *posaderos* hospitable, the landscape magnificent, the meadows and mountain tracks vivid with flowers, the horses stayed sound, and it was altogether a most enjoyable expedition.

There to greet us on our return to Alastair's house in old Ronda, the Moorish Casa de Mondragón, was that tough and gallant traveler, Lady Betjeman, another who knew her Ford very thoroughly, and who, under her maiden name, Penelope Chetwode, and the title *Two Middle-Aged Ladies in Andalusia*, also wrote an interesting book. From this I have cited her description of the preparations she made for her journey from the Duke of Wellington's house through the valleys north of Granada.

Doubtless many visitors to Spain will conjure a picture of the poor *picador's* mount. And perhaps only *aficionados* will admire Ernest Hemingway's *Death in the Afternoon*, written over half a century ago. But, if you can quell your prejudice for a moment, do read his intimate view of this not-so-glamorous aspect of the *plaza de toros*, which I have reproduced.

Foreigners often attribute the callousness of the bull-ring to the fact that Spain is a Catholic nation. "The Roman Catholics believe that animals have no souls," you hear, "therefore their suffering does not matter." In fact bullfighting is not so cruel as the casual observer might think, nor are Spaniards as unfeeling as most foreigners imagine. And I could not resist including in this section A.F. Tschiffely's little anecdote, recorded in *Round and About Spain*, about the coper who has a horse's prayer, beginning "my dear master," nailed to the stable door.

THE ANDALUCIAN HORSE

Richard Ford

1845

WE NOW PROCEED to Spanish quadrupeds, having placed the wheel-carriages before the horses. That of Andalucia takes precedence of all; he fetches the highest price, and the Spaniards in general value no other breed; they consider his configuration and qualities as perfect, and in some respects they are right, for no horse is more elegant or more easy in his motions, none are more gentle or docile, none are more quick in acquiring showy accomplishments, or in performing feats of Astleyan agility; he has very little in common with the English blood-horse; his mane is soft and silky, and is frequently plaited with gay ribbons; his tail is of great length, and left in all the proportions of nature, not cropped and docked, by which Voltaire was so much offended:

> *Fiers et bizarres Anglais, qui des memes ciseaux*
> *Coupez la tete aux rois, et la queue aux chevaux.*

It often trails to the very ground, while the animal has perfect command

162

over it, lashing it on every side as a gentleman switches his cane; therefore, when on a journey, it is usual to double and tie it up, after the fashion of the ancient pig-tails of our sailors. The Andalucian horse is round in his quarters, though inclined to be small in the barrel; he is broad-chested, and always carries his head high, especially when going a good pace; his length of leg adds to his height, which sometimes reaches to sixteen hands; he never, however, stretches out with the long graceful sweep of the English thorough-bred; his action is apt to be loose and shambling, and he is given to *dishing* with the feet. The pace is, notwithstanding, perfectly delightful. From being very long in the pastern, the motion is broken as it were by the springs of a carriage; their pace is the peculiar *"paso Castellano,"* which is something more than a walk, and less than a trot, and it is truly sedate and sedan-chair-like, and suits a grave Don, who is given, like a Turk, to tobacco and contemplation. Those Andalucian horses which fall when young into the hands of the officers at Gibraltar acquire a very different action, and lay themselves better down to their work, and gain much more in speed from the English system of training than they would have done had they been managed by Spaniards. Taught or untaught, this *pace* is most gentlemanlike, and well did Beaumont and Fletcher

> *Think it noble, as Spaniards do in riding,*
> *In managing a great horse, which is princely;*

and as has been said, is the only attitude in which the kings of the Spains, true φιλίπποί, ought ever to be painted, witching the world with noble horsemanship.

Many other provinces possess breeds which are more useful, though far less showy, than the Andalucian. The horse of Castile is a strong, hardy animal, and the best which Spain produces for mounting heavy cavalry. The ponies of Galicia, although ugly and uncouth, are admirably suited to

the wild hilly country and laborious population; they require very little care or grooming, and are satisfied with coarse food and Indian corn. The horses of Navarre, once so celebrated, are still esteemed for their hardy strength; they have, from neglect, degenerated into ponies, which, however, are beautiful in form, hardy, docile, sure-footed, and excellent trotters. In most of the large towns of Spain there is a sort of market, where horses are publicly sold; but Ronda fair, in May, is the great Howden and Horncastle of the four provinces of Seville, Cordova, Jaen, and Granada, and the resort of all the picturesque-looking rogues of the south. The reader of Don Quixote need not be told that the race of Gines Passamonte is not extinct; the Spanish *Chalanes*, or horse-dealers, have considerable talents; but the cleverest is but a mere child when compared to the perfection of rascality to which a real English professor has attained in the mysteries of lying, chaunting, and making up a horse.

The breeding of horses was carefully attended to by the Spanish government previously to the invasion of the French, by whom the entire horses and brood-mares were either killed or stolen, and the buildings and stables burnt.

The saddles used commonly in Spain are Moorish; they are made with high peak and croup behind; the stirrup-irons are large triangularly-shaped boxes. The food is equally Oriental, and consists of "barley and straw," as mentioned in the Bible. We well remember the horror of our Andalucian groom, on our first reaching Gallicia, when he rushed in, exclaiming that the beasts would perish, as nothing was to be had there but oats and hay. After some difficulty he was persuaded to see if they would eat it, which to his surprise they actually did; such, however, is habit, that they soon fell out of condition, and did not recover until the damp mountains were quitted for the arid plains of Castile.

WHERE A HORSE IS BETTER THAN A CAR

Alastair Boyd

1969

WE BOUGHT HORSES ourselves and continued to make the same sort of forays, mostly confined to a day, seldom exceeding two nights – as we made with them. In time we grew bolder and ventured further afield, finally embarking on the longer and more ambitious journeys . . .

It was not long before I came to know the immediate countryside, its farms, tracks, villages, and ruins, rather better than the palm of my hand.

Its paths became much more familiar to me than were my own lifeline or line of fate. Whenever I could get away from teaching, I returned to them. Sometimes I followed them alone, sometimes with Diana, sometimes with friends, but always on a horse.

This means of transport may sound archaic, but there is no doubt that it was far and away the best for the terrain. Very few of the villages I reached were totally without a motor road, but often an immense detour would have been necessary to get from one place to another just over the shoulder of a hill. Then there was the physical pleasure of riding through the last country in Europe where it is still possible to find almost nightly stabling, where rights of way are so ancient and universal that it is practically impossible to trespass even if you try, and where the scenery is seldom less than staggering.

Another factor was the horse's value as a passport to people's conversation and company. The business of arriving by horse at nightfall in a small town or village, of finding stabling and fodder for the animal and a bed and supper for himself involves the traveller in a whole network of people from amongst whom will materialise his companions for the evening, most of them valuable informants on local life. A car will perhaps interest a greater number of small boys but it will not achieve so effective a foothold in the community's door.

PREPARING FOR THE SIERRAS

Penelope Chetwode

1963

IT WAS THE HORSE that brought me to Spain. For years enthusiastic friends had tried in vain to make me go there. I pointed out that two countries, Italy and India, were enough for ten lifetimes. How, in middle age, could I be expected to mug up the history, language and architecture of a country about which I knew next to nothing? I had not even read a line of *Don Quixote*. I knew Italian fairly well and if I now tried to learn Spanish I should inevitably confuse the two and end by speaking neither. I dug in my toes and obstinately refused to be lured to the peninsula by ardent hispanophiles.

Then, in a Sunday paper, I read about conducted riding tours in Andalusia. My resistance suddenly broke down and I booked to go in late October.

St. Thomas says you cannot love a horse because it cannot love you back. This statement proved a serious obstacle to my entering the Holy

Roman Church in 1948. Then Evelyn Waugh pointed out that St. Thomas was an Italian accustomed to seeing his father's old charges sent along to the local salami factory in Aquino. Had he been an English theologian he would never have written like that: his father's chargers would have been pensioned off in the park. Now I was going to a Latin country where old horses ended their lives in the bull-ring. Could I stand such an attitude to animals? I who had always been full of the traditional English sentimentality towards them? This racial antipathy was well illustrated some years ago when I brought my daughter's pony into the kitchen and kissed it in front of Gina, our Calabrian maid: "In Italia bacciamo uomini!" (In Italy we kiss men) she had said in utter scorn.

When I first arrived at Alora, the starting-point of the conducted tour, and saw the wiry little horses of the sierras, I got rather a shock. Standing between fourteen and fifteen hands high they were so much narrower than our own mountain and moorland breeds, and their conformation was decidedly odd: they had ewe necks, cow hocks and unusually straight pasterns. Nevertheless they turned out to be extremely fit, and were surprisingly good rides. They walked out well, never stumbled down the stoniest mountain paths, and had armchair canters. The soles of their feet must have been an inch thick as they never bruised them on the roughest going nor went lame from any other cause. Their narrowness would have been tiring on long rides, but the Andalusian saddles provided the width the animals lacked. They were high fore and aft, had soft sheepskin seats and were almost impossible to fall out of. Beautifully embroidered leather *alforjas* (saddle-bags) were hung over the cantles at the back and it was astounding what a lot one could cram into them.

The feeding of horses in southern Spain is extremely interesting because it is so different from our own. They get neither oats nor hay but *paja y cebada*, which is chopped barley straw chaff and barley corn fed dry. According to Richard Ford 8lb barley is equal in feeding value to 10lb oats because it contains less husk. The manger is first filled with straw chaff then the corn is mixed well into it. In the morning, before giving the first feed, any chaff that remains and any dust in the manger are scooped out onto the floor to form the deep litter on which the animals are bedded. In the *posada* stables this is a muck mystic's dream, with the droppings of horses, mules, donkeys, pigs, goats, hens and human beings perfectly composted with chopped barley straw, wood ash, onion and other vegetable peelings. It is sweet-smelling, as all the best deep litter should be; nor did I ever notice any sign of thrush in the animal's feet. Greenmeat is provided by lucerne cut and fed in the manger, or by grass when it can be found by people with no land of their own on which to grow lucerne. The animals are also taken out to graze when work and time allow, usually along streams or irrigation canals where there is always a bit of grass, or up on the mountains where there are several plants which are eaten with great relish. When grazing they are either hobbled or put in charge of a boy. Morning and evening they are led out to water at the *fuente* (a trough sometimes fed by a spring, sometimes by piped supply) and when on a journey they are encouraged to drink at every stream they ford.

THE PICADOR

Ernest Hemingway

1932

THE PROPINA IS RESPONSIBLE for almost every horror in bullfighting. The regulations provide for the size, sturdiness and fitness of the horses used in the bull ring, and if proper horses are used and the picadors well trained there would be no need for any horses to be killed except accidentally and against the will of the riders, as they are killed, for instance, in steeplechasing. But the enforcing of these regulations for his own protection are left to the picador as the most interested party and the picador is so poorly paid for the danger he undergoes that, for a small addition to this pay, he is willing to accept horses that make his work even more difficult and dangerous. The horse contractor must furnish or have available thirty-six horses for each fight. He is paid a fixed sum no matter what happens to his horses. It is to his interest to furnish the cheapest animals he can get and see that as few of them are used as possible.

This is about how it works out; the picadors arrive the day before the fight or in the morning of the fight at the corrals of the bull ring to choose and test the horses they are to ride. There is a piece of iron set in a stone wall of the corral that marks the minimum height at the shoulder that a horse must have to be accepted. A picador has the big saddle put on a horse, mounts, tests whether the horse minds bit and spur, backs, wheels, and, riding toward the corral wall, drives against it with the shaft of a pic to see if the horse is sound and solid on his feet. He then dismounts and says to the contractor, "I wouldn't risk my life on that lousy skate for a thousand dollars."

"What's the matter with that horse?" says the contractor. "You'll go a long way before you'll find a horse like that."

"Too long a way," says the picador.

"What's the matter with him? That's a handsome little horse."

"He's got no mouth," the picador says. "He won't back. Besides he's short."

"He's just the right size. Look at him. Just the right size."

"Just the right size for what?"

"Just the right size to ride."

"Not me," says the picador turning away.

"You won't find a better horse."

"I believe that," says the picador.

"What's your real objection?"

"He's got glanders."

"Nonsense. That isn't glanders. That's just dandruff."

"You ought to spray him with flit," says the picador. "That would kill him."

"What's your real objection?"

"I have a wife and three children. I wouldn't ride him for a thousand dollars."

"Be sensible," the contractor says. They talk in low tones. He gives the picador fifteen pesetas.

"All right," says the picador. "Mark up the little horse."

So, in the afternoon you see the picador ride out the little horse, and if the little horse gets ripped, and instead of killing him, the red-jacketed bull-ring servant runs with him toward the horse gate to get him back where he can be patched up so the contractor can send him in again, you may be sure the bull-ring servant has received or been promised a propina for every horse he can bring alive out of the ring, instead of killing them mercifully and decently when they are wounded.

I have known some fine picadors, honest, honorable, brave, and in a bad business, but you may have all the horse contractors I have ever met, although some of them were nice fellows. If you wish and will take them, you may have all the bull-ring servants too. They are the only people I have found in bullfighting that are brutalized by it and they are the only ones who take an active part who undergo no danger. I have seen several of them, two especially that are father and son, that I would like to shoot. If we ever have a time when for a few days you may shoot anyone you wish I believe that before starting out to bag various policemen, Italian statesman, government functionaries, Massachusetts judges, and a couple of companions of my youth, I would shove in a clip and make sure of that pair of bull-ring servants. I do not want to identify them any more closely because if I ever should bag them this would be evidence of premeditation. But of all the filthy cruelty I have ever seen they have furnished the most. Where you see gratuitous cruelty most often is in police brutality; in the police of all countries I have ever been in, including, especially, my own. These two Pamplona and San Sebastian monosabios should be, by rights, policeman, and policemen on the radical squad, but they do the best they can with their talents in the bull-ring. They carry on their belts puntillas, broad-headed knives, with which they can give the gift of death to any horse that is badly wounded, but I have never seen them kill a horse that could possibly be gotten on his feet and made to move toward the corrals. It is not only a question of the money they could make by salvaging horses to be taxidermed while alive so they may be reintroduced into the ring, for I have seen them refuse to kill, until forced to by the public, a horse there was no hope of getting on to his feet or of bringing back into the ring purely from pleasure in exerting their power to refuse to perform a merciful act as long as possible. Most bull-ring servants are poor devils that perform a miserable function for a mean wage, and are entitled to pity if not sympathy. If they save a horse or two that they should kill they do it with fear that outruns any pleasure and earn their money as well as the men do who pick up cigar-butts, say. But these two that I speak of are both fat, well-fed and arrogant. I once succeeded in landing a large, heavy, one-peseta-fifty rented, leather cushion alongside the head of the younger one during a scene of riotous disapproval in a bull-ring in the north of Spain and I am never at the ring without a bottle of Manzanilla which I hope yet I will be able to land, empty, on one or the other at any time rioting becomes so general that a single bottle stroke may pass unperceived by the authorities. After one comes, through contact with its administrators, no longer to cherish greatly the law as a remedy in abuses, then the bottle becomes a sovereign means of direct action. If you cannot throw it at least you can always drink out of it.

A PRAYER

A.F. Tschiffely

1952

After having chatted for some time, the Guajiro invited us to accompany him to a nearby stable, where, with visible pride, he showed us his horses. Fine beasts they were, among them two typical Andalusians, all in excellent condition and well-groomed.

On a large board, which was fixed to one of the walls in large clear lettering, was painted the following text, which gave me an insight to the Guajiro's character:

THE HORSE'S SUPPLICATION

My Dear Master,
Please forgive me for putting before you this my supplication.
After the work and fatigues of the day, give me shelter in a clean stable.
Feed me unstintingly, and quench my burning thirst. I can't tell you when I
am hungry, thirsty or ill. If I am looked after properly, I can serve you well,
for I shall have strength. If I leave the fodder untouched, have my teeth
examined. Please don't cut off my tail, for it is my only defence against tor-

menting flies and other insects. Whilst working me, speak to me, for your voice conveys more to me than the reins and the whip. Pat me, and so encourage me to work with a good will. Don't hurry me up steep inclines, and don't pull on my bit when I'm going downhill. Don't make me carry or pull too heavy a load. I serve you uncomplainingly to the limit of my strength. If you forget this, I might die at any moment whilst doing my best to carry out your will. Treat me with the consideration that is due to a faithful servant, and, if I don't understand you immediately, don't get angry, and don't chastise me, for perhaps it's not my fault. Examine my reins, possibly they don't transmit your orders correctly, because they are knotted or twisted. Look at my hooves and shoes, to make sure that they are not hurting me. Dear Master, when old age weakens me, and makes me useless, don't neglect me or let me die of hunger. If you can't keep me any longer, destroy me, but do it yourself, so that my sufferings be less. Above all, when I'm no further use to you, please don't condemn me to the torment of the bullring.

Pardon me for having taken up your time with this my humble supplication, which, I beg you not to forget. This I ask you, invoking the One who was born in a crib . . .

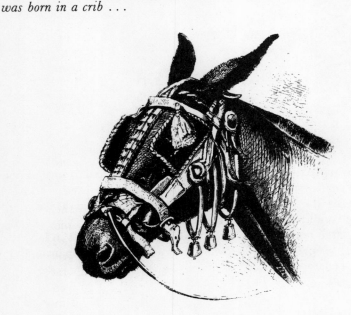

THE
RACE TRACK

I saw the racer coming to the jump,
Starting with fiery eyeballs as he rusht,
I heard the blood within his body thump,
I saw him launch, I heard the toppings crusht.

And as he landed I beheld his soul
Kindle, because, in front, he saw the Straight
With all its thousands roaring at the goal,
He laughed, he took the moment for his mate.

Would that the passionate moods on which we ride
Might kindle thus to oneness with the will;
Would we might see the end to which we stride,
And feel, not strain, in struggle, only thrill.

And laugh like him and know in all our nerves
Beauty, the spirit, scattering dust and turves.

JOHN MASEFIELD,
The Steeplechaser

ALTHOUGH THE ROMANS, Egyptians and Persians rode their horses in races, and such contests were included in the Greek Olympics more than 2,500 years ago, the modern world identifies the wheeled, rather than the ridden, race with the ancients. And I begin this more-or-less chronologically arranged section with the most famous chariot race from the pages of fiction, that won by Ben-Hur, in Lew Wallace's epic.

Of the Western nations, from the earliest of modern times until the present era, England set the pace on the racecourse. In the 12th century William of Malmesbury recorded the competitions of the "running-horses," and, from the time of Henry II, horse-races were held regularly at Smithfield. In the seventeenth century Louis XIV followed where his cousin, Charles II, set the fashion. I have quoted an article by Nimrod (C.J. Apperley) – who appears in more detail in the next section – published in the *Quarterly Review* of 1828, giving a succinct history of the

Turf up to 1764, when Eclipse was foaled, " . . . and from that period" (in Nimrod's opinion) "may English racing be dated."

Eclipse was bred by the Duke of Cumberland, by Markse out of Spilletta, and owned jointly by Mr Wildman and Colonel O'Kelly; he was not run until he was five years old, was said "never to have been touched by the whip," and was unbeaten on the turf. "Eclipse first, the rest nowhere," was the phrase used, both in racing and as a sire, about this most famous of racehorses. Over 100 of his descendants won the Derby.

We next turn to *An Artist's Life*, by Sir Alfred Munnings, with the old horse-portraitist musing over skeletons – among them Eclipse. "Think of that famous horse's skeleton," he commends us, "once covered and articulated with tendon, muscle and nerve, all under the rich, dark chestnut coat, groomed and polished day after day throughout his short span!" Such reflection, surely, is the stuff of history!

Will Ogilvie then described in verse the origin of the steeplechase, the first of which, they say, was run in Ireland, in County Cork, in 1752, between the church steeple of Buttevant and Doneraile, the two contestants being called Blake and O'Callaghan.

No Tolstoy enthusiast will readily forget the scene in *Anna Karenina* when Vronsky leads across a daunting course, only to make a mistake over the last obstacle which brings his Frou-Frou down with a broken neck. ("Incapable of uttering a word, Vronsky answered nothing to all the questions which were put to him: he left the race-course without picking

up his cap, or knowing whither he was going. He was in despair. For the first time in his life he was the victim of a misfortune for which there was no remedy, and for which he felt that he himself was the only one to blame . . .'').

At about the period Tolstoy had Vronsky riding that race, one of the greatest professionals on the English Turf, Fred Archer, had started up the ladder of fame. And here is a pen-portrait of him by a prominent contemporary jockey, the amateur George Lambton. From Archer we focus on Ascot in the Nineties, with the racing commentator, Nat Gould, giving us the line-up for the Royal Hunt Cup – "the prettiest race in England" – with Morny Cannon, Charlie Wood and Tod Sloan riding well to the fore.

After Archer and Cannon, Stephen Donaghue was the champion of the British turf. In *Just My Story*, quoted here, he assures his readers that "a jockey's life before and during the racing season is practically *all work*, his profession is most exacting, and his work never ending; the actual riding in races is the least part of the day's record . . . "

Even as early as the 1920s, which we have now reached, the "gentleman rider" also took his pursuit very seriously – albeit it was probably incumbent on him to appear easy and loosely stylish. Charles Cothill, the (human) hero of John Masefield's narrative poem, *Right Royal* – which is handsomely adorned with drawings by Cecil Aldin – steps straight out of the romantic ranks of the young cavalry officers surviving the First World War. He is brave and good and upright, what used to be termed a "white man." Needless to say, after a dramatically-fought marathon, he and Right Royal win the big race, and readers may be comforted to know that in Masefield's inimitable lilt, Cothill

> *. . . married his lady, but he rode no more races;*
> *He lives on the Downland on the blown grassy places,*
> *Where he and Right Royal can canter for hours*
> *On the flock-bitten turf full of tiny blue flowers . . .*

Hunt race meetings – point-to-points – were first instituted in the late 1870s. They were essentially for hunters, properly "qualified," that is to say seen regularly in the hunting-field fulfilling their true employment and with no immediate or patent pretensions of being ridden "under rules." This was still the form in the 1950s when I rode in point-to-points. But, soon afterward, you required something considerably more streamlined than a "good fast staying hunter." The "qualifying" rule was less strict, and you needed, as you need today, a thoroughbred steeplechaser, which was a pity in a way because it reduced the amateurish charm of the old point-to-point meeting, the aura of which was nicely evoked by H.V. Morton in the 1920s in the short passage I have borrowed from his *In Search of England*.

Perhaps the author who combines most effectively as an authority on race-riding with an ability to write is John Hislop, and, at this point, we return from the amateur to the professional scene by taking a look at his advice on riding tactics from *Steeplechasing*, with one of that book's wonderful economical drawings by John Skeaping. Who, of the British turf, was the foremost master of race-riding tactics? Was it Sir Gordon Richards, who was born in 1904 and did not retire from the saddle to establish himself as a trainer until 1954, having been knighted in the previous year – by which time he had been acclaimed champion jockey on 26 occasions? He broke both Fred Archer's records: in 1933 by passing the old champion's 1885 triumph of 246 winners in the year, with a new record of 259, and, in 1943, when he rode his 2,750th winner, all told. To represent him I have put in the salute given him in *J F–B* (the autobiography of a racing scribe, whom we met in the chapter entitled *Cavalry*, Major Jack Fairfax-Blakeborough) which was published in 1978, and a note from Sir Gordon's *My Story*, describing how he and Pinza overtook Charlie Smirke and the Aga Khan's Shikampur in the Derby.

The section ends with two more famous moments on the racecourse, the first, a tragedy, being taken from Dick Francis's *The Sport of Queens* when he and Devon Loch went down as they rode into the finish of the National; and the second a triumph, an account by a one-time champion amateur jockey, and since, arguably, the best reporter of the racing world, Lord Oaksey ("Audax" of *Horse and Hound*). Just home from Paris, in 1962, he describes how Fred Winter and Mandarin win the Grand Steeplechase de Paris despite broken reins. It was as exciting a finish as any in this anthology. "Mandarin came back," wrote Audax, "mobbed as no film star has ever been, head down, dog-tired, sweating – but surely happy – a cheer went up such as I have never heard on any racecourse."

Let us hope there will always be such graphic pens to portray the great episodes of the turf.

BEN-HUR'S VICTORY

Lew Wallace

1887

IF IT WERE TRUE that Messala had attained his utmost speed, the effort was with effect; slowly but certainly he was beginning to forge ahead. His horses were running with their heads low down; from the balcony their bodies appeared actually to skim the earth; their nostrils showed blood-red in expansion; their eyes seemed straining in their sockets. Certainly the good steeds were doing their best! How long could they keep the pace? It was but the Commencement of the sixth round. On they dashed. As they neared the second goal, Ben-Hur turned in behind the Roman's car.

The joy of the Messala faction reached its bound: they screamed and howled, and tossed their colors; and Sanballat filled his tablets with wagers of their tendering.

Malluch, in the lower gallery over the Gate of Triumph, found it hard to keep his cheer. He had cherished the vague hint dropped to him by Ben-Hur of something to happen in the turning of the western pillars. It was the fifth round, yet the something had not come; and he had said to himself, the sixth will bring it; but lo! Ben-Hur was hardly holding a place at the tail of his enemy's car.

Over in the east end, Simonides' party held their peace. The merchant's head was bent low. Ilderim tugged at his beard, and dropped his brows till there was nothing of his eyes but an occasional sparkle of light. Esther scarcely breathed. Iras alone appeared glad.

Along the home-stretch – sixth round – Messala leading, next him Ben-Hur, and so close it was the old story:

> *First flew Eumelus on Pheretian steeds;*
> *With those of Tros bold Diomed succeeds;*

Close on Eumelus' back they puff the wind,
And seem just mounting on his car behind;
Full on his neck he feels the sultry breeze,
And, hovering o'er, their stretching shadow sees.

Thus to the first goal, and round it. Messala, fearful of losing his place, hugged the stony wall with perilous clasp; a foot to the left, and he had been dashed to pieces; yet, when the turn was finished, no man, looking at the wheel-tracks of the two cars, could have said, here went Messala, there the Jew. They left but one trace behind them.

As they whirled by, Esther saw Ben-Hur's face again, and it was whiter than before.

Simonides, shrewder than Esther, said to Ilderim, the moment the rivals turned into the course, "I am no judge, good sheik, if Ben-Hur be not about to execute some design. His face hath that look."

To which Ilderim answered, "Saw you how clean they were and fresh? By the splendor of God, friend, they have not been running! But now watch!"

One ball and one dolphin remained on the entablatures; and all the people drew a long breath, for the beginning of the end was at hand.

First, the Sidonian gave the scourge to his four, and, smarting with fear and pain, they dashed desperately forward, promising for a brief time to go to the front. The effort ended in promise. Next, the Byzantine and Corinthian each made the trial with like result, after which they were practically out of the race. Thereupon, with a readiness perfectly explicable, all the factions except the Romans joined hope in Ben-Hur, and openly indulged their feeling.

"Ben-Hur! Ben-Hur!" they shouted, and the blent voices of the many rolled overwhelmingly against the consular stand.

From the benches above him as he passed, the favor descended in fierce injunctions.

"Speed thee, Jew!"

"Take the wall now!"

"On! loose the Arabs! Give them rein and scourge!"

"Let him not have the turn on thee again. Now or never!"

Over the balustrade they stooped low, stretching their hands imploringly to him.

Either he did not hear, or could not do better, for halfway round the course and he was still following; at the second goal even still no change!

And now, to make the turn, Messala began to draw in his left-hand steeds, an act which necessarily slackened their speed. His spirit was high; more than one altar was richer of his vows; the Roman genius was still president. On the three pillars only six hundred feet away were fame, increase of fortune, promotions, and a triumph ineffably sweetened by hate, all in store for him! That moment Malluch, in the gallery, saw Ben-Hur lean forward over his Arabs, and give them the reins. Out flew the man-folded lash in his hand; over the backs of the startled steeds it writhed and hissed, and hissed and writhed again and again; and though it fell not, there were both sting and menace in its quick report; and as the man passed thus from quiet to resistless action, his face suffused, his eyes gleaming, along the reins he seemed to flash his will; and instantly not one, but the four as one, answered with a leap that landed them alongside the Roman's car.

Messala, on the perilous edge of the goal, heard, but dare not look to see what the awakening portended. From the people he received no sign. Above the noises of the race there was but one voice, and that was Ben-Hur's. In the old Aramaic, as the sheik himself, he called to the Arabs,

"On, Atair! On, Rigel! What, Antares! dost thou linger now? Good horse — oho, Aldebaren! I hear them singing in the tents. I hear the children singing and the women — singing of the stars, of Atair, Antares, Rigel, Aldebaran, victory! — and the song will never end. Well done! Home to-morrow, under the black tent — home! On, Antares! The tribe is waiting for us, and the master is waiting! 'Tis done! 'tis done! Ha, ha! We have overthrown the proud. The hand that smote us is in the dust. Ours the glory! Ha, ha! — steady! The work is done — soho! Rest!"

There had never been anything of the kind more simple; seldom anything so instantaneous.

At the moment chosen for the dash, Messala was moving in a circle round the goal. To pass him, Ben-Hur had to cross the track, and good strategy required the movement to be in a forward direction; that is, on a like circle limited to the least possible increase. The thousands on the benches understood it all: they saw the signal given — the magnificent response; the four close outside Messala's outer wheel; Ben-Hur's inner wheel behind the other's car — all this they saw. Then they heard a crash loud enough to send a thrill through the Circus, and, quicker than thought, out over the course a spray of shining white and yellow flinders flew. Down on its right side toppled the bed of the Roman's chariot. There was a rebound as of the axle hitting the hard earth; another and another; then the car went to pieces; and Messala, entangled in the reins, pitched forward headlong.

To increase the horror of the sight by making death certain, the Sidonian, who had the wall next behind, could not stop or turn out. Into the wreck full speed he drove; then over the Roman, and into the latter's four, all mad with fear. Presently, out of the turmoil, the fighting of horses, the resound of blows, the murky cloud of dust and sand, he crawled, in time to see the Corinthian and Byzantine go on down the course after Ben-Hur, who had not been an instant delayed.

The people arose, and leaped upon the benches, and shouted and screamed.

Those who looked that way caught glimpses of Messala, now under the trampling of the fours, now under the abandoned cars. He was still; they thought him dead; but far the greater number followed Ben-Hur in his career. They had not seen the cunning touch of the reins by which, turning a little to the left, he caught Messala's wheel with the iron-shod point of his axle, and crushed it; but they had seen the transformation of the man, and themselves felt the heat and glow of his spirit, the heroic resolution, the maddening energy of action with which, by look, word, and gesture, he so suddenly inspired his Arabs. And such running! It was rather the long leaping of lions in harness; but for the lumbering chariot, it seemed the four were flying. When the Byzantine and Corinthian were half-way down the course, Ben-Hur turned the first goal.

And the race was Won!

THE YEAR ECLIPSE WAS FOALED

"Nimrod"

1828

PERHAPS IT MAY NOT be necessary to enter into the very accidence of racing; but on the authority of Mr. Strutt, *On the Sports and Pastimes of England*, something like it was set agoing in Athelstane's reign. "Several race-horses," says he, "were sent by Hugh Capet, in the ninth century, as a present to Athelstane, when he was soliciting the hand of Ethelswitha, his sister." A more distinct indication of a sport of this kind occurs in a description of London, written by William Fitz-Stephen, who lived in the reign of Henry II. He informs us that horses were usually exposed to sale in Smithfield, and, in order to prove the excellency of hackneys and charging horses, they were usually matched against each other. Indeed, the monk gives a very animated description of the start and finish of a horse-race. In John's reign, running horses are frequently mentioned in the register of royal expenditure. John was a renowned sportsman – he needed a redeeming quality – but it does not appear that he made use of his running horses otherwise than in the sports of the field. Edwards II., III., and IV., were likewise breeders of horses, as also Henry VIII., who imported some from the East; but the running horses of those days are not to be too closely associated with the turf; at least we have reason to believe the term generally applies to light and speedy animals, used in racing pursuits, and in contradistinction to the war-horse, then required to be most powerful, to carry a man cased in armour, and seldom weighing less than twenty stone. In fact, the invention of gun-powder did much towards refining the native breed of the English horse; and we begin to recognise the symptoms of a scientific turf in many of the satirical writings of the days of Elizabeth. Take, for instance, Bishop Hall's lines in 1597:

> *Dost though prize*
> *Thy brute-beasts' worth by their dams' qualities?*
> *Sayst thou thy colt shall prove a swift-paced steed,*
> *Only because a jennet did him breed?*
> *Or, sayst thou this same horse shall win the prize,*
> *Because his dam was swiftest Tranchefice?*

It is quite evident, indeed, that racing was in considerable vogue during this reign, although it does not appear to have been much patronised by the Queen, otherwise it would, we may be sure, have formed a part of the pastimes at Kenilworth. The famous George Earl of Cumberland was one of the victims of the turf in those early days.

In the reign of James I., private matches between gentlemen, then their own jockeys, became very common in England; and the first public race meetings appear at Garterley, in Yorkshire, Croydon, in Surrey, and Theobalds, on Enfield Chase, the prize being a golden bell. The art of training also may now be said to have commenced; strict attention was paid to the food and exercise of the horses, but the effect of weight was not taken into consideration, ten stone being generally, we have reason to believe, both the maximum and minimum of what the horses carried. James patronised racing; he gave 500*l.* – a vast price in those days – for an Arabian, which, according to the Duke of Newcastle, was of little value, having been beaten easily by our native horses. Prince Henry had a strong attachment to racing as well as hunting, but he was cut off at an early age. Charles I. was well inclined towards such sports, and excelled in horsemanship, but the distractions of his reign prevented his following these peaceful pastimes. According to Boucher, however, in his *Survey of the Town of Stamford*, the first valuable public prize was run for at that place in Charles I.'s time, viz. a silver and gilt cup and cover, of the estimated value of eight pounds, provided by the care of the aldermen for the time being; and Sir Edward Harwood laments the scarcity of able horses in the kingdom, "not more than two thousand being to be found equal to the like number of French horses"; for which he blames principally racing. In 1640, races were held at Newmarket: – also in Hyde Park, as appears from a comedy called the *Merry Beggars, or Jovial Crew*, 1641 – "Shall we make a fling to London, and see how the spring appears there in Spring Gardens, and in Hyde Park, to see the races, horse and foot?"

The wily Cromwell was not altogether indifferent to the breed of running horses, and with one of the stallions in his stud – Place's White Turk – do the oldest of our pedigrees end. He had also a famous brood-mare, called the Coffin-Mare, from the circumstances of her being concealed in a vault during the search for his effects at the time of the Restoration. Mr. Place, stud groom to Cromwell, was a conspicuous character of those days; and, according to some, the White Turk was his individual property. Charles II. was a great patron of the race-course. He frequently honoured this pastime with his presence, and appointed races to be run in Datchet Mead, as also at Newmarket, where his horses were entered in his own name, and where he rebuilt the decayed palace of his grandfather James I. He also visited other places at which races were instituted – Burford Downs, in particular – (since known as Bibury race-course, so often frequented by George IV. when Regent) as witness the doggerel of old Baskerville:

> *Next for the glory of the place,*
> *Here has been rode many a race.*
> *King Charles the Second I saw here;*
> *But I've forgotten in what year.*
> *The Duke of Monmouth here also*
> *Made his horse to sweat and blow, &c.*

At this time it appears that prizes run for became more valuable than they formerly had been. Amongst them were bowls, and various other pieces of plate, usually estimated at the value of one hundred guineas; and from the inscriptions on these trophies of victory, much interesting information might be obtained. This facetious monarch was likewise a breeder of race-horses, having imported mares from Barbary, and other parts, selected by his Master of the Horse, sent abroad for the purpose, and called Royal Mares – appearing as such in the stud-book to this day. One of these mares was the dam of Dodsworth, bred by the King, and said to be the earliest race-horse we have on record, whose pedigree can be properly authenticated.

James II. was a horseman, but was not long enough among his people to enable them to judge of his sentiments and inclinations respecting the pleasures of the turf. When he retired to France, however, he devoted himself to hunting, and had several first-rate English horses always in his stud. William III. and his Queen were also patrons of racing; not only continuing the bounty of their predecessors, but adding several plates to the former donations. Queen Anne's consort, Prince George of Denmark, kept a fine stud; and the Curwen Bay Barb, and the celebrated Darley Arabian, appeared in this reign. The Queen also added several plates. George I. was no racer, but he discontinued silver plate as prizes, and instituted the King's Plates, as they have been since termed, being one hundred guineas, paid in cash. George II. cared as little for racing as his father, but, to encourage the breed of horses, as well as to suppress low gambling, he made some good regulations for the suppression of pony races, and running for any sum under 50*l*. In his reign the Godolphin Arabian appeared, the founder of our best blood – the property of the then Earl of Godolphin. George III., though not much a lover of the turf, gave it some encouragement as a national pastime; in the fourth year of his reign, Eclipse was foaled, and *from that period may English racing be dated*! . . .

SKELETONS – 1944

Sir Alfred Munnings

1950

NOT LONG AGO I WAS painting at the Pytchley kennels. As I sat at work, with a boy holding a hound on a leash, I could hear a faint rattle coming from a shed adjoining the slaughter-house at the top of the meadow, caused by rats feeding in the mountainous piles of bones stored there. Then I saw, coming through a gate, a groom riding one horse and leading another, both good-looking horses. Being too engrossed with my study of hounds, I took no notice of this entry. A few minutes later there came the report of a gun.

"That's done for him," said the boy holding the hound.

The groom appeared again on his horse, without its lately led stable-companion, and went through the gate as he had come. Out of curiosity, I walked up to the slaughter-house, and found that the kennel-man had already begun to flay the horse, a large thoroughbred chestnut that had belonged to Mr. George Drummond. At the sight of that flayed head and eye I fled, and got to work again.

Belonging to such a man, this horse would have been a good performer, and he looked the sort as I saw him led across to be destroyed; and here he was, in a great pool of blood which was draining away, his glossy skin being torn from him, soon to feed the hounds he had followed from many a cover. Such is life.

Those studies-in-the-making were for a picture of Barker, the Pytchley huntsman. Captain Macdonald Buchanan then was Master, and the picture was for him. Some years before that I had painted Freeman on a black horse called Pilot for Mr. Ronald Tree, Master at that time.

When I find the energy to turn over the heaps of old sketch- and note-books which have accumulated during my life, I realise that I did a lot of work; and, as I find earlier, soiled, old books, I come upon drawings of that Norwich skeleton, of its parts, either from one side or the other; drawings from Stubbs; from the Rosa Bonheur horse; and in much later ones, very carefully done, fore and hind parts from the skeletons of St Simon and Stockwell in South Kensington Museum. I was doing this with fresh interest not long before the war, and now as I write, with the war still on, I wonder where such historic treasures of the equine world are housed. Where is the skeleton of Eclipse which belongs to the Royal College of Veterinary Surgeons? No doubt it is in a safe place. Think of that famous horse's skeleton, once covered and articulated with tendon, muscle and nerve, all under the rich, dark-chestnut coat, groomed and polished day after day throughout his short span! These used to be my thoughts as I looked at the structure standing in its glass case. Yes; indeed those bones had travelled about the country in the 1760s, all once part of a live and famous steed as we see him portrayed in the picture by Stubbs, with Wildman, his owner, and his two sons, in blue coats, cocked hats, white stockings and buckled shoes. That skull had once contained the brain and racing instincts of Eclipse! His eye had moved in and looked out from the dark socket. His lips had covered and been drawn over those teeth, had played with the bit and sneered when smelling something queer, and had played afterwards with many a mare at stud! And what crowds were once attracted by the horse! what betting! what noise of coarse shouting! – and now, here were his white bones in a glass case!

I wanted more paper. I keep reams of it in an old Jacobean oak chest next the fireplace behind me. Before I can open the lid of the chest I have to remove what stands on it. An old copper urn, a large oriental bowl full of rose-leaves, and a white, horse's skull. This skull has stood there for years. Friends say, "How hideous!" I explain to them the beauty of it, although there is a ghostliness about the dark, hollow eye-sockets, the teeth. Being in too much haste to write, the skull is still in the grandfather chair near the chest, where I should have replaced it after closing the lid.

There it sits, showing the frontal bones, the subtle modelling of the bridge of the nose, the dark cavities where the eyes once shone, and lower, where the bony formation ends, and where the velvety expanding surfaces above the nostrils used to quiver. The bone of the lower jaw and its rows of grinders meets the top row, and in the lamplight the whole skull seems alive.

It came from the Pytchley kennels – the skull of a thoroughbred. What a train of imaginary thought is already laid! What a story could be woven about that skull, which seems so alert and listening! And yet a lifeless object to examine, with a magic grain in the bone more delicate than the grain in precious wood. Ivory traceries and shapes. A miracle of creation – of God; a mere trifle in a world of mysteries, of millions upon millions of God's masterpieces.

I lift it from the chair and place it again on the lid of the old oak chest. The grain of the wood is God's design, the grain of the bone is God's design. I know less than nothing. As I placed it, looking down on the perfect symmetry of the forehead, the curve, occipital bones, I was astounded.

What are mere paintings – politics – anything? Nature is lasting – supreme.

ORIGIN OF THE STEEPLECHASE

Will H. Ogilvie

1925

Our forbears saw the Steeple
 Stand bold against the blue,
A landmark to the people
 Who sought for porch and pew;
And while that tall spire bade them
 To prayer and praise withdraw,
How it might further aid them
 Our sporting fathers saw.

So when men matched their horses
 To gallop fast and far,
Before the days of courses
 Built up with birch and bar,
That needle cloud-embordered
 Our fathers chose for guide,
And dropped the flag and ordered:
 "Straight for the Steeple – ride!"

183

Now, o'er the hamlet houses
We watch the lifted spire,
And in each heart it rouses
Some old and smouldering fire;
And many cheery people,
Though far removed from grace,
Look kindly on the Steeple,
That gave the Steeple-chase.

VRONSKY BLUNDERS

Leo Tolstoy

1876

VRONSKY NOW HAD THE LEAD, as he had desired, and as Cord had recommended, and he felt sure of success. His emotion, his joy, his affection for Frou Frou, were all on the increase. He wanted to look back, but he did not dare to turn around, and he did his best to calm himself, so as not to excite his horse. A single serious obstacle now remained to be passed, – the Irish *banquette*, – which if cleared, and if he kept his head level, would give him the victory without the slightest doubt. He and Frou Frou at the same instant caught sight of the obstacle from afar, and both horse and man felt a moment of hesitation. Vronsky noticed the hesitation in his horse's ears; and he was just lifting his whip when it occurred to him, just in time, that she knew what she had to do. The beautiful creature got her start, and, as he foresaw, seeming to take advantage of the impetus, rose from the ground, and cleared the ditch with energy that took her far beyond; then fell again into the measure of her pace without effort and without change.

"Bravo, Vronsky!" cried the throng. He recognized his friends and his regiment, who were standing near the obstacle; and he distinguished Yashvin's voice, though he did not see him.

"O my beauty!" said he to himself, thinking of Frou Frou, and yet listening to what was going on behind him. "He has cleared it," he said, as he heard Gladiator's gallop behind him.

The last ditch, full of water, two *arshíns* wide, now was left. Vronsky scarcely heeded it; but, anxious to come in far ahead of the others, he began to saw on the reins, and to urge on the horse by falling into her motions, and leaning far over her head. He felt that she was beginning to be exhausted; her neck and her sides were wet; the sweat stood in drops on her throat, her head, and her ears; her breath was short and gasping. Still, he was sure that she had force enough to cover the two hundred *sázhens* that lay between him and the goal. Only because he felt himself so near the end, and by the extraordinary smoothness of her motion, did Vronsky realize how much she had increased her speed. The ditch was cleared, how, he did not know. She cleared it like a bird. But at this moment Vronsky felt to his horror, that, instead of taking the swing of his horse, he had made, through some inexplicable reason, a wretchedly and unpardonably wrong motion in falling back into the saddle. His position suddenly changed, and he felt that something horrible had happened. He could not give himself any clear idea of it; but there flashed by him a roan steed with white feet, and Makhotin was the winner.

One of Vronsky's feet touched the ground, and his horse stumbled. He had scarcely time to clear himself when the horse fell on her side, panting painfully, and making vain efforts with her delicate foam-covered neck to rise again. But she lay on the ground, and struggled like a wounded bird: by the movement that he had made in the saddle, he had broken her back. But he did not learn his fault till afterwards. Now he saw only one thing, that Gladiator was far ahead, and that he was there alone, standing on the wet ground before his defeated Frou Frou, who stretched her head towards him, and looked at him with her beautiful eyes. Still not realizing the trouble, he pulled on the reins. The poor animal struggled like a fish, and tried to get up on her fore-legs; but, unable to move her hind-quarters, she fell back on the ground all of a tremble. Vronsky, his face pale, and distorted with rage, kicked her in the belly to force her to rise: she did not move, but gazed at her master with one of her speaking looks, and buried her nose in the sand.

"A-h! what have I done?" cried Vronsky, taking her head in his hands. "A-h! what have I done?" And the lost race, and his humiliating, unpardonable blunder, and the poor ruined horse! "A-h! what have I done?"

The surgeon and his assistant, his comrades, every one, ran to his aid; but to his great mortification, he found that he was safe and sound. Incapable of uttering a word, Vronsky answered nothing to all the questions which were put to him: he left the race-course without picking up his cap, or knowing wither he was going. He was in despair. For the first time in his life he was the victim of a misfortune for which there was no remedy, and for which he felt that he himself was the only one to blame.

Yashvin hastened after him with his cap, and took him back to his quarters. At the end of half an hour he was calm and self-possessed again, but this race was for a long time the most bitter and cruel remembrance of his life.

FRED ARCHER

The Hon. George Lambton

1924

THE FIRST TIME I ever saw Archer (I did not know him till the following year) was on my first visit to Newmarket in 1879. Of course I had read in the papers of his marvellous feats, and I was naturally anxious to see the great jockey. At St. Pancras Station I saw the Duke of Hamilton talking to a quiet, pale-looking young man, dressed in a dark suit with a black tie and a big pearl in it. I asked who it was. "Why, that is Archer," was the answer, much to my surprise, for he was quite unlike what I had pictured him to be.

About 5ft 10in. in height, with a wonderfully slim and graceful figure, and remarkably small hands and feet, there was even at that time the shadow of melancholy in his face which indicated a side to his nature never far absent even in his brightest days, and which was partly responsible for his tragic death. No one seeing him for the first time would have put him down as a jockey, or suspected that such tremendous energy lurked in that frail body. It was that untiring energy which was the secret of his great success, leaving no stone unturned to achieve the one object of his life, the winning of races.

From the beginning of the racing season to the end, health, leisure and pleasure were sacrificed, walking nearer 11st than 10st in the winter he was always ready for Lincoln and Liverpool, riding 8st. 10lb. He had a

Jockey. 1880s.

Turkish bath in his own house, and he used some medicine which went by the name of "Archer's Mixture," prepared by a clever doctor at Newmarket, called Wright. I tried it myself when I was riding races and from my own experience I should say it was made of dynamite.

Archer ate practically nothing all day, but usually had a good dinner which sometimes would send him up in weight 3lb. to 4lb., but the next morning with the Turkish bath and his mixture that would go. How his constitution stood such treatment for ten years was astonishing, but I have no doubt when he was taken ill with typhoid fever in 1886 his health must have been seriously undermined.

Taking him all round, Fred Archer was the greatest of all jockeys. Apprenticed to Matthew Dawson when he was eleven years old, it was not long before his master discovered that in this long-legged boy he had something out of the common. He was only seventeen when he won the Two Thousand Guineas for Lord Falmouth on Atlantic. From that time to the end of his life, at the age of twenty-nine, he was at the head of the winning jockeys. The number of races he won was astounding. In 1876, 209; 1877, 218; 1878, 229; 1879, 197; 1880, 120; 1881, 220; 1882, 210; 1883, 232; 1884, 241; 1885, 246; 1886 (the year of his death), 170. They included five victories in the Derby, four in the Oaks and six in the St. Leger.

He had many great qualities. To begin with, marvellous hands and seat. I think it was Joe Cannon who once said, "When you give Archer a leg-up he drops into the saddle, and in a moment he and the horse are as one; no pulling up or lengthening of stirrups, but away they go, complete confidence between man and horse." I have noticed the same thing myself about Stephen Donoghue.

Jockeys. Seventeenth century.

Archer had a wonderful intuition regarding the character of any horse once he had been on his back, and knew how to get the most out of him. He had undaunted nerve and supreme confidence in himself without any atom of conceit. When he was beaten by a neck for a race he generally thought that if he had just done this or not done that he would have won, and that is how a good jockey can make himself into a great one. Nothing escaped his notice during a race. Not only could he tell you all about his own horse, which is more than most jockeys are capable of, but he knew what the others had been doing. He had a great appreciation of other good riders, and he studied their methods. George Fordham he was always afraid of, saying, "In one race George comes and taps me in the last stride on the post. I am determined not to have this happen again, and then in the next race he just gets home and I beat him a stride past the post; with his clucking and fiddling you never know what the old chap is up to."

ASCOT IN THE '90s

Nat Gould

1900

IT IS A GLORIOUS sight, a picture once seen never forgotten. The dark background of trees, the line of dull brownish green on the top of the rise, the brilliant colours of the riders, the thousands of people looking down the long, straight course, all tend to make up a picture without a rival in the racing world.

And the race itself is generally worthy of its surroundings. The Royal Hunt Cup is one of the most popular handicaps in the year. It is not an easy race to win, but it is a race over which much money can be won, often at liberal odds. It is a race run over a trying course, almost uphill from start to finish. There is a shade of relief from the "collar", after the brow of the hill is reached, but later on, when the finish is near at hand, there is a stiff pinch to try the mettle of the gamest thoroughbred.

I recollect Cradle, Julius Caesar and Mandarin in succession, then that memorable Cup won by Peter, and in 1884 Acrostic, just before I sailed for New South Wales. Then a big blank until I returned home, when Cloraine, Quarrel, Knight of the Thistle, Jacquemont, and Refractor won it, also in succession.

As the horses reach the dip there are anxious eyes looking for the favourite and his nearest attendant in the betting market. Such horses as Victor Wild and Eager rouse the enthusiasm of the sport-loving public. A good horse with a big weight is always sure of a grand reception at Ascot or anywhere else. Victor Wild was a popular idol. He was cheered as he went down to the post, and cheered all the way as he gallantly struggled up the hill. It was the same with Eager.

Coming out of the dip it is seen the favourite has a good position. The "yellow and black" of his rider stands out prominently in the centre of the course. On his right are the familiar primrose and rose hoops. In the front is a lightly-weighted outsider with something between a brown and a purple jacket, or both, close to him. It is a real good race. Of the twenty-five runners, not five are hopelessly beaten. There is plenty of room for them right across the course, and they are spread out wide. There is something sneaking along close on the rails, and a horse going well far away on the outside. There centre divisions are in closer order, and all appear to wish to take the same bee-line for home.

There is a jockey sitting patiently on a horse that is going well, and lying about sixth or seventh.

Perhaps it is Morny Cannon; it looks like him from here. Yes, it must be "Morny" with that graceful seat, those steadying hands, judging the pace as well as his father did before him; no slight praise this, let me tell you. No wonder the Cannons can ride, for was not "Tom", their father, the most finished of horsemen, a perfect miracle on the back of a timid two-year old.

"Look at Cannon, see him, Bill, he's steadying the old horse for a run home. Here goes another half quid on him"; and the speaker, whose appearance is not suggestive of a superfluity of that handy coin, disappears in the direction of the bookmakers with the banners.

There is a jockey crouching low down on his horse's withers, with his body bent almost level with the neck of his mount, his face nearly hidden from view, so low down is it on the opposite side from the occupant of the coach.

He wears a light blue jacket, and the top of a black cap can be dis-

VICTOR WILD CANTERING UP THE COURSE.

tinguished. It is "Tod" Sloan in his crouching attitude. "Tod" at the height of his fame. The little American who has followers by the hundred, whose name is bitter in the bookmaker's mouth, as he says, "Here six to four, Toddy," and before the jockeys' names go up, "I'll lay two to one, Sloan." Generous man. There may be twelve runners, but such is Tod's fame, that two to one is considered a liberal offer.

It is not an elegant way of riding; it reminds one of juvenile days when the pony became an obstructionist, and the lad on its back was precipitated forward, and affectionately clutched him round the neck with both arms. Morny Cannon's style is our style; after all there is something in grace and elegance. It is brought prominently to notice when comparing "Morny" and "Tod".

Yes, Cannon is nursing his mount, and there is Sam Loates keeping an eagle eye on him. Near at hand is Rickaby, the most dapper of men, and Tom Loates and Madden are not far away. There is Charlie Wood come to "jockey life" again surely, and the youngster with somewhat of "Morny's" style is his brother, Kempton Cannon. Bradford and Findlay, Nat Robinson and Seth Chandley, Allsopp and Purkiss, are some others fairly well known.

It is going to be a good race, a ding-dong finish, we can all see that. At least ten horses have good chances as they reach the first carriage enclosure down the course. They are struggling up the hill now, and the pace is hot. There is no time to lose, and Cannon knows it is now or never. He makes a move forward, but cannot shake off Sam Loates, Rickaby and Charlie Wood, while "Brother Tom" and Allsopp are handy. Sailing away in front is "Tod" Sloan, crouching down low on his mount, but not quite so still now; by his movements he is getting a trifle uneasy. "Tod" likes to get in front and keep there; it saves such a lot of trouble.

On this occasion he is destined not to keep in front to the end, the light blue falls back and "Tod" has to taste the bitterness of defeat. He does not like it, but even "Tod" cannot have matters all his own way.

"Sloan's beaten!"

A thousand voices herald the fact that the Royal Hunt Cup is not for the American or popular Lord William Beresford. There is no more thought of Sloan now; he is beaten, and the winner must be looked for elsewhere.

Who will it be? Who will land the Royal Hunt Cup? "the prettiest race in England". The struggle is not over yet. Five horses are fighting it out, neck and neck, and there is no flinching on the part of them or their riders.

It is a hard tussle and shows the pluck of the thoroughbred, the stuff he is made off, the blood that will tell, and has left its mark all over the world. The jockeys know their mounts and strain every nerve to win. The horse has the strength, it must be guided aright, husbanded, until the final and critical moment, when the rider can assist him in this last pinch, and perchance snatch the victory.

A great sight, a glorious sight, a specimen of pluck and endurance seldom seen. It is racing in the truest sense of the word, racing for honour and fame and the spoils of war. There is nothing mean or paltry about it, or those thousands of people would not watch these five men struggling as though their lives depended on the result, with such breathless attention and compressed excitement.

So intense is the strain that there is comparative silence and the thud of the horses' hoofs can be heard.

First one colour in front, then another. A gain of a couple of yards, a loss of a dozen inches, an advantage of a head or a neck, a desperate effort to recover a lost half length. The jockeys' faces firm and set, the horses' heads stretched out towards the winning post. Behind the struggling five a batch of ten, then five more, and the "tail", and beyond that the crowd surging up the course, and the trees rustling in the breeze over the brow of the hill near the starting post.

The Royal Hunt Cup, and a right royal hunt it is for the horses following the leading five, from which the winner and the placed horses must come.

The suspense is ended at last, a momentary advantage is gained and a horse and rider prove their superiority just in the nick of time, and a head and neck are seen by the judge and part of the second horse, with the third close up and number four and five beaten out of places, but by no means disgraced.

The Royal Hunt Cup, the prettiest race in England, is over for another year, and Ascot can now give place to a different scene.

"HIS PROFESSION IS MOST EXACTING"

Stephen Donoghue

1924

LOTS OF PEOPLE seem to imagine that a jockey's life is one round of pleasure, principally spent in riding splendid horses to victory, and then drawing big cheques as presents from grateful owners!

I have had lots of experience and I can assure the reader that a jockey's life before and during the racing season is practically *all work*, his profession is most exacting, and his work never-ending; the actual riding in races is the least part of the day's record.

Early in the morning he is up and out, generally riding work and helping with the horses belonging to one or other of the stables with which he is connected. He probably has to go for long walks daily to get his weight off – or else spend a couple of hours "wasting" in the Turkish baths. Many jockeys are forced to do the latter almost every day. He then usually has hours of travelling to get to the racecourse at which the day's meeting happens to be.

On his return home there is probably a pile of correspondence waiting to be attended to; he has to study the Racing Calendar and consider his

probable rides for the week; there are innumerable telephone calls to make and receive; and, last but not least, many owners to call on and see. Owners usually wish to hear the jockey's opinion afterwards about any animal he has ridden for them. Very often, though, it is considered to be entirely the jockey's fault if a horse runs below expectations. One hears, "What a bad race, Donoghue" (or whoever the jockey happens to be) "rode on mine!" or, "He never tried a yard!" Generally the latter for choice, as if it is finally and comfortably decided that the jockey "never tried a yard" no blame can possibly be attached to the owner, trainer or *horse!*

There are many owners and trainers – especially the former – who cannot see, and do not want to be told, when their horses are moderate, or really bad. It would be imagined that they would prefer to know the truth, and so be in a position to decide to get rid of a bad horse. But no, some people would go on till an animal nearly "broke" them rather than listen to the disinterested advice an experienced jockey would willingly give them.

There is a terrible lot of jealousy, too, between *some* trainers and jockeys, and in this case it is usually the owner who suffers; it makes things most unpleasant, and has caused many owners to wish they had never taken any interest in racehorses.

Many horses go much better for some jockeys than others, and trainers should realise this more, and understand that if a horse goes less kindly for one jockey than another, it is because the animal has his peculiarities and is at least equally in fault.

At this point I would like to anticipate my narrative a little apropos of the diverse views so often expressed by unthinking people on the old type of riding in races and the new.

Very often one hears remarks like the following, in disparagement of the present style. "Ah, what races Fred Archer used to ride in the old days! What a great jockey he was! There are no riders to compare with him nowadays."

Fred Archer no doubt was a wonderful jockey – in those days. But times are very much altered now. Races are run in an entirely different fashion, and competition is infinitely keener.

From all I have learned, on the *best* authority, in the "old days" of race-riding, if any small apprentice got in the way of Archer or any of the older brigade at the start, or during the race, they were "in for it" when they got back to the weighing-room, if they did not get "it" first during the race!

"Here you, take that animal out of the way; get on the outside with it and *stay there*," would be the sort of peremptory orders that would be shouted to any "little kid" whose mount happened to be looking too well at the start, or going too well in the race. And the boy, scared stiff, would instantly obey . . .

RIGHT ROYAL

John Masefield

1922

In a race-course box behind the Stand
Right Royal shone from a strapper's hand.
A big dark bay with a restless tread,
Fetlock deep in a wheat-straw bed;
A noble horse of a nervy blood,
By O Mon Roi out of Rectitude.
Something quick in his eye and ear
Gave a hint that he might be queer.
In front, he was all to a horseman's mind;
Some thought him a trifle light behind.
By two good points might his rank be known,
A beautiful head and a Jumping Bone.

He had been the hope of Sir Button Budd,
Who bred him there at the Fletchings stud,
But the Fletchings jockey had flogged him cold
In a narrow thing as a two-year-old.
After that, with his sulks and swerves,
Dread of the crowd and fits of nerves,
Like a wastrel bee who makes no honey,
He had hardly earned his entry money.

Liking him still, though he failed at racing,
Sir Button trained him for steeple-chasing.
He jumped like a stag, but his heart was cowed;

194

Nothing would make him face the crowd.
When he reached the Straight where the crowds began
He would make no effort for any man.
Sir Button sold him, Charles Cothill bought him,
Rode him to hounds and soothed and taught him.
After two years' care Charles felt assured
That his horse's broken heart was cured,
And the jangled nerves in tune again.

And now, as proud as a King of Spain,
He moved in his box with a restless tread,
His eyes like sparks in his lovely head,
Ready to run between the roar
Of the stands that face the Straight once more;
Ready to race, though blown, though beat,
As long as his will could lift his feet;
Ready to burst his heart to pass
Each gasping horse in that street of grass . . .

POINT-TO-POINT MEETING

H.V. Morton

1926

WE WILL ATTEND that characteristic event of an English spring – a hunt point-to-point.

It is afternoon. It has stopped raining, and the sun has come out; so has the entire county. Those lonely mansions set upon a hill, or lying snug in woods, which six days out of seven appear dead, prove to be inhabited by colonels, majors, Sir Alfred This and Lord That. It is a startling coming-to-life. The recently desolate roads are alive with limousines – luncheon baskets on top, the girls inside, and the major driving – and in a side-lane opposite the gate leading to Farmer Sweetbread's field stands the village bobby, hot and bothered tied up with Fords and Rolls-Royces, to say nothing of Lady Snatcher's hunter, Pinch o' Ginger, favourite for the Hunt Cup, who moves restlessly amid the mudguards with a mustard-coloured blanket on his back and a groom making soothing noises at his head.

A distracted yokel at the gate collects ten shillings from the gentry towards the restoration of Farmer Sweetbread's meadow as each car churns in over the muddy entrance and bumps through a sweet scent of bruised grass and daisies to the car-park.

The clouds are big over the green backs of the hills: enormous sailing gold clouds; and there is a sharp wind. From the hill the country falls away into a crystal-clear patchwork of acres cut by sharp green hedges, with here and there little scarlet flags, which make the course, fluttering in the wind.

On the hill overlooking the course the motor-cars are drawn up on the grass, and near them thirty bookmakers shout and bellow. Behind the bookmakers is an outraged-looking thatched cottage; to the left of the cottage shines a white marquee, the weighing-in tent, and opposite, behind rails, is the paddock.

Here is "the county".

The field is as rich in types as Piccadilly. There are old men with monocles and lined, sagging faces, like bloodhounds. They wear fawn bowlers, and smoke thin cheroots held between fingers in yellow gloves. They wear check clothes that would strike the observer dead in a city; the green grass seems to tone them down. There are still older men bent double, who cup their ears with a hand when addressed, and reply with an asthmatic cough:

"Oh, lord, yes . . . damn good horse! Look at his legs!"

Then there are young men, loose-limbed creatures, who are bred, not born; they are bred to ride horses, so that nature falls into line and fits them out with exactly the kind of legs you need to ride a horse. There is nothing but "horse" in their minds, and when they die surely they become centaurs. Everybody's collarbone has been broken.

Then the girls. Nowhere in the world will you see such trim, neat girls. They sit on shooting-sticks. They wear tweed clothes as perfectly as their brothers wear riding breeches. When quite young their noses have freckles. Most of them have the beauty that comes with health and simplicity, and they stride across a field magnificently, discussing "fetlocks" and "withers" with the man of their choice. They never hesitate at a fence; they are neat-limbed, lovely things. . . .

A flash of colour in the paddock!

Three young men in pink coats ride off over the fields to the starting-point.

"Good luck, sir," says the groom.

"Thank you, Tom."

" 'E'll win it!" says Tom to the chauffeur.

More riders trot out, the crowd streams away after them. . . .

Here they come! A line of horsemen rises and dips over the first brushwood jump; they take the second and disappear. Nothing happens for five minutes . . . ten . . . fifteen . . . twenty; then:

"Here they are! 'Strike-me-Pink' leading. . . . No, no, it's 'Harkaway'. Come on sir; come on 'Harkaway'! Ride him; come on – oh *bad* luck, he's down! – come on 'Strike-me-Pink'."

Over the top of the big water-jump appears the head of a horse, there is a crackle of brushwood, a plash of water, a top-hat floating, a rider catching at the reins, then another horse – a flying horse that clears the jump and thunders to the winning post!

STEEPLECHASE TACTICS

John Hislop

1951

TACTICS IN A RACE are the appreciation and employment of the capabilities and characteristics of one's horse, the short-comings of opposing horses and jockeys, the features of the course, the going, and the circumstances that may arise during the race, in order to further one's chance of victory.

To be skilled in this respect is to be a good jockey, and however expert a horseman a man may be, he cannot be considered a good jockey unless he possess tactical skill, while a good jockey in the tactical sense of the word may quite likely be an indifferent horseman. The top-class race-rider is the one who is fortunate enough to combine both qualities.

Skill in tactics depends upon quick thinking and quick decision, a thorough knowledge of the abilities and peculiarities of one's horse – how often does one hear a jockey say after a race, "If only I'd ridden him before and known him, he would have won" – and experience. Much can be learnt from carefully watching the details of running as a spectator, and anyone whose ambition it is to become a successful steeplechase-rider, should make full use of every opportunity, both of watching from the stands and of walking out to various points of the course from which he can obtain a close-up view of different stages of the race. He will find this more advantageous and economical than gossiping during the race, or "watching it from the bar".

Apart from not falling off or violently interfering with one's horse, tactics are by far the most important aspect of race-riding, and a jockey can often lose a race on the biggest certainty in the world through an error in tactics, while an owner or trainer who has tied a jockey down to orders may find that, owing to unforeseen circumstances arising, the tactics the jockey has been compelled to employ, because of his patron's instructions, will prove the means of defeat.

When a jockey loses a race his tactics are frequently criticised by onlookers, most probably those who have lost their money on the horse he was riding; but no such censure is merited unless expressed by one who knows what orders the jockey was given, what peculiarities the horse possesses, and what has occurred during the race. And since he is unlikely to have a knowledge of the first two conditions at all, and a by no means accurate understanding of the third (some of the running was probably out of sight of the stands, and it is more than possible that he missed seeing a vital incident), the average critic has little or no right to offer adverse comment.

Whatever the natural or acquired tactical skill a rider may possess, in order that he may reap the fullest advantage from it he must be thoroughly familiar with the course over which the race is to be run.

Ignorance of the geography of a course can result in a jockey going many yards out of the way, as was the case with the rider of the French horse, Le Paillon, who was defeated in the Champion Hurdle by National Spirit and afterwards won the Prix de l'Arc de Triomphe against the best flat racehorses in France, and even in going the wrong way altogether, as occurred in the case of Zahia in the 1948 Grand National. And it is of the utmost importance for a jockey to walk the course, not only if he has never ridden over it before, but if he has not ridden over it recently, since it is quite common for slight alterations to be made, without the knowledge of which a rider can easily go wrong. If in doubt he should walk it twice.

Having made himself thoroughly familiar with the ground over which the battle is to be fought, the rider must then take thought about the way in which he is going to ride his horse to ensure that the most can be made of him

Broadly speaking, tactics fall into two divisions: lying up with the leaders all the way, and coming from behind. But before he binds himself to one or the other of these two plans, the rider must learn and appreciate that the dominating factor in all forms of racing is the pace at which the race is run, qualified by such considerations as the state of the going and the wind.

It is not the slightest use leading the field at a hack-canter, under the impression that, through making the running a one-pace stayer is able to benefit from his stamina at the expense of a field of short runners. Conversely, when riding a horse that must be brought with a run from behind, there is no sense in lying so far out of one's ground that the task of catching the leaders is impossible; under some circumstances (when the going is very heavy or the leaders are horses of doubtful stamina) they may "come back" to a jockey lying out of his ground, but on good or firm going and in the case of genuine stayers they most probably will not. It is therefore advisable to form a general and flexible plan rather than a narrow and rigid one, so that room is left for adaptability in the case of the occurrence of the unforeseen.

In the world of athletics it is, I believe, generally recognized that the more even a runner's pace throughout a race, the less energy is he likely to waste, and there seems no reason why this principle should not, with reservations to cover individual characteristics and circumstances, be applied to horses; in fact, the frequently used term "riding a smooth race" suggests an even pace throughout the race, with no periods of violent acceleration or deceleration. The snags to this theory, however, are that horses do not run in "lanes", but are subject to the rough-and-tumble resulting from the presence of other horses in the race, often to the effects of comparatively steep gradients, and to individual idiosyncrasy and temperament, so that it is frequently necessary to accelerate suddenly and violently, to slow down quickly, or to keep a horse in front or covered up as the case may be. And theory must be sacrificed to practice.

In view of this, therefore, I think that, after acquiring a thorough knowledge of the course, the next most important point a rider must consider is the peculiarities of the horse he is to ride, upon which his tactics in the race will largely depend.

The least complicated peculiarity is that of being what is known as a "front runner", in other words, a horse who likes to make the running. In riding this type of horse it is fairly obvious that one's tactics must consist in jumping out of the gate as nimbly as possible, securing the rails, going the shortest way round, and remaining in front from start to finish. Nevertheless, there are times when these tactics must be modified, for if another competitor sets out to do exactly the same it is quite possible that the two horses will "cut each other's throats", that is to say vie with each other to such an extent that they will go too fast in the early stages and be spent forces by the time the finish draws in sight.

When riding a front runner it is essential to be able to gauge the pace one is going in relation to the horse's capabilities, fitness and the state of the going, and to decide, if another competitor draws level or attempts to pass, whether it is policy to increase one's own pace in order to retain one's lead, or to allow one's rival to take the lead, in the belief that he is forcing a pace which he himself will not be able to maintain and which will sooner or later cause him to become exhausted and to drop back, thus enabling one's own horse to reach the front again without having to exert himself to do so.

When horses become well known as front runners, other jockeys frame their tactics to try and make them run themselves into the ground; in fact, the rider of a fancied horse is quite likely to enlist an ally in the shape of one who is considered to have no chance of winning the race but is willing to make the pace so strong that any horse trying to keep with him, or pass him, is bound to exhaust himself before the finish.

Front runners may be inclined to lose heart if they have to relinquish their lead, but if they are over-taxed in being kept in front they will most certainly lose the race, and rather than risk riding his horse into the ground I am sure that it is better policy for a jockey to "sit and suffer" behind a horse who is attempting to make the pace too fast, for, even if his horse drops his bit for the time being, he will, in all probability, take hold of it again when, as assuredly he will, the leader "comes back" to him.

I used to ride a front runner over hurdles who reacted successfully to these tactics, for having been beaten on him through riding him into the ground, I sat still on him the next time I met an opponent trying to take him on at his own game, and though he preferred being in front, and did, indeed, drop his bit when passed, he raced on with determination when the leader came back to him and fell behind.

When riding a front runner, there is a strong temptation to keep looking back to see what is occurring behind. This is a very bad fault: to start with, a rider should have sufficient idea of the pace at which he is travelling to know whether he is going too fast or too slow without having to regulate it according to the proximity of other competitors; besides this, the fact of looking round unbalances and disquiets his own horse, giving a rider following him the advantage of making his challenge at that psychological moment when the horse in front, and his rider, are off their balance. A rider who keeps looking over his shoulder when not protected by the rails on one side enables his opponent behind him to get first run on him by placing his challenge on the opposite side to which he is looking at that moment.

One can sense the presence and approach of a following rider without looking round to see if he is there; and provided one's horse is balanced, collected and kept up into his bridle, it is possible to take the necessary measures to ward off any challenge delivered from behind, as soon as the presence of the challenger makes itself felt, since the better balanced and the more collected a horse is, the quicker will be his response to any demand of his rider, and a rider that is perpetually looking round cannot have his horse as well balanced and as collected as one who is not.

If, then, the particular whim of the horse one is riding is that he likes to be in front, it is advisable to indulge him, but with discretion: to leave the gate with the greatest possible speed – the greater advantage he can gain

Water-jump; in mid-air

at the start, the more effort will his rivals have to exert in trying to catch him; to let him run along in front at such a pace as is consistent with his capabilities, condition and the state of the going, but at the same time being prepared to surrender the lead should another horse attempt to force the pace to an unwise degree.

While the front runner is a type frequently met with, the horse who prefers to come from behind is even more common. Such horses are more difficult to ride, since when brought to the front too soon they are either liable to tear away and run themselves out, or become tired of being in front and slow up.

The way in which a horse who likes to come from behind must be ridden depends upon whether he is calm or impetuous by nature. If the former, he presents no great problem: he can be jumped smartly out of the gate, steadied after he has crossed the first fence or hurdle and then be tucked in behind the leaders in about fourth or fifth place, where he can be allowed to remain until turning into the straight, when he can be brought into a challenging position, finally being ranged alongside the leader or leaders going into the last fence.

Not being an impetuous horse, there will be no difficulty in putting him in any desired position, and it will not matter whether or not he is "shown daylight." He can be kept well up with the leaders, since in the event of one or two of them falling it will not be difficult to pull behind another horse, and will be possible to start moving up into a challenging position gradually and quite a long way from the finish.

In the case of a hard-pulling horse who must be waited with, however, the correct tactics are not so easily carried out.

One's horse must on no account be allowed to tear off in front from the start, or it will be impossible to get him back, and he will find himself, in spite of the efforts of his rider, occupying the role of a front runner; so that considerable care must be taken as regards the way in which he leaves the gate, an aspect dealt with in some detail in the previous chapter.

The rider's next problem will be to keep his horse covered up behind other runners, without being so close on their heels that he has no chance of getting a proper view of the obstacles or is in danger of jumping into the horse in front, which will be certain to happen if the latter is a "sticky" jumper and one's own horse a free one. Quite a number of horses, though they will take a very strong hold when they see daylight, will drop their bits when tucked in behind others, when they will be content to lob along calmly and contentedly until such time as they are pulled out and shown daylight. The riding of these horses is quite a straightforward affair and merely consists of not hustling them out of the gate – this does not mean getting left about six lengths – tucking them in behind the leading horses or in the middle of the field, and bringing them out when the moment arrives to deliver one's challenge.

But the real hard puller is a more difficult problem. If one has any doubts about holding him it is no bad plan to start in the second rank. This will mean that he is covered up from the outset and that, consequently, the rider does not have the task of pulling him back (or trying to do so) in order to get him covered up, which feat, if one is called upon to perform it after the horse has really got into his stride and has seen daylight, is often beyond the task of the average rider.

Before he sets off, the rider should have pulled his stirrup-leathers up as short as is consistent with security in the saddle, in order to have as good a chance as possible of holding the horse. He should be riding the horse on as long a rein as he dares – he will have to take a fairly short hold, but if he overdoes it and "grabs the rings of the bit" he will be in danger of being pulled over the horse's head if the latter blunders. Having planted himself behind another horse he should endeavour to keep a length or more back, to avoid striking or jumping into him. It may happen that one can just manage to keep far enough behind the horse in front to avoid striking into him but not far enough back to enable one's horse to see the obstacle. This is admirable so far as progress on the flat is concerned, but when it comes to jumping, disaster will be inevitable unless measures are employed to cope with the situation.

By moving to one side or the other of one's pilot it is usually possible to get a glimpse of the obstacle, even if there is a horse on either side of him, for they are not likely to be jammed right up against one another, and the best plan, therefore, is to wait until the last moment and then let one's horse see the necessary daylight for him to jump. As he lands the rider will have a chance to take a pull at him and bring him back into his covered-up position. This is neither an attractive nor desirable way of riding in the ordinary course of events, but it is one which sometimes must be resorted to if the rider is going to have any chance of carrying out instructions to ride a waiting race.

THE MANNER OF GORDON RICHARDS

Major Jack Fairfax-Blakeborough

1978

WHAT ALWAYS STRUCK ME most about Sir Gordon was his quiet, unassuming manner. Those of us who spend much of our racing life in weighing-rooms, have an opportunity of seeing and studying jockeys from quite a different angle. It is like being behind the scenes, in the dressing-rooms and wings of a theatre. There actors and actresses, even though dressed and made up, are their natural selves. So it is with jockeys, for they look upon the weighing-room as a sort of refuge and sanctuary in which they are safe from the importuning, questioning, lionising and mobbing of a certain type in the paddock.

I fancy none appreciate the value of the weighing-room in this connection more than Sir Gordon. He never lost his shy, retiring modesty, which made excessive limelight and hero-worship rather repugnant. Unlike many of his contemporaries, there was nothing of the boisterous, excitable hurry and whirl in the weighing-room with him, no shouting for his valet, no last-minute dash to the scale, and bull-in-the-china-shop-like tearing back to the dressing-room.

To look at him, as I have done, patiently waiting his turn in the queue to be weighed out, one might imagine he was some obscure lad, not quite sure of the ropes and anxious to keep in the background. In his humility, his good manners and his restraint lay not only much of his power, but also a natural gentlemanliness and gentleness, which have also stood him in good stead. One admires it all, and it has not detracted in any way from his fame. Sir Gordon certainly lacks the mobile face of Steve Donoghue, the charm of Michael Beary – "Angel Face", as he has been called to his own amusement – the humour of Joe Taylor and Willie Nevett, the vivacity of Joe Caldwell, the quaint piquancy of Johnnie Dines, the assurance and domination of Tommy Weston, the supreme confidence of

Harry Wragg, the seeming wearied detachment of Rufus Beasley, the business-like haste of Charlie Smirke, the grave matter-of-factness of Joe Childs, the alertness and happiness of Henry Jellis, the brightness of eye and smile of Willie Christie, the fun of Davy McGuigan and the buoyancy of Harry Gunn.

Sir Gordon's face, when in repose, would suggest sadness rather than any of those qualities and attributes possessed by some of his contemporaries. I have never seen him "rattled" and I have rarely seen signs of that strain and weariness which are both so often marked in jockeys who have been wasting hard, who are worn out with travelling and with late nights, depressed by a run of bad luck, or the adverse criticisms of owners or trainers. Sometimes criticism enters like iron into a jockey's heart when he knows such censure is not justified. Sir Gordon and I have had many chats in weighing-rooms and during the course of them I have hardly ever mentioned racing. I fancy it is rather a relief to him to find someone who is not so absolutely single-minded as to have no thought or interest beyond the constant striving to find winners.

The right way to fall

HOW TO WIN THE DERBY

Sir Gordon Richards

1955

AFTER WE HAD GONE about three furlongs, I was maybe twelfth, but I was nicely tucked in on the rails. With about six furlongs to go on top of the hill, I had managed to work my way into fifth place, without having to leave the rails. Smirke had now taken up the running on the Aga Khan's Shikampur. As Smirke began to go on, I found myself just in fourth place behind Star of the Forest, who I realised was tiring. I had two or three horses outside me, and my only chance was to go between Star of the Forest and the rails. I gave Pinza a little kick, and he went through like a lion. I found myself, right in the middle of Tattenham, in second place about four lengths behind Shikampur. Pinza came down the hill, and round, quite perfectly, just as he had done that morning. Although I was still four or five lengths behind Shikampur, I already knew that the race was over. I let Smirke lead me until just under two furlongs from home, and then I went by and we won as we liked.

1956: DICK FRANCIS AND THE QUEEN'S HORSE

Dick Francis

1957

DURING THE NEXT MILE Devon Loch was gradually passing horse after horse by out-jumping them, and, as we approached the Canal Turn, we were lying second. Armorial III was in front, but Devon Loch was going so spendidly that there was no need for us to hurry.

Never before in the National had I held back a horse and said "Steady, boy". Never had I felt such power in reserve, such confidence in my mount, such calm in my mind.

Armorial III fell at the fence after Valentine's, and Eagle Lodge took his place, but Devon Loch went past him a fence later, and, with three to jump, he put his nose in front. Amazingly, I was still holding Devon Loch back, and when I saw beside me that E.S.B., Ontray and Gentle Moya were being ridden hard, I was sure we were going to win.

Twenty yards from the last fence I could see that Devon Loch was meeting it perfectly, and he jumped it as stylishly as if it had been the first of thirty, instead of the last.

Well, I had my moment.

I know what it is like to win the National, even though I did not do it, and nothing that happened afterwards has clouded the memory of the seconds when Devon Loch went on to win. One might adapt an old saying to sum up my feelings exactly. Better to have won and lost, than never to have won at all.

An appalling minute after Devon Loch had fallen, I stood forlornly on the course looking for my whip. I had thrown it away from me in anger and anguish at the cruelty of fate; and now felt rather foolish having to pick it up again.

Devon Loch was being led back to his stable, and the stragglers of the race were trotting in, and I took my time over finding the whip, knowing that when I did I would have to face the long walk back to the weighing-room and the turned faces, the curious eyes, the unmanning sympathy of the huge crowd. I wanted very much to be alone for a few minutes to get my breath back, and, as if he had read my thoughts, an ambulance driver came to my rescue.

"Hop in, mate," he said, jerking his thumb at the ambulance.

So I hopped in, and he drove down through the people in the paddock and stopped at the first-aid room, so that I could go straight from there into the weighing-room without having to push my way through the dense crowd round the main door, and I was very grateful to him.

While I was slowly dressing and tying my tie Mr. Cazalet came into the changing-room.

"Dick", he said, "come along up to the Royal box. They want to see you."

We walked across and up the stairs together. Losing the National like that was as disappointing to him as to anybody, and in some ways worse, for twenty years before he had seen Davy Jones break a rein and run out at the last fence with the race in his pocket, and such dreadful luck should not happen to any trainer twice.

It was quiet in the Royal box. It was as if the affectionate cheers for Devon Loch, which had died a long time ago in a million throats all over Britain, had cast a shadow of silence. There was, after all, very little to be said. Their Majesties tried to comfort me, and said what a beautiful race Devon Loch had run; and in my turn I tried to say how desperately sorry for their sake I was that we had not managed to cover those last vital fifty yards.

Her Majesty the Queen Mother said resignedly, "That's racing, I suppose". But she and the Queen were obviously sorrowful and upset by what had happened.

Mr. Cazalet came down again with me from the Royal box, and we went over to the stables to see Devon Loch. He was munching some hay and being groomed, and, apart from looking like a horse which has just had a hard race, there was nothing the matter with him. His intelligent head lifted as we went into his box, and I patted him while Mr. Cazalet ran his hand down his legs to see if there was any heat or swelling in them, but they were cool and firm.

I stood close to Devon Loch and leaned my head against his neck. We were both tired. "Oh, Devon Loch," I was saying in my mind, "Devon Loch, what happened? What happened?" If only he could have answered.

Mr. Cazalet came back to the weighing-room with me, and with a few last sad words, we parted. Still a bit dazed and very unhappy, I collected

Mary, and we drove with Father and my uncle back along the road we had travelled with such hope in the morning, to Douglas's house at Bangor-on-Dee. We hardly spoke a word the whole way.

The little house was full of children, ours and Douglas's, who were too young to understand what the lost race meant to us, and who met us with blunt and penetrating candour.

"The man on the wireless said Devon Loch sat down. Jolly silly sort of thing to do, wasn't it?"

"It's a pity you didn't win, Uncle Dick. I had a shilling on you and now I've lost it, and the stable lads say their beer money's gone down the drain too."

"Never mind, I expect you'll win a race next week."

"Was the Queen cross, Daddy? . . . "

And the youngest, just three, said nothing, but after he had seen the pictures of Devon Loch's spread-eagled fall in the next day's newspapers, I found him playing behind the sofa, running and falling flat on his tummy and saying, "I'm Devon Loch. Down I go, bump!"

NO REINS FOR FRED WINTER

"Audax"

1962

FROM AGINCOURT TO D-DAY, France, I suppose, has been the scene of more brave deeds by Englishmen than any other country in the world. Mostly, of course, they were inspired by the horrid waste of war, but sport in its less serious tragic way, can also lift a man to heights of daring and achievement, and as Fred Winter and Mandarin came back last Sunday after winning the Grand Steeplechase de Paris, I like to think that the ghosts of long-dead English horsemen rode beside them, glad and proud to know that flag for which they fought and died still flies, even in this sad, dull mechanical age.

To win at all would have been a famous victory – to win as Winter and Mandarin did was an heroic triumph over odds so steep that no normal man or horse could have been blamed for giving up long before the end.

None of this, of course, could even be guessed at, as, in the atmosphere of a Turkish bath, the 14 runners swept gaily past the stands for the first of three intricate, twisting circuits.

So far as one could see in the friendly but chaotic tangle that serves Auteuil for a parade ring, the French horses were not a wildly impressive sight. Nor, to someone who had never seen him before, would Mandarin have been, but to the large band of English supporters, the sheen on his coat, the hard muscles writhing over his quarters, and the way he pulled "Mush" Foster round the paddock, all told their own encouraging tale.

Sure enough, after flicking neat and fast over the preliminary hurdle jumped on the way to the start, Mandarin was soon upsides in front, and passed the stands pulling, as usual, like a train. He has always been a "heavy-headed" ride with precious little feeling in his mouth – and always runs in a rubber-covered snaffle to save his lips and jaws.

At the beginning of last season, a brand-new bridle was bought – and Mandarin had worn it only half a dozen times, including both his victories in the Hennessey and Cheltenham Gold Cups. But the trouble with rubber bits is that a fault on wear can develop unseen in the steel chain – and this, no doubt, is what had happened now.

After the first, sharp, left-hand bend the Grand Steeple course comes back towards the stands and there, going to the fourth, a soft but staring privet fence, the best part of six feet high, the bit snapped clean in the middle, inside Mandarin's mouth. I remember thinking at the time "he got a little close to that one," but for another full circuit none of us in the stands realized the dreadful truth.

In fact, of course, Fred Winter now had no contact whatsoever with the horse's mouth or head. The reins, kept together by the Irish martingale (or "rings") were still round Mandarin's neck – and they, together with the thin neck-strap of the breast-girth, were Winter's only hand hold.

To visualize the full impossibility of the situation you must remember first that when a racehorse, particularly a hard-pulling 'chaser, is galloping on the bit, much of the jockey's weight is normally balanced, through the reins, against that of the horse's head and forehand. Now, for both Fred Winter and Mandarin, this vital counterbalance was gone completely. The man, with no means of steering but his weight, had to rely entirely on grip and balance – the horse, used to a steady pressure on his mouth, had to jump 21 strange and formidable obstacles with his head completely free – a natural state admittedly, but one to which Mandarin is wholly unaccustomed.

Small wonder then that, at the huge "Rivière de la Tribune" – the water in front of the stands – he fiddled awkwardly, landing only inches clear of the bank and disaster. Thereafter, save for another nasty moment at the same fence next time round, the little horse jumped unbelievably well – and Fred Winter, sitting still or driving on as the need arose, matched his every move with the sympathetic rhythm that is nine-tenths of horsemanship.

But the fences, needless to say, were only half the problem. Walking the course that morning with Winter, Dave Dick and Joe Lammin, Fulke Walwyn's head lad, we had all wondered afresh at the many turns, and countless opportunities for losing your way. The Grand Steeple is, roughly, two figures of eight in opposite directions and one whole circuit outside both. There are at least four bends through 180 degrees, and to negotiate them all as Winter and Mandarin did, without bit or bridle, was, quite literally, miraculous.

The answer lies, of course, in many things – in the matchless strength of Winter's legs, in Mandarin's own good sense – and in the absolute determination of them both never to give up while there was one shot, however forlorn, left on the board.

It is also, I think, only fair to give some credit – and our thanks – to the French jockeys, several of whom could, had they pleased, have taken advantage of the disaster and, without much risk to themselves, got rid of the biggest danger. Instead, at least one – Laumas on Taillefer – and probably several others, actually did their best to help, proving gloriously that the comradeship of dangers shared can, in *some* sports at least, count far more than international rivalry.

Throughout the race, save for a moment on the last bend, Mandarin was up in the first four – and, as he jumped the Rivière for the last time, the full horror of his situation dawned upon us in the stands.

From that moment on, the nerve-racking suspense, the wild impossible hope, plunging to black despair and back again, were like nothing I have ever known on a race-course – or for that matter anywhere else.

Mandarin cleared with ease the tricky post-and-rails at which he hesitated fatally three years ago – and came to the junction of the courses close fourth – close enough to lift the hearts of those who knew his and Winter's invincible finishing power.

But now disaster almost struck. Before the last right-handed turn a large bush must be passed on the left – but can with equal ease be passed on the right. Mandarin, on the inside, with no rail to guide him, could not know until the last moment which way to go. For a few heart-stopping strides he hesitated, Winter threw all his strength and weight into one last desperate swerve – and somehow they were safe.

But priceless lengths had been lost and now, round the final bend, with only two obstacles to jump, Mandarin was only fifth, some six or seven lengths behind the leader.

On the turn, of course, Winter could hardly ride at all, but then facing the Bullfinch, in a straight line for home at last, it was a different matter. From the stands we saw the familiar crouching drive of the shoulders, and Mandarin, responding as he always had and always will, thrust out his gallant head and went for the Bullfinch like a tank facing tissue paper.

None will ever know what the little horse felt or thought between those last two fences. I have always believe he knows just what it means to win – and now none will ever convince me otherwise. In a hundred desperate yards he passed three horses as if they were walking and, as he landed in front on the long run-in, my eyes, I am not ashamed to say, were half-blind with tears.

But it was not over yet. Mandarin was deadly tired and Winter, the reins gathered useless in his left hand, could do nothing to hold him together. He could only push and drive – and how he drove. Even so, inch by inch, Lumino, the only French horse able to accelerate, crept nearer and nearer.

In the final desperate strides, not knowing the angle, not one of us could really tell who had won. Fred Winter thought he had got up, but he could not speak, so for several ghastly moments we had to sweat it out. But then, there it was – number one in the frame – and as Mandarin came back, mobbed as no film star has ever been, head down, dog-tired, sweating – but surely happy – a cheer went up such as I have never heard on any race-course.

For Fred Winter it was not the end. Riding a dream of a race, he went on, 40 minutes later, to win the Grande Course de Haies on Beaver 11. I have neither time nor space to describe that race and, triumph though it was for Beaver's trainer, Ryan Price, it only served as the perfect ending to an historic afternoon. For on Sunday, Fred Winter and Mandarin had earned themselves a place among the immortal names of sport. I have never seen a comparable feat, never expect to – and can only thank God that I was there.

THE
HUNTING FIELD

Hark! the brave North-easter!
Breast-high lies the scent,
On by holt and headland,
Over heath and bent.
Chime, ye dappled darlings,
Through the sleet and snow,
Who can over-ride you?
Let the horses go!

CHARLES KINGSLEY,
Ode to the North-East Wind

A LARGE PROPORTION, of both those who have ponies as children and those who take up riding later in life, yearn for the hunting-field. Not only is the colorful sight of a huntsman with his whippers-in and hounds on a winter's morning an enticement in itself, but the mutual activity of horse and hound is an entirely natural combination, drawing horsemen and horsewomen of every description into its endeavors. The pursuit is primeval: it was the same chorus of hoof-beat, horn- and hound-music, the same dangerous challenge and uncertainty of direction, and the same sights, sounds and smells of wild Nature, which thrilled and enchanted our remote ancestors. As a hunting correspondent I have seen – not only all over the British Isles, but in the United States and on the Continent, too – great sacrifices made, in terms of money, time and family inconvenience, by people who are determined to "go hunting."

And since there is a constant poetry, as well as adventure and comedy, in the hunting-field, one is not surprised at the wealth of literature it has inspired. Aristotle, Homer, Plato, Virgil and Xenophon were among those who extolled the virtues of the chase, and, in the modern world, Twici, Somerville, Nimrod, Surtees, Whyte-Melville, Trollope, Bromley-Davenport, Somerville and Ross, Theodore Roosevelt, Sassoon and Masefield. Another was the Spaniard José Ortega y Gasset, perhaps the most popular, if not the greatest, of Spain's modern philosophers.

211

His *Meditations on Hunting* is little known outside his own country. The passage I have selected from this book presents a shrewd insight into one of the motivations of the anti-hunting set – jealousy. The philospher might have carried his argument a step forward by discussing the influence of the horse on some of hunting's opponents. For, to quote from a piece I wrote for the "Guest Column" of the London *Times* recently: "As the Freudians tell us, horses are subconscious symbols of feudalism, the squirearchy and the yeomanry. And to whip up the latent hostility for, and jealousy of, the townsman, for the countryman, nothing is more effective than for the former to see the latter on horses, especially if they are dressed in the traditional uniforms of their recreation. . . . "

This envy factor has its roots in class conflict. At least up to the Second World War, to be a hunting man or woman carried social prestige, a fact well evinced in the snobbish dialogue given next from Bernard Shaw's *Heartbreak House*. To "ride well to hounds" of course carried greater *kudos* still, and it must have been satisfying half-a-century and more ago to find your name – or even the names of your parents – on Lady Augusta Fane's list of "the best across the 'Shires," catalogued in her nostalgic *Chit-Chat*. For Lady Augusta was a much-sought-after hunting-field belle, and a thruster, too, who few – even of the young men – could stay with. Following up her list with a brief comment on objections to hunting and that same deduction of jealousy, as you will see, she ends her chapter, by repeating the memorable lines on the wherefore of foxhunting from Will Ogilvie's *Scattered Scarlet*.

Modern foxhunting dates from the 1750s, the period in which Hugo Meynell, with careful scientific application, quickened the pursuit by breeding faster hounds – fundamentally by crossing Northern Beagles with Southern-mouthed hounds – to produce a breed which could catch its foxes in the open. The chase soon became something more than England's leading sport, it became a ritual, not easily understood by foreigners, least of all by the prejudiced French. And this is the background against which Conan Doyle's comical account of how his Napoleonic hero, Brigadier Gerard, slew a fox pursued by Wellington's officers, must be read.

In England by the end of the Napoleonic wars, foxhunting was *de rigeur*. To be a mere patron of sport, what was termed a Corinthian, was no longer admired. People were becoming contemptuous of the Regency's foppishness, and, between 1810–15, everyone was praising Wellington's officers, fresh from the Peninsular, then Waterloo, "returning to England," as one Master of Hounds put it, "to bring out a second edition of cavalry charges over the pastures of the 'Shires." The Prince Regent's dilettante friend, Beau Brummell hunted occasionally at this time from Melton Mowbray, because it was "the thing to do." But, as Captain Jesse, his biographer, points out, finding it not to be a party game, he soon abandoned the practice. Contrast Brummell with that great and eccentric

Master of half-a-dozen different packs, Squire Osbaldeston, as described by "The Druid" in *Saddle and Sirloin* and you understand why, as Jesse says, "it did not suit Brummell's habits."

Melton Mowbray, which was the nearest town to Meynell's home, Quorndon Hall, was the elitist center of foxhunting England from the beginning. And there is none better to describe the gallant and aristocratic scene than that unparalleled authority on the sport, C.J. Apperley, better known as "Nimrod," scholar, coaching expert, horsemaster, hunting correspondent *par excellence* and unashamed name-dropper. His piece appearing here, which first featured in *The Quarterly Review* in the late 1820s, well shows his narrative power and passion for the sport, as well as his *hauteur*.

Nimrod's rival on the *Sporting* Magazine, the satirist, Robert Smith Surtees, who was as contemptuous of the nobility as "Nimrod" was adulatory of it, mercilessly lampooned the older man as "Pomponius Ego," the pedantic and snobbish hunting correspondent, who condescends, in *Handley Cross*, to visit John Jorrocks's motley pack, with a view to a scathing article. My example of Surtees's humor, taken from *Mr. Sponge's Sporting Tour*, shows Soapey Sponge in dire trouble for over-riding Lord Scamperdale's hounds.

The latter part of the nineteenth century boasted a "Nimrod," too. This was Captain Pennell-Elmhirst, who wrote under the name "Brooksby" and was regarded by many of his contemporaries to be superior to his predecessor at describing a run. With the scene again set in Leicestershire, here, too, is "Brooksby's" description of the Quorn's outstanding season of 1883–84.

Between "Nimrod" and "Brooksby" a more famous literary name adorned the hunting-field. Anthony Trollope's interest began during his post office inspectorship in the West of Ireland, his immediate superior there being an MFH. "Then and there began one of the great joys of my life; I have ever since been constant to the sport," he enthused. "Trollope's life as a hunting man and postal official," wrote a biographer, "not only awakened, almost by magic, his hidden powers, it also gave him the materials he was to need. . . . " The eight *Hunting Sketches*, which he wrote for the *Pall Mall Gazette*, were published in volume form, in 1865. *The Lady who Rides to Hounds* is the one given here.

Enclosures, railways, the advent of the automobile and many aspects of modern farming all combined to dictate a different style of foxhunting from Nimrod's mad gallop. Jumping into the twentieth century, this seems the right place to produce a piece of classic advice on how the foxhunter was advised to comport himself, and my chosen savant is the cavalry general, Geoffrey Brooke, who, before the Second World War, was regarded by many as almost a divine oracle on every branch of equitation.

Of all the pen-portraitists who have presented the hunting scene during this century surely the poet-venerer, Siegfried Sassoon, was the most

213

attractively evocative. In *Memoirs of a Foxhunting Man* he conjured, with remarkable economy of prose, the *whole* scene – the delights of a winter's morning, the characters, good and not so good, from stable-yard and kennels to manor-house, the bustle of the meet, the nervous anticipation of the draw and the hectic joy of the chase. I do not believe a cubhunting morning has ever been better portrayed than in the scene included here.

No anthology of the horse's involvement in the chase could be complete without an excerpt from the narrative poem, *Reynard the Fox* by the Poet Laureate, John Masefield. Here are two: his portrait of a high-mettled mare at the meet and his description of that flamboyant couple, the Riddens. To close I cannot do better, perhaps, than quote the following words from Masefield's introduction to *Reynard*:

Hunting makes more people happy than anything else I know. When people are happy together I am quite certain they build up something eternal, something both beautiful and divine, which weakens the power of all evil things upon this life of men and women.

HUNTING AND HAPPINESS

José Ortega y Gasset

1942

THERE IS ONE GENERAL vocation common to all men. All men, in fact, feel called on to be happy, but in each individual that general call becomes concrete in the more or less singular profile in which happiness appears to him. Happiness is a life dedicated to occupations for which that individual feels a singular vocation. Immersed in them, he misses nothing; the whole present fills him completely, free from desire and nostalgia. Laborious activities are performed, not out of any esteem for them, but rather for the result that follows them, but we give ourselves to vocational occupations for the pleasure of them, without concern for the subsequent profit. For that reason we want them never to end. We would like to eternalize, to perennialize them. And, really, once absorbed in a pleasurable occupation, we catch a starry glimpse of eternity.

So here is the human being suspended between two conflicting repertories of occupations: the laborious and the pleasing. It is moving and very sad to see how the two struggle in each individual. Work robs us of time to be happy, and pleasure gnaws away as much as possible at the time claimed by work. As soon as man discovers a chink or crack in the mesh of his work he escapes through it to the exercise of more enjoyable activities.

At this point a specific question, endowed with all the quasi-feminine appeal with which important questions are usually endowed, demands our attention. What kind of happy existence has man tried to attain when circumstances allowed him to do so? What have been the forms of the happy life? Even supposing that there have been many, innumerable, forms, have not some been clearly predominant? This is of the greatest importance, because in the happy occupations, again, the vocation of man is revealed. Nevertheless, we notice, surprised and scandalized, that this topic has never been investigated. Although it seems incredible, we lack completely a history of man's concept of what constitutes happiness.

Exceptional vocations aside, we confront the stupefying fact that, while obligatory occupations have undergone the most radical changes, the idea of the happy life has hardly varied throughout human evolution. In all times and places, as soon as man has enjoyed a moment's respite from his work, he has hastened, with illusion and excitement, to execute a limited and always similar repertory of enjoyable activities. Strange though this is, it is essentially true. To convince oneself, it is enough to proceed rather methodically, beginning by setting out the information.

What kind of man has been the least oppressed by work and the most easily able to engage in being happy? Obviously, the aristocratic man. Certainly the aristocrats too had their jobs, frequently the hardest of all: war, responsibilities of government, care of their own wealth. Only degenerate aristocracies stopped working, and complete idleness was short-lived because the degenerate aristocracies were soon swept away. But the work of the aristocrat, which looks more like "effort," was of such a nature that it left him a great deal of free time. And this is what concerns us: what does man do when, and in the extent that, he is free to do what he pleases? Now this greatly liberated man, the aristocrat, has always done the same things: raced horses or competed in physical exercises, gathered at parties, the feature of which is usually dancing, and engaged in conversation. But before any of those, and consistently more important than all of them has been . . . hunting. So that, if instead of speaking hypothetically we attend to the facts, we discover – whether we want to or not, with enjoyment or with anger – that the most appreciated, enjoyable occupation for the normal man has always been hunting. This is what kings and nobles have preferred to do: they have hunted. But it happens that the other social classes have done or wanted to do the same thing, to such an extent that one could almost divide the felicitous occupations of the normal man into four categories: hunting, dancing, racing, and conversing.

Choose at random any period in the vast and continuous flow of history and you will find that both men of the middle class and poor men have usually made hunting their happiest occupation. No one better represents the intermediary group between the Spanish nobility and Spanish bourgeosie of the second half of the sixteenth century, than the Knight in the Green Overcoat, whom Don Quixote meets. In the plan of his life which he formally expounds, this knight makes clear that "his exercises are hunting and fishing." A man already in his fifties, he has given up the hound and the falcon; a partridge decoy and a bold ferret are enough for him. This is the least glorious kind of hunting, and it is understandable that Don Quixote shortly afterwards, in a gesture of impatience that distorted his usual courtesy, scorned both beasts in comparison with the husky Moroccan lion, provided there by fortune for the voracity of his heroism.

The strongest proof of the extension throughout history of the enthusiasm for hunting lies in the contrary fact – namely, that with maximum frequency throughout the centuries not everyone has been allowed to hunt. A privilege has been made of this occupation, one of the most characteristic privileges of the powerful. Precisely because almost all men wanted to hunt and saw a possible happiness in doing so, it was necessary to stagger the exercise of the occupation; otherwise the game would have very soon disappeared, and neither the many nor the few would have been happy in that situation. It is not improbable, then, that even in the Neolithic period hunting acquired some of the aspects of a privilege. Neolithic man, who is already cultivating the soil, who has tamed animals and breeds them, does not need, as did his Paleolithic predecessor, to feed himself principally from his hunting. Freed of its obligatory nature, hunting is elevated to the rank of a sport. Neolithic man is already rich, and this means that he lives in authentic societies; thus in societies divided into classes, with their inevitable "upper" and "lower." It is difficult to imagine that hunting was not limited in one way or another.

Once we have underlined the almost universally privileged nature of the sport of hunting, it becomes clear to what extent this is no laughing matter, but rather, however strangely, a deep and permanent yearning in the human condition. It is as if we had poked a trigeminal nerve. From all the revolutionary periods in history, there leaps into view the lower

classes' fierce hatred for the upper classes because the latter had limited hunting – an indication of the enormous appetite which the lower classes had for the occupation. One of the causes of the French Revolution was the irritation the country people felt because they were not allowed to hunt, and consequently one of the first privileges which the nobles were obliged to abandon was this one. In all revolutions, the first thing that the "people" have done was to jump over the fences of the preserves or to tear them down, and in the name of social justice pursue the hare and the partridge. And this after the revolutionary newspapers, in their editorials, had for years and years been abusing the aristocrats for being so frivolous as to spend their time hunting.

About 1938, Jules Romains, a hardened writer of the Front Populaire, published an article venting his irritation with the workers, because they, having gained a tremendous reduction in the work-day and being in possession of long idle hours, had not learned to occupy themselves other than in the most uncouth form of hunting: fishing with a rod, the favorite sport of the good French bourgeois. The ill-humored writer was deeply irritated that a serious revolution had been achieved with no apparent result other than that of augmenting the number of rod fishermen.

The chronic fury of the people against the privilege of hunting is not, then, incidental or mere subversive insolence. It is thoroughly justified: in it the people reveal that they are men like those of the upper class and that the vocation, the felicitous illusion, of hunting, is normal in the human being. What is an error is to believe that this privilege has an arbitrary origin, that it is pure injustice and abuse of power. No; we shall presently see why hunting – not only the luxurious sporting variety, but any and all forms of hunting – essentially demands limitation and privilege.

Argue, fight as much as you like, over who should be the privileged ones, but do not pretend that squares are round and that hunting is not a privilege. What happens here is just what has happened with many other things. For two hundred years Western man has been fighting to eliminate privilege, which is stupid, because in certain orders privilege is inevitable and its existence does not depend on human will. It is to be hoped that the West will dedicate the next two centuries to fighting – there is no hope for a suspension of its innate pugnacity – to fighting, I say, for something less stupid, more attainable, and not at all extraordinary, such as a better selection of privileged persons.

In periods of an opposite nature, which were not revolutionary and in which, avoiding false utopias, people relied on things as they really were, not only was hunting a privilege respected by all, but those on the bottom demanded it of those on top, because they saw in hunting, especially in its superior forms – the chase, falconry, and the battle – a vigorous discipline and an opportunity to show courage, endurance, and skill, which are the attributes of the genuinely powerful person. Once a crown prince who had grown up in Rome went to occupy the Persian throne. Very soon he had to abdicate because the Persians could not accept a monarch who did not like hunting, a traditional and almost titular occupation of Persian gentlemen. The young man, apparently, had become interested in literature and was beyond hope.

Hunting, like all human occupations, has its different levels, and how little of the real work of hunting is suggested in words like diversion, relaxation, extertainment! A good hunter's way of hunting is a hard job which demands much from man: he must keep himself fit, face extreme fatigues, accept danger. It involves a complete code of ethics of the most distinguished design; the hunter who accepts the sporting code of ethics keeps his commandments in the greatest solitude, with no witnesses or audience other than the sharp peaks of the mountain, the roaming cloud, the stern oak, the trembling juniper, and the passing animal. In this way hunting resembles the monastic rule and the military order. So, in my presentation of it as what it is, as a form of happiness, I have avoided calling it pleasure. Doubtless in all happiness there is pleasure, but pleasure is the least of happiness. Pleasure is a passive occurrence, and it is appropriate to return to Aristotle, for whom happiness always clearly consisted in an act, in an energetic effort. That this effort, as it is being performed, produces pleasure is only coincidental, and, if you wish, one of the ingredients that comprise the situation. But along with the pleasures which exist in hunting there are innumerable annoyances. What right have we to take it by that handle and not by this one? The truth is that the important and appealing aspect of hunting is neither pleasure nor annoyance, but rather the very activity that comprises hunting.

Happy occupations, it is clear, are not merely pleasures; they are efforts, and real sports are effort. It is not possible, then, to distinguish work from sport by a plus or minus in fatigue. The difference is that sport is an effort made completely freely, for the pure enjoyment of it, while work is an obligatory effort made with an eye to the profit.

THE RIGHT SORT OF PEOPLE

George Bernard Shaw

1921

CAPTAIN SHOTOVER What's wrong with my house?
LADY UTTERWOOD Just what is wrong with a ship, papa. Wasn't it clever of Hastings to see that?

CAPTAIN SHOTOVER The man's a fool. There's nothing wrong with a ship.

LADY U Yes there is.

MRS HUSHABYE But what is it? Don't be aggravating, Addy.

LADY U Guess.

HECTOR Demons. Daughters of the witch of Zanzibar. Demons.

LADY U Not a bit. I assure you, all this house needs to make a sensible, healthy, pleasant house, with good appetites and sound sleep in it, is horses.

MRS H Horses! What rubbish!

LADY U Yes: horses. Why have we never been able to let this house? Because there are no proper stables. Go anywhere in England where there are natural, wholesome, contented, and really nice English people; and what do you always find? That the stables are the real centre of the household; and that if any visitor wants to play the piano the whole room has to be upset before it can be opened, there are so many things piled on it. I never lived until I learned to ride; and I shall never ride really well because I didn't begin as a child. There are only two classes in good society in England: the equestrian classes and the neurotic classes. It isn't mere convention; everybody can see that the people who hunt are the right people and the people who don't are the wrong ones.

CAPTAIN S There is some truth in this. My ship made a man of me; and a ship is the horse of the sea.

LADY U Exactly how Hastings explained your being a gentleman.

CAPTAIN S Not bad for a numskull. Bring the man here with you next time; I must talk to him.

LADY U Why is Randall such an obvious rotter? He is well bred; he has been at a public school and a university; he has been in the Foreign Office; he knows the best people and has lived all his life among them. Why is he so unsatisfactory, so contemptible? Why can't he get a valet to stay with him longer than a few months? Just because he is too lazy and pleasure-loving to hunt and shoot. . . .

THEY WENT WELL TO HOUNDS

Lady Augusta Fane

1926

WHO ARE THE BEST riders is one of the questions which is always a fruitful source of discussion and argument, and I am constantly asked who were the best women to hounds in my day. It is difficult to select individuals when so many rode hard and well. Before my time, Mary, Duchess of Hamilton and Mrs. Sam Garnett (late Marchioness of Winchester) were considered well in the front rank. The former was a strong rider, and would make her horse gallop, which is where so many women fail, and she had undeniable nerve. I have been told that she was a jealous rider, which kept her keen. Lady Winchester was small and very graceful on a horse. She sailed over the fences on her thoroughbred hunter, knew no fear, and went as well in Leicestershire as she had done in Ireland.

Whilst I was hunting I think the best all-round women, who were horsewomen as well as hard riders, were Baroness Max de Tuyll (Mrs. Bunbury), Mary, Lady Gerard, The Honourable Mrs. Lancelot Lowther, Lady Hamilton of Dalziel, Lady Georgina Curzon (Lady Howe), Mrs. Alfred Brocklehurst, The Honourable Mrs. Duberley, Miss Donnisthorpe, Miss Muir, Mrs. Burn (now Mrs. Clayton), and Miss Naylor (now Mrs. Straker).

Many women can ride well on one particular horse or on some days, but it is the woman who goes well every day she hunts, and can ride any horse over any country who counts. And the same thing is applicable to men. During the years I have written about, the men who were always amongst the first flight were: Messrs "Buck" Barclay, Alfred Brocklehurst, Peter Flower, Lord Lonsdale, Count Zorowski, Mr. Foxhall Keene, Major Philip Hubbersby, Teddy Brooks, Colonel Gordon Wilson and his brother Bertie Wilson, Major Algy Burnaby, Mr. Sam Hames, Mr. Charles McNeill, Captain W. de Winton, and last on the list, but always first in the field, Tom Firr.

I am told that some of the best women riders in Leicestershire to-day are Mrs. Jack Harrison, Miss Peggy Brocklehurst, both carrying on the hunting traditions so well started by their mothers; Violet, Duchess of Westminster and her sister, Mrs. Keld Fenwick, and Miss Rosemary Laycock, who was the only lady who saw the whole of the five hours hunt with the Belvoir last January (1926), which will count as one of the record runs for many a long year. The distance travelled was thirty-eight miles, so it was a fine performance for a girl of eighteen to have ridden the whole gallop and been up at the finish.

To the uninitiated it is a mystery why men and women are so passionately devoted to hunting and are ready to sacrifice time, money and everything to the sport they love. But if you are lucky enough to be born with a delight in riding, and can feel the blood racing through your veins from excitement when galloping and jumping fences, and add to that the interest of understanding the science of the game, you need not worry about the sneers of those poor creatures who do not possess your good luck. Probably their objection to the finest sport in the world comes from jealousy – which is the root of most objections! So what they say can be of no importance. Rather go down on your knees and thank God you "are not one of these."

Not for the lust of killing,
Not for the places of pride,
Not for the hate of the hunted
We English saddle and ride,
But because in the gift of our fathers
The blood in our veins that flows
Must answer for ever and ever
The challenge of "Yonder he goes".

1812: BRIGADIER GERARD KILLS THE FOX

Sir Arthur Conan Doyle

1896

IT IS INCREDIBLE the insolence of these English! What do you suppose Milord Wellington had done when he found that Massena had blockaded him and that he could not move his army? I might give you many guesses. You might say that he had raged, that he had despaired, that he had brought his troops together and spoken to them about glory and the fatherland before leading them to one last battle. No, Milord did none of these things. But he sent a fleet ship to England to bring him a number of fox-dogs, and he with his officers settled himself down to chase the fox. It is true what I tell you. Behind the lines of Torres Vedras these mad Englishmen made the fox-chase three days in the week. We had heard of it in the camp, and now I myself was to see that it was true.

For, along the road which I have described, there came these very dogs, thirty or forty of them, white and brown, each with its tail at the same angle, like the bayonets of the Old Guard. My faith, but it was a pretty sight! And behind and amidst them there rode three men with peaked caps and red coats, whom I understood to be the hunters. After them came many horsemen with uniforms of various kinds, stringing along the road in twos and threes, talking together and laughing. They did not seem to be going above a trot, and it appeared to me that it must indeed be a slow fox which they hoped to catch. However, it was their affair, not mine, and soon they had all passed my window and were out of sight. I waited and I watched, ready for any chance which might offer.

Presently an officer, in a blue uniform not unlike that of our flying artillery, came cantering down the road – an elderly, stout man he was, with grey side-whiskers. He stopped and began to talk with an orderly officer of dragoons, who waited outside the inn, and it was then that I

222

learned the advantage of the English which had been taught me. I could hear and understand all that was said.

"Where is the meet?" said the officer, and I thought that he was hungering for his bifstek. But the other answered him that it was near Altara, so I saw that it was a place of which he spoke.

"You are late, Sir George," said the orderly.

"Yes, I had a court-martial. Has Sir Stapleton Cotton gone?"

At this moment a window opened, and a handsome young man in a very splendid uniform looked out of it.

"Halloa, Murray!" said he. "These cursed papers keep me, but I will be at your heels."

"Very good, Cotton. I am late already, so I will ride on."

"You might order my groom to bring round my horse," said the young general at the window to the orderly below, while the other went on down the road.

The orderly rode away to some outlying stable, and then in a few minutes there came a smart English groom with a cockade in his hat, leading by the bridle a horse – and, oh, my friends, you have never known the perfection to which a horse can attain until you have seen a first-class English hunter. He was superb: tall, broad, strong, and yet as graceful and agile as a deer. Coal black he was in colour, and his neck, and his shoulder, and his quarters and his fetlocks – how can I describe him all to you? The sun shone upon him as on polished ebony, and he raised his hoofs in a little playful dance so lightly and prettily, while he tossed his mane and whinnied with impatience. Never have I seen such a mixture of strength and beauty and grace. I had often wondered how the English Hussars had managed to ride over the Chasseurs of the Guards in the affair at Astorga, but I wondered no longer when I saw the English horses.

There was a ring for fastening bridles at the door of the inn, and the groom tied the horse there while he entered the house. In an instant I had seen the chance which Fate had brought to me. Were I in that saddle I should be better off than when I started. Even Voltigeur could not compare with this magnificent creature. To think is to act with me. In one instant I was down the ladder and at the door of the stable. The next I was out and the bridle was in my hand. I bounded into the saddle. Somebody, the master or the man, shouted wildly behind me. What cared I for his shouts! I touched the horse with my spurs, and he bounded forward with such a spring that only a rider like myself could have sat him. I gave him his head and let him go – it did not matter to me where, so long as we left this inn far behind us. He thundered away across the vineyards, and in a very few minutes I had placed miles between myself and my pursuers. They could no longer tell, in that wild country, in which direction I had gone. I knew that I was safe, and so, riding to the top of a small hill, I drew my pencil and note-book from my pocket, and proceeded to make plans of those camps which I could see, and to draw the outline of the country.

He was a dear creature upon whom I sat, but it was not easy to draw upon his back, for every now and then his two ears would cock, and he would start and quiver with impatience. At first I could not understand this trick of his, but soon I observed that he only did it when a peculiar noise – "Yoy, yoy, yoy" – came from somewhere among the oak-woods beneath us. And then suddenly this strange cry changed into a most terrrible screaming, with the frantic blowing of a horn. Instantly he went mad – this horse. His eyes blazed. His mane bristled. He bounded from the earth and bounded again, twisting and turning in a frenzy. My pencil flew one way and my note-book another. And then, as I looked down into the valley, an extraordinary sight met my eyes. The hunt was streaming down it. The fox I could not see, but the dogs were in full cry, their noses down, their tails up, so close together that they might have been one great yellow and white moving carpet. And behind them rode the horsemen – my faith, what a sight! Consider every type which a great army could show: some in hunting dress, but the most in uniforms; blue dragoons, red dragoons, red-trousered hussars, green riflemen, artillerymen, gold-slashed lancers, and most of all red, red, red, for the infantry officers ride as hard as the cavalry. Such a crowd, some well mounted, some ill, but all flying along as best they might, the subaltern as good as the general, jost-ling and pushing, spurring and driving, with every thought thrown to the winds save that they should have the blood of this absurd fox! Truly, they are an extraordinary people, the English! But I had little time to watch the hunt or to marvel at these islanders, for, of all these mad creatures, the very horse upon which I sat was the maddest. You understand that he was himself a hunter, and that the crying of these dogs was to him what the call of a cavalry trumpet in the street yonder would be to me. It thrilled him. It drove him wild. Again and again he bounded into the air, and then, seizing the bit between his teeth, he plunged down the slope, and galloped after the dogs. I swore, and tugged, and pulled, but I was powerless. This English general rode his horse with a snaffle only, and the beast had a mouth of iron. It was useless to pull him back. One might as well try to keep a Grenadier from a wine bottle. I gave it up in despair, and settling down in the saddle, I prepared for the worst which could befall.

What a creature he was! Never have I felt such a horse between my knees. His great haunches gathered under him with every stride, and he shot forward ever faster and faster, stretched like a greyhound, while the wind beat in my face and whistled past my ears. I was wearing our undress jacket, a uniform simple and dark in itself – though some figures give distinction to any uniform – and I had taken the precaution to remove the long panache from my busby. The result was that, amidst the mixture of costumes in the hunt, there was no reason why mine should attract atten-tion, or why these men, whose thoughts were all with the chase, should give any heed to me. The idea that a French officer might be riding with them was too absurd to enter their minds. I laughed as I rode, for, indeed, amid all the danger, there was something of the comic in the situation.

I have said that the hunters were very unequally mounted, and so, at the end of a few miles, instead of being one body of men, like a charging regiment, they were scattered over a considerable space, the better riders well up to the dogs, and the others trailing away behind. Now, I was as good a rider as any, and my horse was the best of them all, and so you can imagine that it was not long before he carried me to the front. And when I saw the dogs streaming over the open, and the red-coated huntsmen behind them, and only seven or eight horsemen between us, then it was that the strangest thing of all happened, for I, too, went mad – I, Etienne Gerard! In a moment it came upon me, this spirit of sport, this desire to excel, this hatred of the fox. Accursed animal, should he then defy us? Vile robber, his hour was come! Ah, it is a great feeling, this feeling of sport, my friends, this desire to trample the fox under the hoofs of your horse. I have made the fox-chase with the English. I have also, as I may tell you some day, fought the box-fight with the Bustler, of Bristol. And I say to you that this sport is a wonderful thing – full of interest as well as madness.

The farther we went the faster galloped my horse, and soon there were but three men as near the dogs as I was. All thought of fear of discovery had vanished. My brain throbbed, my blood ran hot – only one thing upon earth seemed worth living for, and that was to overtake this infernal fox. I passed one of the horsemen – a Hussar like myself. There were only two in front of me now – the one in a black coat, the other the blue artilleryman whom I had seen at the inn. His grey whiskers streamed in the wind, but he rode magnificently. For a mile or more we kept in this order, and then, as we galloped up a steep slope, my lighter weight brought me to the front. I passed them both, and when I reached the crown I was riding level with the little, hard-faced English huntsman. In front of us were the dogs, and then, a hundred paces beyond them, was a brown wisp of a thing, the fox itself, stretched to the uttermost. The sight of him fired my blood. "Aha, we have you then, assassin!" I cried, and shouted my encouragement to the huntsman. I waved my hand to show him that there was one upon whom he could rely.

And now there were only the dogs between me and my prey. These dogs, whose duty it is to point out the game, were now rather a hindrance than a help to us, for it was hard to know how to pass them. The huntsman felt the difficulty as much as I, for he rode behind them and could make no progress towards the fox. He was a swift rider, but wanting in enterprise. For my part, I felt that it would be unworthy of the Hussars of Conflans if I could not overcome such a difficulty as this. Was Etienne Gerard to be stopped by a herd of fox-dogs? It was absurd. I gave a shout and spurred my horse.

"Hold hard, Sir! Hold hard!" cried the huntsman.

He was uneasy for me, this good old man, but I reassured him by a wave and smile. The dogs opened in front of me. One or two may have been hurt, but what would you have? The egg must be broken for the omelette. I could hear the huntsman shouting his congratulations behind me. One more effort, and the dogs were all behind me. Only the fox was in front.

Ah, the joy and pride of that moment! To know that I had beaten the English at their own sport. Here were three hundred all thirsting for the life of this animal, and yet it was I who was about to take it. I thought of my comrades of the light cavalry brigade, of my mother, of the Emperor, of France. I had brought honour to each and all. Every instant brought me nearer to the fox. The moment for action had arrived, so I unsheathed my sabre. I waved it in the air, and the brave English all shouted behind me.

Only then did I understand how difficult is this fox-chase, for one may cut again and again at the creature and never strike him once. He is small, and turns quickly from a blow. At every cut I heard those shouts of encouragement behind me, and they spurred me to yet another effort. And then at last the supreme moment of my triumph arrived. In the very act of turning I caught him fair with such another backhanded cut as that with which I killed the aide-de-camp of the Emperor of Russia. He flew into two pieces, his head one way and his tail another. I looked back and waved the blood-stained sabre in the air. For the moment I was exalted – superb!

Ah! how I should have loved to have waited to have received the congratulations of these generous enemies. There were fifty of them in sight, and not one of them who was not waving his hand and shouting. They are not really such a phlegmatic race, the English. A gallant deed in war or in sport will always warm their hearts. As to the old huntsman, he was the nearest to me, and I could see with my own eyes how overcome he was by what he had seen. He was like a man paralysed – his mouth open, his hand, with outspread fingers, raised in the air. For a moment my inclination was to return and embrace him. But already the call of duty was sounding in my ears, and these English, in spite of all the fraternity which exists among sportsmen, would certainly have made me prisoner. There was no hope for my mission now, and I had done all that I could do. I could see the lines of Massena's camp no very great distance off, for, by a lucky chance, the chase had taken us in that direction. I turned from the dead fox, saluted with my sabre, and galloped away.

But they would not leave me so easily, these gallant huntsmen. I was the fox now, and the chase swept bravely over the plain. It was only at the moment when I started for the camp that they could have known that I was a Frenchman, and now the whole swarm of them were at my heels. We were within gunshot of our pickets before they would halt, and then they stood in knots and would not go away, but shouted and waved their hands at me. No, I will not think that it was in enmity. Rather would I fancy that a glow of admiration filled their breasts, and that their one desire was to embrace the stranger who had carried himself so gallantly and well.

NOT FOR BEAU BRUMMELL

Captain Jesse

1844

THOUGH BRUMMELL WAS so much at Belvoir, and kept a stud of horses there, he was never a "Melton man"; and his friends, as well as everyone else, were amazingly astonished when he joined in the pleasures of the chase; for, like many other gentlemen, he did not like it: it did not suit his habits, and his servant could never get him up in time to join the hounds if it was a distant meet: but even if the meet was near, and they found quickly, he only rode a few fields, and then shaped his course in an opposite direction, or paid a visit to the nearest farmhouse, to satisfy his enormous appetite for bread-and-cheese. I have heard him, but many years after, laugh amazingly over these incidents of his Melton days, and say, in his usual droll way, that he "could not bear to have his tops and leathers splashed by the greasy, galloping farmers."

SQUIRE OSBALDESTON

"The Druid"

1870

WHEN SHALL WE SEE again such a man as Mr. Osbaldeston, on such a horse as Assheton, with three such hounds as Tarquin, Furrier and Vaulter at his side, and two such whips as Tom Sebright and Dick Burton? It was a rare combination of human and brute talent. The ambition of The Squire from his earliest to his latest day was to be talked about. Modern men have the same aspiration but the means are very easy and sybaritic in comparison. They don't care what prices they give for a hunter, a race-horse, a hack or a yacht, provided it is duly chronicled. The Squire, on the contrary, trusted, not to pocket, but to hand and eye for his fame. He never rested till he was at the head of the hunting, the pigeon-shooting, the steeplechasing, the cricket and the billiard worlds. Now it is enough for a man to be prominent in one branch of sporting science, but Mr. Osbaldeston aspired to nearly all, and not a soul breathing could touch him all round. Cue, bridle, trigger, bat, oar and boxing-gloves came alike easy to him. The Meltonians could not outride him, and they crabbed him to make up for it. For society he cared little, and the saddle

THE WHISSENDINE.

was the easy chair he loved. When he got home after a short day he was quite ready to have a second pack out if the humour suited him, and when he got home after a long one, he liked his chop and a pint of port, a chat with his friend Gully, and so to bed. Sport was in fact his business, and when he was fifty-four and generally content to ride 10st. 9lbs. he wasted to ride his King Charles at 8st. 7lbs. in the Two Thousand. A keen limner describes him, even at that age, as "short and awkward, shrivelled and shrunk, with round shoulders and a limping walk, ill-clothed in a brown frock coat with velvet collar, loose grey trousers and cloth boots". Throughout his life he was singularly light of tongue, and the last time we ever saw him, when he was drawn about in a bath-chair on the beach at Brighton, the unruly member was going with its pristine vigour.

HIGH LEICESTERSHIRE IN THE 1820s

"Nimrod"

1828

. . . AT THE END of 19 minutes the hounds come to a fault, and for a moment the fox has a chance; in fact, they have been pressed upon by the horses, and have rather over-run the scent. "What a pity!" says one. "What a shame!" cries another; alluding, perhaps, to a young one, who would and could have gone still faster. "You may thank yourselves for this," exclaims Osbaldeston, well up at the time, Ashton looking fresh; but only fourteen men of the two hundred are to be counted; all the rest *coming*. At one blast of the horn, the hounds are back to the point at which the scent has failed, Jack Stevens being in his place to turn them. "*Yo do it! Pastime*," says the Squire, as she feathers her stern down the hedge-row, looking more beautiful than ever. She speaks! "Worth a thousand, by Jupiter!" cries John White, looking over his left shoulder as he sends both spurs into Euxton, delighted to see only four more of the field are up. Our Snob, however, is amongst them. He has "gone a good one," and his countenance is expressive of delight, as he urges his horse to his speed to get again into a front place.

The pencil of the painter is now wanting; even his pencil would be worth little. What a country is before him! – what a panorama does it represent! Not a field of less than forty – some a hundred acres – and no more signs of the plough than in the wilds of Siberia. See the hounds in a body that might be covered by a damask table-cloth – every stern down, and every head up, for there is no need of stooping, the scent lying breast high. But the crash! – the music! – how to describe these? Reader, there is no crash now, and not much music. It is the tinker that makes great noise over a little work, but at the pace these hounds are going there is no time for babbling. Perchance one hound in five may throw his tongue as he goes to inform his comrades, as it were, that the villain is on before them, and most musically do the light notes of Vocal and Venus fall on the ear of those who may be within reach to catch them. But who is so fortunate in this second burst, nearly as terrible as the first? Our fancy supplies us again, and we think we could name them all. If we look to the left, nearly abreast of the pack, we see six men going gallantly, and quite as straight as the hounds themselves are going; and on the right are four more, riding equally well, though the former have rather the best of it, owing to having had the inside of the hounds at the last two turns, which must be placed to the chapter of accidents. A short way in the rear, by no means too much so to enjoy this brilliant run, are the rest of the *élite* of the field, who had come up at the first check; and a few who, thanks to the goodness of their steeds, and their determination to be with the hounds, appear as if dropped from the clouds. Some, however, begin to show symptoms of distress. Two horses are seen loose in the distance – a report is flying about that one of the field is badly hurt, and something is heard of a collar-bone being broken, others say it is a leg; but the pace is *too good* to inquire. A cracking of rails is now heard, and one gentleman's horse is to be seen resting, nearly balanced, across one of them, his rider being on his back in the ditch, which is on the landing side. "Who is he?" says Lord Brudenel, to Jack Stevens. "Can't tell, my Lord; but I thought it was a queerish place when I came o'er it before him." It is evidently a case of peril, but the pace is *too good* to afford help . . .

Up to this time, Snob has gone quite in the first flight; the "dons" begin to eye him, and, when an opportunity offers, the question is asked – "Who is that fellow on the little bay horse?" "Don't know him," says Mr. Little Gilmour (a fourteen-stone Scotchman, by-the-by), ganging gallantly to his hounds. – "He can ride," exclaims Lord Rancliffe. "A tip-top provincial, depend upon it," added Lord Plymouth, going quite at his ease on a thorough-bred nag, three stone above his weight, and in perfect racing trim. Animal nature, however, will cry "enough," how good soever she may be, if unreasonable man press her beyond the point. The line of scent lies right athwart a large grass ground (as a field is termed in Leicestershire), somewhat on the ascent; abounding in ant-hills, or hillocks, peculiar to old grazing land, and thrown up by the plough, some hundred years since, into rather high ridges, with deep, holding furrows between each. The fence at the top is impracticable – Meltonicé, "a stopper"; nothing for it but a gate, leading into a broad green lane, high and strong, with deep, slippery ground on each side of it. "Now for the timber-jumper," cries Osbaldeston, pleased to find himself upon Ashton. "For Heaven's sake, take care of my hounds, in case they may throw up in the lane." Snob is here in the best of company, and that moment perhaps the happiest of his life; but, not satisfied with his situation, wishing to out-Herod Herod, and to have a fine story to tell when he gets home, he pushes to his speed on ground on which all regular Leicestershire men are careful, and the death-warrant of the little bay horse is signed. It is true he gets first to the gate, and has no idea of opening it; sees it contains five new and strong bars, that will neither bend nor break; has a great idea of a fall, but no idea of refusing; presses his hat firmly on his head, and gets his whip-hand at liberty to give the good little nag a refresher; but all at once he perceives it will not do. When attempting to collect him for the effort, he finds his mouth dead and his neck stiff; fancies he hears something like a wheezing in his throat; and discovering quite unexpectedly that the gate would open, wisely avoids a fall, which was *booked* had he attempted to leap it. He pulls up, then, at the gate; and as he places the hook of his whip under the latch, John White goes over it close to the hinge-post, and Captain Ross, upon Clinker, follows him. The Reviewer then walks through.

The scene now shifts. On the other side of the lane is a fence of this description: it is a newly planted hedge, abounding in strong growers, as they are called, and a yawning ditch on the further side; but, as is peculiar to Leicestershire and Northamptonshire, a considerable portion of the blackthorn, left uncut, leans outwards from the hedge, somewhat about breast-high. This large fence is taken by all now with the hounds – some to the right and some to the left of the direct line; but the little bay horse would have no more of it. Snob puts him twice at it, and manfully too; but the wind is out of him, and he has no power to rise. Several scrambles, but only one fall, occur at this rasper, all having nearly enough of the killing pace; and a mile and a half farther, the second horses are fallen in with, just in the nick of time. A short check from the stain of sheep makes everything comfortable; and, the Squire having hit off his fox like a workman, thirteen men, out of two hundred, are fresh mounted, and with the hounds, which settle to the scent again at a truly killing pace.

"Hold hard, Holyoake!" exclaims Mr. Osbaldeston (now mounted on Clasher), knowing what double-quick time he would be marching to, with fresh pipes to play upon, and the crowd well shaken off; "*pray* don't press 'em too hard, and we shall be sure to kill our fox. *Have at him there*, Abigail and Fickle, good bitches – see what a head they are carrying! I'll bet a thousand they kill him." The country appears better and better. "He's taking a capital line," exclaims Sir Harry Goodricke, as he points out to Sir James Musgrave two young Furrier hounds, who are particularly dist-inguishing themselves at the moment. "Worth a dozen Reform Bills," shouts Sir Francis Burdett, sitting erect upon Sampson, and putting his head straight at a yawner. "We shall have the Whissendine brook," cries Mr. Maher, who knows every field in the country, "for he is making straight for Teigh." "And a bumper too, after last night's rain," holloas Captain Berkeley, determined to get first to four stiff rails in a corner. "So much the better," says Lord Alvanley, I like a bumper at all times." "A fig for the Whissendine," cries Lord Gardner; "I am on the best water-jumper in my stable."

The prophecy turns up. Having skirted Ranksborough gorse, the villain has nowhere to stop short of Woodwell-head cover, which he is pointing for; and in ten minutes, or less, the brook appears in view. It is even with its banks, and, as

"*smooth glides the water where the brook is deep,*"

its deepness was pretty certain to be fathomed.

"Yooi, OVER he goes!" holloas the Squire, as he perceives Joker and Jewel plunging into the stream, and Red-rose shaking herself on the opposite bank. Seven men, out of thirteen, take it in their stride; three stop short, their horses refusing the first time, but come well over the second; and three find themselves in the middle of it. The gallant Frank Forester is among the latter; and having been requested that morning to wear a friend's new red coat, to take off the gloss and glare of the shop, he accomplishes the task to perfection in the bluish-black mud of the Whissendine, only then subsiding after a three days' flood. "Who is that under his horse in the brook?" inquires that good sportsman and fine rider, Mr. Green, of Rolleston, whose noted old mare had just skimmed over the water like a swallow on a summer's evening. "It's Middleton Biddulph," says one. "Pardon me," cries Mr. Middleton Biddulph; "Middleton Biddulph is here, *and here he means to be!*" "Only Dick Christian, answers Lord Forester, "and it is nothing new to him." "But he'll be drowned," exclaims Lord Kinnaird. "I shouldn't wonder," observes Mr. William Coke. But the pace is *too good* to inquire.

The fox does his best to escape: he threads hedgerows, tries the out-buildings of a farm-house, and once turns so short as nearly to run his foil;

but – the perfection of the thing – the hounds turn shorter than he does, as much as to say – *die you shall*. The pace has been awful for the last twenty minutes. Three horses are blown to a stand-still, and few are going at their ease. "Out upon this great carcass of mine! no horse that was ever foaled can live under it at this pace, and over this country," says one of the best of the welter-weights, as he stands over his four-hundred-guinea chestnut, then rising from the ground after giving him a heavy fall – his tail nearly erect in the air, his nostrils violently distended, and his eye almost fixed. "Not hurt, I hope," exclaims Mr. Maxse, to *somebody* whom he gets a glimpse of through the openings of a tall quickset hedge which is between them, coming neck and croup into the adjoining field, from the top bar of a high, hog-backed stile. His eye might have been spared the unpleasing sight, had not his ear been attracted to a sort of *procumbit-humi-bos* sound of a horse falling to the ground on his back, the bone of his left hip indenting the greensward within two inches of his rider's thigh. It is young Peyton, who, having missed his second horse at the check, had been going nearly half the way in distress; but from nerve and pluck, perhaps peculiar to Englishmen in the hunting field, but very peculiar to himself, got within three fields of the end of this brilliant run. The fall was all but a certainty; for it was the third stiff timber-fence that had unfortunately opposed him, after his horse's wind had been pumped out by the pace; but he was too good to refuse them, and his horse knew better than to do so.

The *Aenid* of Virgil ends with a death, and a chase is not complete without it. The fox dies within half a mile of Woodwell-head cover, evidently his point from the first; the pack pulling him down in the middle of a large grass field, every hound but one at his brush. Jack Stevens with him in his hands would be a subject worthy of Edwin Landseer himself: a blackthorn, which has laid hold of his cheek, has besmeared his upper garments with blood, and one side of his head and cap is cased in mud, by a fall he has had in a lane, his horse having alighted in the ruts from a high flight of rails; but he has ridden the same horse throughout the run, and has handled him so well he could have gone two miles farther, if the chase had been continued so long. Osbaldeston's *whohoop* might have been heard to Cottesmore, had the wind set in that direction, and every man present is ecstatic with delight. "Quite the cream of the thing, I suppose," says Lord Gardner, a very promising young one, at this time fresh in Leicestershire. "The cream of everything in the shape of fox-hunting," observes that excellent sportsman Sir James Musgrave, looking at that moment at his watch. "Just ten miles as the crow flies, in one hour and two minutes, with but two trifling checks, over the finest country in the world. "*What superb hounds are these!*" added the Baronet, as he turned his horse's head to the wind. "You are right," says Colonel Lowther, "they are perfect. I wish my father had seen them do their work to-day." Some of the field now come up, who could not live in the first flight; but as there is no jealousy here, they congratulate each other on the fine day's sport . . .

A large party dine this evening at the Old Club, where, of course, this fine run is discussed, and the following accurate description of it is given by one of the oldest members, a true friend to fox-hunting, and to all mankind as well:- "We found him," said he, "at Ashby Pasture, and got away with him, up wind, at a slapping pace over Burrow Hill, leaving Thorpe Trussells to the right, when a trifling check occurred. He then pointed for Ranksborough gorse, which some feared and others hoped he might hang in a little, but he was too good to go near it. Leaving that on his right also, he crossed the brook to Whissendine, going within half a mile of the village, and then he had nothing for it but to fly. That magnificent country, in the direction of Teigh, was open to him, and he showed that he had the courage to face it. Leaving Teigh on the right, Woodwell-head was his point, and in two more fields he would have reached it. Thus we found him in Quorn country; ran him over the finest part of Lord Lonsdale's, and killed him on the borders of the Belvoir. Sir Bellingham Graham's hounds once gave us just such another tickler, from the same place, and in the same time, when the field were nearly as much beaten as they were to-day."

But we have left Snob in the lane, who, after casting a longing eye towards his more fortunate companions, who were still keeping well in with the hounds, throws the rein over the neck of the good little bay horse, and, walking by his side, that he may recover his wind, inquires his way to Melton. Having no one to converse with, he thus soliloquises as he goes:- "What a dolt have I been, to spend five hundred a year on my stable, in any country but this! But stop a little: how is it that *I*, weighing but eleven stone four pounds with my saddle, and upon my best horse, an acknowledged good one in my own country, could neither go so fast nor so long as that heavy fellow Maxse; that still heavier Lord Alvanley; and that monster Tom Edge, who, they tell me, weighs eighteen stone, at least, in the scales?" At this moment, a bridle-gate opens in the lane, and a gentleman in scarlet appears, with his countenance pale and wan, and expressive of severe pain. It is he who had been dug out of the ditch in which Jack Stevens had left him, his horse having fallen upon him, after being suspended on the rail, and broken three of his ribs. Feeling extremely unwell, he is glad to meet with Snob, who is going his road – to Melton – and who offers him all the assistance in his power. Snob also repeats to him his soliloquy, at least the sum and substance of it, on which the gentleman, – recovering a little from his faintness by the help of a glass of brandy and water at the village, – thus makes his comment: – "I think, sir, you are a stranger in this part of the world." "Certainly," replied Snob, "It is my first appearance in Leicestershire." "I observed you in the run," continued the wounded sportsman; "and very well you went up to the time I fell, but particularly so to the first check. You then rode to a leader, and made an excellent choice; but after that period, I saw you not only attempting a line of your own, but taking liberties with your horse, and anticipated the fate you have met with. If you remain with us long, you will be sure to find out that riding to hounds in Leicestershire is different from what it is in most other counties in England, and requires a little apprenticeship. There is much choice of ground; and if this choice be not judiciously made, and coupled with a cautious observance of pace, a horse is beaten in a very short time. If you doubt my creed, look to the events of this memorable day." Snob thanks him for his hints, and notes them in his book of memory.

The fame of Snob and his little bay horse reaches Melton before he walks in himself. "That provincial fellow did not go amiss to-day," says one. "Who was that rural-looking man on a neatish bay horse – all but his tail – who was so well with us at the first check?" asks another, who himself could not get to the end, although he went "a good one" three parts of the way. There is no one present to answer these questions; but the next day, and the next, Snob is in the field again, and again in a good place. Further inquiries are made, and satisfactory information obtained. On the fourth day, a nod from one – a "how do you?" from another – "a fine morning," from a third – are tokens good-humouredly bestowed upon him by some of the leading men; and on the fifth day, after a capital half-hour, in which he had again distinguished himself, a noble *bon-vivant* thus addresses him, – "Perhaps, sir, you would like to dine with me to-day; I shall be happy to see you at seven."

"Covers," he writes next day to some friend in his remote western province, "were laid for eight, the favourite number of our late king; and, perhaps, his Majesty never sat down to a better-dressed dinner in his life. To my surprise, the subject of fox-hunting was named but once during the evening, and that was when an order was given that a servant might be sent to inquire after a gentleman who had had a severe fall that morning over some timber; and to ask, by the way, if Dick Christian came alive out of a ditch, in which he had been left with a clever young thorough-bred one on the top of him." The writer proceeds to describe an evening in which wit and music were more thought of than wine – and presenting, in all respects, a perfect contrast to the old notions of a fox-hunting society:- but we have already trespassed on delicate ground.

It is this union of the elegant repose of life with the energetic sports of the field that constitutes the charm of Melton Mowbray; and who can wonder that young gentlemen, united by profession should be induced to devote a season or two to such a course of existence? We must not, however, leave the subject without expressing our regret that resorting, *year after year*, to this metropolis of the chase should seem at all likely to become a fashion with persons whose hereditary possessions lie far from its allurements. It is all very well to go through the training of the acknowledged school of the craft; but the country gentleman, who understands his duties, and in what the real permanent pleasure of life exists, will never settle down into a regular Meltonian. He will feel that his first concern is with his own proper district, and seek the recreations of the chase, if his taste for them outlives the first heyday of youth, among the scenes, however comparatively rude, in which his natural place has been appointed.

SOAPEY SPONGE WITH LORD SCAMPERDALE'S HOUNDS

R.S. Surtees

1852

IT WAS ONE OF Parvo's going days; indeed, it was that that old Leather and he had quarreled about – Parvo wanting to follow the hounds, while Leather wanted to wait for his master. And Parvo had the knack of going, as well as the occasional inclination. Although such a dray-horse-looking animal, he could throw the ground behind him amazingly; and the deep-holding clay in which he now found himself was admirably suited to his

short powerful legs and enormous stride. The consequence was that he was very soon up with the hindmost horsemen. These he soon passed, and was presently among those who ride hard when there is nothing to stop them. Such time as these sportsmen could now spare from looking out ahead was devoted to Sponge, whom they eyed with the utmost astonishment, as if he had dropped from the clouds.

A stranger – a real out-and-out stranger – had not visited their remote regions since the days of poor Nimrod. "Who could it be?". But "the pace", as Nimrod used to say, "was too good, to enquire". A little further on, and Sponge drew up on the great guns of the hunt – the men who ride *to* hounds, and not *after* them; the same who had criticized him through the fence – Mr. Wake, Mr. Fossick, Parson Blossomnose, Mr. Fyle, Lord Scamperdale, Jack himself, and others. Great was their astonishment at the apparition, and incoherent the observations they dropped as they galloped on.

"It wasn't Wash, after all", whispered Fyle into Blossomnose's ear, as they rode together through a gate.

"No-o-o", replied the nose, eyeing Sponge intently.

"What a coat!" whispered one.

"Jacket", replied the other.

"Lost his brush", observed a third, winking at Sponge's docked tail.

"He's going to ride over us all", snapped Mr. Fossick, whom Sponge passed at a hand-canter, as the former was blobbing and floundering about the deep ruts leading out of a turnip-field.

"He'll catch it just now", said Mr. Wake, eyeing Sponge drawing up on his lordship and Jack, as they led the field as usual. Jack being at a respectful distance behind his great patron, espied Sponge first; and having taken a good stare at him through his formidable spectacles, to satisfy himself it was nobody he knew – a stare that Sponge returned as well as a man without spectacles can return the stare of one with . . . Jack spurred his horse up to his lordship, and, rising in his stirrups, shot into his ear:

"Why, here's the man on the cow!" adding "*It isn't Washey!*"

"Who the deuce is it, then?" asked his lordship, looking over his left shoulder, as he kept galloping on in the wake of his huntsman.

"Don't know", replied Jack; "never saw him before".

"Nor I", said his lordship, with an air, as much as to say, "It makes no matter".

His lordship, though well mounted, was not exactly on the sort of horse for the country they were in; while Mr. Sponge, in addition to being on the very animal for it, had the advantage of the horse having gone the first part of the run without a rider: so Multum in Parvo, whether Mr. Sponge wished it or not, insisted on being as far forward as he could get. The more Sponge pulled and hauled, the more determined the horse was; till, having thrown both Jack and his lordship in the rear, he made for old Frostyface, the huntsman, who was riding well up to the still flying pack.

"Hold hard, sir! For God's sake, hold hard!" screamed Frosty, who knew by intuition there was a horse behind, as well as he knew there was a man shooting in front, who, in all probability, had headed the fox.

"HOLD HARD, sir!" roared he, as, yawning and boring and shaking his head, Parvo dashed through the now yelping scattered pack, making straight for a stiff new gate, which he smashed through, just as a circus pony smashes through a paper hoop.

"*Hoo-ray!*" shouted Jack Spraggon, on seeing the hounds were safe. "Hoo-ray for the tailor!"

"Billy Button himself!" exclaimed his lordship; adding; "Never saw such a thing in my life!"

"Who the deuce is he?" asked Blossomnose, in the full glow of pulling-five-year-old exertion.

"Don't know", replied Jack; adding, "He's a shaver, whoever he is". Meanwhile the frightened hounds were scattered right and left.

"I'll lay a guinea he's one of those confounded writing chaps", observed Fyle, who had been handled rather roughly by one of the tribe, who had dropped "quite promiscuously" upon a field where he was, just as Sponge had done with Lord Scamperdale's.

"Shouldn't wonder", replied his lordship, eyeing Sponge's vain endeavours to turn the chesnut, and thinking how he would pitch into him when he came up. "By Jove", added his lordship, "if the fellow had taken the whole country round, he couldn't have chosen a worse spot for such an exploit; for there never *is* any scent over here. *See!* not a hound can own it. Old Harmony herself throws up!"

The whips again are in their places, turning the astonished pack to Frostyface, who sets off on a casting expedition. The field, as usual, sit looking on; some blessing Sponge; some wondering who he was; others looking what o'clock it is; some dismouting and looking at their horses' feet.

"Thank you, Mr. Brown Boots!" exclaimed his lordship, as by dint of biting and spurring, Sponge at length worked the beast round, and came sneaking back in the face of the whole field. "Thank you, Mister Brown Boots", repeated he, taking off his hat and bowing very low. "Very much obliged to you, Mr. Brown Boots. Most particklarly obl*e*ged to you, Mr. Brown Boots", with another low bow. "Hang'd obl*e*ged to you, Mr.

Brown Boots! D--n *you*, Mr. Brown Boots!", continued his lordship, looking at Sponge as if he would eat him.

"Beg pardon, sir", blurted Sponge; "my horse—"

"Hang your horse!" screamed his lordship; "it wasn't your horse that headed the fox was it?"

"Beg pardon – couldn't help it; I—"

"Couldn't help it. Hang your helps – you're *always* doing it, sir. You could stay at home, sir – I s'pose, sir – couldn't you, sir? eh, sir?"

Sponge was silent.

"See, sir!" continued his lordship, pointing to the mute pack now following the huntsman. "You've lost us our fox, sir – *yes*, sir – lost us our fox, sir. D'ye call that nothin', sir? If you don't, I do, you perpendicular-looking Puseyite pig-jobber! By Jove! You think because I'm a lord, and can't swear, or use coarse language, that you may do what you like – but I'll take my hounds home, sir – yes, sir, I'll take my hounds home, sir".

So saying, his lordship roared "HOME" to Frostyface, adding in an undertone to the first whip, "*bid him go to Furzingfield gorse*".

THIRTY GOOD MINUTES FROM GADDESBY SPINNEY

"Brooksby"

1884

TWENTY COUPLE, young and old, are driving down the wide green slope – the old ladies straining madly on the ravishing scent, the youngsters catching the new excitment that they had never felt to the full before.

We ought to know this bridle path, and should have learned to open its easy gates ere now. But the three leaders find no time nor need to stop – so why should reader and I?

The fence in the valley is but a flying trifle; though little clue can we gather of its make and width till we see that MR. H.T. BARCLAY is safely landed – and we wonder why his horse should have taken no note of the grass-grown rivulet beyond, which ours emphasized with so pronounced a peck on his knees and nose. Up the brow the next is a fair, pleasant jump, and so is the following one. But "Ware wire!" sends a chill down our backbone as we approach the third – and right gladly do we mark the pack turning along the dreaded barrier. At this time of year above all others is wire our phantom, too often our embodied, enemy.

Not only is the light-stretched strand far more difficult to perceive through the leafy branches of October, but the fat stock has not yet found a market, and the farmers are loth to weaken their fences too soon.

Year by year, however, we gladly and thankfully notice a diminution, even during the summer, in the quantity of wire set to guard the fences of the Midlands. It is found to be so fruitful of injury to cattle, so easily knocked out of order and withal so indifferent a protection against the bull-headed pertinacity of a restless shorthorn, that its apparent economy is no longer a recommendation, and very few lines of wire fencing are now either fresh set or renewed. Soon may the old-fashioned oxer again reign paramount, to invite or repel with its rugged honesty, – according to the measure and prompting of our years, (a pun would be a vile thing even in the cause of pusillanimity) and our discretion. But the wire in question stretches only half the breadth of the field; and with the regard for their followers that so constantly characterized the movements of fox and hounds throughout this merry gallop, they now strike through the hedge almost exactly where the metal ends – and while we behind gasp "Wire!" they in front charge a hole in the fence, and sweep down the wide stretching pasture in full content.

Many a gallop have I ridden in LEICESTERSHIRE (as I e'en hope to do again) – and have seen hounds and horses go away from me more often than I should like to say – but never has the pace seemed better than now.

Fast horses are galloping their utmost on the fairest turf, an easy fence comes perhaps in half a mile of galloping, gates are either standing open, or fly back at once to the crop – and yet the pack is going all too fast for us unwilling laggards, till a wandering shepherd throws a chance turn in our favour.

Now we cross the MELTON and LEICESTER turnpike, midway between REARSBY and BROOKSBY; and we have worked through a few pumping acres of newly turned arable, and now we are pushing up the big grass field for the covert of BLEAKMORE, marvelling why the turf seems less elastic, and the stride of our horse less conformable with ridge and furrow, than only a few brief minutes ago.

Yes, lungs and muscle are never in autumn what they may be after Xmas – and 'tis only the commencement of the lesson yet.

Fondly we hug ourselves that BLEAKMORE is just in front; and that in another minute we shall be on foot beside our fat steeds – mopping our foreheads with gusto, and flinging our tongues in noisy exuberant accord on the subject of the pleasant scurry just over.

Not yet.

For the merry ladies race onwards along the ridge – leaving BLEAKMORE and the railway below them on the right.

How now for your "honest oxer"? Here it is in its most laudable ruggedness – and, in plain Saxon, an ugly beast it is too.

The rail on the take-off side is no excuse for the qualm that stabs you like the conscience of a schoolboy caught cribbing his task. But the high laid-fence shows its strong teeth e'en through the heavy foliage; a ditch of unknown dimensions lies beyond; there is a whisper, too, of wire; and any number of predecessors are not likely to bring things to a much lower level.

The huntsman quickly makes up his mind to the inevitable; but his horse (brilliantly as he carries him throughout) on this occasion whips round to take time for a second thought.

MR. BROCKLEHURST clears the whole difficulty a few yards to the right, while the CAMBRIDGESHIRE hero takes the office from FIRR, and makes a bold bid for victory. Post and rails, hedge and ditch are covered gallantly. But beyond them all, and visible only from mid-air, glistens another stout ox rail.

"Forty to one against BENDIGO!" shouts his familiar friend as he himself lands in safety.

But the only response to the liberal offer is a loud cracking of timber, a heavy flounder and another good man fallen on the turf. Matters are a little simpler now; and after seeing the huntsman, CAPTAIN O'NEAL, MR. PEAKE, MR. CRADOCK, MR. ALSTON, and two or three others, surmount the less complicated difficulty, reader and I too may pull ourselves together, put our panting beast through the same process – by help of knee and heel against his well-furnished sides – and even reach the others as, after another half-mile of grass, they muddle at a bridle gate by REARSBY.

The fox had swung to the left, again across the turnpike; but with such a scent as there is today, the pack falters neither on road nor plough, but drives forward over the little fields behind the village, whether they happen to be eddish or arable.

Scarcely so with their followers. The *drive* is wellnigh spent, the steel is out of the iron, and the oil is all but burned out. A horse will gallop in a mechanical sort of way, long after the power to jump has left him. A very limited experience with the symptoms suffices to teach us where such a stage has been reached; also that a mere mechanical stride is of little use against a strong top binder.

It by no means follows that the faculty of appreciation adds greatly to our enjoyment at such moments.

I confess to its having a very contrary effect upon my frail nerves – and I venture to assert, by the way, that the one great drawback to the pleasures of steeplechase jockeyship lies in the frequent necessity of riding a beaten horse home. Now, however, there are gates and gaps to help us.

Again we are on the grass, and at the pace hounds are running they must surely catch a view in another minute or two.

A shepherd – with more than the acumen or consideration of his race, holding his colley in his arms – declares "the fox is nobbut a hoondred yaards afore 'em!" the while he fumbles at an unwilling gate, and we pant and ejaculate, and hope there is no more hunting to be done.

"Forrard, little bitches," rings cherrily out as the pack glides up the hedge-side, and we follow hurriedly to the corner – trusting that, as hitherto, Providence and enlightened agriculture will have provided free means of egress from field to field.

Yes, there's a nice stile for the use of labourers and for people on foot – and well used it evidently is, for the approach to it is worn into a hole, and slimy clay has taken the place of grass. Beyond this, the corner is a veritable *cul de sac*; for lofty bullfinches of an earlier generation enclose either flank – and despair settles upon our souls.

If you, reader, happen to have hunted in the PYTCHLEY country some twenty years ago, when that flying huntsman, and most rapid yet laconic of talkers, CHARLES PAIN, was in his prime, you may remember an oft-quoted incident that eminently illustrated the man.

Reaching a certain corner, from the only apparent escape was retreat – (the last alternative that ever occurred to his mind) he found another hard rider just turning reluctantly away.

CHARLES PAIN was one who suited his words to his actions, the latter being quite as rapid and ready as the former – so, taking his horse short by the head, he pursued his way without further ado, accompanying and explaining his progress only with a single running sentence, "Will do, will do – must do, must do; d—d woolly place – hold up ye beggar – hey bitch!" Men who knew him in those days will easily fill in for themselves the rapidity of his jerky utterances, and the high treble pitch to which the last syllable would raise him.

Alas for the feelings of him who had turned aside; alas for the plight of those who would ride to his lead! Think you they found their situation any more palatable than ours now – FIRR's whitelegged bay having shown us all a clean pair of heels – our fox said to be dead beat, and our horses undoubtedly so?

Well, must do, must do – and Kismet is kind to the next three – *too* kind, for they do nothing to mend matters for those who have yet to come. No. 4 has already declared loudly that he cannot, nay, that he *will* not; for that

> *The heart of his good horse*
> *Was nigh to burst with violence of the beat,*
> *And so perforce he stayed, and overtaken spoke.*

But finding himself, like a bull in a pound, and that neither TENNYSON nor any other man is likely to help him out, unless he helps himself, he too puts his head down and goes for the opening – if so it might be called.

It has every claim to the title when he has done with it; for half a ton of beaten horse-flesh will splinter almost any top-bar in the country, that has been rained upon for more than a single year, – (and this is one of the reasons for our constant assertion that big horses are better than little ones, to carry us in LEICESTERSHIRE).

That such a result, however, cannot always be attained without a certain concussion was, he tells me, instanced in the query of his groom that night – "Wasn't it close at home as you fell, sir? I thought as the colour of the dirt on the chesnut's head looked as if it were."

Meanwhile the hounds have encountered their first momentary check – their fox having been driven almost back among them by two men who shouted in his very face.

But for this they must have pulled him down in a few more fields. Now they of course flash beyond the point; recover themselves, however, and the line very quickly; but lose a very vital half-minute.

By this time the circle is nearly completed, and the boundary brook between the GADDESBY and BROOKSBY parishes is reached where rails must be borne down, while hounds go on alone.

Again we are on the BROOKSBY manor; again hounds are going faster than we can, and we are going very much faster than our horses.

Indeed, as WHO-HOOP sounds over a drain, at the road immediately above the hall, only the MASTER and his man are there at the moment to give it – "the field in varied plight arriving as best they can." We shall see nothing faster, and we may see very few things better this year. I have made a long story of these thirty minutes.

THE LADY WHO RIDES TO HOUNDS

Anthony Trollope

c. 1870

AMONG THOSE WHO HUNT there are two classes of hunting people who always like it, and these people are hunting parsons and hunting ladies. That it should be so is natural enough. In the life and habits of parsons and ladies there is much that is antagonistic to hunting, and they who suppress this antagonism do so because they are Nimrods at heart. But the riding of these horsemen under difficulties, – horsemen and horsewomen, – leaves a strong impression on the casual observer of hunting; for to such a one it seems that the hardest riding is forthcoming exactly where no hard riding should be expected. On the present occasion I will, if you please, confine myself to the lady who rides to hounds, and will begin with an assertion, which will not be contradicted, that the number of such ladies is very much on the increase.

Women who ride, as a rule, ride better than men. They, the women, have always been instructed; whereas men have usually come to ride without any instruction. They are put upon ponies when they are all boys, and put themselves upon their fathers' horses as they become hobble-dehoys: and thus they obtain power of sticking on to the animal while he gallops and jumps, – and even while he kicks and shies; and, so progressing, they achieve an amount of horsemanship which answers the purposes of life. But they do not acquire the art of riding with exactness, as women do, and rarely have such hands as a woman has on a horse's mouth. The consequence of this is that women fall less often than men, and the field is not often thrown into the horror which would arise were a lady known to be in a ditch with a horse lying on her.

I own that I like to see three or four ladies out in a field, and I like it the better if I am happy enough to count one or more of them among my own acquaintances. Their presence tends to take off from hunting that character of horseyness, – of both fast horseyness and slow horseyness – which has become, not unnaturally, attached to it, and to bring it within the category of gentle sports. There used to prevail an idea that the hunting man was of necessity loud and rough, given to strong drinks, ill adapted for the poetries of life, and perhaps a little prone to make money out of his softer friend. It may now be said that this idea is going out of vogue, and that hunting men are supposed to have that same feeling with regard to their horses, – the same and no more, – which ladies have for their carriage or soldiers for their swords. Horses are valued simply for the services that they can render, and are only valued highly when they are known to be good servants. That a man may hunt without drinking or swearing, and may possess a nag or two without any propensity to sell it or them for double their value, is now beginning to be understood. The oftener that women are to be seen "out," the more will such improved feelings prevail as to hunting, and the pleasanter will be the field to men who are not horsey, but who may nevertheless be good horsemen.

There are two classes of women who ride to hounds, or, rather, among many possible classifications, there are two to which I will now call attention. There is the lady who rides, and demands assistance; and there is the lady who rides, and demands none. Each always, – I may say always, – receives all the assistance that she may require; but the difference between the two, to the men who ride with them, is very great. It will, of course, be understood that, as to both these samples of female Nimrods, I speak of ladies who really ride, – not of those who grace the coverts with, and disappear under the auspices of, their papas or their grooms when the work begins.

The lady who rides and demands assistance in truth becomes a nuisance before the run is over, let her beauty be ever so transcendent, her horsemanship ever so perfect, and her battery of general feminine artillery ever so powerful. She is like the American woman, who is always wanting your place in a railway carriage, – and demanding it, too, without the slightest idea of paying you for it with thanks; whose study it is to treat you as though she ignored your existence while she is appropriating your services. The hunting lady who demands assistance is very particular about her gates, requiring that aid shall be given to her with instant speed, but that the man who gives it shall never allow himself to be hurried as he renders it. And she soon becomes reproachful, – oh, so soon! It is marvellous to watch the manner in which a hunting lady will become exacting, troublesome, and at last imperious – deceived and spoilt by the attention which she receives. She teaches herself to think at last that a man is a brute who does not ride as though he were riding as her servant, and that it becomes her to assume indignation if every motion around her is not made with some reference to her safety, to her comfort, or to her success. I have seen women look as Furies look, and heard them speak as Furies are supposed to speak, because men before them could not bury themselves and their horses out of their way at a moment's notice, or because some pulling animal would still assert himself while they were there, and not sink into submission and dog-like obedience for their behoof.

I have now before my eyes one who was pretty, brave, and a good horsewoman; but how men did hate her! When you were in a line with her there was no shaking her off. Indeed, you were like enough to be shaken off yourself, and to be rid of her after that fashion. But while you were with her you never escaped her at a single fence, and always felt that you were held to be trespassing against her in some manner. I shall never forget her voice, – "Pray, take care of that gate." And yet it was a pretty voice, and elsewhere she was not given to domineering more than is common to pretty women in general; but she had been taught badly from the beginning, and she was a pest. It was the same at every gap. "Might I ask you not to come too near me?" And yet it was impossible to escape her. Men could not ride wide of her, for she would not ride wide of them. She had always some male escort with her, who did not ride as she rode, and consequently, as she chose to have the advantage of an escort, – of various escorts, – she was always in the company of some who did not feel as much joy in the presence of a pretty young woman as men should do under all circumstances. "Might I ask you not to come too near me?" If she could only have heard the remarks to which this constant little request of hers gave rise. She is now the mother of children, and her hunting days are gone, and probably she never makes that little request. Doubtless that look, made up partly of offence and partly of female dignity, no longer clouds her brow. But I fancy that they who knew her of old in the hunting field never approach her now without fancying that they hear those reproachful words, and see that powerful look of injured feminine weakness.

But there is the hunting lady who rides hard and never asks for assistance. Perhaps I may be allowed to explain to embryo Dianas, – to the growing huntresses of the present age, – that she who rides and makes no demand receives attention as close as is ever given to her more imperious sister. And how welcome she is! What a grace she lends to the day's sport! How pleasant it is to see her in her pride of place, achieving her mastery over the difficulties in her way by her own wit, – as all men, and all women also, must really do who intend to ride to hounds; and doing it all without any sign that the difficulties are too great for her!

THE GOOD FOXHUNTER

Major-General Geoffrey Brooke

1929

ON THE MORNING of hunting your horse should have a full drink the first thing and a feed of corn. If the meet is near at hand, he may have another small drink and a second small feed a clear hour before he starts, though this will not be possible at the more distant meets.

Some animals realise when they are being prepared for hunting and may not feed in consequence. In such cases, make as little change as possible in their normal stable routine, and such attentions as plaiting of manes should be left to the last moment.

When riding or sending horses on to the meet, the average speed should not exceed six miles an hour.

Insist on your hunters being turned out smartly. A good groom will take pleasure in doing this and a less experienced individual should be

encouraged to do so. It is almost as important to be particular about your own equipment, as it is a reasonable compliment to the Master who is at pains to turn his hunt servants out neatly, and is naturally gratified if the general appearance of his field does him credit.

Before mounting, have a look at your horse's bit and curb-chain, and when in the saddle make sure that your girths are pulled up. Satisfy yourself that there is no pressure on the horse's withers; this should not occur with proper supervision in the stable, but if by any chance it is the case, you will either have to change the saddle or put a knitted woollen pad under the front arch.

On a cold morning do not let your horse stand shivering in the wind. Give him an opportunity to stale, then let him walk about whilst waiting for hounds to move off. Do not ride to where you believe hounds are going to draw first. Your presence and that of others at the covert side may result in the fox going away before hounds arrive, or you may find that the draw has been changed and you are deservedly left out of the hunt.

When hounds are drawing, the field will be marshalled on one side of the covert or possibly in the middle of a big wood; this is done to give the fox a fair chance of breaking covert. Stand clear of kicking horses, and if your own is at all doubtful, you must keep him on the outskirts of the crowd and hold your hand behind your back when going through a gateway or when pulling up in a ride. A horse that stamps or kicks in a crowd should have a red ribbon on his tail.

On no account skirt round the covert on your own, with the intention of getting a start. You are liable to head the fox and will incur the justifiable wrath of the Master.

If necessary, hold open a gate for the huntsman and keep on one side of a ride when he has to pass. On the other hand, take an intelligent interest in the proceedings, be ready for the moment when the fox is holloa-ed away and hounds come out of cover to pick up a line. Remember that they must have a chance to settle, and overriding them now will jeopardise the chances of a hunt. You cannot hunt the fox yourself, a singularly obvious fact that is sometimes forgotten by some of the field.

Once hounds have settled to the line you are at liberty to ride to them, not on their sterns, but about one hundred to two hundred yards on the flank and level with the tail hounds. If there is any choice, ride on the downwind side of the pack, as a fox, unless his mask is set for a definite point, is more likely to turn downwind, and, if you cannot see hounds at times, you may hear them upwind of you.

CUBHUNTING IN EDWARDIAN SUSSEX

Siegfried Sassoon

1928

RINGWELL CUBBING DAYS are among my happiest memories. Those mornings now reappear in my mind, lively and freshly painted by the sunshine of an autumn that made amends for the rainy weeks which had washed away the summer. Four days a week we were up before daylight. I had heard the snoring stable-hands roll out of bed with yawns and grumblings, and they were out and about before the reticent Henry came into my room with a candle and a jug of warm water. (How Henry managed to get up was a mystery). Any old clothes were good enough for cubbing, and I was very soon downstairs in the stuffy little living-room, where Denis had an apparatus for boiling eggs. While they were bubbling he put the cocoapowder in the cups, two careful spoonfuls each, and not a grain more. A third spoonful was unthinkable.

Not many minutes afterwards we were out by the range of loose-boxes under the rustling trees, with quiet stars overhead and scarcely a hint of morning. In the kennels the two packs were baying at one another from their separate yards, and as soon as Denis had got his horse from the gruff white-coated head-groom, a gate released the hounds – twenty-five or thirty couple of them, and all very much on their toes. Out they streamed like a flood of water, throwing their tongues and spreading away in all directions with waving sterns, as though they had never been out in the world before. Even then I used to feel the strangeness of the scene with its sharp exuberance of unkennelled energy. Will's hearty voice and the crack of his whip stood out above the clamour and commotion which surged around Denis and his horse. Then, without any apparent lull or interruption, the whirlpool became a well-regulated torrent flowing through the gateway into the road, along which the sound of hoofs receded with a purposeful clip-clopping. Whereupon I hoisted myself on to an unknown horse – usually an excited one – and set off higgledy piggledy along the road to catch them up. Sometimes we had as many as twelve miles to go, but more often we were at the meet in less than an hour.

The mornings I remember most zestfully were those which took us up on to the chalk downs. To watch the day breaking from purple to dazzling gold while we trotted up a deep-rutted lane; to inhale the early freshness when we were on the sheep-cropped uplands; to stare back at the low country with its cock-crowing farms and mist-coiled waterways; thus to be riding out with a sense of spacious discovery – was it not something stolen from the lie-a-bed world and the luckless city workers?

THE HUNTSMAN'S HORSE

Will H. Ogilvie

1923

The galloping seasons have slackened his pace,
And stone wall and timber have battered his
knees;
It is many a year since he gave up his place
To live out his life in comparative ease.

No more does he stand with his scarlet and white
Like a statue of marble girth deep in the gorse;
No more does he carry the Horn of Delight
That called us to follow the huntsman's old
horse.

How many will pass him and not understand,
  As he trots down the road going cramped in his
    stride,
That he once set the pace to the best in the land
  Ere they tightened his curb for a lady to ride!

When the music begins and a right one's away,
  When hoof-strokes are thudding like drums on the
    ground,
The old spirit wakes in the worn-looking grey
  And the pride of his youth comes to life at a bound.

He leans on the bit and he lays to his speed,
  To the winds of the open his stiffness he throws,
And if spirit were all he'd be up with the lead
  Where the horse that supplants him so easily goes.

No double can daunt him, no ditch can deceive,
  No bank can beguile him to set a foot wrong,
But the years that have passed him no power can
    retrieve —
    To the swift is their swiftness, their strength to the
      strong!

To the best of us all comes a day and a day
  When the pace of the leaders shall leave us forlorn,
So we'll give him a cheer — the old galloping grey —
  As he labours along to the lure of the Horn.

THE HUNTER

John Masefield

1919

A chestnut mare with swerves and heaves
Came plunging, scattered all the crowd,
She tossed her head and laughed aloud
And bickered sideways past the meet.
From pricking ears to mincing feet
She was all tense with blood and quiver,
You saw her clipt hide twitch and shiver
Over her netted cords of veins.

THE RIDDENS

John Masefield

1921

The Riddens came, from Ocle Covers,
Bill Ridden riding Stormalong
(By Tempest out of Love-me-Long),
A proper handful of a horse
That nothing but the Aintree course

Could bring to terms, save Bill perhaps.
All sport, from bloody war to scraps,
Came well to Bill, that big-mouthed smiler.
They nicknamed him "the mug-beguiler,"
For Billy lived too much with horses,
In copers' yards and sharpers' courses,
To lack the sharper-coper streak.
He did not turn the other cheek
When struck (as English Christians do);
He boxed like a Whitechapel Jew,
And many a time his knuckles bled
Against a racecourse-gipsy's head.
For "hit him first and argue later"
Was truth at Billy's Alma Mater,
Not love, not any bosh of love.
His hand was like a chamois glove,
And riding was his chief delight.
He bred the chaser Chinese-White
From Lilybud by Mandarin.
And when his mouth tucked corners in,
And scent was high and hounds were going,
He went across a field like snowing
And tackled anything that came.
His wife, Sal Ridden, was the same,

A loud, bold, blonde, abundant mare
With white horse-teeth and stooks of hair
(Like polished brass) and such a manner
It flaunted from her like a banner.
Her father was Tom See the trainer.
She rode a lovely earth-disdainer
Which she and Billy wished to sell . . .

POLO

~~~~~~

Beneath the rainbow silks they sail
Like birds that wheel and cross;
Then, all their speed of no avail,
Come round to bit and martingale
With heads that reach and toss.

The ceaseless stick beside them swings,
The torn turf marks their track,
To heaving flanks the dark sweat clings
And from their fretted bridle rings
The foam comes feathering back.

But well they know there is no game
That men their masters play
Can fan like this their hearts to flame
And make them one with every aim
That fills the crowded day.

WILL H. OGILVIE,
Over the Grass

POLO, the fastest game in the world, began in the ancient Orient. The name derives from pulu, which is Tibetan for a ball. It was known in Persia as *chaugun*. This brief anthology of the game begins with two sixteenth-century accounts, the first by an Eastern observer, the second by an Englishman, George Manwaring, recording a visit he made to the Imperial court, with the three Sherley brothers – the eldest of whom was the "Sir Anthony" referred to – upon whom he was in attendance.

Western polo was born in 1869, when a group of 10th Hussar officers, stationed at Aldershot read a newspaper account of the game as played by the Manipuris. They promptly saddled their chargers, took a billiard ball, improvized sticks and tried it out. Soon the Life Guards, Blues and 9th Lancers followed suit, and inter-regimental matches began. In India it became the principal recreation of the British *raj*, and Winston Churchill describes the fervor with which it was played when he was serving there as a subaltern in the 4th Hussars: "We . . . devoted ourselves to the serious purpose of life. This was expressed in the one word – Polo. It was upon this, apart from duty, that all our interest was concentrated."

In pre-war days, when the Service officer's existence was considerably more relaxed than in this fully mechanized age, polo, especially in the cavalry, was an integral part of regimental life. The definitive work on the mysteries of the game, however, was written by a sailor, who called himself "Marco," and is better known as Admiral of the Fleet Earl Mountbatten of Burma. All of us, when we started to play, read his *Introduction to Polo* – probably two or three times over, and beginners and veterans alike still read it now.

Major John Board, that rare combination, a skillful artist and a lucid writer, as well as an experienced polo player and umpire, describes to a T the basic requirements of polo horsemanship. I have included with this passage some of his excellent drawings, in which he also shows what a high premium he places on horse-and-rider suppleness.

Polo gained its first literary classic in the early years of this century. *The Maltese Cat*, by Rudyard Kipling, is the tale of an inter-regimental final in British India, between the smart, expensively-mounted Archangels and the Skidars ("what they call a Pioneer regiment"), the leading light of whose string of ponies is the "Cat" of the title. To read the story without

knowing the game, you might think the ponies were endowed with some magic initiative. But, for all the untruth of this, "pony-power" is a far more important factor than most lay spectators appreciate.

An inbalance in pony-power was noted by the artist, G.D.Armour – himself a very keen player in his youth – in his autobiography, *Bridle and Brush*. The excerpt, with which I have closed this section, discusses the talent and strength of the "Big Four" – Dev Milburn, Harry Payne Whitney and the Waterbury brothers, who wrested the Westchester Cup from England for the first time, in 1909, and launched the United States on its career as the leading polo nation, a pride of place which she kept until the rise of Argentina. For the series of maches, which Armour witnessed in 1913, the English team was largely mounted – with the best ponies that money could buy – by the Duke of Westminster, so, if Armour was right and the Americans were "better mounted than our men," their string must have been superlative. Who knows? Perhaps there was another Maltese Cat among them, a leader exhorting them with: "remember we *must* play together, and you *must* play with your heads. Whatever happens follow the ball . . . !"

16th CENTURY PERSIA (1): THE GAME OF CHAUGAN

Abul Fazl-I-Allami

1580

SUPERFICIAL OBSERVERS look upon this game as a mere amusement, and consider it mere play; but men of more exalted views see in it a means of learning promptitude and decision. It tests the value of a man, and strengthens the bonds of friendship. Strong men learn in playing this game the art of riding, and the animals learn to perform feats of agility and to obey the reins. Hence his Majesty is very fond of this game. Externally, the same adds to the splendour of his Court; but, viewed from a higher point, it reveals concealed talents.

When his Majesty goes to the *maidán* (plain or open field) in order to play this game, he selects an opponent, and some active and clever players, who are only filled with one thought, viz. to show their skill against the opponents of his Majesty. From motives of kindness, his Majesty never *orders* any one to be a player, but chooses the pairs by the cast of the die. There are not more than ten players, but many more keep themselves in readiness. When one *ghari* (twenty-four minutes) has passed, two players take rest, and two others supply their place.

The game itself is played in two ways. The first way is to get hold of the ball with the crooked end of the chaugán-stick and move it slowly from the middle to the boundary pillars (hál, i.e. goal). This manner is called in Hindi *rol*. The other way consists in taking deliberate aim and forcibly hitting the ball with the chaugán-stick out of the middle; the (opposing) player then gallops after it quicker than the others and throws it back. This mode is called *béla*, and may be performed in various ways. The player may either strike the ball with the stock in his right hand, and send it to the right forwards or backwards, or he may do so with his left hand, or he may send the ball in front of the horse to the right or to the left. The ball may be thrown in the same direction from behind the feet of the horse or from below its body, or the rider may spit it (*sic* lit., probably meaning "may shove it" with, as it were, a sort of 'cue-stroke), when the ball is in front of the horse, or he may lift himself upon the croup (or crupper) and propel the ball between the feet of the animal.

His Majesty is unrivalled for the skill which he shows in the various ways of hitting the ball; he often manages to strike the ball when in the air and astonishes all. When the ball is driven to a goal they beat a kettledrum, so that all who are far and near may hear it. In order to increase the excitement betting is allowed. The players win from each other, and he who brought the ball to the goal wins most. If a ball be caught in the air, and passes or is made to pass beyond the goal, the game is looked upon as drawn. At such times the players will engage in a regular fight about the ball, and perform admirable feats of skill.

His Majesty also plays chaugán on dark nights, which caused much astonishment, even among clever players. The balls which are used at night are set on fire. For this purpose pálas wood (*Butea frondosa*) is used, which is very light and burns for a long time. For the sake of adding splendour to the games, which is necessary in worldly matters, his Majesty has knobs of gold and silver fixed to the top of the chaugán-sticks. If one of them breaks, any player that gets hold of the pieces may keep them.

It is impossible to describe the excellency of this game. Ignorant as I am, I can say but little about it.

16th CENTURY PERSIA (2): SOME ENGLISH WITNESSES

George Manwaring

1599

AFTER THE BANQUET was ended the King requested Sir Anthony to look through the window to behold their sports on horseback. Before the house there was a very fair place, to the quantity of some ten acres of ground, made very plain; so the King went down, and when he had taken his horse the drums and trumpets sounded. There were twelve horsemen in all with the King; so they divided themselves, six on the one side and six on the other, having in their hands long rods of wood about the bigness of a man's finger, and at one end of the rods a piece of wood nailed on like a hammer. After they were divided and turned face to face, there came one in the middle, and threw a ball between both the companies, and having goals made at either end of the plain, they began their sport, striking the ball with their rods from one to the other, in the fashion of our football here in England; and ever when the King had gotten the ball before him the drums and trumpets would play one alarum, and many times the King would come to Sir Anthony at the window and ask him how he did like the sport.

c. 1900: INDIA AND THE INDISPENSABILITY OF THE GAME

Winston Churchill

1930

WE THREE, Reginald Barnes, Hugo Baring and I, pooling all our resources, took a palatial bungalow, all pink and white with heavy tiled roof and deep verandahs sustained by white plaster columns, wreathed in purple bougainvillia. It stood in a compound or grounds of perhaps two acres. We took over from the late occupant about a hundred and fifty splendid standard roses: Maréchal Niel, La France, Gloire de Dijon, etc. We built a large tiled barn with mud walls, containing stabling for thirty horses and ponies. Our three butlers formed a triumvirate in which no internal dissensions ever appeared. We paid an equal contribution into the pot; and thus freed from mundane cares, devoted ourselves to the serious purpose of life.

This was expressed in one word – Polo. It was upon this, apart from duty, that all our interest was concentrated. But before you could play polo, you must have ponies. We had formed on the voyage a regimental polo club, which in return for moderate but regular subscriptions from all the officers (polo-players and non-polo-players alike) offered substantial credit facilities for the procuring of these indispensable allies. A regiment coming from home was never expected to count in the Indian polo world for a couple of years. It took that time to get a proper stud of ponies together. However, the president of our polo club and the senior officers, after prolonged and anxious discussions, determined upon a bold and novel stroke. The Bycullah stables at Bombay form the main emporium through which Arab horses and ponies are imported to India. The Poona Light Horse, a native regiment strongly officered by British, had in virtue of its permanent station an obvious advantage in the purchase of Arabian ponies. On our way through Poona we had tried their ponies, and had entered into deeply important negotiations with them. Finally it was decided that the regimental polo club should purchase the entire polo stud of twenty-five ponies possessed by the Poona Light Horse; so that these ponies should form the nucleus around which we could gather the means of future victory in the Inter-Regimental Tournament. I can hardly describe the sustained intensity of purpose with which we threw ourselves into this audacious and colossal undertaking. Never in the history of Indian polo had a cavalry regiment from Southern India won the Inter-Regiment cup. We knew it would take two or three years of sacrifice, contrivance and effort. But if all other diversions were put aside, we did not believe that success was beyond our compass. To this task then we settled down with complete absorption.

ADVICE TO PLAYERS

Admiral of the Fleet, Earl Mountbatten of Burma ("Marco")

1931

NUMBER ONE. This is the easiest position in which to keep your place approximately (which is why you will probably play in it when you begin); but it is the hardest in which to keep your place accurately.

You can be certain that you should always be the most advanced player on the side, and near the enemy Back; but you will find it hard to determine when to be ahead of him, level with him, or behind him.

This problem of how far to be an attacker, and how far a defender, is present in all four positions. But in yours it will be aggravated by the fact that, whereas you cannot be excused your fair share of defence, and will be expected not to let the enemy back through, your principal function must be to score goals from passes, and to be lying up-field of the enemy, clear, when the pass comes.

Though you can only really solve this problem for yourself, with regard to the circumstances, the following may help you at first as a rough guide:

When your side is in attack, be ready to slip your Back. Keep a few yards to the side of him, and about half-a-length ahead. Don't gallop up-field at once, to wait for a pass that may never be made, and make it impossible for yourself to get back in time if your side's attack is stopped. But gallop upfield as far as you think a pass can reach you, the moment one of your side is in position to pass up the ball ahead of you and the enemy Back.

The nearer you are to the enemy goal, the further you can afford to be ahead of the opposing Back.

When your side is in defence, *close with your man*; but the moment you see that your Number 2 is going to be able to clear with a backhander, you must disengage. If it is your Number 3 or Back that is going to hit the backhander, you must be more cautious about turning up, as there will then be a greater risk of the enemy Back's meeting the ball successfully.

The nearer you are to your own goal, the more cautious you should be.

You will not be expected to perform the impossible feat of being right back in defence immediately after you have been waiting for a pass before the enemy goal-mouth, or vice-versa; but when your side is neither right up nor right back, you should try to keep your position as flexible as you can.

In placing yourself, you should assume that your side will hit a good long ball. You yourself need not be a particularly long hitter, but you must be able to shoot accurately at goal. To this end, you must practise shooting from every angle; and when practising with another player (preferably your own Number 2), you should learn to shoot from a pass as you pick it up.

NUMBER TWO. You will normally be the player to develop your side's attack: that is to say, when your side has been defending, it is usually to you that your 3 or Back will pass the ball with a backhander.

For this reason you should be particularly quick in turning to a backhander. Practise with your Number 3 and Back until you can tell from their preliminary motions whether they are going to cut or pull the backhander, so that you may turn accordingly.

If ever you allow the opposing Number 3 to get ahead of you when you you are attacking, ride into his backhanders and keep trying to hustle him. If your 3 or Back can meet them successfully, it is not up to you to turn when your opposite number hits them, unless he himself turns.

In placing yourself, you should assume that your side will always succeed in hitting the ball, though you need not rely on their taking a more than average shot. You yourself will have to be a long and strong hitter, so as to be able to get the ball right up to your Number 1. Make use of him whenever you can, for if you try to hit all the goals yourself you will be making your team into a three-man side!

NUMBER THREE. You will be the pivot of the team: the link between the forwards and the Back. It will be your job to feed the forwards, to prevent an enemy attack from getting under away, and to turn defence into attack by a backhand pass up to your Number 2.

You will have ample opportunity to go through yourself in attack, and you must make the fullest use of it. You and the Back should practise going up to one another's backhanders, and interchanging freely, also making short passes across to each other.

You should turn to cover your Back when he is meeting the ball, for this will give him confidence when taking his shot and will reduce the risk if he should miss it. Always be prepared for your Back to miss a shot in defence, and ride to cover him until the ball is actually struck.

In placing yourself, you should assume that your side will make shots below the average, and that your opponents will make them above the average. You yourself must be a steady player, though not necessarily a brilliant one. Reliability in striking is more important for you than long hitting, and you must be the hardest worker on the side.

THE BACK. You can tackle your job in two ways: by staying well back, allowing your Number 3 to do all the half-back work, and only checking attacks that get past him; or else by playing half-back alternately with him.

Unless your Number 3 is a much stronger, more experienced, and better-mounted player than you, your captain is likely to direct you to follow the second plan, as it creates a far more difficult situation for your opponents to cope with.

In attack, you must always follow-up your side closely; for the Back often gets a shot at goal when the other players have all ridden each other over the ball!

Put in constant practise at meeting the ball. There is nothing that will turn defence into attack more effectively; but you should only do this if your Number 3 is turning to cover you.

In defence, you should be prepared for your 3 to miss his backhanders altogether, and continue to mark your opposing Number 1 until the ball is actually struck. You must then gallop up at full speed. When your Number 3 is taking his backhander in the enemy half, however, you will be justified in turning a little earlier, for the risk involved if he should miss the ball is not so great as in your own half.

You should be a long, reliable hitter, the accuracy of your shots being of minor importance.

THE GAME'S HORSEMANSHIP

Major John Board

1956

WITHOUT DOUBT a good natural horseman has a great advantage over others less gifted when beginning the game of polo, and, provided he has the other attributes of a good eye and games' sense, he should with practice, reach a high standard of proficiency. But all the horsemanship in the world is of no avail to a polo player who has no ball-game sense or ability. The one accomplishment can, within reason, be taught and learned, but the other, though it can, indeed must be, developed by practice, cannot be taught to one who does not naturally possess it. Broadly speaking anyone who is keen enough to work hard can learn to ride well enough to play polo. That we used to teach some 20,000 young men to ride well enough to fight for their lives when mounted, seems a reasonable proof of this assertion. But the combined use of eye, wrist, footwork and anticipation, which are the hall-marks of the real games-player, can only be developed; not taught.

Accordingly, the most likely type of boy or young man is he who is a natural ball-game player and, best of all, if he has learned the elements of the game of rackets, in which lie all the items to form a sure basis for all ball games. As examples I need go no further than the late Captain Jack Denning of the P.A.V.O. Cavalry, who was certainly among the half-dozen best players in the world between the Wars – many will aver the best ever. He was a useful rackets player, as I remember well, for we were at school together, and he became also a really fine horseman. Another is Lieut-Col Humphrey Guinness, late of the Royal Scots Greys and an English international. He was in the Eton rackets pair soon after the first German War and I am sure that he owes much of his powerful and accurate hitting to what he learned in the Eton court. Indeed rackets is a marvellous game, not only because of its terrific speed, but because it is absolutely essential to learn and practice the basic action of all strokes correctly. They, in turn, will serve your purpose, whether your ambition lies in the rackets court itself, the cricket field, on the golf links or the polo ground.

In the heat of a hard-fought chukka there is just no time whatever to consider the finer points of equitation. All that matters is, in the words of Kumar Shri Ranjitsinhji of honoured memory, to "see where the ball is, go there, hit it". Accordingly, the better you ride, the more purely instinctive your reactions and aids, the better you and your pony will go together. The reason that no Continental player has ever yet emerged from mediocrity, is that they are so obsessed by the importance of "correct" equitation that even the few who possess some kind of games' sense never lose that stultifying self-consciousness. But all that does not in the least excuse any of us from doing our utmost to become really accomplished riders.

THE MALTESE CAT

Rudyard Kipling

1898

THEY HAD GOOD REASON to be proud, and better reason to be afraid, all twelve of them; for, though they had fought their way, game by game, up the teams entered for the polo tournament, they were meeting the Archangels that afternoon in the final match; and the Archangels' men were playing with half-a-dozen ponies apiece. As the game was divided into six quarters of eight minutes each, that meant a fresh pony after every halt. The Skidars' team, even supposing there were no accidents, could only supply one pony for every other change; and two to one is heavy odds. Again, as Shiraz, the grey Syrian, pointed out, they were meeting the pink and pick of the polo ponies of Upper India; ponies that had cost from a thousand rupees each, while they themselves were a cheap lot gathered, often from country carts, by their masters who belonged to a poor but honest native infantry regiment.

"Money means pace and weight," said Shiraz, rubbing his black silk nose dolefully along his neat-fitting boot, "and by the maxims of the game as I know it ———"

"Ah, but we aren't playing the maxims," said the Maltese Cat. "We're playing the game, and we've the great advantage of knowing the game. Just think a stride, Shiraz. We've pulled up from bottom to second place in two weeks against all those fellows on the ground here; and that's because we play with our heads as well as our feet."

"It makes me feel undersized and unhappy all the same," said Kittiwynk, a mouse-coloured mare with a red browband and the cleanest pair of legs that ever an aged pony owned. "They've twice our size . . . "

Kittiwynk looked at the gathering and sighed. The hard, dusty Umballa polo-ground was lined with thousands of soldiers, black and white, not counting hundreds and hundreds of carriages, and drags, and dog-carts, and ladies with brilliant-coloured parasols, and officers in uniform and out of it, and crowds of natives behind them; and orderlies on camels who had halted to watch the game, instead of carrying letters up and down the station, and native horse-dealers running about on thin-eared Biluchi mares, looking for a chance to sell a few first-class polo ponies. Then there were the ponies of thirty teams that entered for the Upper India Free-For-All-Cup – nearly every pony of worth and dignity from Mhow to Peshawar, from Allahabad to Multan; prize ponies, Arabs, Syrian, Barb, country bred, Deccanee, Waziri, and Kabul ponies of every colour and shape and temper that you could imagine. Some of them were in mat-roofed stables close to the polo-ground, but most were under saddle while their masters, who had been defeated in the earlier games, trotted in and out and told each other exactly how the game should be played.

It was a glorious sight, and the come-and-go of the quick hoofs, and the incessant salutations of ponies that had met before on other polo-grounds or racecourses, were enough to drive a four-footed thing wild.

But the Skidars' team were careful not to know their neighbours, though half the ponies on the ground were anxious to scrape acquaintance with the little fellows that had come from the North, and, so far, had swept the board.

"Let's see," said a soft, golden-coloured Arab, who had been playing very badly the day before, to the Maltese Cat, "didn't we meet in Abdul Rahman's stable in Bombay four seasons ago? I won the Paikpattan Cup next season, you may remember."

"Not me," said the Maltese Cat politely. "I was at Malta then, pulling a vegetable cart. I don't race. I play the game."

"O-oh!" said the Arab, cocking his tail and swaggering off.

"Keep yourselves to yourselves," said the Maltese Cat to his companions. "We don't want to rub noses with all those goose-rumped half-breeds of Upper India. When we've won this cup they'll give their shoes to know us."

"*We* shan't win the cup," said Shiraz. "How do you feel?"

"Stale as last night's feed when a musk-rat has run over it," said Polaris, a rather heavy-shouldered grey, and the rest of the team agreed with him.

"The sooner you forget that the better," said the Maltese Cat cheerfully. "They've finished tiffin in the big tent. We shall be wanted now. If your saddles are not comfy, kick. If your bits aren't easy, rear, and let the "saises" know whether your boots are tight."

Each pony had his "sais", his groom, who lived and ate and slept with the pony, and had betted a great deal more than he could afford on the result of the game. There was no chance of anything going wrong, and, to make sure each "sais" was shampooing the legs of his pony to the last minute. Behind the "saises" sat as many of the Skidars' regiment as had leave to attend the match – about half the native officers, and a hundred or two dark, black-bearded men with the regimental pipers nervously fingering the big be-ribboned bagpipes. The Skidars were what they call a Pioneer regiment; and the bagpipes made the national music of half the men. The native officers held bundles of polo-sticks, long cane-handled mallets, and as the grandstand filled after lunch they arranged themselves by ones and twos at different points round the ground, so that if a stick were broken the player would not have far to ride for a new one. An impatient British cavalry band struck up "If you want to know the time, ask a p'leecman!" and the two umpires in light dust-coats danced out on two little excited ponies. The four players of the Archangels' team followed, and the sight of their beautiful mounts made Shiraz groan again.

"Wait till we know," said the Maltese Cat. "Two of 'em are playing in blinkers, and that means they can't see to get out of the way of their own side, or they *may* shy at the umpires' ponies. They've *all* got white web reins that are sure to stretch or slip!"

"And," said Kittiwynk, dancing to take the stiffness out of her, "they carry their whips in their hands instead of on their wrists. Hah!"

"True enough. No man can manage his stick and his reins, and his whip that way," said the Maltese Cat. "I've fallen over every square yard of the Malta ground, and I would to know." He quivered his little flea-bitten withers just to show how satisfied he felt; but his heart was not so light. Ever since he had drifted into India on a troopship, taken, with an old rifle, as part payment for a racing debt, the Maltese Cat had played and preached polo to the Skidars' team on the Skidars' stony polo-ground. Now a polo-pony is like a poet. If he is born with a love for the game he can be made. The Maltese Cat knew that bamboos grew solely in order that polo-balls might be turned from their roots, that grain was given to ponies to keep them in hard condition, and that ponies were shod to prevent them slipping on a turn. But, besides all these things, he knew every trick and device of the finest game of the world, and for two seasons he had been teaching the others all he knew or guessed.

"Remember," he said for the hundredth time as the riders came up, "we *must* play together, and you *must* play with your heads. Whatever happens, follow the ball. Who goes out first?"

Kittiwynk, Shiraz, Polaris, and a short high little bay fellow with tremendous hocks and no withers worth speaking of (he was called Corks) were being girthed up, and the soldiers in the background stared with all their eyes.

"I want you men to keep quiet," said Lutyens, the captain of the team, "and especially *not* to blow your pipes."

"Not if we win, Captain Sahib?" asked a piper.

"If we win, you can do what you please," said Lutyens, with a smile, as he slipped the loop of his stick over his wrist, and wheeled to canter to his place. The Archangels' ponies were a little bit above themselves on account of the many-coloured crowd so close to the ground. Their riders were excellent players, but they were a team of crack players instead of a crack team; and that made all the difference in the world. They honestly meant to play together, but it is very hard for four men, each the best of the team he is picked from, to remember that in polo no brilliancy of hitting or riding makes up for playing alone. Their captain shouted his orders to them by name, and it is a curious thing that if you call his name aloud in public after an Englishman you make him hot and fretty. Lutyens said nothing to his men because it had all been said before. He pulled up Shiraz for he was playing "back," to guard the goal. Powell on Polaris was half-back, and Macnamara and Hughes on Corks and Kittiwynk were forwards. The tough bamboo-root ball was put into the middle of the ground one hundred and fifty yards from the ends, and Hughes crossed sticks, heads-up with the captain of the Archangels, who saw fit to play forward, and that is a place from which you cannot easily control the team. The little click as the cane-shafts met was heard all over the ground, and then Hughes made some sort of quick wrist-stroke that just dribbled the ball a few yards. Kittiwynk knew that stroke of old, and followed as a cat follows a mouse. While the captain of the Archangels was wrenching his pony round Hughes struck with all his strength, and next instant Kittiwynk was away, Corks followed close behind her, their little feet pattering like rain-drops on glass.

"Pull out to the left," said Kittiwynk between her teeth, "it's coming our way, Corks!"

The back and half-back of the Archangels were tearing down on her just as she was within reach of the ball. Hughes leaned forward with a loose rein, and cut it away to the left almost under Kittiwynk's feet, and it hopped and skipped off to Corks, who saw that, if he were not quick, it would run beyond the boundaries. That long bouncing drive gave the Archangels time to wheel and send three men across the ground to head off Corks. Kittiwynk stayed where she was, for she knew the game. Corks was on the ball half a fraction of a second before the others came up, and Macnamara, with a back-handed stroke, sent it back across the ground to Hughes, who saw the way clear to the Archangels' goal and smacked the ball in before any one quite knew what had happened.

"That's luck," said Corks, as they changed ends. "A goal in three minutes for three hits and no riding to speak of."

"Don't know," said Polaris. "We've made 'em angry too soon. Shouldn't wonder if they try to rush us off our feet next time."

The Archangels came down like a wolf on the fold, for they were tired of football and they wanted polo. They got it more and more. Just after the game began, Lutyens hit a ball that was coming towards him rapidly, and it rose in the air, as a ball sometimes will, with the whirr of a frightened partridge. Shikast heard, but could not see it for the minute, though he looked everywhere and up in the air as the Maltese Cat had taught him. When he saw it ahead and overhead, he went forward with Powell as fast as he could put foot to ground. It was then that Powell, a quiet and level-headed man as a rule, became inspired and played a stroke that some-times comes off successfully on a quiet afternoon of long practice. He took his stick in both hands, and standing up in his stirrups, swiped at the ball in the air, Munipore fashion. There was one second of paralysed astonish-ment, and then all four sides of the ground went up in a yell of applause and delight as the ball flew true (you could see the amazed Archangels ducking in their saddles to get out of the line of flight, and looking at it with open mouths), and the regimental pipes of the Skidars squealed from the railings as long as the piper had breath.

Shikast heard the stroke; but he heard the head of the stick fly off at the same time. Nine hundred and ninety-nine ponies out of a thousand would have gone tearing on after the ball with a useless player pulling at their heads, but Powell knew him, and he knew Powell; and the instant he felt Powell's right leg shift a trifle on the saddle-flap he headed to the boundary, where a native officer was frantically waving a new stick. Before the shouts had ended Powell was armed again.

Once before in his life the Maltese Cat had heard that very same stroke played off his own back, and had profited by the confusion it made. This time he acted on experience, and leaving Bamboo to guard the goal in case of accidents, came through the others like a flash, head and tail low, Lutyens standing up to ease him – swept on and on before the other side knew what was the matter, and nearly pitched on his head between the Archangels' goal-post as Lutyens tipped the ball in after a straight scurry of a hundred and fifty yards. If there was one thing more than another upon which the Maltese Cat prided himself it was on the quick, streaking kind of run half across the ground. He did not believe in taking balls round the field unless you were clearly over-matched. After this they gave the Archangels five minutes' football, and an expensive fast pony hates football because it rumples his temper.

Who's Who showed himself even better than Polaris in this game. He did not permit any wriggling away, but bored joyfully into the scrimmage as if he had his nose in a feed-box, and were looking for something nice. Little Shikast jumped on the ball the minute it got clear, and every time an Archangel pony followed it he found Shikast standing over it asking what was the matter.

"If we can live through this quarter," said the Maltese Cat, "I shan't care. Don't take it out of yourselves. Let them do the lathering."

So the ponies as their riders explained afterwards, "shut up." The Archangels kept them tied fast in front of their goal, but it cost the Archangels' ponies all that was left of their tempers; and ponies began to kick, and men began to repeat compliments, and they chopped at the legs of Who's Who, and he set his teeth and stayed where he was, and the dust stood up like a tree over the scrimmage till that hot quarter ended.

They found the ponies very excited and confident when they went to their *saises*; and the Maltese Cat had to warn them that the worst of the game was coming.

"Now *we* are all going in for the second time," said he, "and *they* are trotting out fresh ponies. You'll think you can gallop, but you'll find you can't; and then you'll be sorry."

"But two goals to nothing is a halter-long lead," said Kittiwynk prancing.

'How long does it take to get a goal?" the Maltese Cat answered. "For pity sake, don't run away with the notion that the game is half-won just because we happen to be in luck now. They'll ride you into the grandstand if they can; you must *not* give 'em a chance. Follow the ball."

"Football as usual?" said Polaris. "My hock's half as big as a nosebag."

"Don't let them have a look at the ball if you can help it. Now leave me alone. I must get all the rest I can before the last quarter."

He hung down his head and let all his muscles go slack; Shikast, Bamboo, and Who's Who copying his example.

"Better not watch the game," he said. "We aren't playing, and we shall only take it out of ourselves if we grow anxious. Look at the ground and pretend it's fly-time."

They did their best, but it was hard advice to follow. The hoofs were drumming and the sticks were rattling all up and down the ground, and yells of applause from the English troops told that the Archangels were pressing the Skidars hard. The native soldiers behind the ponies groaned and grunted, and said things in undertones, and presently they heard a long-drawn shout and a clatter of hurrahs!

"One to the Archangels," said Shikast, without raising his head. "Time's nearly up. Oh, my sire and dam!"

"Faiz Ullah," said the Maltese Cat, "if you don't play to the last nail in your shoes this time, I'll kick you on the ground before all the other ponies."

"I'll do my best when my time comes," said the little Arab sturdily.

The *saises* looked at each other gravely as they rubbed their ponies' legs. This was the first time when long purses began to tell, and everybody knew it. Kittiwynk and the others came back with the sweat dripping over their hoofs and their tails telling sad stories.

"They're better than we are," said Shiraz. "I knew how it would be."

"Shut your big head," said the Maltese Cat; "we've one goal to the good yet."

"Yes, but it's two Arabs and two countrybreds to play now," said Corks. "Faiz Ullah, remember!" He spoke in a biting voice.

As Lutyens mounted Gray Dawn he looked at his men, and they did not look pretty. They were covered with dust and sweat in streaks. Their yellow boots were almost black, their wrists were red and lumpy, and their eyes seemed two inches deep in their heads, but the expression in the eyes was satisfactory.

"Did you take anything at tiffin?" said Lutyens, and the team shook their heads. They were too dry to talk.

"All right. The Archangels did. They are worse pumped than we are."

"They've got the better ponies," said Powell. "I shan't be sorry when this business is over."

That fifth quarter was a sad one in every way. Faiz Ullah played like a little red demon; and the Rabbit seemed to be everywhere at once, and Benami rode straight at anything and everything that came in his way, while the umpires on their ponies wheeled like gulls outside the shifting game. But the Archangels had the better mounts – they had kept their racers till late in the game – and never allowed the Skidars to play football. They hit the ball up and down the width of the ground till Benami and the rest were outpaced. Then they went forward, and time and again Lutyens and Gray Dawn were just, and only just, able to send the ball away with a long splitting back-hander. Gray Dawn forgot that he was an Arab; and turned from gray to blue as he galloped. Indeed, he forgot too well, for he did not keep his eyes on the ground as an Arab should, but stuck out his nose and scuttled for the dear honour of the game. They had watered the ground once or twice between the quarters, and a careless waterman had emptied the last of his skinfull all in one place near the Skidar's goal. It was close to the end of play, and for the tenth time Gray Dawn was bolting after a ball when his near hind foot slipped on the grassy mud and he rolled over and over, pitching Lutyens just clear of the goal-post; and the triumphant Archangels made their goal. Then time was called – two goals all; but Lutyens had to be helped up, and Gray Dawn rose with his near hind leg strained somewhere.

"What's the damage?" said Powell, his arm round Lutyens.

"Collar-bone, of course," said Lutyens between his teeth. It was the third time he had broken it in two years, and it hurt him.

Powell and the others whistled. "Game's up," said Hughes.

"Hold on. We've five good minutes yet, and it isn't my right hand," said Lutyens. "We'll stick it out."

"I say," said the captain of the Archangels, trotting up. "Are you hurt, Lutyens? We'll wait if you care to put in a substitute. I wish – I mean – the fact is, you fellows deserve this game if any team does. Wish we could give you a man or some of our ponies – or something."

"You're awfully good, but we'll play it to a finish, I think."

The captain of the Archangels stared for a little. "That's not half bad," he said, and went back to his own side, while Lutyens borrowed a scarf from one of his native officers and made a sling of it. Then an Archangel galloped up with a big bath-sponge and advised Lutyens to put it under his arm-pit to ease his shoulder, and between them they tied up his left arm scientifically, and one of the native officers leaped forward with four long glasses that fizzed and bubbled.

The team looked at Lutyens piteously, and he nodded. It was the last quarter, and nothing would matter after that. They drank out the dark golden drink, and wiped their moustaches, and things looked more hopeful.

The Maltese Cat had put his nose into the front of Lutyens' shirt, and was trying to say how sorry he was.

"He knows," said Lutyens, proudly. "The beggar knows. I've played him without a bridle before now – for fun."

"It's no fun now," said Powell. "But we haven't a decent substitute."

"No," said Lutyens. "It's the last quarter, and we've got to make our goal and win. I'll trust the Cat."

"If you fall this time you'll suffer a little," said Macnamara.

"I'll trust the Cat," said Lutyens.

"You hear that?" said the Maltese Cat proudly to the others. "It's worth while playing polo for ten years to have that said of you. Now then, my sons, come along. We'll kick up a little bit, just to show the Archangels *this* team haven't suffered."

And, sure enough, as they went on to the ground the Maltese Cat, after satisfying himself that Lutyens was home in the saddle, kicked out three or four times, and Lutyens laughed. The reins were caught up anyhow in the tips of his strapped hand, and he never pretended to rely on them. He knew the Cat would answer to the least pressure of the leg, and by way of showing off – for his shoulder hurt him very much – he bent the little fellow in a close figure-of-eight in and out between the goal-posts. There was a roar from the native officers and men, who dearly loved a piece of *dugabashi* (horse-trick work), as they called it, and the pipes very quietly and scornfully droned out the first bars of a common bazaar-tune called "Freshly Fresh and Newly New," just as a warning to the other regiments that the Skidars were fit. All the natives laughed.

"And now," said the Cat, as they took their place, "remember that this is the last quarter, and follow the ball!"

"Don't need to be told," said Who's Who.

"Let me go on. All those people on all four sides will begin to crowd in – just as they did at Malta. You'll hear people calling out, and moving forward and being pushed back, and that is going to make the Archangel ponies very unhappy. But if a ball is struck to the boundary, you go after it, and let the people get out of your way. I went over the pole of a four-in-hand once, and picked a game out of the dust by it. Back me up when I run, and follow the ball."

There was a sort of an all-round sound of sympathy and wonder as the last quarter opened, and then there began exactly what the Maltese Cat had foreseen. People crowded in close to the boundaries, and the Archangels' ponies kept looking sideways at the narrowing space. If you know how a man feels to be cramped at tennis – not because he wants to run out of the court, but because he likes to know that he can at a pinch – you will guess how ponies must feel when they are playing in a box of human beings.

"I'll bend some of those men if I can get away," said Who's Who, as he rocketed behind the ball; and Bamboo nodded without speaking. They were playing the last ounce in them, and the Maltese Cat had left the goal undefended to join them. Lutyens gave him every order that he could to bring him back, but this was the first time in his career that the little wise gray had ever played polo on his own responsibility, and he was going to make the most of it.

"What are you doing here?" said Hughes, as the Cat crossed in front of him and rode off an Archangel.

"The Cat's in charge – mind the goal!" shouted Lutyens, and bowing forward hit the ball full, and followed on, forcing the Archangels towards their own goal.

"No football," said the Cat. "Keep the ball by the boundaries and cramp 'em. Play open order and drive 'em to the boundaries."

Across and across the ground in big diagonals flew the ball, and whenever it came to a flying rush and a stroke close to the boundaries the Archangel ponies moved stiffly. They did not care to go headlong at a wall of men and carriages, though they could have turned on a sixpence.

"Wriggle her up the sides," said the Cat. "Keep her close to the crowd. They hate the carriages. Shikast, keep her up this side."

Shikast with Powell lay left and right behind the uneasy scuffle of an open scrimmage, and every time the ball was hit away Shikast galloped on it at such an angle that Powell was forced to hit it towards the boundary; and when the crowd had been driven away from that side, Lutyens would send the ball over to the other, and Shikast would slide desperately after it till his friends came down to help. It was billiards, and no football, this time – billiards in a corner pocket; and the cues were not well chalked.

"If they get us out in the middle of the ground they'll walk away from us. Dribble her along the sides," cried the Cat.

So they dribbled all along the boundary, where a pony could not come on their right-hand side; and the Archangels were furious, and the umpires had to neglect the game to shout at the people to get back, and several blundering mounted policemen tried to restore order, all close to the scrimmage, and the nerves of the Archangels' ponies stretched and broke like cobwebs.

Five or six times an Archangel hit the ball up into the middle of the ground, and each time the watchful Shikast gave Powell his chance to send it back, and after each return, when the dust had settled, men could see that the Skidars had gained a few yards.

Every now and again there were shouts of " 'Side! Off side!'" from the spectators; but the teams were too busy to care, and the umpires had all they could do to keep their maddened ponies clear of the scuffle.

At last Lutyens missed a short easy stroke, and the Skidars had to fly back helter-skelter to protect their own goal, Shikast leading. Powell stopped the ball with a backhander when it was not fifty yards from the goal-posts, and Shikast spun round with a wrench that nearly hoisted Powell out of his saddle.

"Now's our last chance," said the Cat, wheeling like a cockchafer on a pin. "We've got to ride it out. Come along."

Lutyens felt the little chap take a deep breath, and, as it were, crouch under his rider. The ball was hopping towards the right-hand boundary, and an Archangel riding for it with both spurs and a whip; but neither spur nor whip would make his pony stretch himself as he neared the crowd. The Maltese Cat glided under his very nose, picking up his hind legs sharp, for there was not a foot to spare between his quarters and the other pony's bit. It was as neat an exhibition as fancy figure-skating. Lutyens hit with all the strength he had left, but the stick slipped a little in his hand, and the ball flew off to the left instead of keeping close to the boundary. Who's Who was far across the ground, thinking hard as he galloped. He repeated, stride for stride, the Cat's manœuvres with another Archangel pony, nipping the ball away from under his bridle, and clearing his opponent by half a fraction of an inch, for Who's Who was clumsy behind. Then he drove away towards the right as the Maltese Cat came up from the left; and Bamboo held a middle course exactly between them. The three were making a sort of Government-broad-arrow-shaped attack; and there was only the Archangels' back to guard the goal; but immediately behind them were three Archangels racing for all they knew, and mixed up with them was Powell, sending Shikast along on what he felt was their last hope. It takes a very good man to stand up to the rush of seven crazy ponies in the last quarter of a cup game, when men are riding with their necks for sale, and the ponies are delirious. The Archangels' back missed his stroke, and pulled aside just in time to let the rush go by. Bamboo and Who's Who shortened stride to give the Maltese Cat room, and Lutyens got the goal with a clean, smooth, smacking stroke that was heard all over the field. But there was no stopping the ponies. They poured through the goal-posts in one mixed mob, winners and losers together, for the pace had been terrific. The Maltese Cat knew by experience what would happen, and, to save Lutyens, turned to the right with one last effort that strained a back-sinew beyond hope of repair. As he did so he heard the right-hand goal-post crack as a pony cannoned into it – crack, splinter, and fall like a mast. It had been sawed three parts through in case of accidents, but it upset the pony nevertheless, and he blundered into another, who blundered into the left-hand post, and then there was confusion and dust and wood. Bamboo was lying on the ground, seeing stars; an

Archangel pony rolled beside him, breathless and angry; Shikast had sat down dog-fashion to avoid fallling over the others, and was sliding along on his little bobtail in a cloud of dust; and Powell was sitting on the ground, hammering with his stick and trying to cheer. All the others were shouting at the top of what was left of their voices, and the men who had been spilt were shouting too. As soon as the people saw no one was hurt, ten thousand native and English shouted and clapped and yelled, and before anyone could stop them the pipers of the Skidars broke on to the ground, with all the native officers and men behind them, and marched up and down, playing a wild northern tune called "Zakhme Bagãn," and through the insolent blaring of the pipes and the high-pitched native yells you could hear the Archangels' band hammering, "For they are all jolly good fellows," and then reproachfully to the losing team, "Ooh, Kafoozalum! Kafoozalum! Kafoozalum!"

Besides all these things and many more, there was a Commander-in-Chief, and an Inspector-General of Cavalry, and the principal veterinary officer in all India, standing on the top of a regimental coach, yelling like school-boys; and brigadiers and colonels and commissioners, and hundreds of pretty ladies joined the chorus. But the Maltese Cat stood with his head down, wondering how many legs were left to him; and Lutyens watched the men and ponies pick themselves out of the wreck of the two goal-posts, and he patted the Cat very tenderly.

"I say," said the captain of the Archangels, spitting a pebble out of his mouth, "will you take three thousand for that pony – as he stands?"

"No, thank you. I've an idea he's saved my life," said Lutyens, getting off and lying down at full length. Both teams were on the ground too, waving their boots in the air and coughing and drawing deep breaths, as the *saises* ran up to take away the ponies, and an officious water-carrier sprinkled the players with dirty water till they sat up.

"My Aunt!" said Powell, rubbing his back and looking at the stumps of the goal-posts, "that was a game!"

They played it over again, every stroke of it, that night at the big dinner, when the Free-for-All Cup was filled and passed down the table, and emptied and filled again, and everybody made most eloquent speeches. About two in the morning, when there might have been some singing, a wise little, plain little, gray little head looked in through the open door.

"Hurrah! Bring him in," said the Archangels; and his *sais*, who was very happy indeed, patted the Maltese Cat on the flank, and he limped in to the blaze of light and the glittering uniforms, looking for Lutyens. He was used to messes, and men's bedrooms, and places where ponies are not usually encouraged, and in his youth had jumped on and off a mess-table for a bet. So he behaved himself very politely, and ate bread dipped in salt, and was petted all round the table, moving gingerly; and they drank his health, because he had done more to win the Cup than any man or horse on the ground.

That was glory and honour enough for the rest of his days, and the Maltese Cat did not complain much when his veterinary surgeon said that he would be no good for polo any more. When Lutyens married, his wife did not allow him to play, so he was forced to be umpire; and his pony on these occasions was a flea-bitten gray with a neat polo-tail, lame all round, but desperately quick on his feet, and, as everybody knew, Past Pluperfect Prestissimo Player of the Game.

AMERICA'S BIG FOUR, 1913
G.D. Armour

1937

IT IS A RATHER OLD STORY now and my impressions may not be as fresh or accurate as they were, but "The Big Four" made polo history, and are still spoken of with reverence. For the last few days I had heard of little else, even among people unconnected with the game. The general enthusiasm was such as I have never seen on this side of the Atlantic over any game. Curiously, my recollection is better of the first game than the second, so I confine myself to how that struck me.

The British team consisted of Captain Leslie Cheape, Captain Noel Edwards, Captain Ritson, Captain V. Lockett, in the order named. Spares were Lord Wodehouse and F.M. Freake.

The American side that year was what they called "The Big Four": Harry Payne Whitney (Captain), the two Waterburys and, last but not least, Devereux Milburn, then – as Lord Wodehouse, one of our spares, said to me at one of the matches – worth at least two goals more than any one in the game.

I cannot after this space of time, describe the matches point by point, nor, if I could, would my account be of much value, as, though I have played mild polo, it does not entitle me to give expert opinion. Milburn's play was always a joy to watch, and some of his defending shots marvellous. He could loft the ball over every one's head half-way up the ground, either forehand or backhand, as I do not think I have ever seen done by any one else. Both the Waterburys were strong, good hitters and very certain at all angles before goal, and I think Whitney, the captain, was also exceedingly capable in that respect.

In connection with the first match, I was particularly struck with this – certainly surmise also – that in practice games the American captain had probably noticed that our men were rather given to starting slow – that is, of course, comparatively speaking – and warming up in pace as things developed, and had given instructions to his men to go all out from the throw-in. Be this as it may, they put on two goals within two or three minutes of the start, and it appeared to me, kept the ball out of the middle line of the ground and played as far as possible afterwards.

It struck me that the Big Four were not pretty horsemen, not, at least, so good to look at as our own. But even this they seemed to turn to good account, their forward seat enabling them, sometimes, to hit some most difficult shots round the fore-end of their ponies. L. Waterbury hit one of their goals in this way, when appearing almost to sit on his pony's neck. I think, also, they were rather given to taking chances. I do not remember the detailed score, but so far as I do remember, the penalties cost them three half-goals, with no penalties against the British team. All round, I think they were better mounted than our men, had faster ponies, and, of course, had then, as now we also have, no size limit. One of Milburn's ponies dwells in my memory, though I have forgotten his name. He would not have looked out of place in a Grand National field, and was so good that, I think, he came out for three chukkers in the match. The matches were played in tremendous heat, beneath a literally brazen sky, which was very trying for all concerned. Those in authority allowed me to see the games from the boards, or anywhere I wished, not perhaps the best view to have of the whole points of the game, but offering me a chance to see details of it more useful from a pictorial point of view, and without obstruction from such things – if I may say so – as the expansive hats which ladies then used to wear.

I think the American influence speeded up polo as it did racing, and I am sure that the pace at which these international games go necessitates those taking part being in the youthful prime of life and absolutely fit to stand the strain entailed, to say nothing of the ponies.

LEAPING

The duty will devolve on you of seeing, in the first place, that your horses are well fed and in condition to stand their work since a horse which cannot endure fatigue will clearly be unable to overhaul the foeman or effect escape; and in the second place you will have to see to it that the animals are tractable since, clearly again, a horse that will not obey is only fighting for the enemy and not for his friends.

XENOPHON
On Horsemanship

SHOWJUMPING is a comparatively young sport. Perhaps the earliest instance of a public display of it was the leaping competition at the Royal Dublin Horse Show in 1865. It soon caught on as a military mounted game, with the Italians emerging as the masters of it. And, when it was introduced into the Olympic games in the early 1900s, a team trained and led by Captain Caprilli, using his revolutionary methods, won very easily.

A star-name in the activity after the First World War was Colonel Jack Talbot-Ponsonby, who won the coveted King George V Cup three years running. I begin with the excellent passage from his *Harmony in Horsemanship*, on training the jumper.

Two incidents from the life of that very popular champion of the 1950s, Pat Smythe, follow. The first recounts the jump-off between Colonel Llewellyn, riding Foxhunter, and Pat Smythe on Finality at Harringay, in 1950, the occasion which, as the author, Dorian Williams says, "really persuaded the public that showjumping was one of the most tele-photogenic of all sports." The second is that supremely human passage from her *Jump for Joy* in which she describes herself torn between her sporting aspirations and her desire to marry.

To represent combined training – showjumping, dressage and cross-country riding – otherwise known as "horse trials" or the *concours complet d'equitation*, but more generally referred to by the English-speaking nations as "eventing," I have included the climax of that most charming of equestrian autobiographies, *Up, up and Away*, by Lucinda Prior-Palmer, the girl who followed her Badminton triumphs by gaining the European

275

Championship in 1975 and again in 1977. It is devoid of conceit and full of humor, as indeed her whole book is.

TRAINING THE SHOWJUMPER

Colonel Jack Talbot-Ponsonby

1964

THE COMPONENT FACTORS in the training of a showjumper for his movements on the flat are free forward movement, obedience to hand and leg, balance and impulsion. When a high degree of impulsion can be produced and maintained a certain amount of natural collection will appear for a few seconds. I mean by this that a horse trained to this standard will instinctively gather himself to face an awkward situation, thereby producing collection for a few strides. But the collection is not enforced, and the horse is not moving forward at a collected canter ordered by the rider. He is merely developing, of his own accord, a shade more impulsion than that which the rider is capable of producing. It will therefore be a natural reflex action, and his physical attitude will not be similar to that required for periods of collected movement.

I am entirely opposed to the theory that a showjumper's training on the flat should be based on the search for collection. I maintain that the

accuracy essential for success must come from complete education in the four component factors, resulting in rhythmical and fluent movement, which will always allow the horse's natural freedom and liberty to take effect. Any curtailment of freedom and liberty will restrict his ability to deal with awkward situations and can well sap his courage. The cry should always be "Forward in control", so that when the take-off is reached the forward trend can be pursued in the form of forward propulsion into the air. This will mean that the rhythm and fluency of balanced movement during the approach will join forces with locomotion, to minimise the muscular effort required to make height and distance. The opposite of this, elevated impulsion, will call for a degree of enforced collection during approach, so that the forehand is lightened by each successive step prior to take-off, and the centre of gravity correspondingly moves back. In consequence, one small error of judgement on the rider's part, or a slight disobedience by the horse, will result in the horse being on the take-off platform in a physical state that makes the clearing of the obstacle difficult and sometimes wellnigh impossible.

To foster forwardness at all times and, as will be seen later, to assist in accurate stride control, I reccommend that the horse's head carriage should be low, and, for purposes of showjumping only, even slightly over-bent. During the approach, which means for the whole time spent in a showjumping round on the flat, the horse should resemble a compressed, slightly convex, spiral spring, the centre of his back being the highest point of the bend. If in such a state the loins, quarters, and hind legs, which are the propelling apparatus, and in this instance the back end of the spring, can sweep smoothly downwards and forwards under his centre, thereby producing power and stability. The front end of the spring, the neck and head, should also be bent downwards and forwards, thereby helping the back to round correctly, giving freedom and liberty to neck and shoulder, and obviating the evasive tendency of the head to come up with a change of contact of the bit in the mouth. When proceeding in this way the horse will have full and free use of all limbs and muscles, will be in a position to bounce off the ground from either a short or a long stride, and will automatically keep travelling forward. Vice versa, a high head carriage will produce a ewe-shaped neck. This will lead to a hollowing of the back and a consequent slackening of the loin muscles. The angle of the spine will then prevent the quarters and hind legs from sweeping under the horse, and all power and elasticity will vanish. Conformation, in the form of well-shaped shoulder and neck, and ample room in the jowl, can help greatly in the production of a low and constant head carriage.

DAVID AND GOLIATH

Dorian Williams

1973

THE FIRST OCCASION on which showjumping was televised was at the Olympic Games at Wembley in 1948, but I have always thought that it was a competition at the Horse of the Year Show in 1950 – the second Horse of the Year Show at Harringay – which really persuaded the public that showjumping was one of the most "tele-photogenic" of all sports.

The event to which I am referring was the Puissance competition that year for the Fred Foster Cup, and when finally the course was reduced, as usual, to two great fences, there were only two horses left in the competition. One was the mighty Foxhunter, ridden, of course, by Colonel Harry Llewellyn, and although it was more than two years since their Olympic triumph at Helsinki, they were still the most famous equestrian partnership in the world. The other was a little mare called Finality, ridden by a young rider barely twenty years old, called Pat Smythe. This was her first showjumper. She had, in fact, bought this little mare, whose mother pulled a milk float, for very little money, near her Gloucestershire home. But, although only 15h.h. this mare, thanks to the brilliant training and riding of Pat Smythe, quickly established herself as one of the best jumpers in the country, and only three months after Pat had first jumped it, she had had the honour to represent Britain at Ostend.

Unfortunately, Pat had been unable to afford to refuse the generous offer made for Finality by a North-Countryman – about £1,000! – and so she sold her, but in a new stable, with a different rider, the mare achieved no success. So at the first Horse of the Year Show, Pat Smythe was invited to ride her again. Immediately she won the Leading Showjumper of the Year championship.

Now, twelve months later, she found herself in this final jump-off with Colonel Llewellyn and Foxhunter in the Puissance, a David and Goliath situation if ever there was one. Foxhunter stood nearly 17h.h; his rider an Olympic Gold Medallist. Finality was little more than a pony – her rider barely out of her teens.

Finality had to jump first. The wall stood at over 6ft. The first fence was a huge triple bar with a spread of nearly 7ft. Finality jumped this fence awkwardly, but carefully. She turned at the end of the arena, sailed down to the wall and cleared that too.

It was then Foxhunter's turn. He jumped first the triple bar and then the wall – both clear. Both fences were then raised. Little Finality came in again. She met the triple awkwardly again and, although she made a great jump screwing over it, she had a pole down. She then turned to jump the big wall and, again, only just got over this: 4 faults. This seemed to be handing it to Foxhunter. He sailed down to the triple and jumped as though it were nothing at all, but turning to the wall he appeared to be a little over-confident, jumped it carelessly and, just tapping a brick, it came down, to give him 4 faults, and so they were equal once again.

The fences were raised. There was an absolute hush as the diminutive Finality and the youthful Pat Smythe rode into the ring. She galloped down to the triple bar, screwed over it, landing well to the left-hand side, but she was clear. Then Pat Smythe did a truly remarkable thing. She pulled up Finality altogether, and there were many people who thought that she had decided that the big, red wall was too much and that she was therefore going to retire. But not at all. In fact, she was just giving her little mare a brief opportunity to get properly balanced. She turned at the end of the arena to face the wall, gathered the reins, applied the pressure of her legs to Finality's sides and set off towards this great wall. She only cleared it by an inch or two, just rapping it with the hind hooves, but she *was* clear. And so, to keep in the competition, the great Foxhunter had to go clear again as well.

He came in looking every inch the greatest showjumper in the world – as undoubtedly he then was. He jumped the triple bar safely, and this time Colonel Harry Llewellyn was allowing no careless mistake at the wall. He collected himself, measured his stride, drove forward and cleared the wall.

And so both were clear yet again. There was a pause. The atmosphere in the stadium was by this time as tense as only these great occasions can inspire. Some eight thousand people awaited the appearance of Finality for yet another jump-off.

At this moment the telephone at my commentary position (which is also the control point at the Horse of the Year Show) rang. My assistant picked up the telephone and then whispered something to me. I was asked to make an announcement. But I did nothing. There was a few moments' pause and then my assistant whispered to me, "You were told to give it out." But I declined. I felt that what I was asked to announce could, in fact, be made public in a far more dramatic way. Instead, therefore, I gave the signal to open the gates from the collecting ring into the arena.

The gates were opened and into the arena rode the mighty Foxhunter – nearly 17h.h. – and by his side the little Finality – the David and Goliath that had been thrilling the crowd for the last half hour. When they reached the centre of the arena I gave another signal and the "boxing lights" were switched on, bathing the whole of the centre of the famous arena in a bright amber light. At that moment Harry Llewellyn leant down and offered his hand to Pat Smythe, who took it. Before that vast crowd they shook hands and Harry Llewellyn took off his hat to Pat.

That gesture made it quite clear that they had decided to divide. Another jump-off would mean that they would either equal yet again when already they had jumped quite enough, or one would have to be the loser when neither deserved to lose, so they had decided they would be equal first.

I do not think that I have ever heard a cheer the likes of that one which went up in the Harringay Stadium . . .

THE HEART OF PAT SMYTHE

Pat Smythe

1954

THE HARRINGAY HORSE of the Year Show brought Tosca and Hal together into glory. Hal carried off the Diana Stakes and Tosca the coveted Lonsdale Memorial Cup. But the surprise of the show was undoubtedly Tosca; a trifle over-ambitious, it seemed, I had entered her for the difficult Prix Caprilli, which involved us in stiff tests of dressage as well as jumping. Much to the astonishment of some of the experts who tended to think that showjumpers knew nothing of dressage, Tosca performed in brilliant style – and won. It was on these performances that she gained me, for the second time, the B.S.J.A. Spurs – a major award of the British Show Jumping Association.

The weeks and the shows flew by, and even while I still revelled in memories of our Spanish tour, the news arrived that we had been selected for Zurich, Geneva, Paris and Brussels – Tosca's first experience of show-jumping abroad.

The tour was a good one for the British team, but there was no doubt that our Continental rivals were masters of all the showjumping arts. High on our list of memories was the comedy performance of the showjumping year – starring Prince Hal, Nobbler, Colonel Llewellyn and me. It happened during the international relay at Geneva . . .

As an ex-racehorse perhaps Hal should have gone last, since he is never easy to pull up when he is excited. But in this event he went first, and at the end of our round Harry Llewellyn on Nobbler was to gallop behind us, take from me the traditional relay whip and begin jumping *his* round. It so happened that Hal went round at a fantastic speed, jumping our last fence enormously. Harry came hard on our trail, but not quite fast enough for Prince Hal's tremendous stride; hearing the beating hooves behind him, Hal the racehorse pulled away like a turbo-jet, the Nobbler just managed to catch up as we reached the first fence that Harry was intended to cope with. Unfortunately Harry and I dropped the whip between us as he jumped. So back came the Colonel to retrieve the whip, and I wondered if I should dismount to pick it up in order to save him time. Harry, however, waved me aside with a gallant gesture indicating that it was not a *lady's* task to climb down from her horse; at the same time he began to dismount.

"Began" is the word. He got no further, since with pieces of old string he had tied his stirrups to his spurs after discovering earlier that the stirrups were inclined to become unhitched when jumping Nobbler. Harry Llewellyn was a fixture on his horse.

Frantically he started to untie the strings. By this point the crowd was cheering with delight. Harry solemnly continued, got himself out of the stirrups, picked up the whip and galloped on. If not the most stylish, it was unquestionably the most popular event of the show.

For me, this Continental tour was also marked by a pathetic incident which put a revealing light on the reactions of men and women faced with an emotional disturbance at moments when all emotion should be blending with concentration on the tasks ahead.

In one of the showjumping cities – it does not matter which – I had a friend who was a first-class horseman, until the night that his young, beautiful, and temperamental fiancée decided to break off their engagement. Next morning I found him hollow-eyed and disconsolate, standing at a street corner gazing at the gutter as if his heart lay shattered in the newly collected heap of litter at his feet. We went to a cafe opposite, ordered rolls and large cups of coffee, and waited until the *garçon* laid them before us.

"You've got to pull yourself together. In two hours you'll be representing your Country in a big competition. Can you not try to forget all this till the end of the day?"

The young rider looked at me blankly, then turned his eyes away and murmured, half to himself:

"Can't you see I still love her? That's why I can't stand it. I love her, and I can't. . . . "

And that was more or less all he would say. I tried to make him see sense, but could not shake him out of the lethargy that was now affecting his physical strength as well as his mind.

Later he went into the ring and jumped atrociously. I was convinced that self-pity had lost him that competition. And my thoughts went back to the night, only a few weeks earlier, during Harringay's Horse of the Year Show. I knew what it felt like and the same sort of thing had nearly knocked me off my balance. Was it merely chance, I wondered, or was it some fundamental difference in the mental workings of women and men which determined whether you went to pieces?

I am going to tell this story because it does show that it is not always easy to reconcile showjumping and some of the things one most values in life. But it is not the sort of story one particularly enjoys telling.

For some time I had known someone whom I not only liked very much but who had come to mean more to me than anyone else. I was and still am quite sure that one should not be in a hurry over marriage – it is worth too much. But I was beginning seriously to think and feel that I was ready to consider it. One thing, however, was plain. I would need to be ready whole-heartedly to abandon showjumping if necessary, and I could not honestly say I was as sure about things as that. I thought he understood this – so it came as a shock when he met me at the close of the first day at Harringay and said:

"I suppose it is vital for you to go on this jaunt to Paris and Geneva. Or is it?"

"What on earth do you mean?" I asked.

"Oh, nothing. It's just that I see no reason for waiting much longer before we marry – and I think it's time you began making up your mind about whether it's me or Hal and Tosca you're in love with."

I must have looked rather upset for he added:

"Don't leap to conclusions. I'm not asking you to give up showjumping, merely to think again about this trip to Europe next month. After all, there'll be other opportunities to go abroad."

Before I could comment he went on: "It so happens that I take the whole month off from business. Surely it is worth swopping one tour for our honeymoon. Or don't you think that's important enough?"

Now it was not the first time – nor perhaps will it be the last – that my friends had remarked, "Pat's just a horsey girl, no time for men . . . I play second fiddle to Tosca, of course." . . . I take it in good heart, but never before had it come home quite so forcibly that men might be jealous of my work.

The next forty-eight hours were like a nightmare. Prince Hal was playing up as never before and his temperament had to be nursed with care. The Prix Caprilli and the Lonsdale Memorial Stakes loomed ahead. I had to meet people and to keep up appearances in various official engagements, but they seemed quite unreal. I felt utterly unnerved and unable to concentrate. I did not sleep that night.

Next morning I looked round the Harringay course and scrutinized the teams. They were mostly men. At that moment there came a sudden glow of determination that no man should beat me that day.

Tosca, the grey mare, was magnificent. We pulled off the Lonsdale Cup, the Prix Caprilli, and the B.S.J.A. Spurs.

GIRL CHAMPION OF EUROPE

Lucinda Prior-Palmer

1978

BE FAIR seemed to be enjoying his stay in Germany as much as I was. We went for long gentle rides and surveyed the German countryside together. He ate ravenously, unusual for him once the event was imminent. His ears went back when Jo brought his meals and he stood eating with one front leg bent up under his tummy in his impatient desire to eat quicker. I only did one half-hour session of schooling in the week before the event. I had found that when he became very fit he ran noticeably short of patience when being disciplined and I was much too unsure of the consequences to risk having a bolshy horse on my hands. Peter Scott-Dunn and Colonel Bill did not mind that I did not school him much, but they did object when I refrained from galloping either. I knew him and I knew how easy it was to send him over the top. Since adopting interval training, I had discovered how the horses thrived on a suggested pre-competition diminuendo. Three days before the cross-country we did one short sharp gallop of two furlongs up a hill to keep the peace. Apart from a similar burst after the dressage that was all the work Be Fair did while in Germany.

Before the dressage he still needed a great deal of work to cool a little of his chestnut blood running at a high pitch through his body. Although he was at last learning to contain himself when he went into the arena, I still never felt that I could sit down and ride him when he was inside the boards. Karl Shultz and Madrigal led after the dressage phase. He and another German had marks in the thirties; Be Fair was lying third with a score in the forties. There were a few in the fifties but most had higher penalties. Unbelieveably the British team led the Germans by ten points after the dressage and we were all as delighted as we were amazed. That evening for the last time I carefully studied the routes I was to take over the exquisitely built fences without noticing who I passed as I walked the flat four-and-a-half-mile course, trying to maintain my concentration. The prospect of the steeplechase course made everyone anxious for me because they were very worried that I would lose my way. They were not being sarcastic either; it was a twisty figure of eight course around which we had to describe a series of asymmetrical changes of direction. The fences were beautiful; big and soft, and Be Fair pounded round each turn and flew over each fence with ease and grace. I neither lost the way nor misjudged my time.

Most of the way down phase C I sang in between saying a passing "Guten Tag" to village children playing in the fields and gardens. One family, gathered by their front door, cheered when they recognised the British flag on my saddle cloth. I felt that the Germans cheering the British did not quite add up, but maybe they had mistaken me for Princess Anne.

My father in his accustomed light brown stock-coat, which he always wore when he was playing groom in the box, was ready to receive Be Fair who came in two minutes early off Phase C. Those extra two minutes are invaluable. Twelve minutes seems more than 120 seconds longer than ten minutes. My father assured me that he had counted the paces at the correct speed to the small starting enclosure and timed how long it would take him to lead Be Fair there from a given point. For a year we had employed this method and it worked well. Provided Be Fair did not have to stand still at the start for longer than one or two seconds he could keep his nerves under control and would not suddenly change into a speedy reverse.

On arrival in the box, I dismounted and was sat in the chair, offered some cool grapefruit juice by the ever attentive Mrs. Lithgow and duly briefed, very briefly. Janet had endured two more crashing falls and been eliminated. Princess Anne was clear and without time penalties. Sue had one stop and only a few time penalties. Ammerman, second after the dressage, had had one refusal and Shultz was on the cross-country at that moment.

Richard Meade had flown over to support the side and gave me a piece of advice which was to prove invaluable. He counselled me to line up on a different tree from that which I had intended if I were to succeed in negotiating all three parts of the Normandy Bank Series on a left-hand turn without running out.

I went to the mobile loo to digest the information and on finding them unusually comfortable fell deep in thought. Richard was despatched to bang on the door and tell me that it was time I stopped acting like Rodin's "The Thinker", and come out and go to work. Despite the tension I felt, this incident reminded me of the day I had locked myself in the loo at the age of four and refused to come out until the doctor with his beastly long syringe full of diphtheria vaccine had finally given up hope and driven away.

Emerging into the bright sunlight from the shade of the powder room on wheels, I noticed my mother standing waiting, her chores in the box completed. There is only one thing that makes me more apprehensive than riding across country and that is watching it. I knew that behind the sunglasses and calm exterior she felt even more tense than I. She used to say, "I mind so much about *both* of you. When you are riding a different horse my anxieties are halved."

My riding orders were delivered, they were simple.

"Go for it – the Gold, girl!" And Be Fair went for it like a bullet from a gun. He gave me a truly wonderful ride. A sensation of sheer enjoyment as he leapt from fence to fence, sploshed in and out of the awkward multiple complex of lake fences as if he was a surf board and jumped the final difficult series on a sharp left turn with such accuracy and agility that it was hard to believe that he had not walked the course three times himself.

Shultz was standing by the finish. He need not have asked, for my face and jubilant patting must have told him the answer.

"Okay?" he asked. "Okay," I replied. "And you?" "Von shtop into zee vater." Be Fair had shot into the lead for the European Championships with fifteen points or one showjump in hand. The British team had left the other nine nations behind as they stood nearly thirty-five points clear of the Soviet Union.

Perched on a land other than Earth, I sat drying my hair in my cosy bedroom in preparation for the evening's entertainment, a big dance and supper for all ten nationalities taking part. There was a knock on the window and once again I went cautiously to investigate. This time it was a white moustache which filled one of the small panes of the lead-rimmed glass. Colonel Bill had come to tell me that *none* of his girls were to go to the party that night.

"Oh but Colonel Bill we must – it's Phase E, it's the fifth phase of the speed and endurance test. If you don't go to the party you haven't completed the cross-country day."

No amount of persuasion succeeded. He felt that it was his responsibility to ensure that there were three British girls fit and ready to win two Gold Medals and one silver the following day and not wandering around with a headache and cross-eyed vision. That was that. Mike Tucker went to wave the flag at the party in the company of three eminent spectators: Richard Meade, Mark Philips and Chris Collins. All three had come out for the week-end to support the "Britischen Amazonen".

Somewhat seething we ate dinner in our hotel. Underneath our displeasure we could see our chief's point. Apart from two Irish ladies of less tender years than ourselves, we were the only females out of the fifty-five men in the competition and we were holding the key position. All in all we supposed that we were quite worth "nobbling" that night.

In continued sweltering sunshine the three team horses and the two individuals came up before the panel of vets the final morning. Janet Hodgson was in bed with bad concussion and Larkspur stayed in his stable. Various foreigners remarked on Be Fair's condition as they eyed him being led around the court-yard by Joanna. None of us could remember a Three-Day-Event where he had looked more magnificent. His legs, thankfully, had never given us another moment's worry since prior to Burghley the previous year. He sprang up the asphalt lane towards the vets between a line of shady apple trees. It was plain for all to see that he was not springing through the air to show how sound he was; he was springing through the air to show that he was "The Greatest".

Alas, disaster struck the team in the showjumping.

Princess Anne confirmed her individual Silver Medal with a clear round, but poor Sue Hatherley had an expensive thirty-penalty fall when the sore-legged Harley missed his jerk at a double of uprights. She finished the course with forty-two penalties and the team Gold turned not to ashes but to silver as the Russians reaped the reward for a well polished performance throughout the competition. As I stood on my feet at the entrance to the arena I was not sure if my eyes were telling me the truth as they watched Sue and Harley's mishap. I glanced over to where Richard and Mark stood watching. They returned the look with blank empty faces. I felt for Sue. How can you console someone when they know that they have lost their country a Gold Medal in the eleventh hour. Princess Anne was marvellous. "Absolute rubbish," she told Sue as the latter apologised. "These things happen with horses."

The exhilaration of a brilliant ride across country had given way to a frosty apprehension by the morning of the showjumping. A small error and so much can be lost in this cold-blooded phase. I felt no less frozen when Be Fair cantered into the arena at Luhmühlen than during the same moment at Badminton two years earlier. Be Fair stood still for long enough to allow me to bow hastily to the judges and then fidgeted and wriggled and asked to be allowed to move into action. In under two minutes time either he would or would not be the European Champion. I shut the thought out of my mind and ordered myself to get on with the job in hand.

Be Fair knew. He was more intent on becoming the Champion of Europe than any other horse on the Continent. The papers reported a deafening roar as we came through the finish. I did not hear the crowd; I was already in Wonderland. Be Fair swept me out of the arena and down through a channel of cheering spectators. I had noticed my father on the way out: he was pulling a handkerchief from his pocket, his wet face glistening in the bright sun.

Late in the afternoon of 7 September, in a clearing on Lüneburg Heath, not far from the spot where a more famous British victory had earlier been recorded, Be Fair stood alone, the rest of Europe fanned out behind him.

The loudspeaker announced his name, his new title and his nationality in three different languages. The British flag climbed the highest of the white poles as the band struck up the National Anthem. Be Fair stood like rock, four square, neck and head still and proud. I sat on his tight, short back, holding my whip vertically from my thigh in salute. Looking between his ears I saw the Gold Medal lying on a velvet-covered table. I was not thinking about medals, instead I wondered if Be Fair had ever had ear-ache, like once I had had jaw-ache from smiling too widely. He always wore his ears so tightly pricked.

I wanted to ride Be Fair myself the two miles through the woods back to the stables because I wanted to savour every second with him. Those special moments evaporate all too soon. Instead I was scooped into the Press tent for a "conference". Joanna took him back. She did not ride, she led him because she wanted to talk to him and tell him that he was indeed "The Greatest", all the way back to the stables.

OLD
COACHING DAYS

No horse lives so high as a coach-horse. In the language of the stable, his stomach is the measure of his corn; he is fed ad libitum. *The effect of this is visible in two ways:- first, it is surprising to see how soon horses gather flesh in this severe work; for there is none, as far as muscular exertion goes, more severe while it lasts: and, secondly, proprietors find that good flesh is no obstacle to their speed, but, on the contrary, operates to their advantage. Horses draw by their weight: the heavier a horse is then, the more powerful he is in harness; in short it is the weight of the animal which produces the draught, and the play and force of his muscles serve to continue it. Light horses, therefore, how good so ever their action, ought not to be put to draw a heavy load, as muscular force cannot act against it for any great length of time.*

"NIMROD,"
in The Quarterly Review, 1828

"NIMROD" was not only a very fine horseman, and hunting-field and turf commentator, he was also one of the great experts of his era, possibly the greatest, on coaching. In one of his *Quarterly Review* contributions of the 1820s, which I have reproduced here, he writes about the latest vehicles on the road as a motoring correspondent might discuss new car makes today, while, in the second piece, he mourns the passing of the old-fashioned coachman.

Why this new look? The answer is that, around the end of the eighteenth century, John Loudon MacAdam, with the cooperation of the Office of Works, streamlined the English roads. He gave them firm surfaces, hardened and evened with square-shaped stones, and thus rid them of ruts – or quarters, as they were called – which, until then, had made coach travel slow, dangerous and comparatively very uncomfortable. The consequence was that smarter and lighter coaches became the vogue, coaches drawn more and more by thoroughbred horses. "In 1742" wrote Nimrod,

The Oxford stage-coach left London at seven o'clock in the morning, and reached Uxbridge at mid-day. It arrived at High Wycombe at five in the evening, where it rested for the night; and proceeded at the same rate for the seat of learning on the morrow. Here then were ten hours consumed each day in travelling twenty-seven miles; and nearly two days in performing what is now done with the greatest ease under six hours. To go from London to York – 200 miles – used to take six days; it now occupies 20 hours.

But, as for the coachman, for all the zephyr quality of his new conveyances, it is doubtful whether he had really changed much. That inveterate American traveler and writer, Washington Irving, journeying in the English North Country in the reign of George IV, meets just the same type of charioteer, whose demise Nimrod is, at the same time, repining. Dickens, writing when Victoria was young, seems to find them at least as tough and bluff and so does the early nineteenth-century essayist, Leigh Hunt, as I show.

The Dickens piece cited here is pre-MacAdam, coming from the 1780s and *The Tale of Two Cities*. Every Dickens devotee will remember that muddy misty night at the beginning of the book, when the Dover Mail climbs Shooter's Hill, "with the jackboots of its passengers squashing

along by its side, and the messenger, "Jerry" calling out for "Mr. Jarvis Lorry!" while the gruff coachman cocks his blunderbuss at him.

Travel was from posting-house to posting-house, the nearest equivalent now being changing trains during a railway journey. These staging-posts teemed with post-boys or postilions, unharnessing tired horses, harnessing fresh horses, riding them and leading them, and repairing coaches. They were often old grooms who had come down in the world, and Dickens had a compassionate spot in his heart for them. "Without going so far as to assert," says Sam Weller in *The Pickwick Papers*,

> as some wery sensible people do, that post-boys and donkeys is both immortal, wot I say is this; that whenever they feels theirselves gettin' stiff and past their work, they just rides off together, wun postboy to a pair in the usual way; wot becomes on 'em nobody knows, but it's wery probable as they starts avay to take their pleasure in some other world, for there ain't a man alive as ever see, either a donkey or a post-boy a takin' his pleasure in this!"

But what a contrast the open road was with London. To end, as we began with "Nimrod." At Hyde Park Corner, that authority told the would-be observer that he would

> see what no other country under the heavens can show him . . . in the space of two hours he will see a thousand well-appointed equipages pass before him to the Mall, in all the pomp of aristocratic pride, and in which the very horses themselves appear to partake. Everything he sees is peculiar – the silent roll and easy motion of the London-built carriage – the *style* of the coachmen – it is hard to determine which shine brightest, the lace on their clothes, their own round faces, or their flaxen wigs – the pipe-clayed reins –pipe-clayed lest they should soil the clean white gloves – the gigantic young fellows, in huge cocked hats bedaubed with lace, in laced silk stockings, . . . not forgetting the spotted coach-dog, which has just been washed for the occasion . . .

But then Dickens did not go to Hyde Park Corner for his copy.

THE LATEST ON THE ROAD

"Nimrod"

1831

A WONDERFUL CHANGE has taken place in the English coach-horse, as well as the sort of horses put into other kinds of harness; but this has been progressive. Fifty years ago, the idea of putting a thorough-bred horse into harness would have been considered preposterous. In the carriages of our noblemen and gentlemen, the long-tailed black, or Cleveland bay – each one remove from the carthorse – was the prevailing sort, and six miles an hour the extent of his pace; and he cost from 30*l* to 50*l*. A few years back, a nobleman gave seven hundred guineas for a horse to draw his cabriolet: two hundred guineas is now an every-day price for a horse of this description, and a hundred and fifty for a gentleman's coach-horse! Indeed, a pair of handsome coach-horses, fit for London, and well broken and bitted, cannot be purchased under two hundred guineas; and even job-masters often give much more for them to let out to their customers. In harness, also, we think we have arrived at perfection, to which the invention of the patent shining leather has mainly contributed. A handsome horse, well harnessed is a noble sight; and is it not extraordinary that in no country but England is the art of putting horses into harness generally understood? Independently of the workmanship of the harness-maker, if our road-horses were put to their coaches in the loose awkward fashion of the Continent, we could never travel at the rate we do. It is the command given over the coach-horse that alone enables us to do it.

We may as well say a word or two as to private vehicles ere we close. As a facsimile of the gentleman's family coach of fifty years back has now become difficult to produce, we will describe it. It had a most comfortable and roomy body, quite fit to contain six portly persons, and suspended by long leather braces, affixed to nearly upright springs. To enable the body to hang low, the perch of a bent form, called the compass perch, was used; and the *carriage* was of great length and strength. In fact it was, coachman and all, in strict accordance with the animals that drew it, and came under the denomination of "slow and easy." The fashionable open carriage of this day was a still more unsightly object – the high, single-bodied phaeton, all upon the fore wheels, and looking as if the hinder ones had nothing to do but to follow. This was the favourite carriage of the late King when Prince of Wales, and was commonly driven, by such as could afford it, with four horses in hand. Indeed, it may almost be said to have given birth to our gentleman-coachmanship, as well as to the well-known doggerel epigram:-

> *What can Tommy Onslow do?*
> *He can drive a phaeton and two.*
> *Can Tommy Onslow do no more?*
> *Yes – he can drive a phaeton and four!*

The phaeton was succeeded by the no less classically yclept curricle – a carriage, when properly appointed and followed by two well-dressed and well-mounted grooms, of singular elegance certainly. It had a long run in the fashionable world; but being, like the phaeton, only calculated to carry two persons, and requiring never less than three horses, taxation and economy put an end to it. Then came the reign of the gig. The curate's wife, a gouty attorney, or a rich old farmer, fifty years ago, might be seen boxed up in a "whiskey" – which, being hung on hind and fore braces, with a head to protect its inmates from weather, made a convenient family conveyance, and – with a steady dobbin to draw it – a safe one. Economy induced a leader of *ton* to cast favouring eyes on this snug whiskey; and thence the airy gig, which, with a hundred-guinea horse in it, has been the best friend to doctors and undertakers they have ever yet found. The race has multiplied, and many names and varieties have been adopted in succession. The quiet movement of their wheels, the nice equilibrium in which they are placed on the axle, the evenness of their motion by reason of their being detached from their shafts, and the ease with which they

follow the horse, make gigs delightful carriages to ride in, and we could wish they were not so dangerous. The Stanhope, so named after the Honourable Fitzroy Stanhope, who planned it, succeeded the Tilbury, so called from the well-known coach-maker; and the cost, without harness, of either may be about 70*l*. Now "every dog has his day," and so have our prevailing fashions. The Buggy, Stanhope, Dennet, and Tilbury, have all, during some seasons past, been supplanted by the cabriolet for town work, for which we must allow it is far more suitable – though much too heavy for the road. In London, this has been at the opera, at the theatres, at the club-houses, and at dinner parties, with a neat little urchin on the foot-board, performing all the offices of the chariot with not a third of its expenses. The English cabriolet, however, is rather on the decline in the fashionable world, and the light and airy Tilbury is making its appearance again.

For country work nearly all these open vehicles have given place to the double-bodied phaeton and the britzska, both of which are much used in travelling post. The former is likewise in vogue with citizens and others who have families, and is now made so light as to be drawn by one horse with four persons in it with ease, for a limited number of miles. Descending still lower in the scale, and only one remove from the donkey-cart, is what is called the pony-chaise, out of which more people have been killed than we should like to enumerate here. These vehicles, by far the most dangerous carriages of the whole family they belong to, are so light that an animal even of little power can do what he pleases with them; they are also obliged to be made so short in the carriage, that the least thing upsets them, while the persons in them are not out of reach of heels. Should the animal be alarmed and endeavour to run away, the lowness and lightness of the vehicle nearly destroy all power of resistance; indeed, if he have much power, a carriage of this description may be compared to a canister tied to a dog's tail.

THE OLD-FASHIONED SORT

"Nimrod"

1828

IT IS, indeed, gratifying to contemplate the change that has lately taken place in the whole system of the road; and it is a most humane one. The old-fashioned coachman to a heavy coach – and they were all heavy down to very recent times – bore some analogy with the prize-fighter, for he stood highest who hit hardest. He was generally a man of large frame, made larger by indulgence, and of great bodily power – which was useful to him. To the button-hole of his coat were appended several whipcord points, which he was sure to have occasion for on the road, for his horses where whipped till whipping was as necessary to them as their harness. In fair play to him however, he was not solely answerable for this: the spirit of his cattle was broken by the task they were called to perform – for in those days twenty-mile stages were in fashion – and what was the consequence? Why, the four-horse whip and the Nottingham whipcord were of no avail over the latter part of the ground, and something like a cat-o'-nine-tails was produced out of the boot, which was jocularly called "the apprentice"; – and a shrewd apprentice it was to the art of torturing, which was inflicted on the wheelers without stint or measure; but without which the coach might have been often left on the road. One circumstance alone saved these horses from destruction; this was the frequency of ale-houses on the road, not one of which could then be passed without a call.

Still our old-fashioned coachman was a scientific man in his calling – more so, perhaps, than by far the greater part of his brethren of the present day, inasmuch as his energies and skill were more frequently put to the

293

test. He had heavy loads, bad roads, and weary horses to deal with, neither was any part of his harness to be depended on, upon a pinch. Then the box he sat upon was worse than Pandora's, with all the evils it contained, for even hope appeared to have deserted it. It rested on the bed of the axletree, and shook the frame to atoms; but when prayers were put up to have it altered, the proprietors said, "No; the rascal will always be asleep if we place his box on the springs." If, among all these difficulties, then, he, by degrees, became a drunkard, who can wonder at his becoming so? But he was a *coachman*. He could fetch the last ounce out of a wheel-horse by the use of his double thong or his "apprentice," and the point of his lash told terribly upon his leaders. He likewise applied it scientifically; it was directed under the bar to the flank, and after the third hit he brought it up to his hand by *the draw*, so that it never got entangled in the pole-chains, or in any part of the harness. He could untie a knot with his teeth and tie another with his tongue, as well as he could with his hands; and if his thong broke off in the middle, he could splice it with dexterity and even with neatness as his coach was proceeding on its journey. In short, he could do what coachmen of the present day cannot do, because they have not been called upon to do it; and he likewise could do what they never try to do – namely, he could drive when he was drunk nearly as well as when he was sober. He was very frequently a faithful servant to his employers; considered trustworthy by banks and others in the country through which he passed; and as humane to his horses, perhaps, as the adverse circumstances he was placed in by his masters would admit.

AN AMERICAN ON ENGLISH COACHMEN

Washington Irving

1820

IN THE COURSE of a December tour in Yorkshire, I rode for a long distance in one of the public coaches, on the day preceding Christmas. The coach was crowded, both inside and out, with passengers, who, by their talk, seemed principally bound to the mansions of relations or friends, to eat the Christmas dinner. It was loaded also with hampers of game, and baskets and boxes of delicacies; and hares hung dangling their long ears about the coachman's box, presents from distant friends for the impending feast. I had three fine rosy-cheeked school-boys for my fellow-passengers inside, full of the buxom health and manly spirit which I have observed in the children of this country. They were returning home for the holidays in high glee, and promising themselves a world of enjoyment. It was delightful to hear the gigantic plans of the little rogues, and the impracticable feats they were to perform during their six weeks' emancipation from the abhorred thraldom of book, birch, and pedagogue. They were full of anticipations of the meeting with the family and household, down to the very cat and dog; and of the joy they were to give their little sisters by the presents with which their pockets were crammed; but the meeting to which they seemed to look forward with the greatest impatience was with Bantam, which I found to be a pony, and, according to their talk, possessed of more virtues than any steed since the days of Bucephalus. How he could trot! how he could run! and then such leaps as he would take – there was not a hedge in the whole country that he could not clear.

They were under the particular guardianship of the coachman, to whom, whenever an opportunity presented, they addressed a host of questions, and pronounced him one of the best fellows in the world. Indeed, I could not but notice the more than ordinary air of bustle and importance of the coachman, who wore his hat a little on one side, and had a large bunch of Christmas greens stuck in the button-hole of his coat. He is always a personage full of mighty care and business, but he is particularly so during this season, having so many commissions to execute in consequence of the great interchange of presents. And here, perhaps, it may not be unacceptable to my untravelled readers, to have a sketch that may serve as a general representation of this very numerous and important class of functionaries, who have a dress, a manner, a language, an air, peculiar to themselves, and prevalent throughout the fraternity; so that, wherever an English stage-coachman may be seen, he cannot be mistaken for one of any other craft or mystery.

He has commonly a broad, full face, curiously mottled with red, as if the blood had been forced by hard feeding into every vessel of the skin; he is swelled into jolly dimensions by frequent potations of malt liquors, and his bulk is still further increased by a multiplicity of coats, in which he is buried like a cauliflower, the upper one reaching to his heels. He wears a broad-brimmed, low-crowned hat; a huge roll of coloured handkerchief about his neck, knowingly knotted and tucked in at the bosom; and has in summer time a large bouquet of flowers in his button-hole; the present, most probably, of some enamoured country lass. His waistcoat is commonly of some bright colour, striped, and his smallclothes extend far below the knees, to meet a pair of jockey-boots which reach about halfway up his legs.

All this costume is maintained with much precision; he has a pride in having his clothes of excellent materials; and, notwithstanding the seeming grossness of his appearance, there is still discernible that neatness and propriety of person which is almost inherent in an Englishman. He enjoys great consequence and consideration along the road; has frequent conferences with the village housewives; who look upon him as a man of great trust and dependence; and he seems to have a good understanding with every bright-eyed country lass. The moment he arrives where the horses are to be changed, he throws down the reins with something of an air, and abandons the cattle to the care of the ostler; his duty being merely to drive from one stage to another. When off the box, his hands are thrust into the pockets of his great coat, and he rolls about the inn yards with an air of the most absolute lordliness. Here he is generally surrounded by an admiring throng of ostlers, stable-boys, shoeblacks, and those nameless hangers-on that infest inns and taverns, and run errands, and do all kinds of odd jobs, for the privilege of battening on the drippings of the kitchen and the leakage of the taproom. These all look up to him as to an oracle; treasure up his cant phrases; echo his opinions about horses and other topics of jockey lore; and above all, endeavour to imitate his air and carriage. Every ragamuffin that has a coat to his back thrusts his hands in the pockets, rolls in his gait, talks slang, and is an embryo Coachey.

Perhaps it might be owing to the pleasing serenity that reigned in my own mind, that I fancied I saw cheerfulness in every countenance throughout the journey. A stage coach, however, carries animation always with it, and puts the world in motion as it whirls along. The horn, sounded at the entrance of a village, produces a general bustle. Some hasten forth to meet friends; some with bundles and bandboxes to secure places, and in the hurry of the moment can hardly take leave of the group that accompanies them.

THE DOVER MAIL

Charles Dickens

1859

THE LAST BURST carried the mail to the summit of the hill. The horses stopped to breathe again, and the guard got down to skid the wheel for the descent, and open the coach-door to let the passengers in.

"Tst! Joe!" cried the coachman in a warning voice, looking down from his box.

"What do you say, Tom?"

They both listened.

"I say a horse at a canter coming up, Joe."

"*I* say a horse at a gallop, Tom," returned the guard, leaving his hold of the door and mounting nimbly to his place. "Gentlemen! In the King's name, all of you!"

With this hurried adjuration, he cocked his blunderbuss, and stood on the offensive.

The passenger booked by this history, was on the coach-step, getting in; the other two passengers were close behind him, and about to follow. He remained on the step, half in the coach and half out of it; they remained in the road below him. They all looked from the coachman to the guard, and from the guard to the coachman, and listened. The coachman looked back and the guard looked back, and even the emphatic leader pricked up his ears and looked back, without contradicting.

The stillness consequent on the cessation of the rumbling and labouring of the coach, added to the stillness of the night, made it very quiet indeed. The panting of the horses communicated a tremulous motion to the coach, as if it were in a state of agitation. The hearts of the passengers beat loud enough perhaps to be heard; but at any rate, the quiet pause was audibly expressive of people out of breath, and holding the breath, and having the pulses quickened by expectation.

The sound of a horse at a gallop came fast and furiously up the hill.

"So-ho!" the guard sang out, as loud as he could roar. "Yo there! Stand! I shall fire!"

The pace was suddenly checked, and, with much splashing and floundering, a man's voice called from the mist, "Is that the Dover mail?"

"Never you mind what it is?" the guard retorted. "What are you?"

"*Is* that the Dover mail?"

"Why do you want to know?"

"I want a passenger, if it is."

"What passenger?"

"Mr. Jarvis Lorry."

Our booked passenger showed in a moment that it was his name. The guard, the coachman, and the two other passengers eyed him distrustfully.

"Keep where you are," the guard called to the voice in the mist, "because if I should make a mistake, it could never be set right in your lifetime. Gentleman of the name of Lorry answer straight."

"What is the matter?" asked the passenger, then, with mildly quavering speech. "Who wants me? Is it Jerry?"

("I don't like Jerry's voice, if it is Jerry", growled the guard to himself. "He's hoarser than suits me is Jerry").

"Yes, Mr. Lorry."

"What is the matter?"

"A despatch sent after you from over yonder. T. and Co."

"I know this messenger, guard," said Mr. Lorry, getting down into the road – assisted from behind more swiftly than politely by the other two passengers, who immediately scrambled into the coach, shut the door, and pulled up the window. "He may come close; there's nothing wrong."

"I hope there ain't, but I can't make so 'Nation sure of that," said the guard, in gruff soliloquy. "Hallo you!"

"Well! And hallo you!" said Jerry, more hoarsely than before.

"Come on at a footpace! D'ye mind me? And if you've got holsters to that saddle of yourn, don't let me see your hand go nigh 'em. For I'm a devil at a quick mistake, and when I make one it takes the form of Lead. So now let's look at you."

The figures of a horse and rider came slowly through the eddying mist, and came to the side of the mail, where the passenger stood. The rider stooped, and casting up his eyes at the guard, handed the passenger a small folded paper. The rider's horse was blown, and both horse and rider covered with mud, from the hoofs of the horse to the hat of the man.

"Guard!" said the passenger, in a tone of quiet business confidence.

The watchful guard, with his right hand at the stock of his raised blunderbuss, his left at the barrel, and his eye on the horseman, answered curtly, "Sir."

"There is nothing to apprehend. I belong to Tellson's Bank. You must know Tellson's Bank in London. I am going to Paris on business. A crown to drink. I may read this?"

"If so be as you're quick, sir."

He opened it in the light of the coach-lamp on that side, and read – first to himself and then aloud: "'Wait at Dover for Mam'selle.' It's not long, you see, guard. Jerry, say that my answer was, RECALLED TO LIFE."

Jerry started in his saddle. "That's a blazing strange answer, too", said he, at his hoarsest.

"Take that message back, and they will know that I received this, as well as if I wrote. Make the best of your way. Good-night."

With those words the passenger opened the coach-door and got in; not at all assisted by his fellow-passengers, who had expeditiously secreted their watches and purses in their boots, and were now making a general pretence of being asleep. With no more definite purpose than to escape the hazard of originating any other kind of action.

The coach lumbered on again, with heavier wreaths of mist closing round it as it began the descent. The guard soon replaced his blunderbuss in his arm-chest, and, having looked to the rest of its contents, and having looked to the supplementary pistols that he wore in his belt, looked to a smaller chest beneath his seat, in which there were a few smith's tools, a couple of torches, and a tinder-box. For he was furnished with that completeness that if the coach-lamps had been blown and stormed out, which did occasionally happen, he had only to shut himself up inside, keep the flint and sparks well off the straw, and get a light with tolerable safety and ease (if he were lucky) in five minutes.

"Tom!" softly over the coach-roof.

"Hallo, Joe."

"Did you hear the message?"

"I did, Joe."

"What did you make of it, Tom?"

"Nothing at all, Joe."

"That's a coincidence, too," the guard mused, "for I made the same of it myself."

Jerry, left alone in the mist and darkness, dismounted meanwhile, not only to ease his spent horse, but to wipe the mud from his face, and shake the wet out of his hat-brim, which might be capable of holding about a half a gallon. After standing with the bridle over his heavily-splashed arm, until the wheels of the mail were no longer within hearing and the night was quite still again, he turned to walk down the hill.

"After that there gallop from Temple Bar, old lady, I won't trust your fore-legs till I get you on the level," said the hoarse messenger, glancing at his mare. "'Recalled to life'. That's a blazing strange message. Much of that wouldn't do for you, Jerry! I say, Jerry! You'd be in a Blazing bad way, if recalling to life was to come into fashion, Jerry!"

NO INHUMAN MASS. . .

J.H. Leigh Hunt

c. 1830

THE MAIL or stage-coachman, upon the whole, is no inhuman mass of great-coat, gruffness, civility, and old boots. The latter is the politer, from the smaller range of acquaintance, and his necessity for preserving them. His face is red, and his voice rough, by the same process of drink and catarrh. He has a silver watch with a steel chain, and plenty of loose silver in his pocket, mixed with halfpence. He serves the houses he goes by for a clock. He takes a glass at every alehouse; for thirst, when it is dry, and for warmth when it is wet. He likes to show the judicious reach of his whip, by twigging a dog or a goose on the road, or children that get in the way. His tenderness to descending old ladies is particular. He touches his hat to Mr. Smith. He gives "the young woman" a ride, and lends her his box-coats in the rain. His liberality in imparting his knowledge to anyone that has the good fortune to ride on the box with him, is a happy mixture of deference, conscious possession, and familiarity. His information chiefly lies in the occupancy of houses on the road, prizefighters, Bow Street runners and accidents. He concludes that you know Dick Sams, or Old Joey, and proceeds to relate some of the stories that relish his pot and tobacco in the evening. If any of the four-in-hand gentry go by, he shakes his head, and thinks they might find something better to do. His contempt for them is founded on modesty. He tells you that his off-hand horse is as pretty a goer as ever was, but that Kitty – "Yeah, now there, Kitty, can't you be still? Kitty's a devil, Sir, for all you wouldn't think it." He knows that the boys on the road admire him, and gives the horse an indifferent lash with his whip as they go by. If you wish to know what rain and dust can do, you should look at his old hat. There is an indescribably placid and paternal look in the position of his old corduroy knees and old top-boots on the foot-board, with their pointed toes and never-cleaned soles.

ADVENTURE
AND ADVERSITY

As in the choice of a horse and a wife a man must please himself, ignoring the opinion and advice of friends, so in the governing of each it is unwise to follow out any fixed system of discipline.

GEORGE WHYTE-MELVILLE

IN THE FOLLOWING PAGES we gallop in heroic alarm with Paul Revere from Charlestown to Lexington, giving warning of the march of the British troops; and with Joris and Dirck we gallop in triumph, "bringing the good news from Ghent to Aix." With Cervantes we laugh, wistfully, as Rozinante, Don Quixote's charger, is seen off by the Galician mares, and as the poor knight of La Mancha and his tubby squire, Sancho Panza, challenge the Yanguesians, only to be concussed for their trouble.

With Mazeppa, Byron brings salvation to end a tale of woe. In this narrative poem, which was inspired from an incident in Voltaire's biography of Charles XII of Sweden, the king flees the field of battle after a defeat by the Russians, and sleeps that night in a wood, surrounded by his chiefs, among them the veteran warrior, Mazeppa. During the battle Charles noted the remarkable devotion of Mazeppa's horse and the heroic duo they make in the fight, and he asks the old chief how he came to have such an empathy with horses. Mazeppa replies that when he was a youth of twenty, serving at the court of Casimir, "the Polish Solomon," he fell in love with the beautiful Theresa, who was married to the proud Count Palatine; and she, being thirty years younger than her husband, "grew daily more tired of his dominion." When the Count discovered the affair, his fury was due more than anything else to fear, "lest such an accident should chance to touch upon his future pedigree . . . he being the highest of his line." Mazeppa's punishment is to be strapped to a wild horse, which is lashed away into the night. There my quotation begins. At the point of death, where it ends, Mazeppa was rescued and succoured by peasants, who find him and his exhausted steed in a forest. There's tragedy too, in the vignette I have borrowed from Kay Boyle's *The White Horses of Vienna*, an anecdote involving an old groom, who kills, first his charge, belonging

301

to the Spanish Riding School, and then himself, rather than see the horse go to the Maharajah, who has offered an unprecedented sum for it.

The horse-fight, described in *Njal's Saga*, epitomises the stark violence of the whole of that epic. Widely acclaimed as the greatest of the many powerful sagas stemming from medieval Iceland, the story, whose central figure is Njal Thorgeirsson, a rich and influential farmer, was written in the thirteenth century about events some three hundred years earlier. Magnus Magnusson was the translator of this 1960 edition.

Charles Kingsley has us in eleventh-century Lincolnshire next, with Hereward the Wake as the triumphant winner of his "enchanted mare." Then Percy F. Westerman (who, as boys, we read – along with Kipling, Scott, Twain, Haggard and Henty) sets a seventeenth-century scene, in which the Royalist hero of *The Young Cavalier* finishes a desperate gallop over a cliff-top " . . . and with a heavy splash my horse and I struck the surface of the water simultaneously. Then everything became a blank . . ."

Moyra Charlton, the author of the following piece – a chapter from her *Tally Ho* – was aged eleven when the book was published, in 1930. The foreword is by Lord Lonsdale: "Although there are some 60 years between our ages", the "Yellow Earl" wrote from Lowther, "I think you possess a greater power of writing than I do . . . and your book is full of human feeling and instinct towards animals." Reading *A Night before the Fair* one can readily endorse the old man's verdict. Moyra dedicates the book to "my own darling Dad and Mum as a surprise, because it is to them I owe so much of my love of horses." But, regrettably, in my example of this love, the theme is man's thoughtlessness, resulting in tragedy, albeit a very minor tragedy, for the horse.

Sir Arthur Conan Doyle features now as a versifier in a Kiplingesque narrative, *The Groom's Story*, which was written shortly after the First World War, and is about competition between the horse and the combustion engine, as seen through the eyes of a groom of the old school.

Last of all comes Kipling's black, *The Undertaker's Horse*, which, in the old days, was a leading character in the last chapter of every man and woman whose family could afford a slap-up funeral.

1775: PAUL REVERE'S RIDE

Henry Longfellow

1861

Listen, my children, and you shall hear
Of the midnight ride of Paul Revere,

On the eighteenth of April, in Seventy-five;
Hardly a man is now alive
Who remembers that famous day and year.

He said to his friend, "If the British march
By land or sea from the town to-night,
Hang a lantern aloft in the belfry arch
Of the North Church tower as a signal light, —
One, if by land, and two, if by sea;
And I on the opposite shore will be,
Ready to ride and spread the alarm
Through every Middlesex village and farm,
For the country folk to be up and to arm.

Then he said, "Good night!" and with muffled oar
Silently rowed to the Charlestown shore,
Just as the moon rose over the bay,
Where swinging wide at her moorings lay
The Somerset, British man-of-war;
A phantom ship, with each mast and spar
Across the moon like a prison bar,
And a huge black hulk, that was magnified
By its own reflection in the tide.

Meanwhile, his friend, through alley and street,
Wanders and watches with eager ears,
Till in the silence around him he hears
The muster of men at the barrack door,
The sound of arms, and the tramp of feet,
And the measured tread of the grenadiers,
Marching down to their boats on the shore.

Then he climbed the tower of the Old North Church,
By the wooden stairs with stealthy tread,
To the belfry-chamber overhead,
And startled the pigeons from their perch
On the somber rafters, that round him made
Masses and moving shapes of shade, —
By the trembling ladder, steep and tall,
To the highest window in the wall,
Where he paused to listen and look down
A moment on the roofs of the town,
And the moonlight flowing over all.

Beneath, in the churchyard, lay the dead,

In their night-encampment on the hill,
Wrapped in silence so deep and still
That he could hear, like a sentinel's tread,
The watchful night-wind, as it went
Creeping along from tent to tent,
And seeming to whisper, "All is well!"
A moment only he feels the spell
Of the place and the hour, and the secret dread
Of the lonely belfry and the dead;
For suddenly all his thoughts are bent
On a shadowy something far away,
Where the river widens to meet the bay, –
A line of black that bends and floats
On the rising tide, like a bridge of boats.

Meanwhile, impatient to mount and ride,
Booted and spurred, with a heavy stride
On the opposite shore walked Paul Revere.
Now he patted his horse's side,
Now gazed at the landscape far and near,
Then, impetuous, stamped the earth,
And turned and tightened his saddle-girth;
But mostly he watched with eager search
The belfry-tower of the Old North Church,
As it rose above the graves on the hill,
Lonely and spectral and somber and still.
And lo! as he looks on the belfry's height
A glimmer, and then a gleam of light!
He springs to the saddle, the bridle he turns,
But lingers and gazes, till full on his sight
A second lamp in the belfry burns!

A hurry of hoofs in a village street,
A shape in the moonlight, a bulk in the dark,
And beneath, from the pebbles, in passing, a spark
Struck out by a steed flying fearless and fleet:
That was all! And yet, through the gloom and the light,
The fate of a nation was riding that night;
And the spark struck out by that steed, in his flight,
Kindled the land into flame with its heat.

He has left the village and mounted the steep,
And beneath him, tranquil and broad and deep,
Is the Mystic, meeting the ocean tides;
And under the alders, that skirt its edge,

Now soft on the sand, now loud on the ledge,
Is heard the tramp of his steed as he rides.

It was twelve by the village clock
When he crossed the bridge into Medford town.
He heard the crowing of the cock,
And the barking of the farmer's dog,
And felt the damp of the river fog,
That rises after the sun goes down.

It was one by the village clock,
When he galloped into Lexington.
He saw the gilded weathercock
Swim in the moonlight as he passed,
And the meeting-house windows, blank and bare,
Gaze at him with a spectral glare,
As if they already stood aghast
At the bloody work they would look upon.

It was two by the village clock,
When he came to the bridge in Concord town.
He heard the bleating of the flock,
And the twitter of birds among the trees,
And felt the breath of the morning breeze
Blowing over the meadows brown.
And one was safe and asleep in his bed
Who at the bridge would be first to fall,
Who that day would be lying dead,
Pierced by a British musket-ball.

You know the rest. In the books you have read,
How the British Regulars fired and fled, —
How the farmers gave them ball for ball,
From behind each fence and farmyard wall,
Chasing the red-coats down the lane,
Then crossing the fields to emerge again
Under the trees at the turn of the road,
And only pausing to fire and load.

So through the night rode Paul Revere;
And so through the night went his cry of alarm
To every Middlesex village and farm, —
A cry of defiance and not of fear,
A voice in the darkness, a knock at the door,
And a word that shall echo for evermore!

For, borne on a night-wind of the Past,
Through all our history, to the last,
In the hour of darkness and peril and need,
The people will waken and listen to hear
The hurrying hoof-beats of that steed,
And the midnight message of Paul Revere.

HOW THEY BROUGHT THE GOOD NEWS FROM GHENT TO AIX

Robert Browning

1843

I sprang to the stirrup, and Joris, and he;
I galloped, Dirck galloped, we galloped all three;
"Good speed!" cried the watch, as the gate-bolts undrew;
"Speed!" echoed the wall to us galloping through;
Behind shut the postern, the lights sank to rest,
And into the midnight we galloped abreast.

Not a word to each other: we kept the great pace
Neck by neck, stride by stride, never changing our place;
I turned in my saddle and made its girths tight,
Then shortened each stirrup, and set the pique right,
Rebuckled the cheek-strap, chained slacker the bit,
Nor galloped less steadily Roland a whit.

'Twas moonset at starting; but while we drew near
Lokeren, the cocks crew and twilight dawned clear;
At Boom, a great yellow star came out to see;
At Düffeld, 'Twas morning as plain as could be;
And from Mecheln church-steeple we heard the half-chime,
So Joris broke silence with, "Yet there is time!"

At Aershot, up leaped of a sudden the sun,
And against him the cattle stood black every one,
To stare thro' the mist at us galloping past,
And I saw my stout galloper Roland at last,
With resolute shoulders, each butting away
The haze, as some bluff river headland its spray.

And his low head and crest, just one sharp ear bent back
For my voice, and the other pricked out on his track;
And one eye's black intelligence, — ever that glance
O'er its white edge at me, his own master, askance!
And the thick heavy spume-flakes which aye and anon
His fierce lips shook upwards in galloping on.

By Hasselt, Dirck groaned; and cried Joris, "Stay spur!
Your Roos galloped bravely, the fault's not in her,
We'll remember at Aix" — for one heard the quick wheeze
Of her chest, saw the stretched neck and staggering knees,
And sunk tail, and horrible heave of the flank,
As down on her haunches she shuddered and sank.

So we were left galloping, Joris and I,
Past Looz and past Tongres, no cloud in the sky;
The broad sun above laughed a pitiless laugh,
'Neath our feet broke the brittle bright stubble like chaff;
Till over by Dalhem a dome-spire sprang white,
And "Gallop," gasped Joris, "for Aix is in sight!"

"How they'll greet us!" — and all in a moment his roan
Rolled neck and croup over, lay dead as a stone;
And there was my Roland to bear the whole weight
Of the news which alone could save Aix from her fate,
With his nostrils like pits full of blood to the brim,
And with circles of red for his eye-sockets' rim.

Then I cast loose my buffcoat, each holster let fall,
Shook off both my jack-boots, let go belt and all,
Stood up in the stirrup, leaned, patted his ear,
Called my Roland his pet-name, my horse without peer;
Clapped my hands, laughed and sang, any noise, bad or good,
Till at length into Aix Roland galloped and stood.

And all I remember is, friends flocking round
As I sat with his head 'twixt my knees on the ground;
And no voice but was praising this Roland of mine,
As I poured down his throat our last measure of wine,
Which (the burgesses voted by common consent)
Was no more than his due who brought good news from Ghent.

ROZINANTE AND THE GALICIAN MARES

Miguel de Cervantes

1605

AFTER LEAVING the goatherds Don Quixote and his squire journeyed onward. At last they stopped in a meadow full of fresh grass, near which ran a pleasant and refreshing brook; insomuch that it invited and compelled them to pass there the sultry hours of midday, which now became very oppressive. They alighted, and, leaving the ass and Rozinante at large to feed upon the abundant grass, they ransacked the wallet; and, without any ceremony, in friendly and social wise, master and man shared what it contained. Sancho had taken care to fetter Rozinante. Fortune so ordered it that there were grazing in the same valley a number of Galician mares, belonging to certain Yanguesian carriers, whose custom it is to pass the noon, with their drove, in places where there is grass and water. That where Don Quixote then reposed suited their purpose. Now it so

Mine arms are mine ornaments

happened that Rozinante conceived a wish to pay his respects to the drove, and departed at a brisk trot to interview them. But they received him with their heels and their teeth in such a manner that in a little time his girths broke, and he lost his saddle. But what must have affected him more sensibly was, that the carriers, having witnessed his intrusion, set upon him with their pack-staves, and so belaboured him that they laid him along on the ground in a wretched plight.

By this time the knight and squire, having seen the drubbing of Rozinante, came up in great haste; and Don Quixote said:

"By what I see, friend Sancho, these are no knights, but low people of a scoundrel race. I tell thee this, because thou art on that account justified in assisting me to take ample revenge for the outrage they have done to Rozinante before our eyes."

"What kind of revenge can we take," answered Sancho, "since they are above twenty, and we no more than two, and perhaps but one and a half?"

"I am equal to a hundred!" replied Don Quixote; and, without saying more, he laid his hands on his sword, and flew at the Yanguesians; and Sancho did the same, incited by the example of his master. At the first blow, Don Quixote gave one of them a terrible wound on the shoulder, through a leathern doublet. The Yanguesians, seeing themselves assaulted in this manner by two men only seized their staves, and, surrounding them, began to dispense their blows with great vehemence and animosity; and true it is that at the second blow they brought Sancho to the ground. The same fate befell Don Quixote – his courage and dexterity availing him nothing; and, he just fell at Rozinante's feet, who had not yet been able to rise. The Yanguesians, perceiving the mischief they had done, loaded their beasts with all speed, and pursued their journey, leaving the two adventurers in evil plight.

The first who came to his senses was Sancho Panza, who, finding himself close to his master, with a feeble and plaintive voice cried:

"Senõr Don Quixote! ah, Senõr Don Quixote!"

"What wouldst thou, brother Sancho?" answered the knight, in the same feeble and lamentable tone.

"I could wish, if it were possible," said Sancho Panza, "your worship would give me two draughts of that drink of Feo Blass, if you have it here at hand. Perhaps it may do as well for broken bones as it does for wounds."

"The Balsam of Fierabras, you mean. Unhappy I, that we have it not!" replied Don Quixote. "But I swear to thee, Sancho Panza, on the faith of a knight-errant, that, before two days pass (if fortune decree not otherwise), I will have it in my possession, or my hands shall fail me much."

"But in how many days," said the squire, "does your worship think we shall recover the use of our feet?"

"For my part," answered the battered knight, "I cannot ascertain the precise term: but I alone am to blame, for having laid hand on my sword against men who are not knights like myself."

Sancho, sending forth thirty "alases," and sixty sighs, and a hundred and twenty curses on those who had brought him into that situation, endeavoured to raise himself, but stopped half way, bent like a Turkish bow, being wholly unable to stand upright: notwithstanding this, he managed to saddle his ass, who had also taken advantage of that day's excessive liberty, to go a little astray. He then heaved up Rozinante, who, had he a tongue wherewithal to complain, most certainly would not have been outdone either by Sancho or his master. Sancho at length settled Don Quixote upon the ass, to whose tail he then tied Rozinante, and, taking hold of the halter of Dapple, he led them, now faster, now slower, towards the place where he thought the high-road might lie; and had scarcely gone a short league, when fortune, that was conducting his affairs from good to better, discovered to him the road, where he also espied an inn; which, to his sorrow, and Don Quixote's joy, must needs be a castle. Sancho positively maintained it was an inn, and his master that it was a castle; and the dispute lasted so long that they arrived there before it was determined: and Sancho, without further expostulation entered it, with his string of cattle.

c. 1665: MAZEPPA'S RIDE

Lord Byron

1819

"Bring forth the horse!" – The horse was
*   brought;*
In truth, he was a noble steed,
A Tartar of the Ukraine breed,
Who look'd as though the speed of thought
Were in his limbs; but he was wild,
Wild as the wild deer, and untaught,
With spur and bridle undefiled –
'Twas but a day he had been caught;
And snorting, with erected mane,
And struggling fiercely, but in vain,
In the full foam of wrath and dread
To me the desert-born was led:
They bound me on, that menial throng;
Upon his back with many a thong;
Then loosed him with a sudden lash –
Away! – away! – and on we dash!
Torrents less rapid and less rash . . .

"Away, away, my steed and I,
Upon the pinions of the wind,
All human dwellings left behind;
We sped like meteors through the sky,
When with its crackling sound the night
Is chequer'd with the northern light . . .

"With glossy skin, and dripping mane,
And reeling limbs, and reeking flank,
The wild steed's sinewy nerves still strain
Up the repelling bank.
We gain the top: a boundless plain
Spreads through the shadow of the night,
And onward, onward, onward, seems,
Like precipices in our dreams,
To stretch beyond the sight;
And here and there a speck of white,
Or scatter'd spot of dusky green,
In masses broke into the light,
As rose the moon upon my right . . .

At length, while reeling on our way,
Methought I heard a courser neigh,
From our yon tuft of blackening firs.
Is it the wind those branches stirs?
No, no! from out the forest prance
A trampling troop; I see them come!
In one vast squadron they advance!
I strove to cry — my lips were dumb.
The steeds rush on in plunging pride;
But where are they the reins to guide?
A thousand horse, and none to ride!
With flowing tail, and flying mane,
Wide nostrils never stretch'd by pain,
Mouths bloodless to the bit or rein,
And feet that iron never shod,
And flanks unscarr'd by spur or rod,
A thousand horse, the wild, the free,
Like waves that follow o'er the sea,
Came thickly thundering on,
As if our faint approach to meet;
The sight re-nerved my courser's feet,
A moment staggering, feebly fleet,
A moment, with a faint low neigh,
He answer'd, and then fell;

311

With gasps and glazing eyes he lay,
And reeking limbs immoveable,
His first and last career is done!
On came the troop – they saw him stoop,
They saw me strangely bound along
His back with many a bloody thong:
They stop, they start, they snuff the air,
Gallop a moment here and there,
Approach, retire, wheel round and round,
Then plunging back with sudden bound,
Headed by one black mighty steed,
Who seem'd the patriarch of his breed,
Without a single speck or hair
Of white upon his shaggy hide;
They snort, they foam, neigh, swerve aside,
And backward to the forest fly,
By instinct, from a human eye.
They left me there to my despair,
Link'd to the dead and stiffening wretch,
Whose lifeless limbs beneath me stretch,
Relieved from that unwonted weight,
From whence I could not extricate
Nor him nor me – and there we lay,
The dying on the dead!
I little deem'd another day
Would see my houseless, helpless head . . .

THE MAHARAJAH AND THE
LIPPIZANER

Kay Boyle

1937

WHEN THEY SAT DOWN to supper, the little fox settled himself on the doctor's good foot, for the wool of his stocking was a soft bed where the fox could dream a little while. They had soup and the thick, rosy-meated leg of a pig and salt potatoes, and the children listened to their father and Dr. Heine speaking of music, and painting, and books together. The doctor's wife was cutting the meat and putting it on their plates. It was at the end of

312

the meal that the young doctor began talking of the royal, white horses in Vienna, still royal, he said, without any royalty left to bow their heads to, still shouldering into the arena with spirits a man would give his soul for, bending their knees in homage to the empty, canopied loge where royalty no longer sat. They came in, said Dr. Heine in his rich, eager voice, and danced their statuesque dances, their "Pas de Deux", their "Croupade", their "Capriole". They were very impatient of the walls around them and the bits in their soft mouths, and very vain of the things they had been taught to do. Whenever the applause broke out around them, said Dr. Heine, their nostrils opened wide as if a wind were blowing. They were actresses, with the deep, snowy breasts of prima donnas, these perfect stallions who knew to a breath the beauty of even their mockery of fright.

"There was a maharajah," said the young doctor, and the children and their father listened, and the young wife sat giving quick, unwilling glances at this man who had no blood nor knowledge of the land behind him, at this wanderer whose people had wandered from country to country and whose sons must wander, having no land to return to in the end. "There was a maharajah just last year", said Dr. Heine, "who went to the performance and fell in love with one of the horses. He saw it dancing and he wanted to buy it and take it back to India with him. No one else had ever taken a Lippizaner back to his country, and he wanted this special one, the best of them all, whose dance was like an angel flying. So the State agreed that he could buy the horse, but for a tremendous amount of money. They needed the money badly enough, and the maharajah was a very rich man." (Oh yes, thought the young mother bitterly, you would speak about money, you would come here and climb our mountain and poison my sons with the poison of money and greed!) "But no matter how high the price was," said Dr. Heine, smiling because all their eyes were on him, "the maharajah agreed to pay it, provided that the man who rode the horse so beautifully came along as well. Oh, yes, the State would allow that too, but the maharajah would have to pay an enormous salary to the rider. He would take him into his employ as the stallion's keeper, and he would have to pay him a salary as big as our own President is paid!" said Dr. Heine with a burst of laughter.

"And what then, what then?" said one of the boys as the student-doctor paused to laugh. (The whole family was listening, but the mother was filled with sorrow. These things are strange to us, she was thinking. They belong to more sophisticated people, we do not need them here. The Spanish Riding School, the gentlemen of Vienna, they were as alien as foreign places.)

"So it was arranged that the man who rode the horse so well should go along too," said Dr. Heine. "It was finally arranged for a great deal of money," he said, and the mother gave him a look of fury. "But they had not counted on one thing. They had forgotten all about the little groom who had always cared for this special horse and who loved him better than anything else in the world. Ever since the horse had come from the stud farm in Styria, the little groom had cared for him, and he believed that they would always be together, he believed that he would go wherever the horse went, just as he had always gone to Salzburg with the horse in the summer, and always came back to Vienna with it in the winter time again."

"And so what, what happened?" asked the other boy.

"Well" said the student-doctor, "the morning before the horse was to leave with the maharajah and the rider, they found that the horse had a deep cut on his leg, just above the hoof in front. Nobody could explain how it had happened, but the horse was so wounded that he could not travel then; and the maharajah said that he could go on without him and that the trainer should bring the horse over in a few weeks when the cut had healed. They did not tell the maharajah that it might be that the horse could never dance so beautifully again. They had the money and they weren't going to give it back so easily," said Dr. Heine, and he laughed as if their shrewdness pleased his soul. "But when the cut had healed," he went on, "and the horse seemed well enough to be sent by the next boat, the trainer found the horse had a cut on the other hoof, exactly where the other wound had been. So the journey was postponed again, and again the State said nothing to the maharajah about the horse being so impaired that it was likely he could never again fly like an angel. But in a few days the horse's blood was so poisoned from the wound that they had to destroy him."

They all waited breathless with pain a moment, and then the doctor's wife said bitterly:

"Even the money couldn't save him, could it?"

"No," said Dr. Heine, a little perplexed. "Of course, it couldn't. And they never knew how the cuts had come there until the little groom committed suicide the same day the horse was destroyed. And then they knew that he had done it himself because he couldn't bear the horse to go away."

*c.*AD 950: ICELANDIC HORSE-FIGHT

Anonymous

c. 1250

A MAN CALLED STARKAD, the son of Bork Bluetooth-Beard, lived at Thrihyrning. His wife was called Hallbera. They had three sons, Thorgeir, Bork and Thorkel, and a daughter, Hildigunn the Healer.

The sons were all arrogant, brutal men, who had no respect for the rights of others.

Starkad owned a good red stallion, which they all thought could beat any other horse at fighting. On one occasion, when the brothers from Sandgill were over at Thrihyrning, they discussed at length all the farmers in Fljotshlid; eventually the question was raised whether there was anyone who would pit his horse against theirs in a fight. Some of the men present, wanting to flatter them, said that not only would no one dare to challenge them, but that there was no one who owned such a good horse.

Then Hildigunn the Healer said, "I know someone who would dare to match his horse against yours."

"Name him," they said.

"Gunnar of Hlidarend has a black stallion," she said, "and he would dare to challenge you or anyone else."

"You women all seem to think that there's no one like Gunnar," they replied. "Just because Geir the Priest and Gizur the White were humiliated by Gunnar, it doesn't follow that we would be, too,"

"You would come off even worse," said Hildigunn.

This led to heated words. Starkad said, "Gunnar is the last man I would want you to pick a quarrel with, for you would find it hard to beat his good luck."

"But you will allow us to challenge him to a horse-fight?" they asked.

"I give my permission," said Starkad, "but only if you promise to play fair with him."

They gave their promise, and rode off to Hlidarend. Gunnar was at home, and came outside with Kolskegg and Hjort, his brothers. He gave them a good welcome, and asked them where they were going.

"No farther than here," they replied. "We have heard that you have a good stallion, and we want to challenge you to a horse-fight."

"You can hardly have heard anything very great about my stallion," said Gunnar. "He is only a young horse, and completely untried."

"But you won't refuse a fight?" they asked. "Hildigunn told us that you were very proud of him."

"What made you discuss that?" asked Gunnar.

"There were some men who claimed that no one would dare to match his horse against ours," they replied.

"I would dare to, certainly," said Gunnar, "but that was a very spiteful remark to make."

"Can we consider it settled, then?" they asked.

"You won't think your journey worth while unless you have your own way," said Gunnar. "But I make this request, that we fight our horses only to entertain others and not to make trouble for ourselves, and that you don't try to discredit me; for if you treat me in the way you treat others, I am likely to retaliate in a way you will find hard to bear. Whatever you do to me, I shall pay you back in kind."

With that they rode back home. Starkad asked how they had got on. They replied that Gunnar had made their journey worth while. "He promised to match his horse against ours, and we arranged when the fight was to be held. But it was obvious that he felt his own inferiority, and he was very evasive."

Hildigunn said, "Gunnar may often be difficult to provoke; but he hits very hard when he has to."

Gunnar rode to see Njal; he told him about the horse-fight, and the words that had passed.

"How do you think the fight will turn out?" he asked.

"You will win it," said Njal. "But it will be the cause of many deaths."

"Will it cause my death?" asked Gunnar.

"Not directly," said Njal. "But they will remember their old enmity and assault you with new hatred – and you will have no choice but to retaliate."

When Gunnar came home, he learned that his father-in-law, Hoskuld Dala-Kollsson, had died. A few days later, Thorgerd, the wife of Thrain Sigfusson of Grjotriver, gave birth to a son. She sent a messenger to her mother Hallgerd, and asked her to choose whether the boy should be called Glum or Hoskuld. Her mother asked her to call him Hoskuld, and that was the name he was given.

Gunnar and Hallgerd had two sons, Hogni and Grani. Hogni was a quiet, capable man, cautious and reliable.

A great number of people rode to the horse-fight. Gunnar was there with his brothers and the Sigfussons, Njal and all his sons, too. Starkad and his sons arrived with Egil and his sons. They said to Gunnar that it was now time to bring the horses together, and Gunnar agreed.

Skarp-Hedin asked, "Do you want me to be in charge of your stallion, kinsman Gunnar?"

Gunnar said he did not.

"It would be better if I handled him," said Skarp-Hedin, "for I can be just as violent as they."

"You would not have to say or do much before trouble arose," said Gunnar. "With me, the process will be slower, even if the outcome is the same."

The horses were brought together. Gunnar equipped himself for goading as Skarp-Hedin led the horse forward. Gunnar wore a red tunic with a broad silver belt, and carried a horse-goad in his hand. The horses started fighting, and bit at each other for a long time without needing to be goaded. It was excellent sport. Then Thorgeir and Kol arranged to give their own horse a push when the horses next rushed at each other, to see if Gunnar would be knocked down.

The horses clashed again, and Thorgeir and Kol threw their weight against their horse's rump; but Gunnar pushed his horse against theirs, and in a flash Thorgeir and Kol were flat on their backs with their horses on top of them. They jumped to their feet and rushed at Gunnar, who side-stepped them and then seized hold of Kol and threw him down so hard that he was knocked senseless. Thorgeir struck Gunnar's horse and one of its eyes came out; Gunnar hit Thorgeir with the goad, and Thorgeir fell senseless.

Gunnar went over to his stallion. "Kill the horse," he said to Kolskegg. "He shall not live mutilated."

Kolskegg killed the horse. At that point Thorgeir got to his feet and seized his weapons and made for Gunnar; but he was stopped, and people came crowding up.

Skarp-Hedin said, "I am bored with this scuffling. Men should use proper weapons to fight each other."

Gunnar did not move, and only one man held him, and he did not shout abuse. Njal tried to arrange a settlement, or an exchange of pledges; but Thorgeir refused to give or accept pledges, and said he would rather see Gunnar dead for that blow.

Kolskegg said, "Mere words have never knocked Gunnar down, and they will not now either." And the people rode away from the horse-match, each to his own home.

c. 1065: HOW HEREWARD WON MARE SWALLOW

Charles Kingsley

1866

ON A BENCH at the door of his highroofed wooden house sat Dirk Hammerhand, the richest man in Walcheren. From within the house sounded the pleasant noise of slave-women grinding and chatting at the handquern; from without, the pleasant noise of geese and fowls without number. And as he sat and drank his ale, and watched the herd of horses in the fen, he thought himself a happy man, and thanked his Odin and Thor that, owing to his princely supplies of horses to Countess Gertrude, Robert the Frison and his Christian Franks had not yet harried him to the bare walls, as they would probably do ere all was over.

As he looked at the horses, some half mile off, he saw a strange stir among them. They began whinnying and pawing round a fourfooted thing in the midst, which might be a badger, or a wolf – though both were very uncommon in that pleasant isle of Walcheren; but which plainly had no business to be there. Whereupon he took up a mighty staff, and strode over the fen to see.

He found neither wolf nor badger: but to his exceeding surprise, a long lean man, clothed in ragged horse-skins, whinnying and neighing exactly like a horse, and then stooping to eat grass like one. He advanced to do the first thing that came into his head, namely to break the man's back with his staff, and ask him afterwards who he might be. But ere he could strike, the man or horse kicked up its hind legs in his face, and then springing on the said hind legs ran away with extraordinary swiftness some fifty yards; after which it went down on all fours and began grazing again.

"Beest thou man or devil?" cried Dirk, somewhat frightened.

The thing looked up. The face at least was human.

"Art thou a Christian man?" asked it in bad Frisian, inter-mixed with snorts and neighs.

"What's that to thee?" growled Dirk; and began to wish a little that he was one, having heard that the sign of the cross was of great virtue in driving away fiends.

"Thou art not a Christian. Thou believest in Thor and Odin? Then there is hope."

"Hope of what?" Dirk was growing more and more frightened.

"Of her, my sister! Ah, my sister, can it be that I shall find thee at last, after ten thousand miles, and seven years of woeful wandering?"

"I have no man's sister here. At least, my wife's brother was killed –"

"I speak not of a sister in woman's shape. Mine, alas! – oh woeful princess – eats the herb of the field somewhere in the shape of a mare, as ugly as she was once beautiful, but swifter than the swallow in the wing."

"I've none such here," quoth Dirk, thoroughly frightened, and glancing uneasily at the mare Swallow.

"You have not? Alas, wretched me! It was prophesied to me by the witch that I should find her in the field of one who worshipped the old gods; for had she come across a holy priest, she had been a woman again, long ago. Whither must I wander afresh!" And the thing began weeping bitterly, and then ate more grass.

"I – that is – thou poor miserable creature," said Dirk, half pitying, half wishing to turn the subject; "leave off making a beast of thyself awhile, and tell me who thou art."

"I have made no beast of myself, most noble earl of the Frisians, for so you doubtless are. I was made a beast of – a horse of, by an enchanter of a certain land, and my sister a mare."

"Thou dost not say so!" quoth Dirk, who considered such an event quite possible.

"I was a prince of the country of Alboronia, which lies between Cathay and the Mountains of the Moon, as fair once as I am foul now, and only less fair than my lost sister; and by the enchantment of a cruel magician we became what we are."

"But thou art not a horse at all events?"

"Am I not? Thou knowest, then, more of me that I do myself," and it ate more grass. "But hear the rest of my story. My hapless sister was sold away with me to a merchant: but I, breaking loose from him, fled until I bathed in a magic fountain. At once I recovered my man's shape, and was rejoicing therein, when out of the fountain rose a fairy more beautiful than an elf, and smiled upon me with love.

"She asked me my story, and I told it. And when it was told – "Wretch!" she cried, "and coward, who hast deserted thy sister in her need. I would have loved theee, and made thee immortal as myself: but now thou shall wander ugly and eating grass, clothed in the horse-hide which has just dropped from thy limbs, till thou shall find thy sister, and bring her to bathe, like theee, in this magic well.'''

"All good spirits help us! And are you really a prince?"

"As surely," cried the thing with a voice of sudden rapture, "as that mare is my sister;" and rushed at mare Swallow. "I see, I see my mother's eyes, my father's nose –"

"He must have been a chuckle-headed king that, then," grinned Dirk to himself. "The mare's nose is as big as a buck-basket. But how can she be a princess, man – prince I mean? She has a foal running by her here."

"A foal?" said the thing solemnly. "Let me behold it. Alas, alas, my sister! Thy tyrant's threat has come true, that thou shouldst be his bride whether thou wouldst or not. I see, I see in the features of thy son his hated lineaments."

"Why he must be as like a horse, then, as your father. But this will not do, Master Horse-man; I know that foal's pedigree better than I do my own."

"Man, man, simple, though honest! – Hast thou never heard of the skill of the enchanters of the East? How they transform their victims at night back again into human shape, and by day into the shape of beasts again?"

"Yes – well – I know that –"

"And do you not see how you are deluded? Every night, doubt not, that mare and foal take their human shape again; and every night, perhaps, that foul enchanter visits in your fen, perhaps in your very stable, his wretched bride restored (alas, only for an hour!) into her human shape."

"An enchanter in my stable? That is an ugly guest. But no. I've been into the stables fifty times, to see if that mare was safe. Mare was mare, and colt was colt, Mr. Prince, if I have eyes to see."

"And what are eyes against enchantments? The moment you opened the door, the spell was cast over them again. You ought to thank your stars that no worse has happened yet; that the enchanter, in fleeing, has not wrung your neck as he went out, or cast a spell on you, which will fire your barns, lame your geese, give your fowls the pip, your horses the glanders, your cattle the murrain, your children St. Vitus' dance, your wife the creeping palsy, and yourself the chalk-stones in all your fingers."

"All Saints have mercy upon me! If the half of this be true, I will turn Christian. I will send for a priest, and be baptized to-morrow."

"Oh, my sister, my sister! Dost thou not know me? Dost thou answer my caresses with kicks? Or is thy heart, as well as thy body, so enchained by that cruel necromancer, that thou preferrest to be his, and scornest thy own salvation, leaving me to eat grass till I die?"

"I say, Prince – I say – What would you have a man to do? I bought the mare honestly, and I have kept her well. She can't say aught against me on that score. And whether she be princess or not, I'm loth to part with her."

"Keep her then, and keep her with the curse of all the saints and angels. Look down, ye holy saints" (and the thing poured out a long string of saint's names), "and avenge this catholic princess, kept in vile durance by an unbaptized heathen! May his –"

"Don't, don't!" roared Dirk. "And don't look at me like that" (for he feared the evil eye), "or I'll brain you with my staff!"

"Fool! If I have lost a horse's figure, I have not lost his swiftness. Ere thou couldst strike, I should have run a mile and back, to curse thee afresh." And the thing ran round him, and fell on all fours again, and ate grass.

"Mercy, mercy! And that is more than I ever asked yet of man. But it is hard," growled he, "that a man should lose his money, because a rogue sells him a princess in disguise."

"Then sell her again; sell her, as thou valuest thy life, to the first Christian man thou meetest. And yet no. What matters? Ere a month be over, the seven years' enchantment will have passed; and she will return to her own shape, with her son, and vanish from thy farm, leaving thee to vain repentance; whereby thou wilt both lose thy money, and get her curse. Farewell, and my malison abide with thee."

And the thing, without another word, ran right away, neighing as it went, leaving Dirk in a state of abject terror.

He went home. He cursed the mare, he cursed the man who sold her, he cursed the day he saw her, he cursed the day he was born. He told his story with exaggerations and confusions in plenty to all in the house; and terror fell on them likewise. No one, that evening, dare go down into the fen to drive the horses up; while Dirk got very drunk, went to bed, and trembled there all night (as did the rest of the household), expecting the enchanter to enter on a flaming fire drake, at every howl of the wind.

The next morning, as Dirk was going about his business with a doleful face, casting stealthy glances at the fen, to see if the mysterious mare was still there, and a chance of his money still there, a man rode up to the door.

He was poorly clothed, with a long rusty sword by his side. A broad felt hat, long boots, and a haversack behind his saddle, showed him to be a traveller, seemingly a horse dealer; for there followed him, tied head and tail, a brace of sorry nags.

"Heaven save all here," quoth he, making the sign of the cross. "Can any good Christian give me a drink of milk?"

"Ale, if thou wilt," said Dirk. "But what art thou, and whence?"

On any other day, he would have tried to coax his guest into trying a buffet with him for his horse and clothes; but this morning his heart was heavy with the thought of the enchanted mare, and he welcomed the chance of selling her to the stranger.

"We are not very fond of strangers about here, since these Flemings have been harrying our borders. If thou art a spy, it will be the worse for thee."

"I am neither spy nor Fleming: but a poor servant of the Lord Bishop of Utrecht's, buying a garron or two for his lordship's priests. As for these Flemings, may St. John Baptist save them both from me and you. Do you know of any man who has horses to sell hereabouts?"

"There are horses in the fen yonder," quoth Dirk, who knew that churchmen were likely to give a liberal price, and pay in good silver.

"I saw them as I rode up. And a fine lot they are; but of too good a stamp for my short purse, or for my holy master's riding, – a fat priest likes a quiet nag, my master."

"Humph. Well, if quietness is what you need, there is a mare down there, that a child might ride with a thread of wool. But as for price – and she has a colt, too, running by her."

"Ah?" quoth the horseman. "Well, your Walcheren folk make good milk, that's certain. A colt by her? That's awkward. My lord does not like young horses; and it would be troublesome, too, to take the thing along with me."

The less anxious the dealer seemed to buy, the more anxious grew Dirk to sell: but he concealed his anxiety, and let the stranger turn away, thanking him for his drink.

"I say," he called after him. "You might look at her as you ride past the herd."

The stranger assented; and they went down into the fen, and looked over the precious mare, whose feats were afterwards sung by many an English fire-side, or in the forest beneath the hollins green, by such as Robin Hood and his merry Men. The ugliest, as well as the swiftest, of mares, she was, say the old chroniclers; and it was not till the stranger had looked twice at her, that he forgot her great chuckle-head, greyhound-flanks, and drooping hind quarters, and began to see the great length of those same quarters, the thighs let down into the hocks, the compact lion, the extraordinary girth through the saddle, the sloping shoulders, the long arms, the flat knees, the large well-set hoofs, and all the other points which showed her strength and speed, and justified her fame.

"She might carry a big man like you through the mud," said he carelessly; "but as for pace, one cannot expect that with such a chuckle-head. And if one rode her through a town, the boys would call after one, "All head and no tail – Why, I can't see her tail for her croup, it is so ill set on."

"Ill set, or none," said Dirk testily, "don't go to speak against her pace, till you have seen it. Here, lass!''

Dirk was in his heart rather afraid of the princess: but he was comforted when she came up to him like a dog.

"She's as sensible as a woman," said he; and then grumbled to himself, "may be she knows I mean to part with her."

"Lend me your saddle," said he to the stranger.

The stranger did so; and Dirk mounting galloped her in a ring. There was no doubt of her powers as soon as she began to move.

"I hope you won't remember this against me, madam," said Dirk, as soon as he got out of the stranger's hearing. "I can't do less than sell you to a Christian. And certainly I have been as good a master to you as if I'd known who you were; but if you wish to stay with me, you've only to kick me off, and say so; and I'm yours to command."

"Well, she can gallop a bit," said the stranger, as Dirk pulled her up and dismounted: "but an ugly brute she is, nevertheless, and such a one as I should not care to ride, for I am a gay man among the ladies. However, what is your price?"

Dirk named twice as much as he would have taken.

"Half that, you mean." And the usual haggle began.

"Tell thee what," said Dirk at last. "I am a man who has his fancies; and this shall be her price; half thy bid, and a box on the ear."

The demon of covetousness had entered Dirk's heart. What if he got the money; brained, or at least disabled the stranger; and so had the chance of selling the mare a second time to some fresh comer?

"Thou art a strange fellow," quoth the horse-dealer. "But so be it."

Dirk chuckled. "He does not know," thought he, "that he has to do with Dirk Hammerhand," and he clenched his fist in anticipation of his rough joke.

"There," quoth the stranger, counting out the money carefully, "is thy coin. And there – is thy box on the ear."

And with a blow which rattled over the fen, he felled Dirk Hammerhand to the ground.

He lay senseless for a moment, then looked wildly round.

"Villain!" quoth he. "It was I who was to give you the buffet, not thou!"

"Art mad?" asked the stranger, as he coolly picked up the coins, which Dirk has scattered in his fall. "It is the seller's business to take, and the buyer's to give."

And while Dirk roared in vain for help, he leapt on Swallow, and rode off shouting,

"Aha! Dirk Hammerhand! So you thought to knock a hole in my skull, as you have done to many a better man than yourself? He must be a luckier man than you catches The Wake asleep. I shall give your love to the Enchanted Prince, my faithful serving man, whom they call Martin Light-foot."

Dirk cursed the day he was born. Instead of the mare and colt, he had got two wretched garrons which the stranger had left, and a face which made him so tender of his own teeth, that he never again offered to try a buffet with a stranger.

c. 1643 : IN THE SERVICE OF CHARLES I

Percy F. Westerman

1930

IT WAS AFTER MIDDAY ere I obtained the necessary permission from the provost to leave the camp, and, having made an excuse to my comrade, I saddled my horse and rode off.

This animal was not the one I had ridden from home, neither was it the passable nag that I had had given me on joining Hopton's camp, but a powerful black charger which I bought immediately after the surrender of the rebel army, and was, in consequence ignorant of its temper.

In under two hours I arrived at Liskeard, where I found the host of the "Stag" most amenable to my request, and, protesting that he had been compelled to take my sword and a brace of pistols belonging to Firestone in payment for the cider, he handed them over in consideration of the sum of a crown – a far less amount that I had expected to have had to pay.

Delighted with the success of my mission, I had refreshment, and afterwards set out on my journey back to the camp. But I had barely covered half the distance when my horse began to show symptoms of restlessness, and before I was fully aware of the fact, it suddenly plunged, bounded forward, and, regardless of my effort to retain it, tore headlong over the dusty road.

Thinking it would soon tire itself out, and consoling myself that I was still going in the direction of the camp, I let the creature have a loose rein, till at length it suddenly turned, cleared a low stone wall with a bound, and headed across a field.

Now I sought to rein in the frantic animal, but in vain. Across country it tore, till it reached a wild tract of open country two miles from the highway, and, sinking to its knees in a marsh, I was able to leap from the saddle.

Tugging at the exhausted creature's reins, I succeeded in extricating it from the bog-land; then, loth to take further risk, I walked in the direction from which I had come.

At length I espied a stone hut, or hovel, from which a thin column of smoke was rising. In the excitement of my wild ride I had failed to notice it before. As I drew nearer I saw that at one time it must have been an ancient British cromlech, a massive slab of granite resting upon two uprights. A rough wall of stone had converted the cromlech into a rude dwelling, and here apparently human beings existed. Door there was none, a gap in the wall serving that purpose.

The soft, springy turf deadened the sound of my approach, and, gaining the entrance, I stooped down and peered within, having tied up my horse to a thorn bush, and taken the precaution of holding one of my pistols in my hand.

In front of the fire a hare was roasting on a rough spit, while the smoke and the sudden change from the glare of the sunlight made it impossible to distinguish things clearly. Lying on the ground was a man. He was fast asleep, and even my voice failed to rouse him. The floor of this singular dwelling had been excavated to a depth of about two feet below the surface of the ground outside, so that there was a height of nearly seven feet between the floor and the roof of solid rock.

I stepped within and stirred the sleeper with my foot.

With a sudden start he awoke and jumped to his feet. It was Captain Chaloner!

It was Captain Chaloner, in spite of his scared face, unkempt hair and beard, his torn and travel-stained clothes. Doubtless he thought that a troop of horse stood without.

"Yield yourself, Captain Chaloner," I exclaimed, holding up my cocked pistol.

"I yield," he replied, without hesitation, somewhat to my discomfiture, for I knew not where I was, neither did he know that I was alone, so what was I to do with my prisoner?

"Make ready to go," I continued, "for we must needs journey to Lostwithiel."

"Promise me that your men will not harm me," he said imploringly, whereat I unthinkingly informed him that there was no one without.

"Then on what authority do you arrest me?" he exclaimed, with a sudden change of tone.

"The authority of right and might," I replied, showing him the pistol once more. "You must needs walk five paces ahead of me, and at the first sign of escape I shoot you down."

"What must needs be," he rejoined. "But, Master Markham, consider a moment. I am of opinion that the matter of Ashley Castle being bestowed upon me is the cause of your hatred towards me, though I swear it was not through my asking."

"You are right, though I'll not believe you did not ask it to be conferred upon you."

"Then why seek my life?"

"I do not seek your life, although by doing my duty I have little doubt but that you'll be hanged for your treachery. Had I not struck up the barrel of a musket, you would certainly have been shot down from the tower of Lostwithiel Church when you tried your utmost to burn or blow us up."

"Good lad! Good lad!" sneered Chaloner, "I thank you for the service."

"And now make ready," I continued, ignoring his insolent manner. "For 'tis late in the afternoon, and we must needs be in camp ere sunset."

"Since you are alone, Master Markham, can you not forego the honour of taking me into the Royalist camp? Consider, sixteen good miles of rough road, darkness long before we arrive there, and the chance of meeting some of my men. For, look you, I am not alone. Furthermore, if you let me go free, I'll promise, on my word of honour—"

"Your word of honour!" I repeated scornfully.

"Ay, I'll swear it, if you will, that I'll hand over the deed of settlement of Ashley Castle, and take ship overseas till the war be at an end. I mean what I say," he continued as I shook my head at his base proposal. "See, I have the document here."

Stooping down, he lifted up a pile of clothing that lay on the floor.

There was a sudden flash, a loud report, and I reeled backwards with a sharp pain like a hot iron searing through my shoulder.

I had a dim recollection of firing my pistol straight at him as he still remained huddled on the floor, and seeing him half spring to his feet, only to fall forward with convulsive struggles. Then, with a red mist swimming before my eyes, I staggered to where my horse was tethered, clambered into the saddle, and gave spur.

After a while my senses became clearer. My left arm was paining me, while a dark stain flooded the shoulder and front of my doublet. My horse had settled down to a trot, though whither 'twas bearing me I knew not nor hardly cared. I had some consolation in the thought that I was being borne somewhere, and, providing I could keep my saddle, all would be well at the next village or homestead I came to.

The sun was close on the time of setting, and by the fact that its ruddy glare came from the direction slightly behind my right shoulder, I knew we were heading southwards.

As my senses returned the pain of my wound increased, the incessant jolting caused the blood to flow more freely. I could not help wondering what might have been my fate had I fallen from the saddle during the period of unconsciousness, for my feet were firmly wedged in the stirrups, and, if unable to disengage them, I would have been a shapeless mass of shattered pulp. I had seen a similar thing at Edgehill, and knew full well what it meant.

At length the horse gained the summit of a lofty hill, and before me stretched the seemingly boundless expanse of the English Channel, a gentle declivity of about half a mile separating me from the water, though on either hand a spur of the hill in what must be pair of rugged headlands.

Suddenly the horse was seized with the same unseen terror that had caused it to bolt on the highway. It reared almost on its haunches, and only by keeping a tight grip on its mane with my sound arm was I able to retain my seat. Then, with its freshly-found wind, the startled animal bounded forward.

"'Tis time to cry halt," I exclaimed to myself, and, putting all the strength of my unwounded limb into the pull, I strove to rein in the animal, as I saw that what I took to be a gentle slope actually terminated in a cliff, though considerably lower than the adjacent portions of the coast.

With undiminished speed the horse shot into space.

My efforts, as before, were useless, and only tended to increase the horse's pace and fury. Several times I tried to turn its head, but in spite of this the animal kept straight for the sea.

Not a moment was to be lost. I determined to shoot the brute and risk a headlong fall on the soft turf. Forgetting my wound for a moment, I took the reins in my left hand. Then, drawing my remaining pistol from its holster, I snapped it at the horse's forehead; but, to my dismay, there was no report.

The weapon had missed fire.

At that moment I realised that there were persons riding to my aid. At least a score of horsemen were galloping furiously down the spur on my right, with the evident intention of intercepting my runaway steed and diverting its flight. Some of them had carbines, and made ready to fire, though I had misgivings as to their marksmanship. But the efforts of the horsemen were in vain; my horse thundered past the leader at more than twenty paces, and, defying pursuit, continued its mad flight.

Throwing away the useless pistol, I drew my sword, determined to slay the animal before it carried me to destruction; but before I could shorten the blade for a stroke we had gained the edge of the cliff.

The horse gave a neigh, whether of triumph or of terror I knew not, and with undiminished speed shot into space. In a few brief seconds I must have turned completely round; I saw the red sheer face of the cliff appear to shoot upwards, the air whistled past my head, and with a heavy splash my horse and I struck the surface of the water simultaneously.

Then everything became a blank. . . .

THE NIGHT BEFORE THE FAIR

Moyra Charlton

1930

THE FOLLOWING MORNING the grey did not go out, and he was glad of it, for he felt stiff and aching all over, and he had developed a bad cough.

Wriley, the stud-groom who had accompanied him and his companions in the train, felt he deserved a day off, so he spent the whole morning and all his money in betting and gambling, and the whole afternoon and every-one else's money in drinking their healths at the "Lobster Arms," a dirty low type of pub in the town.

Meanwhile in the damp, low, wooden-ceilinged little shed where the young horse was stabled, the hours dragged slowly by. The dank straw and unhealthy atmosphere were telling on him. He was no longer the fine, active horse that he had been a few weeks ago, although he stood just as straight, and arched his neck just as proudly, as before; his ribs stood out through lack of condition, and his coat looked staring and dull. He was no longer the healthy gelding whose coat shone like silk; his eyes had lost some of their lustre, and a new look had taken the place of the old glance of fearlessness and fun – a look that betokened nervousness and dread. His cough had increased since the morning.

Round about five o'clock a boy thrust a bundle of hay which was not fit to eat. The shadows lengthened and it grew dark inside the dismal little stable. But still Wriley did not return. The grey had long since drained his bucket of water to the dregs, filthy as it was, and his lips were parched and dry. It got damper still, and he had no rug or blanket to keep him warm, and he shivered all over. He paced restlessly up and down the shed. Outside it had started to drizzle. Would Wriley never come?

At last! Footsteps and voices! Down the alley they came, about six of them, rolling and swaying, singing some rollicking Irish song. They were clearly all drunk. Would they stop at his door or proceed up the street? In his anxiety he let out a shrill, penetrating, pitiful neigh. They paused outside his door and waited a moment in silence. At last someone spoke, and the high-pitched, disjointed sentences could hardly be recognised as belonging to the sober-minded Wriley.

"Here, will the baby come to Mither. Sure an' where be his dhrink?"

A small, shrewd man stepped forward.

"Where all yer dhrink goes to, Paddy Wriley," he replied, with a meaning wink.

"Och man! he be arfter . . . " hissed Wriley, turning on him; but the rest was lost in peals of laughter from the others at this coarse joke. When it had subsided a bit he said: "What d'ye mane, Tim O'Brian?"

"What ar says, an' ye can naht git out of it."

"Bad cess to ye," muttered Wriley with an oath – he could not help feeling that he was getting the worst of it – "ye better be arfter havin' the feeding of the bruht thin, eh?"

"Ar will naht," returned Tim, withdrawing hastily.

"And you, Patrick O'Conneley?"

"Catch me afther him."

"And why naht?"

"He has a whicked oi on him," he whined.

Wriley went the colour of a beetroot to his ears, and he swore a good

"HE HAS A WHICKED OI ON HIM."

deal. Everyone laughed and jeered. He eyed Patrick through the corners of his narrow eyes. He was a tall, big-boned, broad-shouldered fellow, while he, Wriley, was but a small, puny man, and his knees bent outwards, the result of spending most of his life in the saddle. But what he lacked in stature he made up for in courage, besides, those pints of beer at the "Lobster Arms," which he had so unwillingly left but half an hour ago, made him feel hot-headed and brave, so he turned boldly to O'Conneley and said mockingly:

"You be afeared, Patrick O'Conneley."

For reply he got a cuff on the ear, after which a regular tussle began, the others not wanting to be left out of the fun, and they all went off shouting, swearing, and fighting, followed by a crowd of enthusiastic street-boys, while the poor horse never got his water after all.

THE GROOM'S STORY

Sir Arthur Conan Doyle

1922

Ten mile in twenty minutes! 'E done it, sir. That's true.
The big bay 'orse in the further stall — the one wot's
    next to you.
I've seen some better 'orses; I've seldom seen a wuss,
But 'e 'olds the bloomin' record, an' that's good enough
    for us.

We knew as it was in 'im. 'E's thoroughbred, three part,
We bought 'im for to race 'im, but we found 'e 'ad no
    'eart;
For 'e was sad and thoughtful, and amazin' dignified,
It seemed a kind o' liberty to drive 'im or to ride;

For 'e never seemed a-thinkin' of what 'e 'ad to do,
But 'is thoughts was set on 'igher things, admirin' of the
    view.
'E looked a puffeck pictur, and a pictur 'e would stay,
'E wouldn't even switch 'is tail to drive the flies away.

And yet we knew 'twas in 'im; we knew as 'e could fly;
But what we couldn't git at was 'ow to make 'im try.

We'd almost turned the job up, until at last one day
We got the last yard out of 'im in a most amazin' way.

It was all along o' master; which master 'as the name
Of a reg'lar true blue sportsman, an' always acts the
    same;
But we all 'as weaker moments, which master 'e 'ad one,
An' 'e went and bought a motor-car when motor-cars
    begun.

I seed it in the stable yard – it fairly turned me sick –
A greasy, wheezy engine as can neither buck nor kick.
You've a screw to drive it forrard, and a screw to make
    it stop,
For it was foaled in a smithy stove an' bred in a black-
    smith shop.

It didn't want no stable, it didn't ask no groom,
It didn't need no nothin' but a bit o' standin' room.
Just fill it up with paraffin an' it would go all day,
Which the same should be agin the law if I could 'ave
    my way.

Well, master took 'is motor-car, an' moted 'ere an' there,
A frightenin' the 'orses an' a poisonin' the air.
'E wore a bloomin' yachtin' cap but Lor'! wot did 'e
    know.
Excep' that if you turn a screw the thing would stop
    or go?

An' then one day it wouldn't go. 'E screwed and
    screwed again.
But somethin' jammed, an' there 'e stuck in the mud of
    a country lane.
It 'urt 'is pride most cruel, but what was 'e to do?
So at last 'e bade me fetch a 'orse to pull the motor
    through.

This was the 'orse we fetched 'im; an' when we reached
    the car,
We braced 'im tight and proper to the middle of the bar,
And buckled up 'is traces and lashed them to each side,
While 'e 'eld 'is 'ead so 'aughtily, an' looked most
    dignified.

*Not bad tempered, mind you, but kind of pained and
   vexed,
And 'e seemed to say, "Well, bli' me! wot will they ask
   me next?
I've put up with some liberties, but this caps all by far,
To be assistant engine to a crocky motor-car!"*

*Well, master 'e was in the car, a-fiddlin' with the gear,
And the 'orse was meditatin', an' I was standin' near,
When master 'e touched somethin' – what it was we'll
   never know –
But it sort o' spurred the boiler up and made the engine
   go.*

*"'Old 'ard, old gal!" says master, and "Gently then,"
   says I,
But an engine won't 'eed coaxin' an' it ain't no use to
   try;
So first 'e pulled a lever, an' then 'e turned a screw,
But the thing kept crawlin' forrard spite of all that 'e
   could do.*

*And first it went quite slowly and the 'orse went also
   slow,
But 'e 'ad to buck up faster when the wheels began to go;
For the car kept crowdin' on 'im and buttin' 'im along,
And in less than 'alf a minute, sir, that 'orse was goin'
   strong.*

*At first 'e walked quite dignified, an' then 'e 'ad to trot,
And then 'e tried a canter when the pace became too 'ot.
'E looked 'is very 'aughtiest, as if 'e didn't mind,
And all the time the motor-car was pushin' 'im be'ind.*

*Now, master lost 'is 'ead when 'e found 'e couldn't stop,
And 'e pulled a valve or somethin' an' somethin' else
   went pop,
An' somethin' else went fizzywiz, and in a flash, or less,
That blessed car was goin' like a limited express.*

*Master 'eld the steerin' gear, an' kept the road all right,
And away they whizzed and clattered – my aunt! it
   was a sight.
'E seemed the finest draught 'orse as ever lived by far,
For all the country Juggins thought 'twas 'im wot pulled
   the car.*

'E was stretchin' like a grey'ound, 'e was goin' all 'e
    knew,
But it bumped an' shoved be'ind 'im, for all that 'e
    could do;
It butted 'im an' boosted 'im an' spanked 'im on a'ead,
Till 'e broke the ten-mile record, same as I already said.

Ten mile in twenty minutes! 'E done it, sir. That's
    true –
The only time we ever found what that 'ere 'orse could
    do –
Some say it wasn't 'ardly fair, and the papers made a fuss,
But 'e broke the ten-mile record, and that's good enough
    for us.

You see that 'orse's tail, sir? You don't! No more
    do we,
Which really ain't surprisin', for 'e 'as no tail to see;
That engine wore it off 'im before master made it stop,
And all the road was littered like a bloomin' barber's
    shop.

And master? Well, it cured 'im. 'E altered from that
    day,
And come back to 'is 'orses in the good old-fashioned
    way.
And if you wants to git the sack, the quickest way by far
Is to 'int as 'ow you think 'e ought to keep a motor-car.

THE UNDERTAKER'S HORSE

Rudyard Kipling

1886

The eldest son bestrides him,
And the pretty daughter rides him,
And I meet him oft o' mornings on the Course;
And there wakens in my bosom
An emotion chill and gruesome
As I canter past the Undertaker's Horse.

Neither shies he nor is restive,
But a hideously suggestive
Trot, professional and placid, he affects;
And the cadence of his hoof-beats
To my mind this grim reproof beats:-
"Mend your pace, my friend, I'm coming. Who's the next?"

Ah! stud-bred of ill-omen,
I have watched the strongest go — men
Of pith and might and muscle — at your heels,
Down the plantain-bordered highway,
(Heaven send it ne'er be my way!)
In a lacquered box and jetty upon wheels.

Answer, sombre beast and dreary,
Where is Brown, the young, the cheery,
Smith, the pride of all his friends and half the Force?
You were at that last dread dak
We must cover at a walk,
Bring them back to me, O Undertaker's Horse!

With your mane unhogged and flowing,
And your curious way of going,
And that businesslike black crimping of your tail,
E'en with Beauty on your back, Sir,
Pacing as a lady's hack, Sir,
What wonder when I meet you I turn pale? . . .

It may be you wait your time, Beast,
Till I write my last bad rhyme, Beast —
Quit the sunlight, cut the rhyming, drop the glass —
Follow after with the others,
Where some dusky heathen smothers
Us with marigolds in lieu of English grass.

Or, perchance, in years to follow,
I shall watch your plump sides hollow,
See Carnifex (gone lame) become a corse —
See old age at last o'erpower you,
And the Station Pack devour you,
I shall chuckle then, O Undertaker's Horse!

LIST OF AUTHORS

LIST OF ARTISTS

Artists of the pictures on the pages listed are:

Cecil Aldin: 194, 195
G. D. Armour: 174, 251
Robert Ball: 245
John Board: 66, 105, 172, 246, 247, 249, 250
Lionel Edwards: 36, 49, 69, 103, 107, 214
Laurien James: 73
Alfred Munnings: 141
Brian Robb: 58, 59